El Dorado in West Africa

*The Gold-Mining Frontier,
African Labor, and
Colonial Capitalism
in the Gold Coast,
1875-1900*

El Dorado in West Africa

The Gold-Mining Frontier,
African Labor, and
Colonial Capitalism in the
Gold Coast, 1875–1900

Raymond E. Dumett

Ohio University Press
ATHENS

James Currey
OXFORD

Ohio University Press, Athens, Ohio 45701
©1998 by Ohio University Press

James Currey Ltd.
73 Botley Road
Oxford
OX2 0BS

Printed in the United States of America

Ohio University Press books are printed on acid-free paper ∞

Book design by inari

Library of Congress Cataloging-in-Publication Data
Dumett, Raymond E.
    El Dorado in West Africa: the gold mining frontier, African labor,
and colonial capitalism in the Gold Coast, 1875-1900 /
by Raymond E. Dumett.
        p.   cm.
    Includes bibliographical references (p.) and index.
    ISBN 0-8214-1197-7 (alk. paper). —
    ISBN 0-8214-1198-5 (pbk. : alk. paper)
    1. Gold mines and mining—Ghana—History—19th century.
    2. Gold miners—Ghana—History—19th century.
    3. Capitalism—Ghana—History—19th century. I. Title.
    HD9536.G5D86 1998
    338.2'741'09667—dc21   97-46494
                                                      CIP

British Library Cataloging in Publication Data available
    ISBN 0-85255-769-8 (cl)
    ISBN 0-85255-768-X (pbk)

To my wife
Ardis Ivarson Dumett

CONTENTS

LIST OF ILLUSTRATIONS

ILLUSTRATIONS

African Laborers Working for the Mechanized Companies 256

African skilled surface workers and early company sawmill
African "shovel men" at entrance to adit level of mechanized mine
Women headloading sacks of gold ore to crushing mills
Workers clearing ground for construction of crushing mill
Mining company hammockmen
Woman carrying her child plus a 100 lb. load of mining equipment

Kru men from Liberia, Important for the Unskilled Mines Labor Forces at the Wassa Mines, 1979–1900 259

Kru mariners manning surfboard between steamship and shore
Contemporary sketch of Kru men in Liberia
Kru and Akan unskilled laborers on the Gold Coast

Expansion of the Akan Gold Miners and Trader Frontier in the Late Nineteenth and Early Twentieth Centuries 291

Nana Efoa Tenkroman, Queen Mother of Konongo
Chief Kofi Kyei of Heman-Prestea
Nzeman traditional gold miner
Entrance to advanced African pit mine

Akan Goldsmiths and Gold Traders Who Played a Part in the Expansion of the Indigenous Gold Mining Frontier 294

Traditional African goldsmith and gold trader with villagers
    preparing to weigh gold dust
Traditional Akan goldsmith melting gold dust

FIGURES

MAPS

TABLES

ACKNOWLEDGMENTS

A number of friends and institutions assisted me in the production of this book. Research was conducted at archives in Great Britain, Ghana, and the United States whose staffs were unfailingly courteous and helpful. Early work centered at the Public Record Office, Kew, England. Further investigations were carried on at the School of Oriental and African Studies, London University; the British Library; the Balme Library, University of Ghana; Rhodes House Library, Oxford University; the Library of Congress; Purdue University; and the Ghana National Archives. Tommy Rowe offered me every assistance in the retrieval of documents and the use of photographs from the archives of the Ashanti Goldfields (Lonrho Corporation, Ltd.), now housed at the Guildhall Library, London. Over several years I benefited from research and travel grants awarded by the National Endowment for the Humanities, the Hoover Institution, the American Philosophical Society, and the Purdue Research Foundation, which were essential for the completion of archival and field research in both West Africa and the United Kingdom. The following scholars read portions of the manuscript at various stages and offered useful suggestions: Bob Kubicek, the late Marion Johnson, Timothy Garrard, Kwame Arhin, David Henige, Enid Schildkrout, Colin Newbury, Larry Yarak, and Ian Phimister. I am grateful to Tony Hopkins of the University of Cambridge and Eugenia Herbert of Mount Holyoke College for extensive comments on the entire manuscript. None of them are responsible for any errors or flaws that remain.

Words cannot express what I have gained in understanding of the people and cultures of Ghana from travel and research over the years in that country. Their warmth and friendliness was wonderful. Albert Van Dantzig and his wife, Eti, not only offered me the hospitality of their home; but also the use of their car in one of several trips to the Wassa mining districts. The staffs of both the Ghana State Mining Corporation (Tarkwa) and the Ashanti Goldfields (Obuasi) allowed me free rein to tour their premises and to interview retired mine workers. Particular thanks go to Robert Addo-Fening, Department of History, University of Ghana and Edward Reynolds, University of California, San Diego, both of whom checked the manuscript for the accuracy of Twi vocabulary and offered other valuable comments. In several of my earliest trips to Ghana, Stephen Marfoh assisted me as a translator and guide in field interviews up-country. Many Ghanaian elders were extremely generous with their time in relating their experiences and recollections to me in taped interviews, which are listed in the bibliography at the end of this volume. These encounters were exhilarating and I cherish the memory of them. I am especially appreciative of the assistance given by Augustine Mensah, assistant director at the main branch of the Ghana National Archives (Accra) during the 1980s.

Finally, without the yeoman work of Judy McHenry, administrative assistant, and the fine secretarial staff in the Department of History, Purdue University, who aided me in the typing of numerous drafts, the final manuscript would never have taken shape. I also would like to thank Gill Berchowitz and the editors of Ohio University Press for guiding the book through to publication. Above all, I express gratitude to my wife, Ardis, and my two daughters, Susan and Ann Marie, for their steadfast love, support, and encouragement over the many years of this project.

ABBREVIATIONS IN NOTES AND BIBLIOGRAPHY

actg.	acting
ADM	Additional Manuscripts
AGC	Ashanti Goldfields Corporation
BL	British Library
BLG	Balme Library, University of Ghana
BT	British Companies Records
CO	Colonial Office
Col. Sec.	Colonial Secretary
conf.	confidential despatch or memorandum
DC	District Commissioner
dist.	district
encl.	enclosure
FO	Foreign Office
G.C.	Gold Coast
GHL	Guildhall Library, London
GNA	Ghana National Archives
Gov.	Governor
IAS	Institute of African Studies, Univ. of Ghana
LRC	Lonrho Corporation
min.	minute(s)
ord.	ordinance
PP	*Parliamentary Papers*
PRO	Public Record Office
Q.	quarterly
RHO	Rhodes House Library, Oxford University

RJSC	Registrar of Joint Stock Companies
UB-CWAS	University of Birmingham, Centre for West African Studies
UBL	University of Birmingham Library
UK	United Kingdom
U.Sec.	Under-Secretary of State
W	West
WGCMC	Wassa (Gold Coast) Mining Company

1

Introduction

The story of gold blazes a spectacular path across the history of the Akan region of West Africa from the late Middle Ages onward.[1] Long before the first Iberian seafarers reached the Mina Coast at the end of the fifteenth century, the local people had mined for gold. And though the exact origins and dates are still open to dispute, there is now a consensus among scholars that the long-distance overland gold trade between the Akan forest zone and the entrepôts of the Western Sudan was already in existence when the Portuguese first appeared on the scene in 1471.[2] The most recent research tends to confirm what has long been suspected—that gold from the Akan region was one of the three major sources (along with Bambuhu on the Upper Senegal and Bure on the Upper Niger) for the Trans-Saharan caravan trade,[3] whence African gold found its way into the minted coins of Morocco and Egypt, to Florence, Venice, Spain, and other states of late Medieval and Renaissance Europe.[4] To tap supplies of Guinea gold closer to their sources as a means of compensating for gold shortages in Lisbon had been one of the primary goals of Henry the Navigator and his successors in Portugal's grand design of African reconnaissance. The Lusitanian merchant adventurers, who built the famous trading castle at São Jorge da Mina at the mouth of the Benya Lagoon on the Gold Coast in the 1480s, were astonished by the resplendent gold ornamentation of the local African women, chiefs, and other dignitaries and by the willingness of ordinary people to part with their gold dust and nuggets for European merchandise of seemingly lesser value.[5] As the emerging Akan states were gradually absorbed into the Atlantic commercial system, the European contact—with gold as the most potent initial lure—opened up a new era in the history of West Africa.

THE EARLY GOLD TRADE AND
GOLD IN THE AKAN CULTURE

The overseas gold trade based on traditional African mining reached its peak when Dutch and English traders joined the competition in the early 1600s, and it flourished for more than four centuries before the advent of mechanized mining, which is the main focus of the present study. It is worth keeping in mind that it was the gold trade, rather than the infamous trans-Atlantic slave traffic, that provided the impetus for the imposing forts and castles—Axim, Shama, Butre, Kommenda, Cape Coast, Mouri, Kormantine, and Anomabu—built along the littoral in the 1500s and 1600s.[6] Among the major European powers, the Portuguese earned a reputation as the overlords of the African gold trade by nearly monopolizing its export from the Mina Coast for about one hundred fifty years. On the other hand, in the midst of the dazzle, it is important to recognize the persistent obstacles and odds against successful gold mining on the Mina Coast from the age of the Portuguese exploration and settlement through to the period covered in this volume. Thus, as A. Teixeira Da Mota and P. E. H. Hair have pointed out, stories about the ease and abundance of profit making from overseas export of the yellow metal in the early modern period have been "overblown" by economic determinists. The estimated average of 450 kilograms exported per year by the Portuguese during the heyday of their monopoly (from 1450 to 1520) was probably not equaled in the succeeding decades of their hegemony. Older publications failed to take sufficient notice of the debit side of Portuguese accounts on the Gold Coast, including shipping costs to and from Portugal, maintenance of the coastal forts, rising costs in local trade on the coast, and growing competition from northern European interlopers.[7]

The Dutch, who succeeded the Portuguese as the dominant European trading nation of the Gold Coast in the 1640s, continued to earn their largest profits from the export of gold rather than from slaves for more than a hundred years. It was only about the middle of the eighteenth century, as surface gold deposits became depleted and as interior warfare and competition for trade by new European merchant adventurers (Danish, French, Spanish, Flemish, Swedes, and Brandenburgers, as well as English) intensified, that slaving finally superseded gold in profitability as the dominant export in this part of Africa. The stagnation in gold exports lasted beyond Britain's prohibition of the overseas slave trade in 1807, but gold revived in importance in the 1840s and 1850s.[8]

Over the years a number of scholars have attempted with varying success to estimate the total amounts of the yellow metal exported from the Gold Coast by all European nations, together with annual averages. Writing in the 1930s, Norman R. Junner suggested a total of 11,200,000 crude ounces, or about 40,000 ounces (1,243 kilograms) per year for the peak period, 1471-1750; and a total of 500,000 ounces, with an average of 10,000 ounces per year, during the half century 1751-1800.[9] More recently, Timothy Garrard has suggested 9,350,000 ounces total and 21,750 ounces (about 659 kg.) annual average from 1471 to 1900.[10] Fairly reliable statistical series on gold imports to Europe are available for the state-controlled Guinea and Mina House of Lisbon and the Dutch West Indian Company during segments of the sixteenth and seventeenth centuries.[11] It has to be emphasized, however, that these estimates derive from available figures on individual *importing* countries only. Philip Curtin, who has written the best general survey of the literature on this subject, points out that attempts to calculate total overseas gold exports by all European trading nations, let alone total West African gold production over the long term (which would have to include the overland gold trade and local uses in currency and jewelry), are so beset by methodological difficulties as to endow such estimates with limited scholarly value.[12]

Equally important in setting the scene for the present study were the political, religious, and aesthetic roles of gold that developed in Akan societies over the centuries. Ivor Wilks has drawn attention to the "northern factor," centering on the market town of Bigho and the early Akan gold-trading state of Bono-Mansu on the fringes of the forest and savanna belts, which became a crossroads for itinerant traders from the coast and for Malian middlemen from the bend of the Niger. It was at Bono-Mansu that the ritualistic regalia (the gold sword, mace, and stool—later associated with the kingly office of the great forest states: Denkyera, Akwamu, and, above all, Asante) first became the central symbols of office. Furthermore, the main towns of these and other Akan kingdoms and chieftaincies sometimes grew up around or near mining centers. Thus the presence of valuable gold deposits at the ancient town of Tafo is said to have been one of the factors that led to the consolidation of chiefdoms into the great Asante kingdom about 1700.[13] In Asante the glittering sunlike metal became at once the mirror of kingship and imperial splendor and the nexus that undergirded the state, the social order, and the entire culture.[14] Gold dust formed the base of the currency system; furthermore, tributes on conquered states were most commonly levied in gold, as were taxes, judicial fines, and other imposts on ordinary citizens. Skilled artisans in Asante and other Akan states became known far afield for the artistic quality of their gold jewelry and brass castings (the famous Akan brass weights, used for weighing gold dust), which have continued to play such an important part in royal regalia and ceremonies of state. (For details on traditional gold mining see chap. 3 and photos throughout this chapter.)

ORGANIZATION AND SCOPE OF THE STUDY

I shall make no attempt here to complete a lengthy exegesis of the published literature on gold mining in Ghana. Instead detailed references to the most pertinent prior research in various subfields will be made in subsequent chapters when appropriate to the issues at hand. Considering its importance to the economy and cultural traditions of the nation, it is surprising that the gold industry of the Akan region has not received greater in-depth attention in historical and anthropological scholarship. Obviously the yellow metal has been mentioned at various points in a number of surveys of Gold Coast colonial history and of Ghanaian political history as well as in scholarly monographs of the "trade and politics" genre.[15] Historians such as Kea and Daaku did a good job in highlighting the intricacies of the trade during the Dutch, Danish, and early English periods on the Gold Coast.[16] Yet in only a few rare instances has the African side of the gold industry itself been subjected to lengthy and systematic analysis from the standpoint of production as well as trade and taxation by modern economic and social historians.[17] One reason for this is the immensity and complexity of the subject and the fact that the thrust of Africanist scholarship in both the history and anthropology of Ghana in the immediate postindependence decades was more toward the intricacies of indigenous political and social systems. Pioneering works in Ghanaian economic history focused on trade and farming, with primary emphasis on the history of cocoa cultivation. Cocoa was viewed, correctly, as central to twentieth-century economic development and more representative of African entrepreneurial skills than mechanized mining, which tended to be disparaged as a narrow arm of expatriate colonial capitalist intervention. Today, as historians attempt to expand the horizons of what should be included in African economic history,[18] it is possible to examine Ghanaian gold mining from a more balanced perspective as a pursuit that embraced an indigenous

sector and a modern sector. The latter, which included important contributions by Africans, and not just Europeans, is worthy of study in its
own right, irrespective of the historical period and the associations with
colonialism, because it was an industry that occupied a central place in
the economic evolution of the country.

In the past several decades one of the dominant interests of scholars
writing about modern African mining history—whether from liberal,
conservative, or Marxist perspectives—has been on labor, including
mobilization, relations of production, wage payment, worker resistance, health and disease, class formation, and, for the twentieth
century, protest movements and trade unions. And of these studies,
it is safe to say that a majority have focused on southern Africa.[19]
African labor also occupies an important place in the present study;
and the evidence leads to what some readers may view as surprising
and paradoxical conclusions. At the same time there is room for a
broader history that takes a multidisciplinary perspective and attempts to integrate the analysis of labor relations to gold mining in
all of its dimensions, including capital, management, technology,
finance, control over land, and government policy. An encyclopedic
history of gold mining in the Gold Coast/Ghana from precolonial
times through the colonial period to the present—which would have
to include not only history, anthropology and economics, but such
topics as geology, engineering, metallurgy, religion, art, politics, management, African social systems, labor, and transportation—remains
a daunting task for the future. The present work tries to overcome
some of the obstacles to such a broad survey by concentrating in
some depth and technical detail on features of both indigenous mining and early European mechanized gold mining, but over a shorter
span of time: from 1877 to about 1900.

Historiographical Debate

I did not set about this task in order to test any single model or
paradigm. The methodological guidelines are those of traditional nar-
rative history. The book attempts to reconstruct the past in a realistic
way and to explain a complex set of interactions between several
fundamental historical forces, institutional structures, and human
agency rather than to make grand theoretical evaluations or pass moral
judgments about the long-term impact of Western technology and
colonial capitalism. In defense of the empirical approach taken here, I
shall argue that there is no single unified field of social science theory

(Marxist or otherwise) that can possibly comprehend the complex range of sectoral changes—in technology, labor, capital, land, entrepreneurship, mines management, transportation, health and housing, incipient urbanization, and government policy—when a prototype capitalistic mining industry gains a foothold in an undeveloped country or territory. For an accurate reconstruction of the past as it was lived, it is essential to examine individual and group actions and attitudes, at least in part, within the political and economic framework, technological capabilities, and cultural ethos that prevailed at that time, without exaggerated concern for what came after. In mining history, this means that it is extremely important to examine the efforts of the leading actors against the backdrop of daunting physical and geological barriers, coupled with the rudimentary mining technology and limited mining engineering expertise that were available at the time. None of this implies an avoidance of critical analysis, interpretation, moral judgment, or a sense of irony. Indeed, as we shall see throughout the chapters, the subject of Gold Coast gold mining history and mining labor history is crisscrossed by a number of wrenching and controversial issues for historiographical and interpretive debate. Many of these have been thrashed out in scholarly symposia and monographs on West Africa over the past twenty years; others are explored in this book for the first time.

Examples of older interpretations and received opinion that are modified or challenged in the ensuing chapters include the following notions: (1) that African traditional mining was inefficient and uneconomic for the farmer-miners who engaged in it; (2) that precolonial African mining was based fundamentally on local slave labor, and that when the British outlawed indigenous slavery in 1874 it destroyed traditional gold mining; (3) that the introduction of "modern" or "industrialized" mining to the Gold Coast was entirely the work of Europeans and that no middle-class Africans played any part in it; (4) that gold mining in Third World countries invariably brought easy and early riches to the entrepreneurs who participated in it; (5) that the mobilization of local African workers as underground wage laborers at the mechanized mines was never a genuine problem, except as it existed in the minds of biased Europeans; (6) that the pioneering capitalist companies made no use of older forms of African "nonwage" labor at their mines; (7) the stereotype (based primarily on the experience of southern Africa) that all European mining companies in Africa invariably used force to recruit labor; or the opposite view, (8) that the early

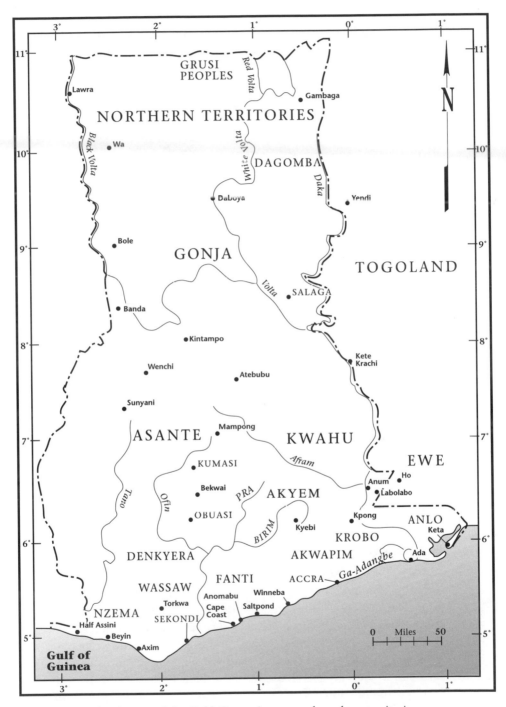

Map 1.1. Sketch map of the Gold Coast, Asante, and northern territories

expatriate mining companies of West Africa treated their African labor so fairly that no regulation or intervention by the colonial government was needed; (9) the commonly held view that from the beginning the British imperial government recognized the great value of mechanized mining and that the local colonial administration worked hand-in-glove with the concessionaires to support their interests and needs; and (10) that the expatriate companies exaggerated the problem of transportation between the coast and the interior and that from the beginning machinery and equipment could be moved efficiently by riverboat and human porterage without the existence of a railway. Reference books, speeches, and articles—both contemporary and modern—that ventured these opinions are cited in the chapters that follow. Furthermore, throughout the book I challenge hypotheses put forward by a number of scholars (11) that recruitment of the first wage laborers at the Wassa gold mines led to the genesis of an unskilled industrial wage labor force and that capitalistic gold mining ignited the first stirring of a working-class consciousness. Instead, I argue (12) that when measuring economic and social change, the transforming impact of capitalistic mining is revealed far less in the mobilization of a permanent unskilled wage labor force than in the individualization of *land* transfers as a consequence of concessionaire activity. Other important issues that emerge in this study include gender, ethnicity, business organization, pressure groups, and exploitation.

WORLD MINING BOOMS IN
THE NINETEENTH CENTURY

As just noted, the continuing role of gold in the economies of the Akan states of Ghana forms one central theme for this study. Another vastly different historical framework that also shaped the forces of economic change and the mentality of colonial miners and company agents is found in the literature on the great gold rushes in the larger global arena. From a cross-cultural perspective it is extremely interesting how from almost the beginning of recorded time gold mining, both in preindustrial (Europe, Asia, Africa, and the Americas) and in industrial societies, has given rise to a vivid set of myths and fantasies, from Jason and the Golden Fleece to the fabled Ophir and Coronado's Seven Cities of Cibola.[20] In fact, the legends, exaggerations, and delusions surrounding the North American and British Empire gold rushes of the nineteenth century were quite phenomenal. The second half of the nineteenth century embraced the greatest mining migrations in world history when dreams of bonanza lured thousands of gold and silver seekers to the far corners of the earth—to California in 1849, to Australia and British Columbia in the 1850s, to Colorado for gold in 1859 through 1865 and for silver in the 1870s, and to New Zealand for gold in the same decades. By century's end the gold fever had penetrated the eastern frontiers of Russia, Mexico, the Kolar goldfields of India, and Nevada; and it rose to frenzied levels at the Transvaal from 1886 through 1895, the Yukon and Klondike in 1896 through 1899, and many other colorful locales. The drive for control of precious metals became a vital theme in both the romance and the realities of European imperialism and American Manifest Destiny. Nearly everywhere mining had aggressive, disruptive, and exploitative, as well as heroic features. As part of the euphoria of the mining frontier, motley groups of driven and rough-hewn men launched a host of mining camps and boom towns. Names like Sacramento, Ballarat, Virginia City, Deadwood, Leadville, Johannesburg, Cripple Creek, and Dawson Creek became legendary and notorious. Some modern writers have even gone so far as to speak of a nineteenth-century "gold crusade."[21]

To this list of highly publicized mining regions must be added the southwestern Gold Coast, which attracted worldwide attention in two main gold rushes, known as the jungle booms. These booms pulled in prospectors, skilled laborers, and a few professional engineers, as well as assorted land speculators, share pushers, and con artists—some of whom had gained experience in the earlier rushes. As mining historians know, there was a natural momentum and continuity from one gold rush to the next. In the nineteenth century the pattern of booms was governed by the timely happenstance of new ore discoveries, as if according to a cycle. After each boom passed its zenith there was generally a lull or period of stagnation when members of the international mining fraternity regrouped and looked for fresh fields to conquer.[22] Diggers who had been lucky, or not so lucky, were often ready to follow the flock and move on to the next mining frontier. The first modern rush to the Gold Coast occurred in the lull prior to the "Rand" gold strike in South Africa during the second half of the 1880s. Thus, Cornishmen (always prized for their skills as timbermen and blastmen), Englishmen, Australians, and even some North Americans made their appearance in the Akan region of West Africa.

London, Center of World Mining Capitalism

What was the role of British metropolitan-centered capitalism in this process? The investment boom in West African gold mines was swept along by a broad surge in the issue and purchase of shares in foreign and colonial mining companies worldwide on the London Stock Exchange in the late 1870s and 1880s.[23] This movement was the product of a complex combination of interacting "push" and "pull" factors, difficult to disentangle, operating at both the empire-wide and local colonial levels. The Hobsonian question of whether there was a vast reservoir of "surplus capital" in domestic savings and investment that was suddenly drawn into overseas corporate and government securities in the last quarter of the nineteenth century was debated by contemporaries and has continued to intrigue historians.[24] More recently, writers such as Peter Cain and Michael Edelstein have suggested that there was indeed a "tendency for British savings to push down [domestic] interest rates and drive investors to look for more profitable opportunities abroad as the economy, after 1870, adjusted to a permanently lower rate of growth."[25] In addition, based in large part on its prior and ongoing role in the financing of corporate mining ventures in the United States of America, London by the 1870s had become the pivot point for the expansion of capitalistic gold-mining ventures around the globe. With the concentration of financial resources and mechanisms for floating share issues in the City, there developed also an expertise in mine management, where firms of engineering consultants could evaluate ore samples and offer technical advice to pioneering companies in the Americas, Australia, and the continent of Africa.[26] Some of these consultation firms might themselves engage in mining operations or establish their own mining investment syndicates.

On top of this, the general movement toward the gold standard as a backing for national currencies by major industrialized countries of the world quickened stock market interest in new and untried gold-producing regions of the world, such as the Gold Coast. As the foundation for Britain's internal and international credit system, the Bank of England by law had to maintain a gold reserve equal to one-fourth or more of all banknotes in circulation. The key point in this connection was that gold mines are a wasting asset. The world's output of gold, for which there was an unrelenting demand, particularly after 1873 when the United States turned to the gold standard, could be maintained only by bringing as many new mines as possible into production throughout the world.[27] Every new and distant El Dorado was always a gamble for investors; but as part of the shift from domestic savings toward increased overseas investment there was a substantial volume of capital available in London and the south of England for more speculative and risk-laden overseas investments—which included colonial mining ventures. This did not mean that new mining companies, especially those working in far-off tropical territories, necessarily had to entice well-to-do rentiers or members of the city's ruling elite of merchant bankers to invest in their companies—though occasionally they were fortunate in attracting two or three. My own researches in the Register of Joint Stock Companies reveals rather that there were hundreds of faceless shareholders drawn from various rungs of the middle classes—stock brokers and jobbers, estate agents, solicitors, owners of apothecary shops, clergymen, solicitors, scores of unemployed gentlemen, and even occasional greengrocers and shop assistants (residing in London and the southeast), most of who bought shares in small increments.[28] By the 1880s, according to one estimate, British-based companies were raising about £9,000,000 sterling per year for overseas mining operations, and the figure would continue to rise into the 1890s.[29] The risk-taking, speculative element was not the sole driving force behind investment in overseas mineral ventures, but it was obviously significant. Lance Davis and Robert Huttenback have calculated that there was a seven-fold increase in the quincennial averages for capital called up for mining and agricultural ventures on the continent of Africa between 1880 and 1884 and again in 1905 through 1909, as against a much smaller multiplier for increased investment in domestic manufacturing enterprise and public utilities during the same periods.[30] And the period of renewed interest in mining on the Guinea Coast of Africa occupied a lull between the New Zealand and Colorado gold rushes of the 1860s and 1870s and the great stampede to the Rand in South Africa in the second half of the 1880s.

STAGES OF DEVELOPMENT ON
THE MINING FRONTIER

What was the process by which mining enterprise penetrated the Gold Coast hinterland? Although the literature on frontiers in colonial history is voluminous, the concept of mining frontier used in this study is straightforward and uncomplicated; I make no attempt to elaborate on existing definitions with new theoretical edifices. Focusing mainly on the economic and geographic definition of a frontier, I follow J. C. Hudson in describing it simply as "the fluid outer boundary of a growth region."[31] The attractions of mining frontiers drove people outward to settle new lands and establish colonies; and by drawing hosts of supporting traders, shopkeepers, and hangers-on inward to sprawling shanty towns, the frontier could also ignite incipient urbanization. But mining frontiers also had a reputation for collapsing very quickly if promises of early bonanzas failed to materialize.

Penetration of Indigenous Economic Systems by Expatriate Technology and Capital

Machine technology probably played a larger part in the extension of mining frontiers than in cases of cattle-herding or trading frontiers. Complex and cumbersome heavy machinery and hand-powered equipment would be required to overcome formidable environmental and geological obstacles. These included efficient steam pumps for getting rid of groundwater, railways to ship machinery and supplies over long hauls, sawmills to cut lumber for building construction, and powerful explosives and crushing machinery to attack the extremely fine particles of gold that were sometimes embedded in very dense rock. On the other hand, European mining machinery was still quite rudimentary in this period. It is important not to exaggerate the force of technology on the mining frontier at this juncture. And I shall underscore the fact that indigenous African miners were also innovative, having developed their own tools and technology over the centuries in methods of extraction that were far from static or backward. In general, mining frontiers had less spatial sweep and permanence than the archetypal ranching and farming frontiers associated with vast prairies, veld, and pampas. By its very nature mining technology is highly specialized and restricted in its uses. Mining corporations deployed much of their research knowledge (geology and mining engineering), capital (expenditures on wages, tools, and equipment) and power (steam engines and explosives) in both a vertical and a downward (or subterranean) direction. And though the resulting mining elevator headgear and crushing installations might cut a strange silhouette in the midst of the tropical rain forest, they tended to be concentrated in pockets or fingerlike enclaves along river valleys or the crests of ridges, as at Heman-Prestea or Tarkwa and Aboso. Nonetheless, as with other colonial frontier movements of the nineteenth century, African mining frontiers had broader dimensions and consequences—both short term and long term, both positive and negative. An alien capitalism could contribute to social and political upheaval by bringing in new money, by impinging on indigenous labor and traditional relations of production, and especially—as we shall see in later chapters—by altering the authority of chiefs and upsetting traditional land-holding relationships.

Mining Cycles

Comparisons between the early history of expatriate gold mining in the Gold Coast and trends in technological innovation and organizational change among mining companies worldwide can be framed in roughly parallel patterns or waves of development: first ore discovery, then the big "rush," followed by capitalization, the building of underground and surface installations, adaptation of new machinery, and recruitment of labor. If these stages passed successfully, mines would move to production, the inculcation of effective management practices, a period of profitable operations, and, a final phase of decline, collapse, and reconsolidation. In the first stage of the Wassa gold boom described here, small groups of prospectors sought to make an easy killing from placer deposits along the banks of rivers and streams. A closely related activity was digging for surface level alluvial gold and reef outcrops through shallow shafts or short hillside adits in a manner not far different from the African peasant miners who preceded them. This was then followed by the full-scale rush—claim jumping by swarms of frontier individualists, as the news of quick riches was spread by propaganda. Such early rumblings on miners' frontiers in all parts of the world were accompanied by extravagant outpourings of promotional puffery in which slick share pushers in the metropole and swindlers in the mining camps sold worthless claims to naive and unsuspecting newcomers.[32]

After the initial placer and alluvial deposits were combed out or became depleted and dreams of easy and early riches faded, the miners invariably turned to the tough work of "hard-rock" or reef gold mining for the middle and late stages of development. And whereas the earliest phases of prospecting, panning, and shallow digs were the work of isolated individuals and small partnerships, the heavy capital requirements of the deep-level mining phase increasingly required the formation of joint-stock companies and the employment of trained professionals and experienced skilled workers.[33] It must be understood, therefore, that this transition to what can be called scientific and systematic mining stretched out over many decades. We can observe the rudiments of the process in these chapters. Because the geological map of the Gold Coast was largely unknown in the 1870s and 1880s and because veins of gold were located far underground, isolated from one another and often interrupted by long stretches of barren rock, the mining of deep-level gold posed monumental technical and logistical difficulties. Ordinarily the "free gold" of alluvial deposits could be separated fairly easily using manual methods. Even gold derived from surface outcrops was usually recoverable to its full value. But deep-level reef gold—whether of the quartz or banket type—tended to be more tightly bonded with other minerals and compounds to the parent rock. To release this gold companies had to install heavier and more sophisticated devices for drilling, crushing, extraction, and separation, all of which required ever larger capital inputs. For effective ore location, this stage urgently required consultation with geologists and professional mining engineers.[34] But such skilled professionals with advanced training were relatively few in the mining world in the second half of the nineteenth century; and they gravitated to the higher-paying jobs with top European and North American companies. If they traveled to West Africa at all, it was for brief tours as visiting consultants. Neither the mining companies, nor the colonial government had the will to undertake the kind of large-scale geological survey that was fundamental for long-range success. Experts acknowledged that the normal strictures against scientific ore discovery, not to mention expert installation of machinery and efficient production, were doubled or quadrupled in tropical regions like the Gold Coast over other mining regions of the world.

Decline and Exhaustion

The final stages in the cycles of the nineteenth-century mining booms in Europe and the Americas were also replicated in the Gold Coast. The capital requirements and ordinary working costs for deep-level reef gold mining were exceptionally burdensome and the longer a company maintained its operations, the heavier the burden became. Under these circumstances it became a cardinal principle of pioneering nineteenth-century capitalistic gold mining that working costs had to be pared to the bone if a company was to survive; and it was unskilled labor that was invariably selected to bear the burden of cost reductions. Unless paying streaks of gold were found reasonably early, most moderately capitalized companies found to their dismay that they lacked the liquidity to replace worn-out machinery, to press ahead with new exploration and development, and sometimes even to meet their payroll. Yet the successful raising of sufficient capital through the sale of new blocks of shares was contingent upon the maintenance of public confidence in continuous production. Pressured by shareholders to demonstrate profits and by workers for regular payment of wages at the accepted market rate, a majority of the companies were caught in a vice of their own making because they often wasted money in the initial purchase of concessions. At this point strong pressures for state-supported colonial public works entered the debate. Recognized mining experts of the day were united in the belief that cheap and effective road and rail transport were sine qua nons for getting requisite heavy machinery into place[35] and maintaining same in good working order through replacement of components. But for a variety of reasons, which were in some ways paradoxical, colonial administrators—while preaching "development"—tended to distance themselves from the miners. Later, in the face of disappointment, it was no wonder that a majority of the Wassa mining companies of the late nineteenth century blamed many of their problems on the failure of both the imperial and colonial regimes to provide the necessary financial assistance for the construction of railways and roads, geological and topographic surveys, mining-town administration, and sanitary works. The relatively short life of most of the mining companies whose stories are told here should not surprise the reader: minerals are an exhaustible resource. In many respects, considering the congeries of physical and institutional barriers that confronted them, it was remarkable that any of the first wave of Gold Coast ventures survived as long as they did. The fever chart of slow decline in West African, as in North American and other frontier mining regions, was marked by the familiar cycle of companies reconstituting themselves under new articles of incorporation and raising loan capital through the sale of debentures. In the Gold Coast, machine breakdown in the face of intractable geological and climatic obstacles brought forward progress to a standstill by the turn of the century.

EXPATRIATE MINERS AND
INDIGENOUS POPULATIONS

Despite their many similarities, there were also a great many ways in which the mining booms of the Gold Coast differed from the classic gold strikes of North America or Australia. Thus, the book also turns its attention to the impact of mining capitalism on Africans. For example, in the Gold Coast the mining rushes did not lead to a flood tide of European migration and large-scale settlement. Another major contrast lay in the expatriate miners' and their governments' treatment of the indigenous peoples who owed the land. In places such as Colorado, the Black Hills of the Dakotas, and the Arizona territory, nobody paid the slightest heed to the land and mineral rights of the Native Americans. The U.S. government had arrogated to itself sovereign control over all unsettled lands of the West, and the government viewed the Indians as nonpersons, without any proprietary rights in the land whatsoever. In some instances, it is true, the mineral-bearing lands "appeared to be uninhabited"; but the reality was that all but the most precipitous mountains were essential parts of nomadic hunting grounds. In many instances the miners and their cohorts ran the Indians off at gunpoint; a terrible number were killed in massacres by soldiers or settlers, and most others were ultimately forced to live in reservations.[36] Seldom did Native Americans become a part of the miners' work force—although this could happen on rare occasions.

In West Africa conditions for the use and takeover of mineral lands were different. The Akan peoples were sedentary cultivators who looked to their kings and chiefs as trustees for the care of land owned by all the people. Even though the European gold seekers and diggers in West Africa had the same aggressive propensities as their counterparts in North America or Australia, and sought to take advantage of kings and chiefs over the grant of mineral concessions at every turn, they could not sweep away African land rights, and they soon became aware that colonial authorities on the coast took at least a nominal responsibility that expatriate mining leases were bona fide legal instruments with provision for consideration and the payment of regular rents to chiefs. On the other hand, it soon became clear that successive Gold Coast governments fell far short in their regulation of these standards without adequate powers of enforcement in the interior districts where mining took place. As we shall see, countless misunderstandings and abuses occurred in the Gold Coast mining hinterland, owing to confusion over whether African or English law would apply and because the colonial regime lacked the personnel and nearby district courts to enforce either English or African law on the transfer of land rights in the interior. A related key issue that emerged from the gold rush would be the slow deterioration in the authority of kings and chiefs under the disruptive force of a grasping expatriate-led capitalism and frontier individualism. African farmers fought to retain their old surface farming and mining rights in tracts of land that their own chiefs and concessions middlemen leased to European companies. Many injustices did occur, but there were no wholesale expulsions of people nor vast land grants to giant expropriations during the period prior to 1895, owing to the resistance of Africans, the small capitalization and limited capabilities of companies, and constraints on the aggressiveness of the imperial and colonial governments.

LABOR MOBILIZATION: THE PERSISTENCE OF TRADITIONAL MINING IN THE FACE OF CAPITALISTIC ENCROACHMENTS

I began in-depth work on the history of mining in Ghana with curiosity to learn more about indigenous mining techniques before the establishment of British colonial rule. The deeper I became immersed in the topic, the more I discovered how varied, complex, and innovative traditional African mining methods were. Several illuminating parallels to my own findings come from the writings of Ian Phimister on the mining activities of the Shona people and their ancestors in what is now Zimbabwe.[37] At the same time cross-cultural analysis of work by archaeologists and classicists into ancient mining in the classical world shows how closely periodic and seasonal extractive methods by smallholding farmers in West Africa had a universal quality, resembling techniques used by Greek and Spanish miners in the ancient Mediterranean world and by counterparts in the Near East, Asia and elsewhere.[38] The data presented in chap. 3 revises and expands considerably on work I have published elsewhere on Akan precolonial gold mining.[39] Another area where a fair body of theoretical and comparative literature has offered insight is the history of colonial mining labor, particularly in the areas of recruitment and the attempted transformation of part-time farmer-miners into full-time wage earners under capitalist relations of production. Here studies on regions as diverse as Medieval Europe and Latin America, as well as other parts of Africa, have added nuance to what writers in the Marxist or materialist tradition call the "articulation of capitalism."[40] Interesting and provocative though this literature is, I do not use this terminology or methodology to any great extent here, but refer instead at various points to the advance, the penetration or the encroachment of capitalistic forms on precolonial or peasant relations of production. Some of the best recent studies in both the Marxist and non-Marxist traditions show that it is well to be wary of overarching and simplistic theoretical models that treat the ultimate domination of capitalism over peasant relations of production—whether in a progressive or regressive context—as a foregone conclusion.[41]

Marxist and Non-Marxist Interpretations

The analysis presented here suggests that scholars should raise new questions about the presumed inevitable drift toward capitalist/wage-earning relations of production, generated by industrialized gold mining and abetted by the colonial state in African and other Third World countries. My conclusions in African labor history differ from a number of mainstream determinist studies.[42] Fundamental to the conventional materialist approach is the premise that important road-blocks, shifts, reverses, and even changes of direction in labor migration during specific decades of history are of little account and constitute mere blips on the screen in the supposedly inevitable and central movements toward the creation of an African working class. I disagree with these assumptions. Instead I argue that the perpetuation of older forms of family-based peasant production, which included not only subsistence farming, but also occasional hunting, fishing, and traditional gold mining, were much more than short-term setbacks, but were the norm, and that they often stood in the way of the formation of a working class, even in the midst of inroads by colonial capitalism, to a far greater degree than is commonly supposed. The conclusions presented here also find support from studies in the history of mining labor in Bolivia that demonstrate that, even in the twentieth century, the development of capitalistic relations of production often proceeded by fits and starts and may in the end have replaced older kin-based relations of rural production only in a partial or fractured form—and sometimes not at all.[43] As we shall see, European mining capitalism in West Africa could be potent in its impact; but it did not necessarily sweep everything before it, nor did it affect every sector of life.

Of course some radical historians may contend that studies such as the present one, which focus on working conditions over a single generation, neglect the magnetic pull of wage labor over the long term and that most rural people who reside within the locus of a modern mining complex must sooner or later be absorbed, one way or another, into the all-powerful embrace of an advancing capitalist order. The present study takes issue with this contention on two cogent grounds. First, not all historical writing must deal with long-range movements (which may be, after all, no more than models in the mind of the historian); nor is it mandated that one must reconstruct the past in Whiggish fashion—that is, in terms of a natural evolution toward capitalist-proletarian class relationships or other "end product" institutions of the twentieth century. Historical phenomena are worth studying in their own time period, without regard to what came later. Second, even though the present study ends at the turn of the century, ongoing research by other scholars shows that many of the constraints against mobilization of a genuine proletariat in the mining industry, enumerated in this monograph, persisted in Ghana throughout the greater part of the twentieth century.[44] In short, I shall argue that there was no sign of either an emergent class consciousness or class formation evinced in the Gold Coast mining industry during the period surveyed here.

One of the salient points of interpretation in this book is, then, the survival and continuity of traditional village-based and family-based relations of production in gold mining. When examined in this light, the notion of an expanding miners' frontier takes on an added meaning. All too often the concept of frontier has Eurocentric overtones, owing to its derivation from the famous thesis of Frederick Jackson Turner. But a new mining frontier may embrace more than the activities of interloping foreign diggers and alien corporate interests; it can also include the expansion of an indigenous or peasant mining sector. Standing apart from the formal mechanized mining centers with their massive iron headgear, crushing mills, and chemical extractive plants were the armies of traditional African gold farmer-miners, who migrated with their adzes and shovels in the age-old way and opened up hundreds of new pit mines. Some of these new sites lay in the immediate vicinities of the Tarkwa, Aboso, and Prestea mines, which fell under the control of Europeans, others lay far off the beaten track at more distant and sparsely populated sites in the forest hinterland. Thus it was said that all along the River Ankobra, from its mouth east of the port of Axim and for more than fifty miles upstream, one could observe myriads of small riverbank settlements of Africans panning for gold in the traditional way during the dry season. One of the central conclusions of this book, driven home in the final chapter, is that there was an expansion of the indigenous African miners frontier, during the gold rush of 1877-1897 that existed and continued quite apart from the activities of the expatriate companies.

THE ROLE OF BRITISH AND AFRICAN
MERCHANTS IN THE GOLD RUSH

I have stressed the role of "push factors" in the West African gold rush that emanated from the City of London's role as the center of a worldwide network of mining investment and technical expertise. Yet one important "pull factor," which also drew mining investment to the Gold Coast, derived in part from the depression in the export of palm oil—a crisis throughout British West Africa in the late nineteenth century—and one that impelled merchants and traders to seek new outlets for their entrepreneurial energies. In a number of ways the winding down of the era of "legitimate trade" and "informal empire" on the Gold Coast mirrored trends all along the Guinea Coast during the years between about 1865 and 1890—just prior to the advent of the "new imperialism." It is, of course, possible to argue that the buildup in the export of palm oil as a substitute for the traffic in slaves gained a fair success during the first half of the nineteenth century.[45] The Gold Coast could not have survived commercially without it. During the first five decades of the nineteenth century, clusters of African, Eurafrican, and European traders, some of whose family links with overseas commerce extended back to the slave trading era, had eked out of a living from small-scale exporting and importing at various towns along the Gold Coast. In the early 1860s the competition between two British-owned West African steam shipping lines, by driving down freight rates and permitting cargo shipment in small lots, had widened the business opportunities for independent African traders competing with expatriate firms on the coast.[46]

Unfortunately, the appearance of this new entrepreneurial niche coincided with the start of an undulating downward price trend in Europe for palm oil, the demand for which was dependent on the state of the international fats and oils market. Unit prices and annual export values for Gold Coast palm oil dropped precipitously in the 1860s, but recovered again in the second half of the 1870s and early eighties, only to hit the doldrums again from 1886 to 1892.[47] The causes of this protracted phenomenon, which are too complex to unravel here, varied to some extent with the locale—the Gold Coast, Lagos, Bonny, Old Calabar. But the Gold Coast suffered more than the other countries because the quality of its oil was rated as inferior in Liverpool and Hamburg to the product of the Bights of Benin and Biafra.[48] "The main point here, to use A. G. Hopkin's words, is that there developed in the last quarter of the nineteenth century a "commercial crisis" all along the West African littoral that prompted a range of adaptive reactions in various regions and among different trading groups.[49] Some of these were well designed and constructive economic innovations; others, hastily conceived, aggravated the existing economic decline. For example, many of the merchants and traders of the Gold coast engaged in "tonnage hunting"—paying higher than market rates palm for oil to up-country producers in order to retain clients and engross export volumes—which only added to the glut on the worldwide fats and oils market and aggravated the depression.[50] Another reaction was seen in the cacaphony of complaints from local merchants and trade associations about severe impediments to interior market expansion and the disruption of existing trade flows to the coast by the frequency of internecine warfare, which at Cape Coast and Accra focused on the aggressive tactics of the powerful Asante kingdom and led to commercial pressures for "imperial" political solutions to the Gold Coast's hinterland problem.[51] Such accumulated protests from both European and indigenous traders would serve as one of the colonial government's strongest justifications for the conquest of Asante at century's end.

More constructive responses toward diversification came with the commercial development of palm kernels (used in the production of oleomargarine), experimentation with new products of commercial agriculture, such as citrus fruits, coffee, and cocoa (which took hold in the 1890s) and, finally, with the entrance of merchant adventurers into modern mechanized gold mining. Viewed from the vantage point of both the expatriate and indigenous coastal trading firms, then, the investment boom in gold mining and concessions presented itself as a possible way out of the ongoing commercial crisis. What has not been treated in the historical literature before is the way in which a significant number of the new mining companies and concessions syndicates were spawned directly by the old-line legitimate traders and palm oil dealers, frustrated by the trade depression, who sought to diversify their exports and find new outlets for their capital and entrepreneurial energies. One of the most direct connections between the palm oil depression and orchestration of the Gold Coast gold rush— which will be treated in chapter 4—was exemplified in the activities of James Irvine, a leading Liverpool consignment merchant and oil broker, who had sold off many of his West African holdings and whose speeches to U.K. business groups and articles in the commercial press pounded home the theme of expanding and diversifying West African

trade.[52] The other leading example was Francis Swanzy, senior partner
of the most powerful and longest lived of all the British trading companies active on the Gold Coast. With his home offices in London, his
Wassa (Gold Coast) Mining Company would become the leader of the
pack in the unfolding gold rush. Not all the new mining company
organizers and backers were Englishmen: there was also a pioneering
group of Parisian investors. Liverpool was represented as well. Still, a
majority of the companies had headquarters in London. Though by no
stretch of the imagination can it be said that they were members of the
gentlemanly elite of high finance and aristocratic connections, these
entrepreneurs were not without contacts and associations in the City
and they knew the mechanics of company flotation.

The Coastal African and Eurafrican Business and Professional Elites

Nearly as important, particularly in the early promotional and concessionaire phase of the gold boom, was the coterie of leading African merchants
and professional men whose contributions to the genesis of industrial
mining and other aspects of the Gold Coast's nineteenth-century commercial revolution still have not been treated adequately in a book-length
monograph.[53] Since mid-century a score of these members of the Gold
Coast's educated middle class had built up successful businesses in several
lines of endeavor and had become extremely prosperous. But they too had
fallen prey to the unpredictable gyrations of the palm products market;
and like their European competitors, they were searching desperately for
new business outlets.[54] Two great future achievements would be their
pioneering roles in actuating the first wild rubber exports in the 1880s and
the development of the Gold Coast's timber industry, based on the export
of West African mahogany from the western districts in the 1890s and the
early twentieth century. Soon after the ending of the Sixth Anglo-Asante
War (1873-1874), this same group of African entrepreneurs (some of
whom had served with distinction on the British side) were among the first
to seize on the window of opportunity for profits in a world-class "gold
rush." As a consequence of long-standing contacts with up-country chiefs,
they were among the first to buy up tracts of mineral-bearing lands in the
African kingdom of Wassa Fiase for later resale or lease to expatriate
concessionaires and claim jumpers.

A number of the African and Eurafrican promoters (like their British
rivals) took advantage of opportunities for windfall profits through
speculative real estate ventures; but the visionaries among them also

dreamed of a viable gold-mining industry that would augment exports and bring lasting prosperity to their country. The leading projectors— who included Dr. J. A. B. Horton of Sierra Leone, Ferdinand Fitzgerald of Liberia and London, and such Gold Coast luminaries as F. C. Grant, Swanzy Essien, James Amissah, and John Sarbah—truly believed that mechanized gold mining could serve as a launching vehicle for the creation of a "native capitalist class." Against overwhelming odds, a few tried to turn the dream to reality by opening up and working their own pit mines. Considering the prejudices and discrimination of the time, it was nothing short of astounding that William E. "Tarkwa" Sam and his two sons, springing as they did from Akyem roots and local mission schools, could become bona fide mining engineers, who were respected in the United Kingdom, as well as in West Africa, and who would play a leading role in the management of one of the central producing companies of the period—the Wassa (Gold Coast) Mining Company. At the end of my story I shall also show that there was a connection between indigenous African entrepreneurship and the estab- lishment of the world-famous Ashanti Goldfields Corporation at Ob- uasi in Asante. Although members of the Gold Coast's educated middle class occupied a secondary position in terms of numbers of individuals involved and the volume of capital subscribed, the very idea of indige- nous African entrepreneurs taking the lead in modern mining conces- sionaire activity deserves emphasis because it was extraordinary on the continent of Africa at this early juncture.

In brief, the Anglo-West African merchants and professional men of the Gold Coast were searching for a radical solution—a golden key—to their trading and business dilemmas. Expansion of coastal and interior markets for a wider range of imported manufactured goods, diversification into new export products, assistance to commercial agriculture (the miracle of cocoa lay further in the future), and the discovery of new and profitable outlets for capital investment were all put forward as worthy targets for govern- ment and private programmatic action and a way out of mid-nineteenth- century commercial stagnation. The development of a modern gold-mining industry seemed to come at an opportune time. Both the African middle class and the major English mercantile houses had good reason to hope that the gold rush (which they not only participated in, but helped to generate) would trigger general economic development for the entire colony. Two main focal points for this resurgence would be the gateway port towns of Axim in the west, near the mouth of the River Ankobra, and Cape Coast, in the central, or Fante, area (see map 1.1, above). The expatriate and

African promoters hoped that the substantial sums of money spent there and further north by prospectors, company agents, foremen, and mine workers would have a multiplier effect on the general economy. Both towns became steamer disembarkation points for industrial freight and equipment and rest points and staging areas for weary miners, traders, and transport carriers with heavy loads traveling to and from the inland mining centers.[55]

RELATIONS BETWEEN THE WEST AFRICAN GOLD-MINING INTEREST AND THE COLONIAL STATE

A final leitmotiv, which runs through each of the chapters and has something in common with mining histories in other parts of the British Empire, focuses on relations and tensions between the mining promoters and the British colonial and imperial elites. An enduring myth in the conventional wisdom on European mining in tropical Africa (perhaps overinfluenced by the experience of southern Africa) is that of a close identity of interests between colonial governments and mining capital. By compressing time and the minutiae of daily human interaction, both general surveys and doctrinaire tracts (whether from the right or left) miss or gloss over the most intriguing details on the day-to-day political economy of mining capitalism, which often reveals neither unity nor harmony between private enterprise and the colonial state, but rather constant argument, friction, and the clash of interests. In the case at hand, the Anglo-West African merchants of Cape Coast and Accra had long been suspicious of Whitehall and had complained vociferously both to the Gold Coast and imperial governments about official inattention and indifference to the general economic and social improvement of the colony and to the needs of the indigenous community in particular. To the African business class the frequent promises of government assistance to education, commercial agriculture, and public health on the coast in this period were hypocritical, smacking less of cooperation and development than of "subjugation."[56] Strange though it may seem, considering the long-term revenue advantages that mining might be expected to bring to a starved colonial treasury, the convoluted laissez-faire lens through which British officialdom normally viewed ordinary commercial enterprise, distorted to an even greater extent their perspective on colonial miners and mining activity. One reason for this is that Britain's West African possessions—whether the Gold Coast, Lagos, or Sierra Leone—could not hope to reach the export levels of the more prosperous tropical possessions, such as Ceylon or Jamaica, let alone India (the "diamond in the imperial diadem"), where there was a long tradition of state intervention in social and economic improvements under potent governors-general stretching back to mid-century.[57] A second reason for the discrepancy was that the Anglo-West African merchants and miners had not yet organized themselves into a potent lobbying organization, like that of the East India or China merchants, which could gain the ear of London.[58] When, after 1895, Whitehall did decide to move forward with direct assistance to the mining companies, the advance came about in part as the result of years of pressure and the natural evolution of policy on the spot and also from a dramatic new configuration of power relationships and pressures on the international scene that would totally alter the nature of economic imperialism.

Gold Ornamentation and the Adornment of Royalty in the Akan State

King Prempeh of Asante and several of his officials at Kumasi (c. 1889).
From Francis Hart, *The Gold Coast, Its Wealth and Health* (London, 1904).

State Officials of the Royal Court of the Asante Kingdom, Kumasi,
Asante. Courtesy Herbert M. Cole.

Selection of jewelry from the Royal Family of Asante. From Herbert M. Cole and Doran H. Ross, *The arts of Ghana* (Fowler Museum of Cultural History, U.C.L.A., 1977).

Fine artistic examples of the famous Akan gold weights, used in weighing gold dust. Courtesy Doran H. Ross.

2

Geological Structures and the Location of Gold in Ghana

MAIN GEOLOGICAL FORMATIONS

Before proceeding to a description of traditional African gold production and the more detailed history of European mechanized mining, it is necessary to introduce several broad generalizations and definitions concerning geological structures, ore classifications, and the locations of major mining sites. There are a bewildering variety of preconditions and essential ingredients required for a successful mining enterprise, but the most basic is that there must be a valuable mining property. Though the point may seem obvious, the serious natural barriers and technical difficulties that impede the discovery and development of rich ore zones are often slighted or ignored in popular and generalized accounts by historians and political economists who, for understandable reasons, have tended to emphasize only the human and governmental aspects of minerals exploitation in Africa.

Even a cursory understanding of geology and mining engineering helps modify the misconception that expatriate mining firms in Africa have invariably operated with overwhelming advantages in their favor. The history of gold mining, in particular shows few successes and a far greater number of false starts and failures. This is partly because gold occurs in far more minute and dispersed quantities than most of the other metallic ores and is highly insoluble. Moreover, the most valuable gold deposits normally lie below the water table. Even where gold reefs were sighted, companies foundered owing to the lack of sustainable paying lodes. These and other factors help explain the strong odds against discovering, let alone extracting, gold in rich-paying quantities in West Africa at this period (1875-1900) in history.

Still, the Gold Coast/Ghana was especially well-endowed in possessing at least two, and arguably four, important gold-mining zones. Both the "banket" deposits of the Wassa district and the more conventional quartz reef deposits of southern Asante ultimately proved to be extremely valuable. Of course there were variations in the quality of ore recovered depending on where particular mines pierced the vein. By the time scientific mining took hold in the Gold Coast in the 1930s, geologists and engineers with knowledge of South Africa contended that the banket deposits of Tarkwa were similar, and nearly equal in grade, to those of the Rand.[1] Professional assays demonstrated that the quartz reef deposits reefs of the Ashanti Goldfields Corporation further north yielded some of the highest precious metal contents per ton of ore of any gold deposits in the world.

I shall not dwell at length on the detailed geological map of Ghana (see map 2.1) except to note that the underlying strata have been grouped into approximately nine major systems that conform to the conventional schemes of geological time. The most important of the basic zones for the story here were the Birimian (named after the Birim River in Akyem) and the Tarkwaian, formed in the Precambrian period (approximately 2 to 2.8 billion years ago). Other major formations that proceeded forward (and upward) in time include the Akwapimian and the Voltaian—both of which are practically devoid of gold deposits—and, the Tertiary to Recent formations, which contain the major alluvial and lateritic deposits of subsurface gold. In fact, virtually all the gold deposits of Ghana derive from the basic Birimian rocks that underlie about one-sixth of the total land surface of the country south of the Kwahu escarpment (see map 2.1). And the Birimian greenstone belts (named from the greenish tinge of many metamorphosed volcanic rocks) were of special importance, since gold tended to be concentrated where these belts were penetrated by later igneous intrusions.[2]

Sedimentary or Alluvial Deposits

Gold ore, as is well known, falls into two main types: alluvial, or placer, and lode, or reef, gold. During the precolonial period, African miners extracted gold chiefly from the alluvial deposits, of which there are

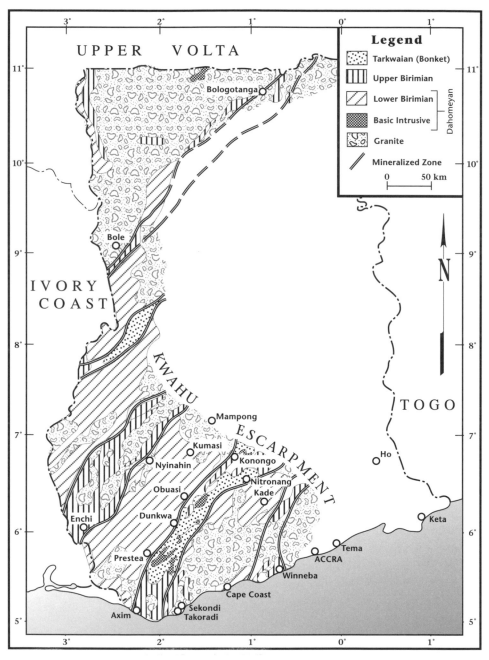

Map 2.1. Geological map of the gold belts of the Birimian and Tarkwaian systems

several subtypes: (1) those panned from rivers and streams that flowed over the Birimian and Tarkwaian formations, (2) those found along coastal sands washed down from the interior by rivers and rains, and (3) gold mines from denuded outcrops and subsurface sediments along the sides of dried-up valleys and gulches carved by antediluvian streams that had long since been obliterated. In addition, modern geologists sometimes make a further subdivision for surface deposits, called (4) eluvial gold.[3] In the Gold Coast/Ghana oxidized gold ore in the second and third categories was commonly found beneath layers of hard laterite or intermingled with strata of blue clay, which rested in turn on hard rock or in layers of gravel.[4]

Important traditional African alluvial washing sites could be found along the banks of practically every river in Ghana. Proceeding from west to east, some well-known examples were the Tano River, the southern part of which formed part of the boundary with the French Ivory Coast; the River Ankobra and its tributary the Bonsa, which formed the gateways to the key mining areas of Wassa, emphasized in the present study; the smaller Butre and Fimi Rivers; the rivers Pra and Ofin, which divided the Kingdom of Asante from the South-Central Akan states; and the Birim River Valley of the Akyem region in the east. The River Volta was used for placer mining in the far north (the Black and Red Volta); but was much too deep and powerful for gold washing in its southern reaches. In precolonial times, much of this river gold washed down to the seashore and turned towns and villages near the coastal towns at the river mouths into particularly active areas for panning by women and children at the time of the spring and summer rains.[5] Though commonly observed throughout the seventeenth and eighteenth centuries, shoreline gold collection had dwindled by the end of the nineteenth century.

Although this study will concentrate primarily on the state of Wassa Fiase, one of the main regions where European deep-level, mechanized mining took place, it would be incorrect to assume that all mining—and especially African mining—was restricted to Wassa. Three other great areas for both indigenous African gold mining and for mechanized mining by European companies were the western interior state of Sefwi and the great kingdoms of Asante and Akyem. The kingdom of Gyaman, subsequently absorbed into the hinterland of the French-controlled Ivory Coast was also famous for its gold. And in such other Akan states as Denkyera Twifo, Nzema, and Gwira, riverbed placer mining by traditional diggers and panners continued long after the advent of expatriate-controlled industrial mining. And in other districts, early explorers reported that almost the whole of the sandy gravel beneath the surface soil was auriferous.

Lode Gold

Lode gold or reef gold, the second major type of deposit, has played the dominant role in the history of capitalistic, mechanized mining in Africa. In Ghana such deposits were classified according to two main subtypes—banket formation and quartz vein gold. Now considerable confusion exists among laymen about *banket* and *conglomerate,* causing the two words to be used interchangeably, as if they were synonymous. The word *banket* was not known when the first substantial groups of British miners hit Wassa in the late 1870s; and it required several years of experience and research before miners understood the complexities of this kind of rock structure.[6] In fact, *banket* was first applied in South Africa in the mid-1880s, and it described any ore where extremely fine particles of a mineral are found embedded in a matrix of compressed gravel and clay.[7] Banket ores varied greatly in mineralogical composition and in degree of hardness. Conglomerate on the other hand, is a more specific type of rock, sometimes grouped with the breccias, grits, and quartzites: it is essentially a very hard natural concrete made up of closely packed pebbles of quartz cemented in clay or detritus. It would take us too far afield to cover the various contending theories as to the origins of the banket deposits of both West Africa and South Africa.[8] For the most part pioneering miners of the nineteenth century using crude machinery were pessimistic about the potentialities of banket ore, owing to the difficulty of recovering the extremely fine particles of gold so widely dispersed throughout the matrix. Still, most of the deeper gold deposits of Wassa state of the Southwest were found in one of the basic Tarkwaian substrata known as the Banket Series.

THE GEOLOGY OF THE TARKWA AND ABOSO GOLDFIELDS

Speaking generally, the lode gold deposits of southwestern and central Ghana are concentrated in a narrow rectangle approximately 100 miles long running from the confluence of the Ankobra and Bonsa Rivers in

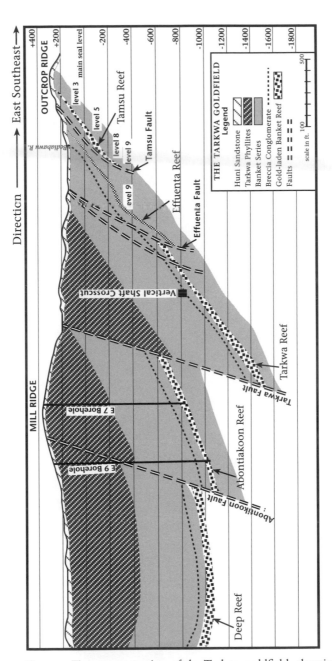

Fig. 2.1. Transverse section of the Tarkwa goldfield, showing
main geological levels and location of gold-bearing banket reefs,
Tarkwa. Based on A. M. Robinson, "The Gold Coast Banket:
Some Aspects of Its Geology in Relation to Mining," *Transactions
of the Institute of Mining and Metallurgy* 52 (1942–43): 311–46.

Wassa through southern Asante in a north-northeast direction to the edge of the Kwahu escarpment near Mpraeso (see fig. 2.1). At the Tarkwa and Aboso goldfields, one of the main centers of mining activity in Wassa state, the basic Tarkwaian System averages approximately 8,000 feet thick: It is composed of a number of substrata of varying thickness, including (1) the Kawere Group (the lowest level), made up of alternating bands of breccias, conglomerates, and quartzites; (2) the Banket Series, about 2,100 feet thick (just noted) composed of three sublayers—one of which contains the main gold deposits; the Tarkwa Phyllites; the Huni Sandstones (about 1,500 feet thick) formed by the leaching of silica from quartzite matrices; and (3) a top layer of secondary placer deposits, consisting primarily of decomposed quartzites and phyllites.[9]

Few of these geologic details were understood by European prospectors in the nineteenth century. Thanks in part to the pioneering work of the British geologist Norman Junner, and strengthened by modern Ghanaian geologists, such as G. O. Kesse, we know today that virtually the whole of the Tarkwa and Aboso area is part of a single great fault zone that houses clusters of many smaller structures. The advantageous feature of these upward-thrusting faults is that they forced the banket gold deposits closer to the surface. Places where sharp anticlines broke the surface of the ground coincide with some of the earliest Akan mine shafts and tunnels. Without trained geologists in their company or deep-boring equipment to test the lower strata, the first European prospectors to Wassa fared rather poorly and had to proceed by trial and error (see chap. 4). But they had the advantage of being able to follow the pathways marked by African pit miners who had worked these districts for centuries. To the English and French miners, the Banket Series quartzites appeared as stark ridges, as at the Tarkwa and at Aboso mines, where the main camps were built. Most of the early European probes were by horizontal adits or tunnels, which could be dug straight into the sides of these ridges so as to intersect the banket. By contrast, gold embedded in the clays and sandstones of the Huni Sandstone and Kwawere groups tended to be found in low-lying ground, sometimes with sharp "whaleback" outcrops.[10] These surface deposits continued to be the bases for the pit or trench mines dug by traditional African miners, as well as for the gold panned from river bottoms and seashores. Early British reports optimistically observed that the Banket Series were relatively free from metallic elements other than gold, but that extraction was made "troublesome" by the excessive fineness of the gold scattered throughout the matrix.

THE GEOLOGY OF SOUTHERN ASANTE

The auriferous deposits of the Obuasi region of southern Asante, which are touched on only briefly in this study, were quite different from the Tarkwa banket formations. In southern Asante, where Birimian rather than Tarkwaian formations predominated, the main sources of gold were not banket but dense quartz reefs. Again, the recognizable north-northeast angle of the general geological system and the numerous folds and faults within the various reefs were the results of complex deformation. It was at the breaks or sheer zones resulting from overthrusting faults that the gold veins, originating from igneous intrusions, were most likely to be found. Thus, the main ore channel stretching from the village of Sansu to beyond Obuasi, taken over in 1897 by the Ashanti Goldfields Corporation, appeared as one strong and persistent zone of overthrust and shearing. The main gold deposits occurred in Birimian phyllites and schists transversed by myriads of chutes and lenses of quartz.[11] But the value of a particular deposit depended on the length and thickness of these ore pockets, which varied greatly. Largely because the locations of many traditional African mines were secrets, zealously guarded by the paramount rulers of the Akan states, next to nothing was known about the location of Asante mines at the time of the first European gold rush to Wassa in the 1870s and 1880s. However, one early surveyor reported that the richness of the Asante reefs appeared to increase with their depth and that the first samples had yielded over four ounces of gold to the ton.[12]

Obuasi, which became the most famous center for mechanized gold mining in Ghana (see chap. 8), was but one of many important traditional Asante mining sites in precolonial times, which also included Manso-Nkwanta (in Kumase division), Kontsiabu, Atobiase, and Konongo (in Dwaben division). Lesser mining areas for African traditional mining in Asante were along the Owiri River, north of Odumasi in eastern Kumasi division; Kokobin, south of Lake Bosumtwe in Bekwai division; and Wam in the Brong-Ahafo region.

Again, there was no sure way that the first companies could determine the gold content of quartz ore without extensive testing, since the fine particles were seldom observable with the naked eye. Depending on the region, gold might be found in quartz of either the gray, bluish, or black-banded varieties. Much of the gold in the quartz vein existed in a free state and therefore could easily be milled; but some was contained in sulfides, such as arsenopyrite and pyrite, which required complex techniques for separation.

THE PRESTEA-BRUMASI DISTRICT

Quartzitic vein gold also formed the basic deposits of the third major mining district of southern, Ghana, that of Prestea-Brumasi, situated about twenty-two miles northwest of Tarkwa (see chap. 7, map 7.3). Though located in Upper (or northwestern) Wassa, the geology of the Prestea and Brumasi mines more closely resembled that of southern Asante than that of the Tarkwa district. Here the yellow metal was found, first, in Birimian sediments and lavas that had faulted many times and been intruded by granite and porphyry, and, second, in younger Tarkwaian sediments, also penetrated by igneous rocks. As with the quartz lodes of Obuasi, gold at Prestea and Brumasi was found in conjunction with a number of other minerals: arsenopyrite, carbonates, silver- and copper-bearing sulfides.[15] Like all the major mining zones described here, the Prestea district had been mined since early times by Africans, using traditional methods; and it quickly became one of the major targets for the expatriate concessions of the 1880s and 1890s. Over the next forty years an estimated £6,000,000 worth of gold was extracted by the major companies of Prestea-Brumasi.

THE BIBIANI GOLDFIELDS

One other distinct mining zone, which figures tangentially in my story of mechanized mining, is the Bibiani goldfields, located in Sefwi state, about fifty miles due west of Bekwai, in Asante. It was part of a wide belt of Birimian greenstones that stretched all the way from the south-eastern part of the Ivory Coast through Enchi in Aowin, north-north-east to Wiawso, the capital of Sefwi, through to Chicheware in the Ahafo region of western Asante. Some of the most noticeable and reliable outcrops of this greenstone belt were found in the Bibiani hills, which became a target for European company activity after 1895. The gold deposits here were found mainly in deep quartz reefs, which generally followed dykes of porphyry surrounded by gray and black phyllites.[16] As with the majority of mining districts mentioned in this study, Bibianiha first was opened up by traditional Akan gold diggers long before Europeans had heard of the area. It became an important advanced outpost of the expanding indigenous mining frontier under the leadership of traveling miners from Nzema state in the second half of the nineteenth century (see also chap. 8). The British company Bibiani Goldfields Limited took over mechanized mining in this area in the early twentieth century.

OTHER GOLD-BEARING ZONES IN GHANA

Other gold-containing greenstone strata that attracted both African and European prospectors included (1) eastern Asante (also called Asante-Akyem), coupled with the Birim River Valley of Akyem-Abuakwa; (2) a zone that followed a northeast line beginning in Gyaman (present Ivory Coast) and centering on the Tain River Valley and the Banda Hills district of present day Brong-Ahafo; and (3) the Black Volta river system, with goldfields near Bole and Lawra in the northwestern part of modern Ghana. Although the gold-containing strata of eastern Asante and western Akyem were thick in places, their interruption by frequent faults and fractures meant that the reefs were often extremely difficult to follow. Gold of the quartz vein type was derived entirely from Birimian strata, with the richest concentrations at or near the town of Konongo. Activities by European companies in Asante-Akyem (for example, the Lyndhurst Deep Level and Konongo Gold Mines), which became stable only in the 1930s, lie outside the bounds of this study.[17] Surface outcrops and gold from alluvium in the riverbeds, such as those of the Owiri in Konongo and the Birim in Akyem-Abuakwa, had yielded fair returns to African miners in times past and also beckoned European placer mines in the early 1900s. Similarly, the denuded oxidized ore of the Banda Hills,[18] northwest of Asante, and the deposits of the Bole and Lawra districts of the Black Volta region, in the northern territories, had yielded fair results to African surface miners in precolonial times. And several European dredging companies were projected during the early colonial decades examined here. But when tested at deeper levels in the 1930s by members of the Gold Coast geological survey, these northern districts were found to be either "barren of gold" or to possess deposits of insufficient value to merit substantial expatriate investment.

Of these tertiary areas then, only eastern Asante (particularly the Konongo mine) proved remunerative to modern deep-level mining companies. Mechanized dredging was attempted for a time at various points along the Birim and Black Volta Rivers but with limited and uneven success.

African merchant's house at the port town of Axim
which served the mining districts. Photo by the author.

An outcrop of gold ore in Asante

An African geologist with an example of banket gold ore (1987). Photo by the author.

Rapids on the Lower Ankobra River. Photo by the author.

An Akan village on the middle reaches of River Ankobra (c. 1890). Photo from the Rev. J. T. F. Halligey, "A Visit to the West African Gold Mines," *Work and Workers in the Missionary Field*, Vol. II (London, 1893).

Man with typical cargo-carrying canoe on River Ankobra near Bonsa junction (c. 1890). Photo from the Rev. J. T. F. Halligey, "Mission Work on the River Ankobra, West Africa," *Work and Workers in the Missionary Field*, Vol. III (London, 1894).

3

Traditional Gold Mining in the Southwestern Akan Region

African States, Technology, Political Economy, and Gender

No serious study can hope to analyze the origins of mechanized or industrial gold production in the Gold Coast/Ghana without first investigating the richness and complexities of African indigenous gold mining that stretched back for centuries prior to the coming of the first Portuguese traders and adventurers. The *sikadifo,* or gold miners, occupy an extremely important place in the economic history and culture of the Akan people.[1] Traditionally, gold dust, or *sika futuro,* was the major currency of practically all the Akan states. In Asante *sika,* or gold, in every form (tiny grains, nuggets, or jewelry and ornamentation) was the touchstone for judging both personal and institutional wealth throughout the realm. Over the centuries revenues from gold mining provided one of the most important building blocks for state formation and state consolidation in all the important kingdoms—Akwamu, Denkyera, Asante, Akyem-Abuakwa, Wassa Fiase, and others—of the Akan region. No one who aspired to any status or influence in Akan society could go far without gold; and most men would do anything they could to get their hands on it. It is one of the arguments of this study that traditional or preindustrial gold mining retained its vigor to a greater degree than was appreciated in many early-twentieth-century histories, and that it survived long after the Akan farmer-miners were supposed to have withered in the face of the onslaught by European mechanized companies.

Within the considerable and expanding literature on the economic history and anthropology of West African societies, the story of precolonial mining is still a relatively neglected area.[2] Of course, most of the classic European sources on the history of the greater Akan region refer to gold mining as one of the central occupations of the people; and these accounts affirm that surface-level gold could be found to some extent nearly everywhere throughout the coastal states and their hinterlands. In fact, the richest centers, where gold could be mined in substantial quantities, were found in five or six major kingdoms, or states: Wassa (emphasized in this volume), Asante, Denkyera, Akyem, Sefwi, and Gyaman, in the northwestern Brong-Ahafo region. Other secondary gold-mining areas included Nzema, Gwira, Aowin, Ahanta, Assin, Twifo, and Kwahu. To treat exhaustively every aspect of indigenous mining in each subzone or to trace the shifting patterns of the overland and overseas gold trades from the fourteenth through the eighteenth centuries would require a separate volume. Although the present chapter on African mining methods will include some evidence from each of the major mining states for a general overview, principal attention will focus on Wassa Fiase and neighboring states of southwestern Ghana because this was the first enclave of modern European capitalist penetration and the main action zone for this volume.

This chapter compresses time and space in that it covers a range of beliefs and practices about gold that varied to some degree from state to state, and sometimes even within districts, but which evolved over centuries of experimentation into a recognizable set of extractive methods and relations of production throughout the Akan world. Among the questions which we try to answer are: Who mined for gold? What kind of labor inputs were required in small-scale gold mining? What was the role of immigrant strangers? How was the typical gold mining labor unit organized? Was there any functional specialization or role differentiation in gold mining based on age or gender? To what extent were slaves involved in mining? What were the complementarities between gold mining and traditional agriculture? What part did religious belief play in attitudes toward gold and the practice of mining? What were the connections between gold mining and the powers of precolonial Akan states? And, finally, What were the economics of traditional gold mining? How profitable was it?

Against the view of some earlier chroniclers and historians, who argued that preindustrial gold mining by farmer-foragers was an overly arduous, inefficient, and essentially uneconomic activity, this chapter argues that digging for gold made great economic sense as a seasonal activity within a range of alternative choices.

A BRIEF SUMMARY OF POLITICAL HISTORY

Of the four or five major kingdoms of the Akan gold-mining region, the political and economic history of Wassa is perhaps the most kaleidoscopic and elusive. A region called Wassa, or Warsha, "a land rich in gold," had been well known since Portuguese times, and its approximate location was noted in the famous Dutch map of 1629.[3] Certainly the early Portuguese and Dutch merchants at the trading factories of Axim, Shama, and Elmina were aware of the importance of Wassa, since gold traders from that country were in constant passage to and from the coast. The original heartland of the kingdom lay north of the River Bonsa, south of the River Ofin, east of the River Ankobra, and west of the Bosum-Pra. "Old Wassa" was bounded on the west by the state of Gwira, which contained rich goldfields, and on the south by Ahanta (also important for mining), which William Bosman described as a "Commonwealth" of small states or chieftaincies.[4] The famous Duarte Pacheco Pereira, Portuguese Governor of São Jorge da Mina, had sent a representative to the court of Wassa as early as 1520, subsequently using his offices to settle a quarrel between the Wassa people and their neighbors the Adoms.[5] The period of Portuguese hegemony was followed by that of the Dutch and the English. Dutch takeover of Elmina Castle and Fort St. Anthony, Axim, at the expense of the Portuguese, between 1637 and 1642, gave them direct access to the gold trade of Wassa and of the Ankobra region. Kormantine, the first English post on the Gold Coast (obtained by agreement with the Fante states) dates from the 1630s, and it remained the only English fort until the capture of Cape Coast Castle from the Dutch in 1664.[6] Among many complex features, Dutch documents gathered by Albert Van Dantzig show that one of the unceasing aims of European commercial and diplomatic activity on the coast in the seventeenth and eighteenth centuries was "to keep the trade paths open," but that this also entailed the more insidious practice of the Dutch and the English competing to support one African state against another and either allowing or abetting "one more little war in order to achieve the desired peace."[7] Even during the height of the slave trade era in the eighteenth century, European interest in Wassa continued to center mainly on the gold trade.[8]

The political history of the Kingdom of Wassa in the eighteenth and nineteenth centuries can be written in terms of its conflicts with the great Asante Kingdom as well as its relations with the European powers.[9] From the early 1700s Old Wassa became well known as a potent military state as well as a significant commercial entity. Under the leadership of its greatest king, Ntsiful I (ca. 1721-52), Wassa stood as a primary obstacle to efforts by Asante to control the trade between the European forts of the central coastal districts and the interior. The main interest of the Dutch and the English lay in reducing the sources of friction and conflict between the African states, even as they continued to supply the various contending parties with the firearms and powder used to wage war.[10] Contrary to earlier theories advanced by Eva Meyerowitz that a division of Wassa into two kingdoms took place in the 1730s or even earlier,[11] the recent work of Larry Yarak demonstrates that that the modern states of Wassa Amenfi and Wassa Fiase did not exist during the first three centuries of the gold trade, but were, in fact, the products of early-nineteenth-century developments.[12] In a very general way the split into the two separate kingdoms of Wassa Amenfi and Wassa Fiase is traceable to overextension of the kingdom's territorial base under King Ntsiful I and his successors, coupled with exhaustion of the state's resources in the long series of conflicts with Asante. So long as Wassa maintained its military alliances with Twifo, Fante, and other "middle" states, it was able to resist Asante invasion (as it did in 1765 and 1776). But in 1785 this alliance system collapsed, and a successful Asante assault on the isolated Wassas led to full-scale conquest and occupation.[13]

The process of Wassa fragmentation was aggravated by the weight of Asante intervention and tribute exaction over the years, combined with the impotence of later Wassa kings and the fact that they were frequently at odds with their own chiefs and *abirempon*.[14] Even though a King, Ntsiful III, in the early 1800s continued to style himself as the legitimate sovereign over all Wassa from the old capital at Abrade, near the River Pra, nineteenth-century Dutch and English sources speak of at least three other centers of Wassa power that grew up near leading gold-mining and trading centers. These were Asemankro, near the heart of the Tarkwa and Aboso gold district; Daboasi, near the lower part of the River Pra on the southern gold route to Shama; and Enerhebi, near the present Heman-Prestea gold-mining region in northwestern Wassa Fiáse.[15] Exactly when Wassa became polarized into two separate king-doms is uncertain from the sources.[16] Whereas the Dutch at Elmina favored the pro-Asante faction in Wassa and sought to restore peaceful relations between Wassa and Asante, the British, under administrators such as Charles McCarthy and George Maclean, sought to detach

Wassa from Asante; and the existence of two separate Wassa kingdoms was affirmed in policy pronouncements of the 1830s.[17] By the 1850s the once powerful former "king" at Abrade, near the River Pra, had shrunk to a cipher; the centers of the two kingdoms were now further west in the Valley of the River Ankobra; and it became the practice to speak of the two states of Wassa Fiase (eastern or lower Wassa), with its capital at Amentin (not far from Asemankro), and Wassa Amenfi (western or Upper Wassa), with its capital at Enerhebi (see map 3.1).[18] Both of these capitals were within reach of a myriad of traditional gold-mining centers.

According to F. G. Crowther, a leading authority on Wassa in the early twentieth century, both Wassa Fiase and Wassa Amenfi, in theory, maintained strong kingdoms with centralized political systems. For each there existed a three-tiered pyramidal structure with a king, or *omanhene*, at the apex. Under the king's central authority were a set of *aman*, or stools (from 22 to 25 in Wassa Fiase), ruled by an *ohene*, or chief (also according to Crowther, called *asafohene*);[19] under this layer was a third division of villages ruled by *odikro* or village headmen (also called *koranti* in Wassa). At each level the rulers were advised by councils of elders *(mpanyimfo)* which were characteristic of the Akan tradition. Whenever the stool of an *ohene* fell vacant, whether by death or another cause), his successor, elected by local elders, had, nonetheless, to be confirmed by the *omanhene* (the king of Wassa Fiase or Wassa Amenfi). Similarly, the election of a village *odikro* had to be confirmed by the supervising *ohene*. Crowther also argued that the various *asafohene (omanhene)* of the two Wassas possessed less independence of action than in the normal subdivisions of most Twi-speaking states.[20] Kings and chiefs possessed authority over the land and over revenues (see also later sections in this chapter). Thus, whenever a local chief granted the right to a stranger to mine for gold on stool lands, the *omanhene*, as paramount ruler, was entitled to a one-third, or *abusa*, share of the proceeds.

State administrative claims over proceeds from gold mining operated as a double-edged sword. Under powerful rulers, it could strengthen the central resource bases of the two Wassa kingdoms; on the other hand, it could serve as an incentive for refractory chiefs to seek greater freedom from the king's authority. As with most of the Akan states, power wielded by the Wassa Fiasehenes over mining areas waxed and waned, depending on the capacities and energies of individual rulers. Theoretically, as Crowther has specified, the two major Wassa states possessed

Map 3.1. Southwestern Gold Coast, including the political and mining centers in the states of Wassa Fiase and Wassa Amenfi

sufficiently bureaucratized state structures for the kings' subordination of lesser chiefs and collection of revenues. In practice, however, important substools, like that of Apinto (which controlled the mines of Tarkwa) and that of Heman (within whose jurisdiction fell the mines of Essaman and Prestea), gradually tried to reduce their subordination to the paramount stool as more opportunities for mining wealth accumulated.[21] This is one of the subthemes that runs through this and succeeding chapters—how the accelerated intrusion of an alien capitalism, coupled with colonialism, gradually weakened the hold of the centralized state and encouraged decentralization. A significant part of mining history turns on *local* history. And though my main emphasis in this study focuses on the social relationships and technology of mining, one of my subordinate questions will be, What were the fluctuating centers of power inside Wassa Fiáse? During the early and middle decades of the nineteenth century, one or two strong Apintohenes gradually widened the political and territorial powers of the Apinto substate. As a consequence the kings of Wassa Fiase increasingly came to rely on the Apintohene as one of the major protectors and guarantors of the larger Wassa state.[22]

THE PRECOLONIAL ECONOMY OF WASSA

A number of early Dutch and English colonial sources stated that the Wassa people were poor or indifferent farmers.[23] During the period covered in the present volume, Wassa was categorized as a sparsely populated region, whose soil was not particularly fertile and where agriculture did not flourish.[24] It is now necessary to flesh out these surface observations with a more complete explanation from a more balanced perspective. In the first place a number of these early commentators never visited Wassa and, therefore, could not have known this vast area, which contained numerous topographical subdivisions and districts, capable of sustaining different kinds of vegetation and food crops.[25] Second, many expatriate observers, then and later, did not understand the ecological exigencies and practical efficiency of forest bush fallow (often described as slash-and-burn) agriculture. And because they did not see families toiling arduously in the fields every day, they assumed that labor exertions were weak, when, in fact, the seasonal labor inputs for clearing forests (especially heavy), planting, and harvesting could be intensive and taxing.[26] Third, it is certainly true that many parts of Wassa, and indeed much of the Akan region, were sparsely populated, even up to the early twentieth century. Forests blanketed much of the land; and villages with extensive cleared fields were few and far between.[27] Eurocentric terminology may have been a problem. Victorian travelers' accounts sometimes gave their readers a mistaken impression by referring to Akan farms generally as "estates," or even "plantations."[28] In reality most cultivated family plots, surrounding *nkuro,* or hamlets (ranging from, say, five to twenty domiciles), were small, dispersed, and difficult for strangers to discern.[29] This conforms to Wilks's estimate of the average size of Asante forest farms during this time as about 2.5 acres (one hectare); though plots for some families could be less than one acre.[30] Fourth, it is possible that low soil fertility was a factor that limited which crops could be grown extensively in certain districts of Wassa. True, in many parts of the Akan region, especially some of the nearer hinterlands of the coastal states (Ahanta would be one example) expatriates recognized that a rich variety of garden vegetables (for example, tomatoes, beans, maize, onions, red peppers, and okra), plus citrus fruits, flourished in addition to the starchy root crops (yams, cassava, coco-yams), and that farmers in these areas sometimes produced these vegetables as a surplus for market sales.[31] This was far less true in many parts of the more distant forest zone—Sefwi, Aowin, Akyem, Kwahu, as well as parts of Wassa—where it was said that markets were rare and that the main food crops were those more easily grown plantains, supplemented in the diet by game and fish.[32] At the same time, some parts of the two Wassas and Gwira, contained highly fertile areas—as for example, in the valley of the Ankobra. One Dutch official traveling upriver said that the people lived by agriculture and appeared "to be well supplied with food." The main crops were plantains and maize.[33]

Persistence of the stereotyped view that the Wassa people were not good farmers[34] can also be explained in part by the tendency to provide simple explanations for complex phenomena and to place African peoples, or ethnic subgroups, into a single economic niche. The Wassa people were, indeed, farmers; but they alternated between tilling the soil and a number of other economic pursuits, including hunting, fishing, foraging, and, of course, mining. Persistence of the hunting mode in the Akan region, even into the modern era, has often been slighted by scholars. Thus, the flesh of wild animals (rabbits, "bush puppies," deer), plus wildfowl, fish from rivers, and snails gathered from the forest floor added balance to the diet. Nor should we neglect the fact that the Wassa people were active as middlemen and earned a good deal in trade with the coast. This point has been strongly underscored by Yarak.[35] Finally—and this gets to the core of my story—we should not neglect the central fact that many (perhaps a majority) of the Wassa people in key gold districts spent a high percentage of their time in mining activities. This, added to all the above factors, explains seemingly paradoxical expatriate observa-

tions about the apparent neglect of farming coupled with the noticeable wealth of numbers of people:[36] for many Wassa men and women
mining became practically a full-time activity during certain months
of the year—particularly the dry season—when the chances for a
lucrative return were most propitious.[37] Robert Addo-Fening makes
a set of nearly identical points about the high importance of gold
mining and the relative neglect of farming in his penetrating analysis
of the economic pursuits of the people of Akyem-Abuakwa, the
leading gold-producing state in eastern Ghana.[38] Historians and an-
thropologists will continue to press for greater precision in their
search for concepts that mirror the realities of regional ecological
diversity and economic change in Africa. Some Africanist scholars
feel comfortable with the term *peasants* as a broad category for rural
people not fully absorbed into full-time capitalistic farming.[39] There
is at present no perfect conceptual framework. Recognizing the awk-
wardness of terms such as *farmer-hunter-miners* or *farmer-forager-
trader-miners,* I shall continue to use the term *farmer-miners,* as well
as *traditional miners,* or *indigenous miners* throughout this study,
with the understanding that these simplified terms do not do justice
to the complexities of what actually took place.

Migrant Groups Who Mined in Wassa:
The Gold Miners of Nzema

It is unfortunate that early European reports on Wassa and Asante tell
us precious little about the ethnic subgroups and classes—let alone
individuals—who developed special prowess in gold mining. Not all the
Wassa miners were indigenous to the area. There was a sizable group
of diggers who migrated to Wassa and also to Asante from such
southwestern states as Ahanta, Aowin, Gwira, and from Assin, Twifo,
and Denkyera. One of the most interesting features of Akan gold-mining history concerns the prominent role of the Nzeman people (or
Apollonians as they were still called in most nineteenth-century accounts). Closely related by language and ethnic affinity to the Anyi
people of the eastern Ivory Coast, they lived in the region between the
Ankobra River and the Tano Lagoon. An expansionistic people, the
Nzemans originally occupied a small patch of coastal territory centered
around their capital city of Beyin. For a variety of complex reasons,
most notably the pressure of an expanding population, they fanned out
from their original homeland and became peripatetic traders, farmers,
and gold miners, settling in small communities as far west as the Comoé

and Bia river basins in the Ivory Coast hinterland, northeast into Wassa, and as far north as Sefwi, Asante, and Gyaman.[40] According to Nana Ezonle, the Tutohene of Atuabo, the coastal heartland of Nzema was a densely populated area with a narrow and limited agricultural base. This, coupled with early contacts with Portuguese and Dutch merchant vessels, propelled the people into overland commerce as middlemen between the coast and interior from an early period.[41]

I cannot delve here into the complex political history of Nzema, except to note that under a series of strong rulers, including Yanzu Acka, Kwaku Acka, and Kofi Blay, the Nzemans simultaneously expanded their base of territorial and administrative control so that it embraced virtually all the lands east of Axim and the River Ankobra, stretching westward to the River Tano (see map 3.1).[42] More important, the Nzemans stretched their own gold-mining frontier to the interior by opening up new mines in virgin or sparsely populated areas long before the first European gold rush of the late 1870s and early 1880s. Under the supervision of one of their own subchiefs or headmen, they would move into an area, obtain permission from the local stool authority to remain for a period of time, and start to dig.[43] The Nzeman people were known for their physical vigor and for bringing improvements (through tools and working methods) to the miners' art. One of their most innovative techniques was that of "fire setting" in difficult-to-penetrate deep-reef gold mines,[44] a technique that became common in Wassa and other Akan gold-mining states as well. Setting fire to bundles of straw or faggots deep underground, they might let them burn for as long as several days and then douse the red-hot rock with buckets of cold water, causing the brittle quartz to crack. In most cases, Nzeman families appear to have migrated to Wassa in small groups only for the duration of the mining season; but, in some instances, they settled permanently and took up farming as well. Some accounts also credit the Nzemans with being the first to mine for gold at a number of the famous Asante sites, such as Obuasi at Adanse state in Asante.[45] Later they were instrumental in developing the timber trade of the Ankobra, Huni, and Tano rivers. The Nzemans were skillful entrepreneurs who transmitted knowledge of new trade goods and useful methods in mining and agriculture to some of the more remote and less populous areas of the western interior. (For a map of Nzema and surrounding states see also chap. 8, map 8.1.)

MINING CATEGORIES, TECHNIQUES,
AND SPECIALIZATION

Traditional gold mining can be analyzed according to three main categories. The most common type was washing or panning for alluvial gold along the banks of streams and rivers—the Ankobra, the Ofin, the Tano, and the Birim—and along ocean shores, particularly those near river estuaries. The second, and probably the most important form of mining in terms of numbers of workers involved and returns of gold, was shallow-pit surface mining on either the crests or sides of hills or in the sedimented valleys of ancient river beds. The third type was deep-shaft mining for reef gold. Gold mining was largely a seasonal activity. Some panning for river gold, particularly as the rivers emptied near the seashore, tended to be best in the early rainy season, as the resurgent rushing waters brought down loose soil from the upland regions.[46] But deep-shaft mining (sometimes called digging for "mountain gold") was essentially a dry-season activity—occupying the time of men after yam harvesting in December and reaching a peak just before planting in April, while the underground water table was still low. As we shall see, there were clear-cut divisions of labor in mining, but mainly along lines of gender, rather than of "slave versus free," as some writers have suggested.

Placer Mining

Panning for alluvial gold (Twi: *apoa*) in up-country stream beds and along coastal shorelines was primarily the work of women, adolescent girls, and young boys, organized on a family basis. Early Dutch accounts, such as that by John Barbot, stating that young boys could find rich stores of gold by diving into the most rapid streams or underneath waterfalls, must be taken with a good deal of skepticism.[47] The fact is that the most rapid reaches of the most powerful rivers, such as the Volta and the Pra, were not suitable for alluvial mining. The most common and effective method was for people to scoop holes in the gravel beds of small and slow-moving up-country streams or in eddying pools on the shallow sides of larger rivers (see photo of women washing for gold), rather than descend into the centers of rushing torrents. Adult males might also participate in digging holes close to the river banks. Women's alluvial gold washing could be dictated in some states by strict custom. Thus in one Wassa substate panning for gold was restricted to

Tuesdays, Thursdays, and Sundays.[48] Still placer gold washing was not always organized as a group or family activity. Informants in Denkyera, Akyem, and Asante stated that individual women could go to the local river at any time and pan for gold. Furthermore, it was not a pursuit fit only for slaves, as some accounts have suggested (although some female household slaves might participate); any member of a family or surrounding community could engage in it. In some districts gold washing might be the almost daily occupation of women during the appropriate season. Among the interesting and colorful names the Akan miners gave to rich areas were: Omampah, "the place where gold nuggets are"; Mudaso, "the forge in the stream"; Yirama, "choke-full (of gold)"; and Obuasi, "that which is under the rock."[49] In panning for gold grains on the sandy coastal beaches the best results were gained shortly after the start of the rainy season, or just after a violent thunderstorm, when the rising rivers and streams—not yet swollen—deposited gold-laden sand along the beaches near their estuaries.[50]

Separation of the gold dust from its parent sand and gravel was an extremely time-consuming process. The methodology entailed repeated swirlings of a given amount of riverbed sand for even the smallest amount of pure gold to be isolated. Experienced Akan panners for placer gold—nearly always women—washed the mixture by a circular motion in a series of stages requiring successively smaller bowls or trays known as *akorow, posie, aposna,* and *korowa*[51] until at last all the sand and gravel was washed away, leaving only the heavier gold grains at the bottom of the last pan. In some instances the final and smallest bowl was painted with black vegetable dye to better expose the gold. In Wassa, Nzema, Akyem, and Asante, I talked to elders who had seen their mothers and grandmothers pan for gold along the riverbanks and had heard stories about the practice going back to earlier generations. All agreed that it was an arduous process requiring great experience, care, and patience. In Akyem and in Asante, the general term used for all gold-washing bowls was *sika kodoo.*[52] In Nzemaland the name for gold was *nduke,* and the calabashes or wooden bowls used for swirling the gold-laden sand were known as *bondo* (or *bondoo*). And among Nzemans, in contrast to the general norm for Akan mining, informants said that it was as common for adult men as well as women to both dig and pan for gold in streambeds and along the shores. John Ansah Quino of Awiebo village, Eastern Nzema, a modern miner using traditional methods showed the writer a twentieth-century innovation wherein the gold-containing sand was quickly separated from rocks and gravel by means of a wire screen sieve (see photo, chap. 8).[53] Henry Meredith observed in 1812 that the seashore gold panners of the Cape Coast area exercised "much dexterity and ingenuity" and that this only could be "acquired by much practice."[54] After the 1880s, as European-style mechanized mining opened up, seasoned sourdoughs from Australia and South Africa marveled that the skill of a West African woman with a wooden bowl or brass pan far exceeded anything they had seen at Ballarat or on the Rand (see photos at the end of this chapter).

Tools and Innovations

Over the course of time, indigenous gold miners demonstrated innovative ability in devising a variety of mining tools and extractive techniques. According to J. A. Skertchly, pioneering prospector of the 1870s, the most commonly used implement in shallow-pit mining was the ordinary digging hoe, or adze (which the Akan people used in farming), known as the *aso* or the *soso*, with a metal head about two inches broad and six inches long.[55] For centuries this was the local version of the miner's pick ax. But G. E. Ferguson, the Fante geologist and surveyor, when passing through the Upper Birim Valley of Akyem-Abuakwa in 1890, noted that local diggers had developed another more specialized digging tool—a kind of long-handled chisel—known in Twi as the *soso toa*, which miners could use for chipping and prying open cracks in the rock. Pressing the ends of this digging tool against the walls of the shaft, the miner also used it for support in descent and ascent. Dredgers for river gold sometimes also used the *soso tupre*, a kind of shovel.[56] As they labored, miners placed the loosened earth and rock in a basket, a clay pot, or a calabash, which was raised to the surface by coworkers using a handmade raffia rope. As a result of long experimentation, ever more sophisticated mining techniques evolved among Akan miners, in some districts to the point where miners were using European-made picks and shovels and substituting wooden ladders for the previous hollowed-out hand- and footholds for descent and ascent down and up shafts. In some instances, with larger mine shafts, miners built frame sheds or palm leaf coverings to keep out the rain (see fig. 3.1). There is also evidence that by the late nineteenth century indigenous miners were using metal and wooden buckets to raise the ore. In Akyem, according to informants, these buckets were called *bokiti*; and ropes were made from the bark of a tree known as *mutua*.[57]

Shallow-Pit Mining

Shallow-pit subsurface digs constituted the most common form of indigenous gold mining and were undoubtedly the principal source of the gold dust and nuggets produced in the Akan states and exported overland both north and south to the coast over the centuries (see photos at the end of the chapter). Most of the gold deposits worked in the precolonial period were in the softer oxide ores, located closer to the surface, rather than the deeper and harder quartz and sulfide ores. As John Beecham noted in 1841, much of the gold wealth of Asante "appeared more like an impregnation of the soil than a mine."[58] The surface was opened either in small holes, dug by individuals, or in larger excavations, such as trenches or broad circular pits (sometimes eight to ten feet in diameter), carved out by families, or even entire villages, working together. Despite what has been said here about underground mining being restricted to men, there appears to have been no absolute gender division of labor for *surface-level* excavations: some accounts say that men, women, and children dug side by side. The pits usually were no more than three to ten feet deep. Miners found little difficulty in getting at the sedimentary deposits of fine gold and occasional nuggets that underlay the upper strata and that sometimes could be found at each of the following levels—topsoil, laterite, blue clay, and gravel—before reaching the hard rock.[59]

The central importance of this intermediate type of mining—neither placer nor deep-level hard-rock—where work could be carried on by two, three or four family members—is one of the key points to which I referred in my criticism of Emmanuel Terray's contention that a major part of Akan traditional mining was in quartz reefs, so hard and impenetrable that only large numbers of slaves could do the work.[60] In the years that have passed since this debate began we have come closer to agreement that at least two categories of traditional mining labor existed. I still hold firmly to my contention that in the main areas that I have studied—such as Wassa, Denkyera and Akyem—that a family or kin-based mode of production in mining was the general rule. In this common type of family mining small numbers of slaves might work alongside the head of the household. Informants who recalled kin-based mining did tell the writer that if a family mining group had slaves, then such slaves might well be the first to descend the deepest parts of a pit and perhaps undertake some of the more dangerous and difficult work.[61] But such deep level work was not left exclusively to

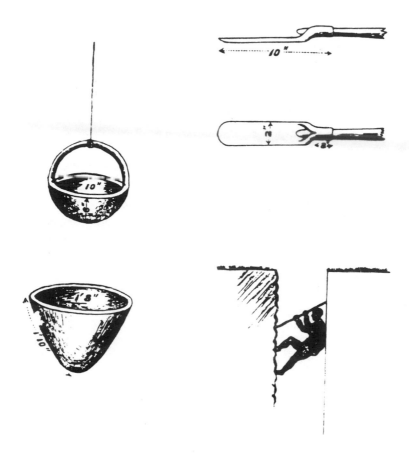

Fig. 3.1. Contemporary drawing of traditional mining implements. From a drawing by the African surveyor, G. E. Ferguson, reproduced in R. A. Freeman, *Travels and Life in Ashanti and Jaman* (London, 1898), 531.

slaves. And it is extremely important to keep in mind that not all families owned slaves.[62] On the other hand, I am prepared to accept that in certain highly centralized kingdoms—notably Asante and Gyaman (the area Terray has studied most closely) that kings and chiefs sometimes employed their own cadres of royal miners which could have consisted mainly of slaves. There is also some evidence of this in Wassa. More significant—and this is the point emphasized here—even if it could be asserted that deep level reef gold ore extraction was so tough that only slaves would do it, such hard-rock mining tended to be the *exception* and not the rule; it definitely was not the most important source for gold production throughout the Akan region. This pride of place was, as we have just seen, reserved for intermediate level or shallow pit surface mining.

Norman Junner, the geologist who became the leading authority on Ghana rocks and minerals in the twentieth century, stated that even though they certainly possessed the skills for hard-rock mining, the typical free Akan miner was too intelligent to want to waste his time and energy on this aspect of mining when easier and quicker sources of gold retrieval lay open to him. Thus, even when first coming across a rich lode of quartz or banket, Gold Coastans would first attack the extremities of the ore body—the shattered and crumbled portions—"particularly on the hanging wall side of the outcrop."[63] Oral data gathered in Wassa reinforces contemporary written evidence that much gold was extracted from the crumbled detritus of reefs or of sedimentary-level *nkron,* seldom more than eight to twenty feet deep, reached by shafts that averaged about two to three feet in diameter.[64] And the key point, which all these sources are quick to confirm, is that on the average these small shafts and working areas could accommodate no more than two or three men at a time—certainly not the large gangs of slaves that were central according to Emmanuel Terrays "slave-based mode of production model."[65]

Deep-Level Reef Gold Mining

Beyond this, there were indeed *instances* of deep-level reef gold mines (known in Twi as *amenapeaa,* or *nkron nkomena*) in the major Akan gold-bearing states. Considering the prejudices of Victorian times, it comes as no surprise to read that some European travelers, many of whom had never traveled to the mining districts, continued to voice serious doubts about the technical expertise of African gold miners and their capacity to attack quartz reefs. In the jaundiced eyes of many expatriate traders and colonial administrators, African gold mining could be described only as primitive and inefficient. Even some reputable London mining experts sent to Tarkwa on brief inspections thought that Akan miners were incapable of sinking truly deep shafts, or of knowing how to cut adits and tunnels. On the other hand, several hard-slogging sourdoughs, who had traveled widely abroad before becoming heavily immersed in deep-level mining up-country in Wassa knew differently. For instance, C. J. Harvey, a mining engineer from Victoria, Australia, who would be among the first Europeans to observe indigenous hard-rock mining firsthand at Wassa in the 1870s, mapped instances where African miners, having skimmed off the surface gold, would penetrate (on the average) thirty to sixty feet or more down through the various gold-containing sedimentary layers and attack the main reef.[66] Though the presence of ground water was an ever-present threat below those levels, examples of mine shafts 100 to 200 feet long (not necessarily vertical) were recorded. Since the fiercely determined diggers appeared willing to follow almost any lead, underground shafts and chambers could at times take on bizarre shapes and patterns. Centuries earlier, the Dutch chronicler Pieter de Marees noted that "if they find a vein, they follow it down to the end," so that "a gold mine is like a tree with roots spreading out in all directions."[67] In addition to the original tools already named, Akan miners during the 1870s and 1880s were reported to be making increased use of short-handled hammers and chisels, fashioned by local blacksmiths from imported bar iron, to assist in splitting the toughest rock.[68] Shafts came in a variety of shapes and sizes, ranging from the chimney type, large enough for one man (the most common form), to a rectangular type, to sloping types with steps cut in, and long snakelike tubes that bent to follow the line of the reef. If miners struck a rich lode, they worked extremely hard—often around the clock—to gouge out all the gold-laden ore: "All day and night" one observer reported in 1860, "nothing is heard but the noise of digging, grinding and washing the soil ."[69] To say that vision was impaired deep underground—whether by night or day—is an understatement. To help brighten the darkness, miners might use candles or they developed special lamps, made of clay and lighted by wicks of cotton cloth soaked in palm oil.

While large, deep-level hard-rock mines with open chambers and galleries did exist, oral and written sources confirm that the most common type of dig was still the narrow tubular shaft—about two feet in diameter—often sufficient to accommodate only one man with two or three confederates.[70] A characteristic intermediate-depth mine was the bell-shaped or bottle-shaped *nkron*, narrow at the top but widening at the lower levels into a dome-shaped mining chamber.[71] In one instance sketched by E. Wray, miners found a huge dome-shaped mass of gold-laden quartz that had intruded into the surrounding clays and shales (see chap. 4, fig. 4.1). The conventional wisdom that indigenous miners knew nothing about horizontal adits and timbering also was off the mark.[72] Tunneling was not the norm, but African miners did use short tunnels to connect vertical shafts on occasion. Edwin A. Cade, the Londoner who later purchased the rich Obuasi concession, noted in passing through southern Asante in 1895 that the twenty-foot shafts, most common there, tended to "occur in pairs about 6 feet apart, the intention being to tunnel at the base from the one to the other and so obtain a portion of the underlying rock."[73] For disconnected vertical shafts, the diggers got protection against cave-ins by using "lagging" — long bamboo poles or lath, kept in place by rope or horizontal strips nailed at intervals (see photos at the end of this chapter).[74] Though less frequent, they also used heavy timbers to shore up the hanging walls of longer horizontal tunnels and adits. Such signs of technical change became more common in the 1880s and 1890s. Whether it was true, as two popular writers alleged, that such innovations could only have been developed in emulation of European practices, is beside the point.[75] Most innovations are the products of the diffusion of knowledge. Akan miners displayed their resourcefulness by constant alertness to new challenges and opportunities using local adaptations. If traditional African miners benefited to a limited extent from brief contacts with European prospectors, it is also well to point out that the early expatriate companies frequently built their first vertical shafts on the exact sites of earlier African pit mines. Though many expatriates continued to doubt it, the skill and success of Akan deep-level miners was confirmed in a report by Louis Wyatt, one of the first Gold Coast government officials to visit the Wassa mining districts:

> The natives sink shafts from 40 to 90 feet, then drive under the hill, supporting the roof with timber. I personally descended the richest and deepest of these, and it was a matter of surprise that with the primitive tools and appliances used, and the toughness and hardness of some portions of the rock to be pierced, that such [large] workings should have been successfully prosecuted.[76]

Fire Setting and Explosives

Several stages were involved in excavating and crushing quartz reef and banket gold. In the absence of explosives, the best way of loosening the gold ore from its parent rock was by the ancient technique of fire setting. Now many European written accounts of the eighteenth and nineteenth centuries referred to fire setting in bare outline; but few filled in the nuances of how it actually worked. Informants in Wassa in the 1980s disclosed to the writer that their parents and other kinsmen would attack a pillar of reef gold by trying first to dig the earth and broken rock out from around it, thus exposing the gold-laden pillar or block on all sides. Next the family group would go into the bush to gather a special kind of dense, slow-burning wood, known in Wassa Fiase as *krodze,* which would be stacked in big piles against the rock. These detailed narratives make one doubly aware of the formidable nature of reef mining and how much time and effort went into heating the rocks to red-hot temperatures. Incredible though it may seem, elders at Tarkwa stated that underground bonfires had to be kept burning for three to four days and perhaps longer in order to be effective.[77] One or two people might be left to tend the fire, while the rest might return to their home village or else probe further into the bush for gold or to hunt or fish. At the end of the necessary period the miners would return to douse the fires and crack the rock with buckets of cold water. Then they would attack it with their adzes or hammers and chisels if available. But fire setting was seldom a once-and-for-all operation. With a particularly lengthy or refractory quartz vein it might be necessary to repeat the process of roasting followed by sudden dousing many times over as the diggers advanced along the line of reef.[78] Not every mining group possessed this degree of persistence. Obviously many indigenous miners evaded the burden of fire setting by going around, under, or over the top of the hardest sections of reefs and simply gathering gold from the detritus of broken fragments at the margins. This made economic sense. Evidence for a rich lode had to be extraordinarily good in order for fire setting to pay off. Still, tough obstacles had a way of sparking the African initiatives for more effective solutions—namely, the use of explosives. Yarak has provided evidence from Dutch sources that African miners were experimenting with gunpowder for the cracking of hard rock from in states nearer the coast, such as Ahanta, from at least the 1840s.[79] The spread of this technique among Akan miners was also reported with greater frequency in Wassa with the coming of British mechanized mining in the 1870s and 1880s;[80] though, as with some of the other modern tools and techniques earlier described (iron hammers and chisels, shovels, horizontal tunneling, supportive timbering) the use of explosives by traditional miners, partly owing to the expense and quantity required, was still far from a common practice.[81]

RELIGION AND MAGIC IN
RELATION TO GOLD MINING

Belief in strong spiritual forces and taboos remained an important factor in indigenous mining throughout the period surveyed. As noted in chapter 1, gold possessed a sacred aura in Akan folklore as a symbol of both godly and royal splendor and power. As in many African religions, the Supreme Being, called *Nyame* or *Onyame* among the Akan, was viewed as the somewhat remote Creator and Lord of the Universe, but not one who intervened regularly in the lives of people. In Wassa the most important local deity to whom people prayed for special favors and deliverance from misfortune was Mankouma (or Mankuma). As an earth deity, Mankouma was closely associated not only with the forest, the hunt, and farming but also with gold mining. Informants at Tarkwe stated that before anyone would go gold mining it was common to obtain a blessing for the journey. "To do this you would pour some libations of schnapps on the earth and pray to Mankouma to release the gold to you."[82] Elders and court advisers to the present Apintohene, Nana Faibill III, stated that their people traditionally believed that all the gold that lay under the earth and in the rivers fell under Mankouma's custody or guardianship. Therefore, when villagers went on gold-finding expeditions they would frequently pray to him for personal safety and good luck on their journey. (In the Apinto substate of Wassa Fiase one of the most important traditional mines was, in fact, called the Mankouma Mine.) For the people of Konongo, Dwaben State (in eastern Asante), the name of the local deity endowed with similar powers over gold and the mines was Apuntea.[83]

Gold itself was deemed to have magical properties. To some it was like a living organism that could move through the ground and pop up anywhere like quicksilver. According to some Akan traditions nuggets could be planted in the ground and would sprout up and multiply like the nodules on a coral reef.[84] Just as miners would offer up prayers and libations before embarking on a mining expedition, so too they performed rituals after the discovery of an unusually rich lode of gold. Writing in the eighteenth century, the Danish trader R. F. Rømer noted that if the Akyems found a rich nugget, "they had to bring a fowl or a hen into the mine, kill it near the place where gold was found, and . . . appease the god of earth with its blood." The richer the deposit, the larger the animal that might be sacrificed.[85]

There were also definite prohibitions and bad omens associated with mining—especially underground mining—in which transgressions would be punished by an accident or injury. In Apinto informants stated that Tuesday was a sacred day when people were not permitted to dig for gold.

In some other areas, Friday was also a taboo day for gold mining. Women in the Akan culture were not permitted to go deep underground at any time for the well-known reason that menstruation was associated with uncleanliness and that any emission of blood, especially underground, would have been viewed as a defilement of sacred soil. Misfortune might also be associated with offenses against those lesser deities or spirits in the Akan pantheon known as *abosum* or *bosum*. These unseen forest spirits were often seen as capricious and mischievous, lying in wait to entrap the unwary miner or hunter who might stumble into an abandoned mine shaft. If a group digging deep underground suffered death or injury from a cave-in or a collapsed shaft, it might be suspected that they had provoked or angered an *abosum*.[86] Some mining areas were deemed so sacred that a total ban existed that prevented anyone (European or African) from digging in the earth or desecrating the surrounding forest lest they rouse the local spirits.[87]

Though the product of genuine belief, supernatural explanations could also serve a strategic function. Some of the early Dutch traders thought that the kings and the chiefs of inland states of the southwestern Gold Coast used *juju* (magic) and the threat of injury or death to deliberately scare off intruders—and especially to prevent white men from learning the location of the most valuable gold mines.[88] Underlying nearly all of these religious beliefs and legends was a very genuine human response to the danger of losing one's life. Numerous instances were recorded where whole groups of family workers were caught under a crumbling shaft or collapsed hanging wall.[89] Barbot thought that the justifiable fear of being "buried alive" was probably a far more potent deterrent to deep level mining "than any religious or superstitious conceits."[90] Even during the period described in this book European prospectors were turned away from certain valleys in Wassa with the warning that it was "fetish" or taboo. These prohibitions also extended to educated Africans and Eurafricans from the coastal towns who desired to travel inland to mine. Another underlying explanation is that local chiefs wanted to keep these mines isolated and uncontaminated for their private gold needs. Thus the stories of doom served a very practical purpose. There was a persistent rumor among the people of Apinto that the French prospector M. J. Bonnat, discussed in the next chapter, lost his life to fever in Wassa for the very reason that he had provoked or angered the gods by veering off prescribed pathways or transgressing against a taboo (or both).[91]

Obstacles and Limitations on Deep-Level Mining

When we consider the engineering and production barriers that troubled European companies in the 1870s and 1880s, it is scarcely surprising to learn that African peasant miners in Wassa and elsewhere also could be discouraged by unusually tough geological and environmental obstacles. When confronted by a shelf of feldspar, diorite, or granite that stood between them and an ore chute or lens, they astutely generally preferred to dig around it, if possible, in order to attack the reef from a more exposed angle. As we have seen, the possibility of pushing directly forward by cracking the rock with fire setting was always open; but the practice required moving or resetting new fires at intervals down the entire reef—a staggeringly time-consuming task. Lack of sufficient fresh air at the deeper levels was more than a minor irritant. It is difficult for the unfledged to capture the feelings of "closeness" and claustrophobia that easily could set in after an extended period of hard work underground,[92] and how the simple function of breathing could be stressful with limited oxygen and practically no ventilation.[93] Imagine what it was like for miners to grope about and find a seam of gold ore in half-light or semi darkness. Lamps or candles were not always available; more often miners had to operate as best they could from dim natural light transmitted down the shafts. Obviously darkness added greatly to the aura of mystery that surrounded gold mining.

Above every other factor, the most common cause for total work stoppage at the deeper levels was the ever-present threat of seepage from groundwater. This could be especially bad—even dangerous—after a big rain, which was the main reason for concentration on deep-level mining during the dry seasons. Still, ordinary groundwater might intrude into mining chambers at anywhere from 40 to 100 feet, depending on the height of the water table and the month of the year when miners might be working. As already noted, some of the sikadifo built swish lean-tos or sheds with angled roofs over their mine shafts to protect against rain.[94] Such improvisations might allow them to finish a day's work, but they could not prevent ultimate flooding. Here we see one of the most serious technological thresholds between precapitalist and late-stage mechanized mining. But it is important to realize that not even the early expatriate capitalist companies, which are the focus of later chapters, would be able to cross this technological threshold effectively during the period under

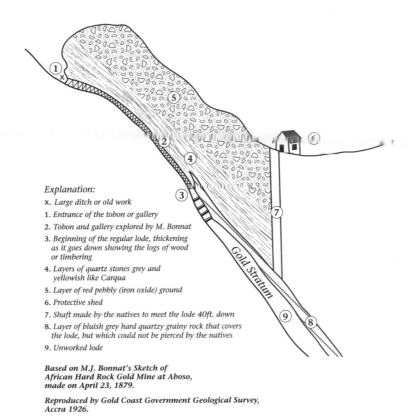

Explanation:

x. Large ditch or old work

1. Entrance of the tobon or gallery

2. Tobon and gallery explored by M. Bonnat

3. Beginning of the regular lode, thickening
   as it goes down showing the logs of wood
   or timbering

4. Layers of quartz stones grey and
   yellowish like Carqua

5. Layer of red pebbly (iron oxide) ground

6. Protective shed

7. Shaft made by the natives to meet the lode 40ft. down

8. Layer of bluish grey hard quartzy grainy rock that covers
   the lode, but which could not be pierced by the natives

9. Unworked lode

Based on M.J. Bonnat's Sketch of
African Hard Rock Gold Mine at Aboso,
made on April 23, 1879.

Reproduced by Gold Coast Government Geological Survey,
Accra 1926.

Fig. 3.2. Sketch of African hard-rock gold mine at Aboso by M. J. Bonnat (1979). Note use of: (a) vertical shaft, forty feet deep: (b) shed to protect against rain: (c) tunneling to pierce gold lode: (d) timbering to protect against falling rock.

survey here. The problem of deep-level flooding would be overcome only through the introduction of the most sophisticated differential steam pumping machinery after 1900. Mine shafts deluged by the sudden onrush of water into subterranean sinkholes or drowning pools were the ultimate bugbear for all deep-level miners—African and European; and it was mainly for this reason that so many mines had to be abandoned, often at the richest point of the lode.[95] When considering all these problems and the limited available technology, knowledgeable British prospectors and engineers of the period—J. A. Skertchly, Louis Wyatt, C. J. Harvey, and Edwin Cade—could only express amazement at the continued ingenuity and perseverance of African traditional miners against such daunting odds.

How in the name of fortune the men of that nation of born gold seekers could have twisted and turned themselves down those wretched
holes—how they lived when they got there in the deuced foul air—
or how they cracked rock and got it out absolutely passes my com-
prehension.[96]

CRUSHING, WASHING, AND GOLD EXTRACTION

After excavation came the equally arduous process of pulverization,
washing, and separation. All during the day diggers and their female
companions would pile chunks of ore at the head of their mine shafts.
After a hard day's digging the miners and their family helpers would
either transport the rough-hewn chunks back to their homes, or (if
they had traveled great distances from their villages) crush the ore in
the makeshift camps constructed near the mining site. (There were
many of these temporary camps—some used for hunting as well as
mining—scattered throughout Wassa and, indeed, the entire Akan
forest zone.) In the first step, the men would place the chunks of ore
on granite slabs, using their hammers to pound the ore into small
bits. Beginning after the evening meal, miners might work for many
hours in order to grind down one cubic foot of stone.[97] Commenting
on the cooperative work ethic of these mining groups, eyewitnesses
said it was not uncommon for the family head and his helpers to
work straight through the night and into the next day in order to get
the job done. Boredom was relieved by singing, small talk and a
demijohn of rum or palm wine.[98] Women played a large part in every
phase of extractive activity above ground.

In the second stage, which was entirely women's work, a handful of
the pounded ore would be placed on a block of granite about two feet
square held on a wooden frame. A woman would then take an oblong
stone shaped stone like a baker's roller and rub it forward and back
across the slab (these were the "mullerstone" and the "bedstone") until
the ground quartz became powder to be collected in a calabash bowl
at the base of the slab. It is almost certain that this technique was an
adaptation of the traditional method of preparing *kenkey,* the cornmeal
of the Akan, made by crushing maize between two stones.[99] According
to Nana Efoa Tenkromaa, Queen Mother of Konongo in Dwaben,
Asante, the rolling or crushing stone was called the *mobaa.* (For an
example of the stones used for grinding grain, see photo at the end of

this chapter.) But she added that, in her experience, this roller was not identical with those used for making *kenkey;* rather it was painted black in order to highlight the tiny gold grains that invariably stuck to its surface.[100] For the third phase the pulverized grains (which included much sand) were turned over to the women and children of the family for final separation by washing and panning in the same manner as for river gold. If the crushing site lay some distance from any river or stream, women would prepare washing pits adjacent to the hillside shafts. In the last phase the wet gold grains were normally dried in a shell in the open air and sun. Some informants stated that the drying process might be speeded by roasting in a pan over a fire. After this the gold dust, or *sika futuro,* would be "given back to the men, who," after "weighing it in their little scales," then "put it carefully away in a small piece of cloth or quill."[101]

Here we can touch only briefly on a related question that lies outside the purview of the present study. What did the Akan people do with their gold after they had extracted it? Keep in mind that until about 1890 gold dust, or *sika futuro,* was still one of the main currencies of the realm—especially in the interior.[102] And it was the only officially acceptable currency in Asante. At the time some hypercritical government officials and coastal merchants contended that Gold Coastans lacked a natural "saving spirit," that they tended to spend any earnings all too quickly and that, therefore, they fell easily into debt.[103] To any one who has studied the history of the Akan states or has talked with rural Ghanaians such statements appear far from the truth, then or now. It is necessary to reemphasize that the wealth of every individual and family, every lineage head and chief, was tied up with both the possession and the effective use or investment of gold, or *sika,* in productive enterprise. Older informants from Wassa, Asante, and Akyem insisted that they and their forbears were extremely conscious about thrift.[104] Most family heads saved a portion of the gold dust and nuggets that they extracted over time. A number of elderly gentlemen stated that they had been able to invest in cocoa farming as a result of the money they had saved from previous economic pursuits such as gold mining and rubber tapping.[105] Furthermore, the penchant of the ruling orders of society—particularly in Asante—to have plenty of gold in the form of jewelry for display is also well known. When an important family member died, a certain amount of gold would be buried with him or her. Another strong motive for saving gold was so that elders could leave a legacy for their families.

Several eyewitnesses recounted that when all the aforementioned tasks of separation had been completed, their fathers might again roast the gold grains in a brass pan over an open fire in order to melt them down for making their own jewelry or transforming them into solid lumps for easier safekeeping. Others said it was common for them to turn over a portion of their gold grains to traveling goldsmiths who for a fee would do the melting down into jewelry. (Incidentally, the presence of a greater number of goldsmiths in remote up-country villages has been an indicator of healthy and expanding mining operations in the surrounding districts.)[106] (See photos of goldsmiths at end of ch. 8.) With open doors to every domicile, householders were naturally concerned about possible theft of the gold they saved. According to Efoa Tenkromaa, "After that [winnowing the gold grains] we made some holes in the house and put the gold into pots and covered it with stones and earth." Referring to her parents she added, "They would also pour sheep's blood on it as a kind of protection."[107] This evidence on what European travelers used to put down as "hoarding" bears on another major research issue. We shall never be able to estimate the total or annual amounts of gold produced by indigenous miners in the Gold Coast and Asante from the narrow and spotty figures on overseas gold exports alone (see also chap. 8). Not only does this leave out gold used in internal exchange and overland trade; it ignores the large portion of mined gold that was retained by the people and their rulers in the forms of nuggets, gold dust currency, and jewelry.

MODES OF PRODUCTION AND APPROPRIATION OF SURPLUS BY THE PRECOLONIAL AKAN STATES

In several earlier publications I have discussed in broad outline labor organization in precolonial gold mining, the question of who had access to mining areas, and the administration of gold mining for the appropriation of surplus by the state.[108] Based on more recent research, I would like to venture several further conclusions coupled with one or two qualifications on the extent of state intervention in gold mining that may help us to get a bit closer to what really happened. Although there will continue to be controversy on this issue, I am more convinced than ever that traditional gold mining took place mainly within the small family group. In other words, the search for gold centered on small-scale patriarchal and kin-based relations of production with husband, wives, and other members of the conjugal family comprising the basic work unit.[109] Contemporary accounts that talk of hundreds of people mining in a rich goldfield do not detract from this supposition (see chap. 4). That numbers of separate families and individuals might congregate side by side in a particularly rich zone does not necessarily prove the invariable existence of centralized or coercive direction by some external or royal authority—although this could exist.

Characteristic Family Work Routines

Much of the information presented in these sections on the nuances of traditional African attitudes toward gold mining and methods of gold extraction is relatively fresh, having been acquired in oral field interviews in several recent trips to Ghana. Though the broad outlines have been known, many of the of the details on the daily routine of family mining and gold saving presented here have not (to my knowledge) been recounted in the same way in other written sources. Typically, families would set out for the gold fields in the morning and return in the evening. According to my informants, two or three men of the family would start out at the crack of dawn without any morning meal. If the mining area was not too far away, the women of the family might bring cooked food to them for a break later in the day. Normally, any individual or group could mine for gold anywhere they chose within the limits of their own lineage or stool lands. If two men were fortunate in finding a lucrative area on a given day they would return home and bring other family members to the location. It was natural that they would not wish to share this information with everyone in their village, unless they had to. Of course, informants conceded, it was not always possible to keep such news secret. But if other villagers followed to the new site, they would most often respect the exclusive rights of the discovering family or group to the pits that they had developed.[110] It is quite possible that the picture of an entire village mining for gold helped to foster European images of gang slave labor (see also chap. 4). From data on states like the two Wassas, Akyem-Abuakwa, and others, however, one finds little or no basis for the model of a massive or dominant "slave-based mode of production." Once again, if slaves were used at all in Wassa they functioned mainly in very small numbers as part of the family unit. Slaves under state auspices may have been used to a somewhat greater extent in parts of Asante; however, even there I would argue that the bulk of exportable gold was the product of work by free individuals and ordinary family groups.[111] Again, informants did say that if a family possessed slaves (known as *odonko*), then they might order them to do some of the more risky deep-level work; but other informants stated that, as a general rule, it was the senior male family members who did the toughest underground work. Keep in mind, however, that this still would not have constituted "gang slavery" functioning as large cadres under a royal official or overseer, as in the Terray model. As an added point, I must repeat that most of the shallow- or intermediate-level *nkron* I have emphasized here tended to be small (two feet across), circular shafts into the upper sedimentary layers that could accommodate only a few men at one time. One elder stated that two men—one above, hauling up the earth, and another below, doing the digging—were sufficient for the average soft-earth mining job.

Customary Land Law

The constitutional and theoretical foundations for state and lineage control over gold-bearing lands and expropriation of a percentage of profits by rulers—which are basic to an understanding of both African and European mining— have been the subjects of lengthy treatises by specialists.[112] Fundamental were, first, the concept of varying "clusters of rights" in land, in contrast to the simplistic formula of "individual" versus "communal" ownership (a dyad prevalent in the older anthropological literature), and second, the threefold classification of the land into (1) stool land, (2) family or lineage land, and (3) individual land. The idea of multiple and overlapping interests (or clusters of rights) implies that we should look not to notions of land tenure relationships, but rather to such issues as the varying uses made of given parcels of land, who had access to land, possible limitations placed on that access, and, finally, to the administrative rights exercised by the ruling authorities, which were those of allotment, regulation, and collection of a portion of the proceeds.

As for general access to gold-bearing lands, most traditions concur that any individual or group could mine for gold almost anywhere it chose within the limits of their own lineage or stool lands. And because so much of the Akan interior was sparsely populated in the nineteenth century—with vast reaches unsettled—free and open access also applied to many mineral-bearing lands outside a miner's home area. In the case of the stool lands of a neighboring state or stool, under a strong king or chief a stranger would first have to obtain permission to mine, then pay a token fee and perform a ritual in order to commence working.[113] In Wassa Fiase it was common for an official to kill a goat in sacrifice before allowing a stranger to mine on stool lands. Rules of access generally would be much tighter in those lands under the direct control of a king's own lineage (so-called royal lands). In those cases a king or chief might restrict mining to his own family and retainers and keep out strangers altogether. The overarching method by which Akan kings and chiefs appropriated economic surplus for state administration was through "tribute," or "royalty," based on customary land law and the patriarchal principle. There were two fundamental connections between production—whether of mineral or forest products—and the rights and powers of a ruling hierarchy: first, the traditional obligation by family heads or farmer-occupiers to pay a portion of the usufruct to local stool authorities (chiefs, or *ahenfo,* and kings, or *amanhene*) and, second, the direct power of a political authority to tax, which derived from both the traditional territorial controls of the ruler as well as from the kinship obligations of the people to him.[114]

Tribute and Taxation

The linchpin of the system for surplus appropriation by rulers and the state was the one-third, or *abusa,* share. In fact, the working out of the exact proportion paid to the various parties varied with the situation and the persons involved. The discovery of gold nuggets was treated in a special way. In some states the local stool authority claimed an absolute right to all nuggets found within his custodial lands; in practice, some informants said, he would take no more than half of a large nugget. Similarly, stool interests in land created additional rules in many Akan states allowing for (1) absolute right of chiefs to ownership of all treasure trove; (2) a one-half interest in all ivory tusks from any elephants killed; (3) one leg or shank of any wild animals killed on the hunt; and (4) the right to a one-third share in the profits from tree products (palm oil, timber, rubber, or kola nuts collected).[115] The exact methods by which each party received his legal share could be quite complicated and take time to resolve. Robert Addo-Fening notes that in Akyem, there was a strict rule that all nuggets (called *epo*) had to be surrendered to the chief of the area where the miner was working; the chief would pay the miner a small fee for his trouble and then take the nugget to the *okyenhene* (king), who would decide on its ultimate disposition.[116] Though pathways of state appropriation (or confiscation) might vary considerably in practice, normally the miner retained one-third of his proceeds, and turned over one-third to the local chief or stool authority, leaving the remaining third for the king or paramount ruler. In some usufruct relationships a one-half, or *abuna,* share distribution might be arranged.[117] On top of this, an ordinary farmer in a strong centralized kingdom might be subject to other exactions and incidences through kings, chiefs, and subchiefs, including court fines and fees and special levies to defray the costs of enstoolments, funeral customs, and religious festivals.

The kingdom of Asante was a case unto itself that cannot be analyzed in depth here. Nowhere in the Akan world did the administration of taxes, imposts, and incidences on trade and the produce of the land lead to such weight and complexity as in Asante.[118] At the zenith of Asante power in the nineteenth century, revenue included a poll tax, levied at the rate of one-tenth of an ounce of gold per man; a luxury tax on any chief who increased the amount of his gold jewelry or ornaments; court fines and fees; and death duties based on the rationale that the Asantahene was "the heir to the gold of every individual." In addition, judicial fines in a variety of court cases, involving both serious and lesser offenses, were also exacted in gold dust. According to Wilks, the ability to tax gold was the fundamental bulwark in the material power of the Asante state. The pervasive quality of the royalty system throughout Akan culture is shown by the fact that when the first European companies came to Tarkwa and Aboso in the late 1870s and found it difficult to recruit and adapt Africans to capitalistic wage labor, they decided to continue the *abusa* share method of payment as a transitional scheme to attract workers (see chaps. 4, 5, and 7 of this volume). It is undoubtedly true, as both Thomas McCaskie and Wilks underscore, that the Asantehene was always short of gold needed for a variety of state and personal purposes, and that he would use any means to acquire more—including mining for gold on his own. But the totality of returns from structured channels for the accumulation of state surplus through tribute from conquered states, trade tolls, and the taxation of ordinary citizens probably outweighed what might be garnered by a king or chief from direct gold mining using a personal corps of slave miners, as in the Terray hypothesis.[119]

Slavery or Corvée?

Once again, none of this is to suggest that the above channels for surplus appropriation excluded direct gold mining by a stool holder, using his own retainers. However, it is still highly debatable, at least for the period and region under detailed discussion here, whether such communal laborers under a king's supervision consisted entirely of slaves. In an earlier publication on gold mining and state surplus in the Akan region, I argued that Joseph Dupuis (not a wholly reliable nineteenth-century source), on whom Terray depended for several of his assumptions concerning centralized coteries of slave labor in Gyaman,[120] could have confused the supposed extensive use of slaves in gold mining with the much more common use of communal labor, or what might be called corvée.[121] I interpret such compulsory labor as emanating more from a ruler's custodial rights over the land and his mastery over his subjects *(nkoa)* than from his control of large numbers of slaves. This is substantiated by the fact that in most of the great Akan kingdoms, a king or chief could call out ordinary people to help augment the royal gold supply—just as he could to build roads—at almost any time. Thus, in conducting oral interviews with the chiefs and elders of villages and towns in Denkyera, Kwame Daaku found that almost invariably special days were set aside for all the citizens to mine solely on behalf of the paramount ruler.[122] This was true in most other Akan states as well. Speaking of the Nanwa mines on the southwest bank of the Ankobra River, controlled by King Kofi Blay of Eastern Nzema, one British observer wrote: "The Nanwa mines had been known to the natives, and have indeed been an important source of the local gold supply for the last 75 years, and were worked by a system of corvée or forced labor."[123]

We may conclude, therefore, that there were three principal methods by which the rulers of precolonial Akan states used their powers to extract surplus from the soil: the *abusa* share system, direct taxation, and, finally, compulsory community labor during set and limited periods. Finally, it can be argued that in some kingdoms and chieftaincies these theoretically distinct justifications merged with one another as methods of administration shifted over time. Thus, in Wassa a special tax or royalty on gold took the form of the "Saturday Earth," or what John M. Sarbah labeled *Tikororo*.[124] According to Enemil Kuma, chief of Aboso in the late 1880s, every Saturday during the mining season all miners were expected to turn over a portion of the gold ore from their day's labor directly to the agents of the king or paramount ruler. In extraordinary circumstances when a new and particularly rich gold field was opened, the king himself might set up a temporary headquarters at the nearest village in order that he might supervise operations more closely. Such a location was Egtapa, noted by Alfred Moloney in 1875 as the place where King Enemil Kuow "at present resides." There

he observed 2,000 to 3,000 men and women digging for gold. Moloney
did not go into detail on the exact nature of the labor relations between
chiefs and subjects. But he added that such a number "work on the
gold fields, but one day in the week as a rule."[125] Again, this does not
rule out the occasional use of royal slaves to mine for gold, especially
in the more centralized states such as Asante and Gyaman. In an
attempt to put the seal on the Dumett-Terray debate, it is my conclusion
that there were at least three different ways of organizing gold production in Akan traditional gold mining and that we should cease to speak
of a single dominant "mode of production" or unified set of labor
relations in mineral production.[126]

THE ROLES OF WOMEN

I cannot do full justice here to every important social issue related to
mining. The work of Eugenia Herbert on iron metallurgy demonstrates
that a wealth of material remains to be investigated concerning the role
of women in African traditional mining and smelting.[127] For centuries
female winners of gold aroused the curiosity and respect of foreign
travelers to the Akan region. I have noted that women virtually mo-
nopolized panning operations at seashore washing sites; and, aided by
young boys, they also dominated placer mining in small holes alongside
or near the riverbanks known as "womens washings."[128] But these brief
descriptions scarcely do justice to their overall contributions. A close
study of the available literary evidence combined with field data indi-
cates that, if anything, we have greatly underestimated both the numbers of women and female adolescents involved, and the functional
tasks they performed, in gold production. One extremely important yet
neglected point is that women served as the major transport carriers
for the gold trade, lugging sacks of earth or huge chunks of unmilled
ore from the mines to the crushing and separation sites. This tradition
of women serving as porters was not overlooked when the first European mechanized companies tried to recruit transport labor in Wassa
and Asante (see photos at end of chapter 7).[129]

Women also participated with men in prospecting—both as a regular
occupation and indirectly in the course of other tasks. This was particularly true in the discovery of new river panning sites; but they might
also direct their husbands to promising outcrops or topographic features that suggested the existence of rich underlying reef gold. Of

course, the whole question of Akan gold discovery methods is one that deserves far greater attention. Over the centuries the reputation of the people of the Gold Coast and its hinterlands as "born gold finders" grew in the literature. Whether this was traceable, as some supposed, to special psychic powers of certain individuals in detecting gold through the presence of a mysterious "mist" above auriferous ground, or, more scientifically, to perceptions about the chemical content of soils passed down through the generations, British geologists who toured Wassa and Asante in the early twentieth century did not doubt that many rural Akan people possessed an extraordinary talent for discerning the presence of underlying gold from innocuous signs in the surface topography. One method was to locate the presence of gold in the yellow or pink silicaceous streaks in the weathered outcrops of oxidized ores. Much more ingenious was "loaming"—Akan miners ability to locate the presence of deeper underlying gold from ordinary samples of surface soils.[130]

Finally, I must repeat that the presumably rigid division of labor between men (digging) and women (washing and pulverizing) stressed in most early written accounts of Akan gold mining did not always hold. As we shall see in the next chapter, we have examples of open cast mines—literally "gold fields"—where very large numbers of women, men, and children labored side by side to carve out long trenches, which could sometimes reach a quarter mile in length. In such instances eyewitnesses reported that females outnumbered the males two to one.[131]

In terms of the numbers who participated at all stages of the extractive process, then, it is possible to argue that in a given year more women than men participated in mining operations. Let us take hard-rock gold extraction first. When we consider the fact that both a part of the pulverization (at least one day's work per cubic foot of quartz), practically all washing and separation (another day or sometimes two) of reef gold, plus carrying sacks of ore, tended to be women's work, it is not unreasonable to suggest that female labor accounted for at least one-half of all the labor inputs in Akan reef gold mining—considered to be mainly mens work. In addition, their traditional supporting roles in collecting firewood (for both the men's fire setting and for cooking) plus gathering food, water and preparing meals for their husbands and work crews during the mining season, would have to be factored into any calculation.[132] And yet this estimate does not even include traditional alluvial mining for river and seacoast gold, which was, as we have seen, almost entirely the work of females. Of course, we can never know the proportions of exported African trade gold derived from hard-rock versus alluvial sources. All factors considered, it does not seem an exaggeration to guess that women contributed anywhere from two-thirds to three-fourths of all labor inputs connected with traditional gold mining in the Akan region.

Another issue on which we need much more historical data concerns the degree of women's independence from, or subordination to, male supervision on mining projects in the nineteenth-century context. One interpretation is that their leeway was considerable, demonstrated in the fact that a wife or mother could take her children and female servants to pan for river gold whenever and wherever she chose. The question of the distribution of earnings also reenters our discussion here.[133] Informants from Ghana say that given the patriarchal structure of the Akan household, it was highly unlikely that women of 100 or more years ago, particularly rural women, would have retained any of their earnings in a personal savings box in the manner of market women today. Rather the earnings from deep-level gold mining and pulverization by the nuclear family probably would have been kept by the head of the family under one account.[134]

DYSFUNCTIONAL FEATURES OF THE LINKAGES BETWEEN MINING AND STATE ADMINISTRATION

It is nearly always a mistake to force the facts of economic history into exaggerated functional symmetry; and any notion of a smoothly operating state bureaucracy quickly and easily collecting surplus in the form of gold dust, through a well-ordered multitiered revenue-gathering system, without tensions or friction, may convey an idealized conception of reality. Even with the efficient state administrative cadres at Kumasi, it may be questioned whether all taxes and dues owed to the Asantahene invariably flowed in without a hitch from subordinate tiers according to the exact amounts expected. In Wassa Fiase the tax-gathering mechanisms were much more segmented. As two inveterate Victorian travelers (who observed the revenue-gathering process firsthand) put it in their inimitable fashion, the state administration in Wassa functioned something like a European "squirearchy" with the immediate chief or stool holder having to turn a portion of his mine royalties over to the next higher official and thence on to the king. Thus the dwindling amount of money might "pass through three or four hands before reaching its final destination."[135] In noting the weakening of traditional revenue collection methods in certain areas, such as Wassa, one must also take cognizance of the impact over time of an alien colonial capitalism. Though customary land law dictated that the proceeds from any mining operation be divided three ways—one-third to the miner, one-third to the local stool holder (such as the chief of Apinto), and one-third to the paramount ruler (the king of Wassa Fiase)—during the period under review in this volume we find that there was increasing tension between the *omanhene* of Wassa Fiase and the supposedly subordinate Apintohene to increase their respective shares at the expense of the other. Clearly, the chief of Apinto was in the more advantageous position because the most productive European mines lay within his direct sphere of control. By the 1880s, the Wassa Fiasehene was complaining to the British Gold Coast authorities that he lacked the leverage to ensure that his traditional imposts on local mining were always effectively collected.[136] It may be that stranger-miners from neighboring states such as Nzema, Gwira, or Ahanta, mining around Tarkwa, felt no special obligation to honor a weakened Wassa king's decrees. It is also clear from older sources that ordinary Wassa miners had long nurtured secretive ways of avoiding the king's collectors and of concealing their true gold earnings. Despite the acknowledged rule that all nuggets belonged to the stool authority, diggers had probably always managed to hide or cut up highly prized nuggets before the king's agents learned about them. At the same time, as we shall see in later chapters, the very presence of the new European mining companies and concessions middlemen could either strengthen or erode the traditional political powers of African rulers. Techniques of avoidance also undermined the effectiveness of Saturday Earth collections. As Paul Rosenblum aptly points out, upon testing the king's Saturday Earth bowl, royal agents often found that it contained just that—dirt or sand with a non existent gold content.[137]

At the other end of the spectrum, some traditional state officials went to the opposite extreme of exercising undue force in collecting the *abusa* share. For the farmer-miner the dividing line between legitimate taxation and extortion by rulers who exceeded their authority was sometimes a thin one. Reports from Akyem indicate that petty chiefs and their functionaries might enter a mining district any time they chose and, in total defiance of the *abusa* share and legitimate taxation systems, forcibly confiscate all gold dust and gold jewelry possessed by miners and their families.[138] Wilks has provided evidence that the Asantehenes at Kumasi could become greedy and use state power to siphon off far more than their accepted and legitimate shares of state revenues. Thus Mensa Bonsu, taking more than his usual tribute from the mines at Manso-Inkwanta, also imposed an onerous 50 percent tax on gold mining in general.[139] As one eyewitness who traveled through Wassa in the 1870s observed, "the villagers are subjected to incessant plunder, under the name of taxation, by their kings, who descend with their warriors as often as convenient upon these gold-diggers, and carry off every particle of the precious metal that has not been buried."[140] I do not suggest that such excesses were the constant and uniform pattern. What the record shows is that state tax-gathering systems did not function in so regularized a fashion as proclaimed in some general accounts. Disruptive external conditions, such as wars, could create undue pressures to expand revenues for reasons of defense.[141] There were obviously wide variations as to time and place in the effectiveness of collection methods; and the impulses of some kings and chiefs to expropriate gold collected by ordinary farmer-miners in ways that exceeded customary norms, must have been strong indeed.

PROFITS, OPPORTUNITY COSTS, AND LINKS TO THE GENERAL ECONOMY

A perennial question that crops up in the literature on traditional gold mining in the Gold Coast concerns the return per man-day of labor and per ton of earth extracted. How profitable was gold mining to the individual worker? The weight of opinion from both nineteenth-century chroniclers and some recent historical studies is that traditional African nonmechanized gold mining was not worth the great effort expended. Timothy Garrard has worked out the returns for a single woman panning for river gold to be on the average of about one-sixth of a cubic yard of sand or soil per day, valued at 10d. to 1s. 2d. per person.[142] J. A. Skertchly, one of the first Europeans to record in detail how reef gold was extracted, crushed, and separated by traditional miners, also reached a pessimistic conclusion on the returns for hard-rock gold mining. Observing that it took two men one entire day to cut out a one-cubic-foot block of ore, a second day to pound the ore into powder, and two more days for four women to separate the gold from the sand and powdered rock by traditional separation methods, Skertchly calculated that it would take four days to retrieve a mere three dwt. of gold (20 dwt. equals one ounce).[143] This average of three dwt. of gold per one cubic foot of rock would then, according to Skertchly, have had to be divided among eight people. This works out to 1s. 4d. per person for the four days, but only 4d. per person for the daily rate. Reasoning along similar lines, G. A. Robertson, an early-nineteenth-century observer, concluded, "Working for gold was not a profitable form of employment."[144] The question is, by whose standard?

While Skertchly's low guesstimate might appear accurate in theory, one can take issue with the verisimilitude and practical applicability of his premises. For example, I criticize his estimate in that it invariably required eight people, or at the least six people, a full four days to break down one cubic foot of ore. These numerical stipulations are purely arbitrary and do not square with the facts from other sources. Furthermore, we should bear in mind that Skertchly based his estimates on crushing some of the hardest reef gold ore, rather than on the looser and easier-to-work surface-level oxides and sedimentary deposits, which, I have emphasized, were by far the most commonly excavated types. In point of fact the attempt of Europeans to calculate an average return of the ounces of gold that African workers (presumably throughout the whole of Wassa and perhaps across a wider area) could glean from one cubic foot of ore was not a worthwhile exercise. The variations were too great—ranging from many pounds sterling for a single nugget (see below), to 2s. 6d. for a women washing for river or shoreline gold on a "good day," down to nothing for deep -level miners on an "unlucky day." The fact that other contemporary chroniclers came up with higher estimates than Skertchly for the average returns per man-day of labor in traditional gold mining, is not even the main issue.[145] What is at fault is the entire Eurocentric perspective of measuring the importance or worth of gold mining, according to a set yardstick of an average daily return per individual according to man-hours of labor per day.

The question of the worth of mine labor must be analyzed from the perspective not only of an archetypal miner but from the perspective of an idealized "economic man." What is or is not profitable is very much a relative matter that varies with the culture, the locale, and the specific case. Indeed, in the case of the typical family mining group, described earlier, informants declared that it is not accurate to state that the proceeds from a kin-based group mining trip invariably were divided up according to individual contributions. Rather, they said, the male head of the family group would most likely have retained the bulk of it. Obviously, in some instances—that of three or four male village miners from different families, for example—there could have been such a division of proceeds. In precolonial times, and after, with the coming of the first mechanized companies, many forest miners did make broad comparisons of estimated returns from traditional gold mining in relation to the up-county cost of living (which was extremely low at this time) plus reports on average wages for unskilled labor paid by European mining firms or by merchants in the coastal economy at that time. In these rational choices (see chap. 7), the latter pursuits came up wanting. At the same time most miners did not judge the worth of their work from the standard of a single days meager or average returns, but rather from the prospect of an exceptional day's returns over a reasonable span of time. This is what kept the intrepid family groups pressing on for days on end without realizing any immediate return. Kwame Yeboa of Kyebi, Akyem-Abuakwa, shared with me a revealing recollection:

> Author: What would you say was the average return from gold mining for, say one day or one week's work?
> Kwame Yeboa: Gold Mining is a gift from God. It is not as if when you go mining you will set your mind that you will get such and such a return by digging. It is only by luck if you can get some gold. So you may get £10, £8, or whatever you can get.[146]

Furthermore, the typically pessimistic European view on what appeared to be the low profits from traditional African gold mining overlooked the very genuine and overarching hope that Akan miners harbored of finding a nugget. Two large nuggets, worth £39 and £82, were found near Tarkwa in 1891; and George Ferguson observed that nuggets worth £100 were not uncommon.[147] Discovery of smaller nuggets, the size of a kernel of maize, was said to be far more frequent. This dream of finding the elusive gold nugget was probably sufficient in most instances to cancel out the disappointments over rounds of monotonous labor and low returns in ordinary gold recovery. In one sense gold mining, whether by colonial corporations or by indigenous farmer-miners, has always been governed by a different set of economic principles than ordinary business ventures. It is a high-risk enterprise, more akin to gambling, in which the mere hope of a lucky strike may justify long hours of tedious effort.

Beyond this, many previous commentators on gold mining in the Akan region have neglected to point out the subtler economic connections between mining and the seasonal cycle in West African agriculture. Traditional mining was (and in some locales still is) a useful replacement activity for farming in those areas where minerals can be found. First, it offers a satisfactory supplementary income for entrepreneurial farmers who may earn a reasonable profit from marketing agricultural produce during the year but who have almost unlimited free time between the harvesting (end of November) and planting (beginning of April) seasons. As Philip Curtin has noted for the Bambuhu region of the Upper Senegal River, the upswing in gold mining during the months of January through April coincides with the main period of underemployment in agriculture, when the opportunity cost of labor is low.[148] Put another way, during the dry season especially, the productivity loss of removing a worker from agriculture tended to zero.

Second, there was another possible connection between gold mining and the general economic structure of Wassa. Mining seems to have offered an income supplement for farmers who produced at generally low levels (i.e., those who were marginal farmers). Polly Hill, for example, has cited a complex concatenation of elements that have led to inequality among and between groups in rural northern Nigeria. People known as poor (or "unlucky") farmers often have to make ends meet by engaging in other types of work—such as transport carriers, wood gatherers, petty traders, or by hiring themselves out as casual wage laborers on the farms of others.[149] I would suggest that a similar set of circumstances prevailed in a general way in Wassa. Early-twentieth-century sources also noted that the some of the best farmers in Wassa were immigrants from other Akan states. Thus the common observation that the Wassas were rather indifferent farmers, but, very vigorous and effective gold miners can now be placed in sharper focus. There was a direct casual connection between the two phenomena.

Present-day Ghanaian peasant miners removing gold ore in sacks from hillside pits. Photo by Albert Van Dantzig.

Akan farmer using the *aso* (or short hoe), used in both traditional farming and in gold mining. Photo by the author.

The entrance to an *nkron* or traditional Akan mine. (Note a shovel is barely observable.) Photo by the author.

African pit mines following the line of a reef at In-sintsiam, Asante, c. 1895. (Note dark holes at right of steps up the reef and pile of earth near pit in lower right corner.) Photo courtesy Ashanti Goldfields Corporation.

A traditional African pit mine, showing bamboo lagging for reinforcement and prevention of cave-ins. Photo courtesy Ashanti Goldfields Corp.

An example of the rudimentary timbering sometimes used by African traditional miners. Photo by the author.

The Role of Women in Traditional Gold Mining

A rare photograph of Akan women washing for river gold in the traditional way. Photo courtesy Ashanti Goldfields Corporation.

Women pulverizing maize using mullerstones and bedstones similar to those which women adapted to grinding ore for extraction of gold dust. Photo from exhibit at "Ashanti Kingdom of Gold." American Museum of Natural History. (Mrs. Enid Schildkrout and M. D. MacLeod, coordinators.)

4

The Wassa "Gold Rush" of 1877-1885

African and European Promoters of Mining Capitalism

Mechanized gold mining in the southwestern Gold Coast followed a zigzag course from the 1870s into the first decades of the twentieth century: there were innumerable detours, dead ends, and no straight pathways to success. As with other famous gold booms in history, glittering early forecasts of quick riches were tarnished by the harsh reality of an unknown geology and difficult working conditions. Ebullient publicists in London and earnest spokesmen for an indigenous African capitalism on the coast were convinced that exploitation of mineral wealth presented a direct route to industrialization in West Africa. But the forerunners of capitalistic mining soon found to their dismay that, despite stories of fabulous wealth in Wassa and elsewhere, the creation of effective installations in the thickly forested southwestern interior would be a long and arduous task. Among the scarce elements in the 1870s and 1880s were sustained capital investment, professional training in geology and mining engineering, workable machinery, and cheap mechanized transport. How far the Gold Coast Colonial Government would extend itself to assist British mining companies remained from the start problematic. It would take an optimal combination of solid management, technological expertise, good labor relations, and an extraordinary measure of good luck for neophyte companies to achieve success.

THE LURE OF GOLD AND EARLY
GOVERNMENT POLICY

Most previous accounts have traced the birth of modern mining enterprise on the Gold Coast to a European-sponsored "gold rush" that
followed on the heels of victorious British troops in the Sixth Asante
War of 1873-74,[1] but this enduring legend glosses over the complexities of what really happened. It is true that a handful of expatriate gold
seekers were lured to Wassa in 1875 following rumors of great untapped mineral wealth circulated by journalists and officers who accompanied Sir Garnet Wolseley's expeditionary force.[2] But administrators acted swiftly to curb further European travel to the interior because
of the unsettled state of the Gold Coast-Asante frontier in the aftermath of the war. Advisers to Earl Carnarvon, the Secretary of State for
Colonies, agreed that "the resources of the county [were] undoubtedly
capable of great development . . . ," but recommended that the government take a "cautious" approach in investigating the possibilities
for "opening up the gold fields of the Wassaw District."[3]

Three factors prompted government hesitancy at this juncture: (1)
distrust of freebooting miners and concessions dealers, many of whom
had no real interest in development, coupled with (2) an alarm about
the potentially destabilizing effects of expatriate mining on interior
African states, and (3) long-standing adherence to laissez-faire principles in colonial political economy. It is necessary to point out that we
are speaking here of historical conditions that were still eons away from
those that produced the post-1895 concept of African "tropical estates," which allowed for the grant of huge tracts of mineral lands to
giant concessionaire companies under government backing. Not even
the notion of a new "gold-mining frontier" in West Africa had capti-
vated the official imagination with its potentialities. In the British
Colonial Office's essentially Cobdenite mindset, the question was
whether the Gold Coast was ready or even suitable for this kind of
corporate capitalism. In the ten years following the Sixth Asante War
of 1873-74 the Gold Coast Government's primary objectives were to
establish a framework for military defense—primarily against the possibility of a resurgent threat from the powerful Asante Union—and to
stabilize financial administration for the colony. Preoccupied with the
twin problems of drafting controversial new legislation on local slave
dealing and slave emancipation,[4] plus preventing disintegration of the

recently defeated Asante Union, the new Gold Coast Governor George Strahan was not about to create additional causes for upheaval.[5] The last thing he wanted on his hands was a gold rush.

With the recent experience of the Australian and New Zealand gold booms of the 1850s and 1860s fresh on their minds, the Colonial Office staff took a jaundiced view of the peripatetic "diggers" and claim jumpers of the Empire as riffraff and troublemakers. And in a series of sharply worded edicts, Governor Strahan warned that concession hunters from Britain would get no help from the local government. Only one party of four Europeans traveled to the Wassa mining area in 1875, and their project was soon abandoned.[6] Several other small parties of English and North American miners entered Wassa in 1877, but their efforts also ended in early failure.[7] Until internal tensions between the government and the defeated Asante power were mollified, Strahan told his superiors, it would be utterly reckless to encourage any movement of foreign miners to the Coast.

THE UNDERMINING OF TRADITIONAL AFRICAN POLITICAL AUTHORITY

Nowhere were the contradictions in colonial attitudes more blatant than in the Gold Coast government's relations with the African mining state of Wassa Fiase. Unwilling to offer direct assistance to European prospectors and company agents on grounds of the potentially disruptive consequences of a gold boom, the government nonetheless unwittingly undermined the Wassa king's authority by direct and indirect actions. In 1877 the nominal overlord of the mining districts was King Kwamena Enemil Kuow, whose residence was variously at Manso and Egtapa in Wassa Fiase. Yet Kuow proved to be an irresolute and ineffective leader. Though he had tried to persuade his people to back the British and coastal Fante military effort in the late Asante war, King Enemil's support from his own subordinate chiefs melted away, owing partly to the former's weak leadership and to the misconceived policies of the British government.

The single most important ruler with whom European concession hunters had to deal in the 1870s and 1880s was not King Enemil, but Chief Kwabena Ango of Apinto, whose seat was at Aodua on the River Ankobra, twenty-two to twenty-five miles northwest of Tarkwa.[8] Another subordinate chief, nominally under the authority of both Wassa and

Apinto but who ruled semi-independently, was Enemil Kuma, who controlled the mining site of Aboso, just north of Tarkwa. (I alluded to some of the causes of this internal rivalry in chapter 3.) The supposed paramount ruler of Tarkwa, Afrenen Asante, also subordinate to King Enemil, was described by one traveling commissioner as a cipher—"a blind old man" who "hardly, if ever, leaves his house."[9] While much of this loss of central control had local roots in age-old disputes between rulers in Wassa, coupled with the long history of interventionist actions toward Wassa by Asante, part of it was traceable to the eroding effects of colonialism and, by the late 1870s, of mining concessionaire activity.

Among other traditional rulers at the time of the first capitalist penetration of Wassa was Chief Kofi Kyei of Heman (see photo at the end of chap. 8) on the Upper Ankobra, who controlled both the Essaman/Prestea and Gie Appanto mines and also the Heman and Brumasi concessions northwest of Tarkwa in the state of Wassa Amenfi. On the basis of sheer territory, the most powerful king of the entire southwestern region was Kofi Blay of Eastern Nzema (Apollonia), who controlled most of the southwestern littoral from Axim as far as the Ivory Coast (see chap. 8, map 8.1).[10] Another important deputy of the king of Wassa Fiase was Kwabena Sensense, who controlled the Apatim and Akankoo mines west of Tarkwa—both of which were leased to British companies in the early 1880s. But Chief Sensense's proprietary rights to these mines were strongly contested by Kofi Blay (see above), Kwaku Bukari, and Chief Ebba, who controlled lands on the lower Ankobra inland from Axim.[11]

These brief comments from contemporary observers on indigenous politics suggest how difficult it is to make clear-cut statements about either the boundaries of territorial divisions or the exact channels and range of hierarchical control between paramount rulers (amanhene) and subordinate chiefs (ahenfo) in the histories of precolonial Akan states. It is often more useful, as Van Dantzig has noted, to think of Akan state structures as a patchwork quilt of overlapping and shifting obligations between paramount and subordinate rulers, and of linear controls by chiefs, not by blocks of territory, but along spiderwebs of roads and pathways that connected particular population towns and centers. It is important to add that not every traditional ruler wilted before the advancing tide of mining capitalism. Some kings and chiefs increased their wealth and influence through the very considerable leverage placed at their disposal by the lease of mineral properties to Europeans. Uncertainty and confusion over stool boundaries and the lines of kingly authority certainly impeded the colonial government's effort to understand the traditions of Wassa concerning land use and control and to establish procedures regulating the lease of mining lands to strangers. Throughout the decades covered here British officials misinterpreted the "relative ranks of chiefs, their powers [and] the boundaries of their districts."[12]

A RESURGENCE ON THE
AFRICAN MINER'S FRONTIER

There was, indeed, a major inrush of new miners to the Wassa goldfields in the late 1870s, but this differed radically from its depiction in contemporary popular accounts and later political histories of the Gold Coast/Ghana. The image handed down is that of a first wave of capitalistic mining initiated by heroic European prospectors. The reality was rather a massive migration into Tarkwa and Aboso of hundreds of traditional *African* miners from other districts and regions. Many of these miner-cultivators were from the two Wassas, plus Ahanta and Gwira; but the majority appear to have come from Nzema, the coastal state west of the River Ankobra. As stated at the outset, the activities of the energetic and expansionistic Nzeman miners constitutes an important background theme in my story. From 1875 through 1880 they not only continued to mine in well-known locations, they flocked to new and untouched areas such as the large Ntaya complex of mines, which had not been a great center of attention before.[13] The Frenchman M. J. Bonnat, whose career will be discussed presently, recorded no less than "1,306 natives working at the [various] Tarkwa mines" in 1879 and double that number if women and children were included. Another observer estimated that anywhere from 3,000 to 6,000 Africans were working the open-pit surface mines at the peak of the season.[14] One British manager exclaimed that this huge onrush of miners to lower Wassa was undoubtedly a new phenomenon, as demonstrated by the fact that so many of the mine shafts were freshly cut.[15]

In reality this "new" African gold rush was the logical outgrowth of historic patterns. Wassa Fiase was, after all, one of the premier gold states in the Akan region; indigenous miners had worked the Tarkwa Ridge probably since Portuguese times and perhaps earlier. But it is important to discern an important phenomenon, not sufficiently analyzed by other historians (who have emphasized the central role of expatriate capital), wherein traditional miners using supposedly primitive mining techniques, intensified their efforts in the 1870s, 1880s, and 1890s. Thus, farmer-miners were not displaced or superseded by the new mechanized companies but in fact competed with them for an extended period on an equal basis.[16] Precolonial relations of production endured.

Recent research on mining among peasant societies in Latin America demonstrates that it is not uncommon for two disparate systems of production (precapitalist and capitalist) in mining to exist in tandem.[17] In a similar way indigenous miners in the Akan region, showing remarkable resilience, continued to work in the traditional way alongside the struggling European companies for decades, up to and even after the turn of the twentieth century (see chap. 8). This parallels a trend that Bill Freund has recounted for tin miners in Nigeria.[18] It can be explained in part by the effectiveness of traditional production systems, and in part by the ineffectiveness of the poorly organized European firms in their attempts to recruit local African workers and find and extract the gold in the most effective way. British "pacification" of the frontier of "friendly" states between Asante and the coastal polities also played a part in the process. As noted in the last chapter, the king of Wassa Fiase at this time regarded the Asantehene as his enemy on the ground that the Asante kingdom in various times in the past had deigned to treat Wassa as its vassal.[19] Traditional mining at Tarkwa and surrounding sites had suffered setbacks in the 1860s and early 1870s owing to repeated Asante intervention in Wassa political affairs. Indeed, Asante invaded Wassa at least seven times during the 1873–74 war, and the fighting and depredations had left Wassa in an unstable and demoralized condition.[20] Now, with the return of peace and the normalization of trade, African miners from Wassa and elsewhere had a strong incentive to move back to Tarkwa in larger numbers than before.

It is also likely that stranger miners—especially from Nzema—poured into Wassa because they believed they could take advantage of weakened political structures in Wassa and thereby flout the one-third *abusa* share or other payments to local chiefs with impunity. Furthermore, weather conditions were invariably a consideration in the success of traditional mining. In a revealing comment, one eyewitness observed that most of the Tarkwa mines had been inoperative in 1875–76 owning to flooding with groundwater. The favorable "Dries" of December 1876 through March 1877 presented African miners with their first big opportunity in several years for deep digging without flooding at every turn. Indeed, many new shafts were sunk in 1877 through

1879. But other contemporary reports also noted that older tunnels and shafts that touched the main reef were being reworked.[21]

Against these facts, the story of the first Gold Coast gold rush formerly credited entirely to expatriate initiatives has to be interpreted in a new light. The main initial spark was a definite resurgence along the "traditional African miner's frontier" in 1877 through 1880. Of course, the European presence became stronger as the last quarter of the nineteenth century unfolded. But it is also clear that the entrance of the first trickle of English and French miners to Wassa Fiase stimulated a renewed African interest in their valuable patrimony as the rush progressed. Thus it was reported that, quite apart from the preexisting concentration of African diggers at Tarkwa in 1879, there was a further movement of peasant miners north to the neighboring town of Aboso in 1881 soon after the first expatriate companies settled in. In other words, the sudden presence of European intruders reinforced and expanded the beliefs of African miners about the great value of their inherited gold-bearing properties. "Ten months ago, Aboso contained 40 to 50 head of negroes, now it may number 3,000," said one account.[22] In subsequent chapters I will show that all during the struggling period of European capitalistic company formation the bulk of the colony's gold dust exports continued to come from traditional African sources.

EARLY EUROPEAN PROSPECTORS

Who were the pathfinders of modern mechanized mining in southwestern Ghana? Most earlier histories lavished praise on the French trader Marie Joseph Bonnat as the founder of modern gold mining in the Gold Coast and Asante.[23] But this claim has been overblown. Limited credit for being the first machine users should go to a party of Dutchmen who experimented with mechanized mining in the valley of the River Butre as early as the 1840s. Van Dantzig and Yarak have shown how a party of three Dutch engineers, nine European miners, plus two carpenters and two blacksmiths was dispatched to the village of Hotopo on the Butre by the Dutch governor at Elmina in 1844 (see map 4.1).[24] They recruited a fair-sized crew of local African workers and installed hand-powered machinery, including pumps, crushers, and wooden rockers (using techniques similar to those used by the famous forty-niners of California); and they remained on the job excavating ore for

nearly four years. But twentieth-century scientific surveys demonstrated that the Butre Valley was not propitious for large-scale reef
mining. The Dutch cadres recorded meager gold returns for all
their efforts, owing to the perennial problems of underground
floodings plus the incapacitation or death of more than half of
their staff by malaria.[25] The Butre Valley lay, of course, not in
Wassa, but within the borders of Ahanta State to the south. And it
is clear that there was no continuity whatever between these early
Dutch efforts and the "boom" of the late 1870s, which is one of
several reasons for the enduring legend of Bonnat as the father of
the Ghanaian gold mining industry.

M. J. Bonnat and J. A. Skertchly

In fact there was no single promoter of the 1877–82 gold rush nor a
single founder of the modern gold industry. From all accounts the first
European miner to take out a concession and dig for reef gold on the
famous Tarkwa Ridge was the Englishman J. A. Skertchly beginning in
March of 1877.[26] That Bonnat's name appears so often in the literature
is explainable in part by the fact that he was such a prolific writer and
effective booster for his own commercial adventures. We cannot delve
at length into the whole of Bonnat's colorful if checkered career here.
For some years a thorn in the side of British officialdom, both at London
and Cape Coast, his name had cropped up repeatedly in government
dispatches on account of his petitions for British government support of
grand schemes for opening up the River Volta to regularized freight-car-
rying boat traffic for the trade with Asante and the far north.[27]

  The Frenchman was certainly an energetic traveler and entrepreneur, but
he was also a spinner of fantasies about untapped African bonanzas. And
just as his pleas for government-backed commercial projects fell on deaf
ears, so most of his early gold extraction projects also foundered. Bonnat
had first learned of the gold wealth of Wassa while a prisoner of the Asantes
at Kumasi between 1864 and 1874. But he was always more interested in
commerce than in mining; and on his next journey to the Gold Coast
(1874–75) he concentrated wholly on a trading expedition to the market
town of Salaga in the northern territories in the hope of establishing a chain
of trading stations for ivory, indigenous salt, and the sale of Birmingham
and Manchester goods.[28] But in the face of the twin obstacles of distance
and terrain plus uncertainty about the reactions of Asante in the aftermath
of war, the scheme failed to attract government support. Returning to
France, Bonnat accepted an offer from a consortium of Parisian business-

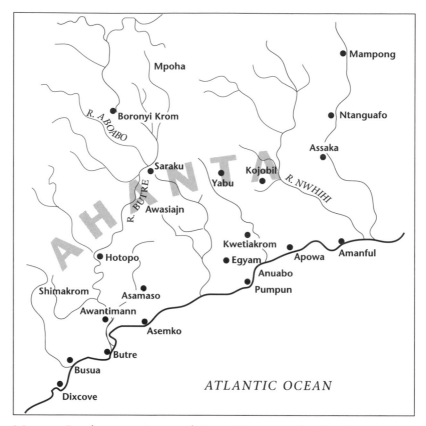

Map 4.1. Dutch prospecting expedition to Hotopo on the River Butre (Ahanta state), ca. 1840

men, led by M. Bazin, and called the Societé des Mines d'Or l'Afrique Occidentale, to purchase concessions and undertake a mineral survey of the Gold Coast in 1877.[29]

In attempting to come to grips with the euphoric bonanza imperialism that infected so much of the Western world in the second half of the nineteenth century, it would be difficult to overestimate the compelling imagery of California symbols like Sutters Mill, the Sacramento River, and the gilded city San Francisco.[30] Bonnat, like other exuberant adventurers of the time, developed a fixation for river mining based on secondhand accounts from the goldfields of Ballarat in Australia and the Sacramento Valley,[31] where sluicing for river gold indeed had been the central mode. And he was led astray by the hope that easy profits might be gained through use of similar placer techniques in the Gold

Coast. Arriving at Axim in May of 1877 (two months after Skertchly started mining at Tarkwa Ridge), Bonnat and three companions used up the greater part of a year in experimenting with bizarre diving suits and hydraulic suction devices while negotiating with Chief Ango of Apinto for leases to innumerable washing sites of doubtful value along both the Ankobra and Bonsa rivers.[32] All this ended in fiasco. It was only after the riverbank concessions failed to pan out that Bonnat's colleagues turned the next year to inspecting the far more valuable and extensively used African pit mines in the vicinity of Tarkwa.

Yet Bonnat had no practical knowledge of reef gold mining and made no serious attempts to purchase or work the banket concessions of Tarkwa until pressed to do so by his board of directors. And so, despite the frequency of references to his name in the sources, Bonnat's role should be placed in perspective. It is necessary to repeat that there were a number of European prospectors and promoters in the Tarkwa district at this same time—J. A. Skertchly, E. T. McCarthy, C. J. Harvey, E. Wray, Paulus Dahse, F. J. Crocker, and others—"whose efforts," in the words of H. J. Bevin, "were in no way dependent on Bonnat."[33] Furthermore, as I shall show presently, few of the early histories paid any credit whatever to the *coastal African pioneers* of the mechanized gold industry.

The African Gold Coast Company

After Bonnat's first riverbank prospecting foray, his Parisian backers— Albert Verillon, I. E. Illurant, M. Luc, E. Begoran, and Emile Bassot— together with a group of Liverpool investors headed by M. Radcliffe, Colonel C. Steward, and J. C. Wray reconstituted themselves as the Compagnie Minière de la Côte d'Or Afrique, better known in Britain as the African Gold Coast Mining Company.[34] In February 1878 these men dispatched a party made up of three Englishmen, Major General E. Wray (Royal Engineers), Colonel J. C. Lightfoot, and C. J. Harvey, to inspect more closely the riverine properties in which Bonnat had acquired an interest. Harvey, a bona fide mining engineer, who had served as manager of the Port Philip Mining Company of Victoria, Australia, should have known what he was doing. Yet even this group dallied interminably, inspecting the large number of low-value placer sites that Bonnat in his initial ebullience had purchased along the East bank of the Ankobra. Bonnat's movements during the latter part of 1877 are unclear, but it appears he was still working the riverbanks in and around Aodua, with an encampment at "Bush Castle," when the three Englishmen arrived in early 1878.[35] In a fresh agreement, drawn up in November of that year, the company expanded Bonnat's original lease to include the entire bed of the Ankobra to the limits of the Apinto substate, including banks 500 yards wide on both sides of the river.[36]

Why the Anglo-French team did not move to the richer Tarkwa banket area straightaway is hard to fathom. But we should keep in mind that the group had a fixation, based on the still potent images from California and Australia, about the supposedly quicker and easier gains from river-bank and placer mining. It is also apparent that the artful Chief Ango kept the group on leading strings as long as possible, enticing them with the hope that each new washing site would be better than the last, while withholding information on Tarkwa Ridge until the last possible mo-ment. Finally after pressure from Wray and Harvey, who trekked to the ridge and conducted on-the-spot assays, Chief Ango relented: he agreed to lease the 400-by-2,000-yard property that comprised the Compagnie Minière's Tarkwa concession for the modest terms of £200 cash and 3 percent of future profits[37] (see map 4.2 for the location of the first European concessions on Tarkwa Ridge). As a result, General Wray and his colleagues got far better terms than if concessions agents or middle-men had placed themselves between the chief and the foreign intruders.

While it is true that there was some continuity between Bonnat's first claims and later productive concessions, the first manager of the main Anglo-French mine was not Bonnat (as some scholars have supposed), but another Frenchman named M. Moulton. Moulton took his mana-gerial assignments more seriously than Bonnat, but the second man's professional mining expertise was also limited.[38] He confessed that he was totally perplexed by the peculiar (banket) rock formations in Wassa (see chap. 2). As the accompanying maps and drawings show, Moulton, Wray, and their cohorts would have made little headway without their reliance on scores of earlier African underground work-ings for determining the location of the main gold reefs and the best places to attack them. Most commonly the line of traditional African pit mines on a ridge (see photos at the end of chap. 2) determined the direction of angle at which a company would blast its shafts and adits into a hillside (see fig. 4.1). But this was only a beginning. Moulton still faced the daunting tasks of organizing transport carriers, recruiting a mines work force, and installing a crushing plant in rapid order.

Few early miners and mine managers had any conception of the awesome physical and environmental barriers that awaited them in West Africa. That the Anglo-French Company could have expected to overcome the problem of underground flooding without efficient steam

Map 4.2. Major mining concessions at Tamsu, Tarkwa, and Aboso

pumps was pure folly. As with African miners over the centuries, Moulton found it next to impossible, even with the fair-sized work force at his disposal, to deal with ever-present groundwater or the unstable claylike rock strata, encountered just twenty feet below the surface, which was constantly crumbling away.[39] Without air-powered rock drills to help set explosive charges, initial hard-rock excavations were extremely time-consuming. Some of the companies started simply by penetrating outcrops with small shafts at the top of ridges in the old African manner (see photo at the end of this chap.). Nonetheless, after three months on the job, Moulton's work crews had succeeded in driving three horizontal tunnels into the side of Tarkwa hill for up to forty or fifty feet. By early 1879 Moulton had installed one eight-horse-power "Bellville" steam engine, which drove a ten-stamp crushing mill.[40] But rain and seepage became the company's undoing. During one rainy season the manager had to keep 600 men working day and night on bucket relays and drainage.[41] Much rock was excavated dur-ing 1881 and 1882 but little or no gold retrieval took place. The annual report of the African Gold Coast Company was forced to concede a high operating cost of £550 per month. After extracting only a few ounces of gold, and exhausting the major portion of its capital on exploratory digging, the company suspended operations in January 1882.[42] Even so, the promoters were convinced that the site was a potentially valuable one; and the workings were converted to more effective use under a new company—the Tarkwa and Aboso Gold Mining Company—which will be dealt with in succeeding chapters.

AFRICAN PROMOTERS AND
THE GOLD RUSH OF 1879-1882

Meanwhile a separate force for the promotion of capitalistic mining emanated from a different area—the educated West African mercantile and professional elite, who came primarily from the port of Cape Coast and the "Fante districts" surrounding it. Here it is necessary to say a brief word about the relationship of Cape Coast to the so-called Fante area, or Fante region, of the Gold Coast, since there frequently has been confusion over the historical use of these terms. Strictly speaking the town of Cape Coast was not originally a formal part of "Fante," nor the home of the Fante king. Rather the traditional political center of Fante was the Abura state to the northeast, while the spiritual center was the town of Mankessim further east, inland from the port of Saltpond. The traditional Twi name for Cape Coast was Oguaa, which was, in fact, the chief town of the larger Efutu State on the coast. In the mid-nineteenth century, however, Efutu joined with other nearby coastal and interior states to form the landmark Fante Confederation (1868-73), an early protonationalist political organization. A large number of the African mercantile entrepreneurs and professional men of Cape Coast, some of whom occupy a key role in the present story, contributed mightily to the philosophical base and financial backing of

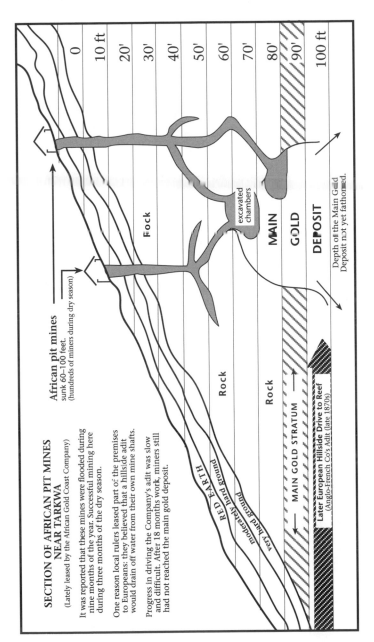

Fig. 4.1. Cross-sectional sketch of traditional African deep-level mines at Tarkwa. This record shows that Africans often penetrated through hard rock to levels 60 to 100 feet or more below the surface. The dark arrow at the lower left shows that pioneering European companies, like the Anglo-French Company and later the Tarkwa and Aboso Company, relied to a great extent for gold discovery on traditional African prospectors. From a sketch by E. Wray (1879) of the Tarkwa and Aboso Mining Co. Reproduced by G.C. Geologocal Survey (Accra, 1926).

the Fante Confederation movement. One of the few early West African nationalist associations, which included both chiefs as well as representatives of the educated community in the leadership, its goals were to establish a strong unified political presence on the coast that could counter the power of the interior Kingdom of Asante and provide at the same time the foundations for African self-government. The failure of British colonial authorities to appreciate its true value, as a genuine experiment in African democracy, contributed in large measure to the confederation's demise.

Contrasting Interpretations

It is one of the arguments of this study that the modern gold-mining industry rose not only on the backs of African labor but also with the vision and leadership provided by pioneering African commercial entrepreneurs. Most of the early European prospectors lacked substantial mining experience in the tropics: they knew next to nothing about local geology and topography. They had no knowledge of who the local African rulers were or the boundaries of states. They had to rely on Fante guides and interpreters to get to Wassa, to enter negotiations with local chiefs, and to learn about the locations of the best gold deposits. According to J. A. B. Horton, who was certainly in a position to know, the first person to experiment with mining machinery in the interior states of the southwestern Gold Coast—the claims of early Dutch miners, Skertchly, and Bonnat notwithstanding—was the Eurafrican merchant Thomas Hughes of Cape Coast. A trader and civic leader, Hughes journeyed up the Ankobra sometime in the late 1850s or early 1860s and secured a mining lease in Wassa Amenfi near one of the richest gold-bearing areas. Operating on his own, he hired a team of bearers from Cape Coast who transported several hundred tons of crushing machinery to the mining site. But Hughes incurred the wrath of the king, then Kwaku Mensa, and was forced to flee, before he could produce much gold, on the grounds that a "black man in white man's clothes" digging for gold would surely offend the local gold fetish.[43] His machinery confiscated by the Wassa ruler, and unable to get British government backing for recovery of his losses, Hughes was left a ruined man; and no further Western-style mining projects were initiated for another eighteen years.[44]

Scholars have diverged in their interpretations of the role of the African and Eurafrican mercantile elite in Ghanaian economic and political history. These merchants and traders constituted a substantial and highly visible group at Accra, Cape Coast, and other towns along the coast. There is no time to expatiate here on the all of the reasons for their rise to prominence in the Gold Coast export economy or the reasons for their later decline that both I and Edward Reynolds have analyzed elsewhere.[45] As the work of David Kimble and Francis Agbodeka has shown, the mercantile and professional elite became well known for their pioneering protonationalist role in Gold Coast politics; and they constituted the mainspring for the both Fante Confederation and the Aborigines Rights Protection Society of the late 1890s.[46]

On the other hand, one or two studies from the Marxist perspective have taken a less sympathetic view of this African bourgeois class—referring to them as compradors—who served as pathways for the spread of capitalism in West Africa and appendages of a European system that eventually plunged African local economies into underdevelopment.[47] While there is undoubtedly some truth to this charge, I would place more emphasis on their constructive attempts to strengthen an indigenous capitalist class as a bulwark for future economic development and self-government. Considering the barriers placed in their path, including their lack of access to European capital markets and inability to get loans from British-controlled banks, it is difficult to represent these African entrepreneurs as the lackeys of alien forces. Though they were willing to work with colonial governments in some instances, where it would serve their interests, they were at the same time the harshest critics of colonial laws and policies that were antithetical to African needs and fulfillment.

Clearly there were paradoxes and contradictions in this indigenous commercial capitalism, just as there were in capitalism generally. But it is also necessary to analyze the movement in realistic human terms. Where else could these African entrepreneurs have found an outlet for their considerable dynamism and abilities if not through the existing coastal brokerage system? The interest of many African merchants in making money from gold mining during the late 1870s and early 1880s was in part a reflection of the stagnating trade and declining profits from the Gold Coast's two staple exports, palm oil and palm kernels.[48] In addition to their interest in gold mining, these African businessmen, along with their expatriate competitors, also attempted to expand and diversify the Gold Coast economy through new forest products that would bring them and the country considerable success and profit in the years ahead. These achievements included the mahogany-cutting industry of the Ankobra River Valley, the "rubber boom" of the 1880s and 1890s,[49] and especially in the cocoa-growing revolution of the early twentieth century. Gold mining must be seen as one part of a broader spectrum of attempted diversification and development. The Gold Coast African and European entrepreneurs also had to struggle against the inherent white man's racism of the time—though it was not so flagrant on the Gold Coast as in many other areas of colonial Africa. These African business and professional leaders should be respected for what they achieved and tried to accomplish, including their resistance to total domination by the colonial economic power, rather than condemned or pitied because they at times cooperated with and profited from European business connections.

The Promotional Leadership of Ferdinand Fitzgerald

From the 1860s through the mid-1880s the most vociferous spokesman for capitalistic gold mining as the key to general economic development in the Gold Coast was Ferdinand Fitzgerald, editor of the London-based *African Times*. A Liberian by nationality, Fitzgerald (ca. 1807–1884) had launched his career in the West African palm oil trade in the 1830s, and as a result of numerous contacts built up in produce brokerage, had moved to Great Britain, where he earned a living as the London agent for a variety of commercial and political organizations, including British export-import houses, African traders, the Kingdom of Bonny (east of the River Niger), and numerous other groups. Fitzgerald began his newspaper in 1861 as a vehicle for the African Aid Society, an association devoted to promoting representative government and economic self-sufficiency for African peoples everywhere; and this body subsequently became the mouthpiece for the Fante Confederation in the United Kingdom.[50] Almost from its inception the *African Times* took up the call for industrialized gold mining in the Gold Coast as one of the cardinal themes in its editorials. Thus in 1863 we find Fitzgerald exhorting his fellow West Africans to emulate the example of the Americans in the Great West by discovering undreamed-of El Dorados of mineral wealth. "Whenever the day for extracting their precious stores may arrive, we feel convinced that they will prove to be among the greatest gold deposits of our globe." What made Fitzgerald's appeal doubly provocative was his belief that mineral development was inseparable from African economic "self-help" and the drive to modernization and political independence. For if

the natives did not take the mining industry in their own hands, armies of English, French and American miners will rush in and dispossess, if not exterminate the populations that have been left from the ravages of the slave-traders and the constant butcheries of a relentless and most bloody superstition.[51]

During the 1860s and first half of the 1870s, Fitzgerald had written on a wide range of political, social, and administrative issues, such as the suppression of slavery in West Africa,[52] new educational opportunities for indigenous peoples, increased expenditure on public health, and most important, a greater say for Africans in the colonial government. But in 1879, as the concessions boom gathered force, he focused increasingly on West African economic issues—the call for imperial government-assisted transportation projects (roads and harbors), the promotion of an indigenous Black capitalism and especially, the development of the gold-mining industry.[53] Indeed, the determined and articulate Liberian did more than perhaps any other person to popularize the notion that there was indeed a West African Gold Rush. As time wore on, Fitzgerald became less blatantly anticolonialist. Though he never forsook his call for African nationalism and self-government, his earlier idealism merged with the understandable practical search for business deals and earning a living; and he himself became an investor, director, and promoter of six to eight different London-centered mining and concessions companies. Again, these separate goals were not necessarily incompatible. Fitzgerald and his colleagues saw no contradictions between their long-term hopes for African self-determination, the concomitant need for powerful doses of both private and public investment as a base for general economic development, plus the natural desire to earn a personal profit from within the capitalist system.

James Africanus Horton

Probably the most famous African involved in the gold rush of the later 1870s and 1880s was Dr. James Africanus Beales Horton.[54] A Nigerian Saro (descendant of freed slaves), raised and educated by missionaries in Sierra Leone, Horton had attended what became Fourah Bay College, Freetown, and later studied medicine at Kings College, London, and the University of Edinburgh before taking up practice as assistant surgeon in the Army Medical Service of the Gold Coast. As a medical practitioner of great intellectual breadth, he had conducted research on the disease of guinea worm and had written four books on various aspects of tropical medicine.[55] But in the latter part of his career he turned away from medicine toward educating both his fellow West

Africans and the colonial authorities about the necessary strategies for West African political liberation, economic development, and social change. His name, like that of a number of other Africans in this story, was closely linked with the Fante Confederation. While his mining projects are the focus of attention here, one should not forget that Horton's career spanned an impressively broad spectrum of service to public health and medicine, political activism, and scientific and professional activities quite apart from his forays into private business.[56]

Some may ponder why a man of Horton's stature became deeply involved in so many mineral development schemes of a risky and dubious nature. There is no doubt that Fitzgerald, Horton, and their colleagues engaged in some promotional practices and deals for the sublease of mining lands from chiefs to gullible foreign buyers that cut a fine line between acceptable "sharp dealing" and outright misrepresentation. At the same time, exaggerated stories and rumors played into the hands of biased British journalists and colonial officials, who frequently criticized the actions of educated coastal Africans by the most hypocritical double standards. On the one hand Horton and Fitzgerald had talked of—and continued to truly believe in—the highest civic ideals and national political and economic goals. On the other, these two leaders, and many of their colleagues from the business and professional elite of the coast, desperately needed money—especially after they had expended so much of their time and personal fortunes in the failed Fante Confederation over the preceding years. Besides, this group had observed and borne the brunt of sharp practices by European "old coasters" and wholesale suppliers of manufactured goods for decades. Why should they have felt any compunction about trying to attract as much European capital as possible, whether from London, Paris, or Liverpool? All gold mining was uncertain, dangerous, and to a great degree speculative. Who expected any guarantees? As emphasized throughout this study, respectable bourgeois nearly everywhere (Europe, North America, South Africa), viewed mining speculation as a special kind of game—with no holds barred—almost totally divorced from the canons of ordinary business enterprise. Horton's diverse interests included not only West African medicine and the Fante Confederation, but ventures in Sierra Leone such as the first African-owned commercial bank—an enterprise he hoped would provide low-interest loans for hard-pressed indigenous businessmen in the Gold Coast, Lagos, and Sierra Leone.[57]

During 1880 and 1881, amid rapidly spreading news about the gold rush, Horton urged his deputy, Swanzy Essien, another prominent coastal African entrepreneur and a former employee of the F. and A. Swanzy Trading Firm, to buy up as many concessions as possible from Wassa rulers, such as Kwamena Enemil and Chief Ango of Apinto. Horton then resold these leases to the directors of London-based companies, who paid him partly in cash and partly in paid-up shares. All told, between May 1878 and June 1882 the government noted that 109 different mining concessions for the western districts (Wassa, Nzema, Ahanta, etc.) were registered at Cape Coast. And of these the largest number were owned by Horton, with about thirty-one.[58] Not all were underground banket mining tracts; many were river washing sites of the sort purchased by Bonnat and others. By the mid-1880s Horton had overextended himself and was deeply in debt. Nevertheless, a number of Horton's concessions *were* turned to productive account after he sold them to London-based operating companies.

Joseph Dawson

Horton's leading associate and main up-country agent at the mines was Joseph Dawson, another well-known alumnus of local Wesleyan missionary schools, and representative of the African middle class of Cape Coast. Along with Horton, John Sarbah, F. C. Grant,[59] Jacob W. Sey, and George Blankson, Dawson too had played an active role in framing the constitution of the Fante Confederation and had served as a roving ambassador between its leaders and the rulers of interior states like Wassa Fiase and Asante. After appointment as official emissary to Kumasi by the Gold Coast government before the 1873-74 war, Dawson was taken prisoner by the Asantehene, along with Bonnat, and the missionaries F. A. Ramseyer and J. Kuhn. According to more than one account it was Dawson, rather than the Asantehene or his advisers, who first drew Bonnat's attention to the wealth of the Tarkwa district.[60] After the war, through prior contacts and familiarity with Akan customs and society, he played a central major role in negotiating mineral leases from the chiefs and subchiefs of Wassa. Dawson wore several different hats and he moved freely between the European, Eurafrican, and traditional African communities. It was not long before officials at Accra became apprehensive about what they termed his extraordinary political and personal influence with Chief Ango of Apinto. British traveling commissioners who toured Tarkwa spoke of him disparagingly (and probably excessively) as a gray eminence, a so-called bush magistrate, whose political and judicial advisory power "rivalled that of the king himself."[61] Future critics of the gold rush would trace this as one more example of the causal connections between an advancing capitalism, excessive Westernization, and the deterioration of traditional African political structures.[62]

Grant, Sarbah, Amissah, and Brew

This did not exhaust the record of African middle-class participation in the first gold rush. It also included the formation of the first fully African-owned mining syndicate. In the spring of 1882 four members of the Cape Coast business community—F. C. Grant, a leading exporter, shipowner, and member of the Gold Coast Legislative Council (who was elected chairman); James Amissah, his brother-in-law, also a trader (elected vice-chairman); James Hutton Brew, lawyer and editor of the *Gold Coast Times* (elected secretary); and John Sarbah, prosperous merchant (elected managing director),[63] formed the Gold Coast Native Concessions Purchasing Company. This was the first of at least three examples (for others see chap. 7) of mineral lands and mining companies with headquarters in the Gold Coast, boasting wholly African managing directorates. Though primarily a real estate venture, established to purchase and sell mining lands in Wassa, the directors intended eventually to undertake mining operations. The company started with a nominal capital of £25,000 in twenty-one shares with, the promoters taking up 10,000 shares and advertising the remainder to the general public. The company stands as an interesting might-have-been of Gold Coast mining history. Sarbah, Amissah and Sey hoped that it might serve as a forerunner for "developing industrial tendencies among our peoples."[64] Its failure underscores the formidable obstacles that any African-owned company had to face in the harshly competitive world of late-nineteenth-century Atlantic capitalism. In the 1970s two of the latter-day heirs of this enterprising group of Cape Coast African entrepreneurs, S. Sey and W. S. Kwesi Johnson, explained to me the limited entrepreneurial success of their forefathers in terms of lack of access to European capital markets, lack of local banking facilities, and lack of experience in the tough-minded ways of the European corporate world.[65] The downturn in the fortunes of the G.C. Native Concessions Purchasing Company was traced at the time to the inability of the promoters to secure the service of a professional mining engineer (which they knew was essential),[66] and to the unwillingness of the colonial government to acquiesce to their application for local incorporation under the English Companies Acts of the 1850s and 1860s— which were in fact applicable to the Gold Coast.[67]

Swanzy Essien and the Essaman Gold Mining
Company of Heman-Prestea

The hypersuspicious Colonial Office view that practically all the African-owned and most of the European concessions syndicates of the 1880s were purely speculative real estate ventures, devoid of serious productive intent, was far from accurate. It was common practice for most of the concessionaire directors to maintain their hold over at least one bona fide producing mine, while floating simultaneously a host of less secure speculative ventures. One of Horton's best-known companies, the Wassa and Ahanta Syndicate, formed in 1882 with a capital of £10,000, controlled some of the most valuable riverbank and hinterland concessions of the Heman-Prestea region, twenty-three miles northwest of Tarkwa.[68] Another member of the embryonic African "middle class" who played a more than passive role in the development of operational mining as well as promotion was Horton's close associate Swanzy Essien. He knew the western region well, having served as a trader for the Swanzy interest at Sekondi, Axim, Beyin, and at Assini on the French Ivory Coast. More important, Essien, who had negotiated the original lease with Chief Kofi Kyei for the valuable 2,000-square-yard block of territory at Heman-Prestea, was the first man to transport machinery to this subdistrict with the serious purpose of developing its rich lode in 1885.

Essien was practical and energetic. Thus, contrary to official opinion, not all the early indigenous mining entrepreneurs were mere real estate promoters. Essien singlehandedly tried to bridge the gap from land acquisition and prospecting to mechanized plant installation and ore production. Working from old African diggings at the Essaman or "Arsarman," mine he drove 180 feet straight into the side of the hill, along what came to be known as Essien's Adit, until he had reached the paying lode.[69] Unfortunately, rapid depletion of its small working capital forced the Wassa and Ahanta Syndicate to liquidate without retrieving much gold. Access to European capital markets remained the bugbear for pioneering African and Eurafrican mining capitalists. As a last resort the firm sold its various properties to an offshoot, the new Essaman Mining Company, in which Essien, Horton, and Fitzgerald retained an interest.[70]

The Essaman Company was capitalized in 1885 at £50,000, of which about £15,000 was paid up by the end of the first year (table 4.1). Its properties were valuable enough: in addition to its main leases at Prestea, it also gained control of the nearby Brumasi mines, later developed into a major producing lode by a separate company.[71] Ultimately the mines of the Heman-Prestea and Brumasi zone, which stood northwest of Tarkwa, proved to be among the most valuable in Ghana (see map 7.3). But, in a pattern characteristic of the first wave of active companies, the Essaman enterprise was plagued by a lack of capital, transportation problems, underground flooding, and the constant breakdown of machines, which were hard to fix owing to lack of skilled mechanics and spare parts. A small number of primitive "elephant" type stamping machines were carried in, none of which functioned properly when emplaced.[72] (For further developments at Prestea, see chap. 7.)

The Sam Family of Cape Coast and Tarkwa

Of all the African mining pathbreakers of the Gold Coast, the most redoubtable were the members of the Sam family—William Edward Sam and his two sons, Thomas Birch Freeman Sam and William Edward Sam Junior. The Sams were the descendants of an eastern Akan family who traced their roots back to one of the chiefdoms of Akyem. Educated at Christian mission schools, they were by mid-century recognized leaders among the middle class of Cape Coast and points west. This trio of father and two sons reflected many of the dynamic traits and attitudes noted elsewhere as part of the tradition of indigenous entrepreneurship in the Gold Coast.[73] Inspired by the teachings of the distinguished Eurafrican pastor Thomas Birch Freeman in the 1840s, the elder Sam began his adult life as a teacher in the local Methodist schools, but later shifted to trade and commerce (see photo). During the 1860s William Sam worked as an agent for a number of European and African merchants on the coast, including J. A. B. Horton and the Swanzy firm, where he gained a solid reputation not only as a businessman but as a skilled negotiator and arbiter. So considerable were the elder Sam's linguistic and diplomatic skills that the colonial government employed him off and on in settling disputes between the Dutch, English, and African rulers on the coast. Partly because of Britain's traditional support for the Fante (central coastal) states against the expansionistic power of Asante, the Sams (father and sons), like most of their friends in the coastal African community, tended to identify with the aims and policies of the colonial occupying power. After service in the Gold Coast volunteer regiment in the Sixth Asante War, William Sam Sr. was rewarded with the post of chief magistrate and commandant for the Axim fort,[74] and it was from this post that he made numerous expeditions to

Table 4.1

Major Operating Mining Companies with Concessions in Wassa, 1878–1895

Name of Company and Date of Registration	Nominal Capital £	Called-Up Capital £	Amt. Paid for Purchase of Concessions £	Date of Resolution to Liquidate
1 Compagnie Miniere de la Côte d'or Africain The African Gold Coast Co. (1878) (E. Wray, A. Verillon, I. Illurant, C. Stewart, M. Radcliffe)	50,000 increased to 200,000	21,921 (1878)	No middleman. £200 & 3% of future profits paid to local chief	Taken over by Tarkwa & Abosso Co. in 1888
2 Akankoo Mining Cost (1881) (J. A. Horton, J. Irvine)	150,000	100,019 (1887)	50,000	April 1888
3 Compagnie Mines d'Or Aboso (1880) (Aboso Mining Co. Ltd)— combined with the African Gold Coast Co. in 1882 (E. Wray, J. C. Wray, A. Verillon, M. Radcliffe)	30,000		30,000	Taken over by Tarkwa & Abosso Co. in 1888
4 Cinnamon Bippo Gold Mines Ltd. (1889) (Aboso) (F. Swanzy, W. Cleaver, J. Irvine)	75,000		Initial leascholder paid £180 per year to chief. Lease later sold for 65,000 shares	Taken over by Wassau (G.C.) Mining Co. in 1895
5 Effuenta Mining Co. Ltd. (1879) (F. Fitz-gerald, Solomon Hecht, Paulus Dahse, Samuel Cearns)	60,000	57,000 (after 2nd year)	33,000	August 1883
6 Essaman Gold (1885) Mining Co. Ltd.	50,000	40,950 (1890)	15,000 for piece of land near Himan-Prestea	Combined with Gie Appantoo Company in 1892
7 Gie Appanto Gold Mining Co. Ltd. (1888) (Sir S. Cawston, G. E. Burnell, C. Wise, A. H. Baker, Louis Wyatt, Swanzy Essien)	110,000 (1890)	33,550 (1891)	7,250	Properties trans-ferred to the new Appanto Mining Co. in 1893 and later to Prestea Mining Co.

Continued on next page

Table 4.1 *(continued)*

	Name of Company and Date of Registration	Nominal Capital £	Called-Up Capital £	Amt. Paid for Purchase of Consessions £	Date of Resolution to Liquidate
8	Appantoo Mining Co. (1893) [reconstruction of Gie Appantoo Co.] (above)	150,000	80,000	(paid 80,000 to shareholders of Gie Appantoo Co.)	Taken over by Prestea Mining Company in February 1885
9	Gold Coast Mining Co. (1880) (Abontiakoon Mining Co.) (Ferdinand Fitzgerald, J. A. B. Horton)	65,000	40,349 (1880)	37,000 paid to J.A.B. Horton	
10	Guinea Coast Gold Mining Co. (1881) (The Izra Mines) (J. Irvine, Jasper Johns, Solomon Hecht, London Mercantile Assn.)	125,000	100,000	33,333 in July 1885 deferred shares plus 17,000 in cash	
11	Swanzy Estates Co. Ltd. (1881) (Aja Bippo Mines) (F. Swanzy, F. J. Crocker, William Cleaver)	25,000	21,921 (1887)		Taken over by Cinnamon Bippo (1887) and by Wassau (G.C.) Mining Co. (1897)
12	Tarkwa and Abosso Gold Mining Co. (1888) (A. Verillon, W. F. Morecroft, P. Luc, T. J. Foster, L. Gruning)	100,000	80,000 (1890)	64,000 in paid-up shareholders of the Africa Gold Coast Co.	Still in operation after 1900
13	The Wassau Gold Coast Mining Co. (1882) (Francis Swanzy, Frederick Crocker)	100,000	100,000 (1887)	Paid 75,000 to Swanzy Estates Co. for Aja Bippo lease	Still in operation after 1900

Sources: Companies Records; Registrar of Joint Stock Companies. Also Quarterly District Reports for Wassa; and *Annual Colonial Reports, Gold Coast*: PRO.

the Ankobra gold districts, cementing ties of friendship with the leading kings and chiefs of Wassa. I shall return to the even more remarkable professional mining careers of the Sams in a subsequent chapter on the producing mines of Wassa (see chap. 7).

EUROPEAN CONCESSION MONGERS
AND COMPANY PROMOTERS

It goes without saying that the ingress of foreign capital into both legitimate and bogus mining companies in two significant Gold Coast booms (1879–85 and 1900–1904) would not have been possible without the increasing availability of English surplus capital seeking new speculative outlets from about the 1860s onward. In an overlooked scholarly article on this subject, J. R. Jeffreys substantiates that in the wake of the companies acts of 1855 and 1856 a multitude of new corporations, inexperienced with limited liability, permitted a heavy proportion of the capital on the shares they *issued* (not simply their nominal capital) to remain unpaid by their subscribers.[75] This was particularly true of nonferrous mining companies (especially in gold, silver, and copper) and other overseas concessionaire ventures. Keep in mind that the first South African gold boom still lay in the future, so that the total amount of British capital implanted in the foreign and colonial gold mining schemes in the 1870s, while significant, still did not rank with the investments of later decades.

> The exhaustion of British mines and the development of limited compa-
> nies engaged in mining enterprises abroad changed radically the charac-
> ter of the companies but not the character of the shares. The overseas
> ventures were regarded as frankly speculative; few investors would risk
> much capital, and the average life of the company was short.[76]

We should not, therefore, exaggerate the importance of capital outflows to African mines (whether in West or South Africa) in the total basket of British overseas investments at this juncture. In spite of intensive efforts by both the coastal African and European promoters, the companies of the 1880s were unable to attract many major individual investors (well-to-do landowners, financiers, merchants), let alone banks or financial institutions in London. For the greater part of the period under review the norm was small-scale bourgeois capitalism.[77]

Francis Swanzy of London

A shadowy but potent force behind mineral development in Wassa during both the formative (1877–95) and productive (1902–14) phases, was Frank Swanzy, partner of the long-established Anglo-West African mercantile firm of F. and A. Swanzy, Cannon Street, London. The long and complex history of the Swanzy family's contact with the Gold Coast, which had its beginning in the late eighteenth century and covered the transition from the slave trade to legitimate trade, has been told elsewhere. In fact, the managers of the nineteenth-century trading firm, Francis and Andrew Swanzy, were the third generation of this family associated with West Africa. These two had been instrumental in developing the palm oil trade of the Gold Coast and had weathered the trade doldrums of the 1860s, when many other African and expatriate firms had foundered.[78] With their extensive financial outlay in numerous ventures (retail stores, warehouses, docks, and ships) in Britain and North America as well as West Africa, the Swanzys had the capacity to spread their risk. Quite apart from any lingering stigma about possible involvement in the eighteenth-century slave trade, the Swanzy commercial record on the coast, even after 1870s, was not without blemish. One suspicion, which particularly rankled critics in London, was that the Swanzy firm had knowingly allowed firearms and gunpowder imports to reach Asante during the late war against British imperial forces.[79]

When Andrew Swanzy, the senior partner, died in 1880, leadership passed to his son Francis. Under Frank Swanzy's management, mining investment in the Gold Coast became an important subsidiary interest, but it was never a high-priority, all-or-nothing affair in which a profit had to be realized immediately. This firm had the necessary capital and could afford to take its time. Much of the initial investment came from members of the family, close friends, and other leading members of the firm. More important, the highly solvent trading firm itself could provide loans to the mining company whenever necessary. This gave the Swanzy mines a clear-cut edge over their competition—a broader financial base and staying power. Unlike the field agents for a majority of the London-based mining companies of the period, the manager-in-chief of the Swanzy firm's trading operations on the coast, William Cleaver, had resided in the Gold Coast for many years and knew the country and its people well. He and other members of the Swanzy organization had traveled up-country and examined some of the best mineral-bearing properties in Wassa with a fair degree of care and economy.

Well aware that the Sam family's long-standing familiarity with traditional chiefs and with the terrain might be trump cards, Swanzy had cajoled the father—William Edward (then in government service)—back into the firm's employment. Sam, together with another of Swanzy's senior agents at Cape Coast, Frederick Crocker, trekked to Wassa in 1878 (about the same time as the Anglo-French prospectors) and negotiated numerous leases with Kwabena Ango of Apinto, along with another 1,800-acre concession from Chief Enemil Kuma at Aboso. These became the core properties of two of the most solid and potent mining organizations of the 1880s and 1890s—the Swanzy Estates Mining Company and the Wassa (Gold Coast) Mining Company— whose operations will be analyzed in detail in chapter 7.[80] William Edward Sam and his two sons remained loyal to the Swanzy firm and adjunct mining companies throughout their illustrious careers. Because they had to protect their long-standing commercial reputation among Gold Coastans, Swanzy and his agents were more circumspect in their dealings with chiefs and African workers than some of the get-rich-quick European mining promoters and their agents. And, compared with other concessionaires, the Swanzy mines were known in this period for relatively good labor relations with the local communities where they worked.

James Irvine of Liverpool and the Irvine Block of Companies

The most aggressive and controversial of all British mining company directors from the 1870s through to the late 1890s was James Irvine of Liverpool. Both he and Swanzy conform to the model, outlined in chapter 1, of Anglo-West African palm oil dealers and general merchants on the West African coast who sought business diversification by moving into gold mining. A Merseyside palm product broker and consignment merchant with long experience, Irvine had served his apprenticeship on the Guinea Coast during the early days of the palm oil trade and while still in his twenties had formed his first export-import partnership. A self-proclaimed pietistic Christian who took great pride in his church membership, charitable public service, and circumspect business dealings, he exemplified the contradictions in European entrepreneurship in West Africa during the mid-Victorian period of informal empire and "the three Cs" (Christianity, Commerce, and Civilization). He was, for example, a close friend and confidant of

several of the leading pioneering African nationalists and colonial reformers of the day: not only did he cooperate with Fitzgerald and
Horton in a number of mining ventures, he provided financial support
and advice (on the basis of a common Christian heritage) to the great
Liberian educator and Pan-Africanist spokesman, Edward Wilmot
Blyden.[81] An ardent temperance advocate, Irvine steadfastly proclaimed
that he totally separated himself from such questionable segments of
West African trade as the traffic in liquor and firearms. Yet, in a kind
of "doubling" style[82] well known in the business practices of Mark
Twain's America and other capitalist countries at this time,[83] he saw no
conflict between his service on the boards of numerous Victorian phil-
anthropies on the one hand[84] coupled with the most shameful false
advertising, and stock manipulations in London in connection with
mining schemes on the other. No doubt one explanation for these
hypocrisies lies in the fact that many reputable business leaders in
Manchester, Liverpool, or London viewed speculative real estate deals
in distant "wilderness areas" as a totally separate sphere of action,
where (despite the existence of vulnerable "native cultures") a ruthless,
no-holds-barred ethic somehow appeared (or was rationalized as)
justifiable. Yet Irvine, and other mining projectors of the period, continued to believe they were performing useful work and spreading
Christian civilization. During a business career that spanned more than
sixty years, he vigorously championed heavy doses of government
assistance for a new Empire of West Africa, where corporate gold
mining and railways would play a fundamental role.

As early as 1877, Irvine had employed two main agents on the coast,
an African trader, William Grant, and a British prospector who went by
the colorful, if pretentious, name of Robert Bruce Napolean Walker,[85] to
buy up supposedly valuable riverbank properties in the lands immediately
north of Axim. Walker, strongly influenced by Grant and by King Kofi
Blay of Nzema, lingered too long in the immediate hinterland of Axim,
unwisely buying up well-known African mines and alluvial concessions
near the mouth of the River Ankobra, without proceeding to the main
reefs at Tarkwa.[86] From Blay and his subchiefs and headmen, such as
Kwaku Apo of Asanta, Kwaku Joma of Nanwa, and Etie of Kikam,
Walker acquired extensive mining rights to the Ingotro concession, the
Nanwa Mines, the Izrah mine, the St. John's River concession, plus
numerous other (mainly riverbank) properties in the Lower Ankobra
valley.[87] Already worked out by Nzeman miners, these pit mines had the
advantage of easy access. To control the leases, Irvine then established

the African Gold Coast Syndicate in 1882 (see table 4.2) with a nominal capital of £45,000. But after paying £40,000 for the concessions to the local vendors (unclear in the sources—but most likely Irvine himself plus Grant), the company had a working capital of only £5,000.[88] It later transpired that Grant was a wheeler-dealer of no mean repute (related by marriage to Joseph Dawson and closely involved with King Blay) who had built up a small personal fortune from multifarious shrewd deals between chiefs and naive representatives of European companies. With properties covering ten square miles, the African Gold Coast Syndicate took control of ten times more land than any other single capitalist company of this decade. But, since the area in question lay a mere sixteen miles from the coast and probably had been well-known since Portuguese times, Irvine and his underlings should have been far more skeptical about its value. Most of the surface layers on the banks of the Ankobra had been mined out long before, and the deposits proved utterly devoid of the rich deep reefs suitable for sustained mechanized mining.

The financial structure of Irvine's pyramid of London-based companies rested on equally shaky ground. Among the subsidiary firms he personally controlled were the Guinea Coast Mining Company, the West African Gold Fields, Egwira Mines, the Akankoo Mining Company, and the Effuenta Mining Company. In addition, Irvine held shares in several of the Horton-Fitzgerald ventures, such as the Gold Coast Mining Company's Abontiakoon concession. Irvine's Guinea Coast venture was floated in 1881 primarily for working the Izra concession south of Tumento (not shown on maps) with a nominal capital of £100,000. Here was a classic case of stock watering through the issue of a large segment of vendors shares. By special agreement the company agreed to pay Irvine £75,000 for rights to the Izra lease—£41,667 in cash and £33,333 in fully paid-up shares.[89] Only a negligible amount of the share capital represented investment in buildings, equipment, or productive technology. The whole enterprise was scarcely more than a scam for the benefit of promoters. The amount paid to Irvine and his cohorts for the mere transfer of lease to the new company amounted to 86.7 percent of the available working capital. This was quite a return for Irvine's original down payment of £3,000; and in order to make such payments to themselves, the directors had to siphon off monies that belonged to bona fide investors.[90] Except for the Essaman and Abontiakoon mines (see below), the greater part of Irvine's concessions satrapy consisted of riverbank placer properties on the Lower and Middle Ankobra that were never developed. It was difficult to reconcile

Irvine's self-serving pronouncements about business rectitude and con-cern for African welfare and development with the most flagrant squan-dering of his companies' capital stock on land of little value, purely for personal enrichment.[91]

Richard Francis Burton and Verney Lovett Cameron

More than one colorful character from the international fraternity of explorers, adventurers, and fortune seekers made their way to the goldfields of Wassa, Akyem, and Asante in these decades. To follow up on Walker's and Grant's initial claims and to prop up the evaporating market for his proliferating stock flotations, Irvine hired the intrepid and flamboyant Victorian pathbreakers Captain Richard Burton and Commander V. L. Cameron to journey to the Gold Coast in late 1881 and early 1882.[92] Burton, of course, was already a household name for being the first European to sight Lake Tanganyika on his expedition with John Hanning Speke to East Africa in search for the sources Nile in 1858–59. In addition he had created a sensation as the first Christian to penetrate the Muslim holy city of Medina in Arabia; and he had traveled across the great American desert to observe the Mormon City of the Saints at Salt Lake in 1860. Cameron, who deserved to be better known, had trekked across Central Africa in the late 1870s; and had campaigned against the inland slave trade. He was a hard-working professional and less of a self-promoting publicist than Burton. Still neither man had found his niche in life; and Burton, according to one biographer, after writing numerous books and wandering in and out of different careers, including British Consul to Trieste, had come to view himself as a failure.[93] Seeking new horizons, the two travelers interpre-ted their West African assignment precisely the way Irvine intended. They were to write, not a critical evaluation on the technical prospects for successful Gold Coast mining, but a piece of propaganda that would restore the confidence of skeptical investors in an already flagg-ing market. In banner articles and popular lectures Burton extolled the hinterland north of Axim as an "El Dorado" whose "soil was as rich as California."[94] After three months tramping around Wassa and in-specting mining sites mainly along the banks of the Ankobra, he sailed for England in late April 1882, leaving Cameron behind to map and report on the mines in detail. The published account was not without value, if read at two different levels. Burton had long been adept at presenting himself as a quasi-expert on exotic regions and cultures of the world and in turning out best-selling books on his adventures at

short notice. Their jointly authored *To The Gold Coast for Gold,*
published in two volumes (London, 1883), revealed scant professional
understanding of geology or mining technology and was scathingly
reviewed by critics at the time;[95] but it remains (despite hyperbole about
the richness of gold discoveries along the Ankobra) a useful eyewitness
account of the topography of southwestern Ahanta and Gwira, the
location of mines in Wassa, and details of encounters with African
rulers and European prospectors in the early years of the "rush."

Did the Izra mine contain rich and untouched lodes deep beneath the
levels already worked by African traditional miners? The two explorers
were certain that it did. Burton had personal reasons to hope that his
effusions would attract new shareholders, since Irvine had appointed
him to the board of directors of the Guinea Coast Mining Company
(the supervising body of the Izra mine), and he held hoards of shares
in other Gold Coast mining ventures. Three years elapsed, however,
before it became apparent that Burton, Cameron and Irvine had been
hoodwinked by Walker and Grant. The Izra mine proved to be "utterly
destitute of gold," largely because the local Nzeman miners had
combed out the subsurface strata over many decades of prior working.
A qualified engineer who inspected the area in 1886 told Irvine that the
mine had been salted "by some designing rascal you had in your
employ."[96] Burton, according to his biographer, lost money on all his
Gold Coast misadventures. Forced to pay back the money Irvine had
advanced him, he failed to develop his numerous claims on the Ankobra and ended up "poorer than before."[97] A more thorough survey
by experienced mining engineers fifty years later suggested that the
Lower Ankobra Valley indeed may have contained some deeper gold-
containing strata not seen by these early prospectors, but that the
minable areas were "patchy."[98]

The Guinea Coast Mining Company

The story of the Guinea Coast Mining Company and its various concessions was typical of the unsystematic purchase of unknown tracts of
land by the Gold Coast mining projectors of the late 1870s and early
1880s. Nearly everything about the company was tainted by muddle
or deception, including the initial prospecting, R. B. N. Walker's survey
of the boundaries (which failed to show conflicting rights by different
chiefs), the assays of ore, the flotation of stock, and the manipulation
of company funds. Equally disappointing were the fates of Irvine's
Egwira Mines, Ltd., and the West African Goldfields, Ltd. None of

these concessions, despite the full stamp of approval by Grant, Walker, Burton, and Cameron, ever yielded paying quantities of gold. Quite apart from dubious management practices (including skimming off the top) by the directors, these companies failed simply because gold did not exist in sufficient quantities to defray operating costs.

To be fair, Irvine was not all puffery, and the Liverpool entrepreneur apparently intended to start productive operations at several sites run by his companies—including the riverbank concessions. He spent about £3,000 in Britain and the Gold Coast on salaries and equipment.[99] But disease was a genuine bugbear, and the notorious image of the "fever coast" made if difficult for the companies to attract expert field engineers and supervisors. The first manager, imported from Chile, directed his tunneling operations in the opposite direction from the lode and died of acute alcoholism after less than three weeks on the job. Of the next two managers, one succumbed to sunstroke and the second to dysentery.[100] All told, five Europeans died at the Izra mine within a short period. On the other hand, Irvine bore responsibility for the irresponsible powers wielded by his board of directors, who continued to vote themselves substantial fees out of the dwindling capital stock of the Guinea Coast Company even after its mines had failed. It was against such a background of legalized embezzlement that the secretary of the company was driven to suicide. Desperately afraid that the shock waves would depress the market value of shares in all his companies, Irvine concealed news of the Izra mines failure from shareholders for two years, until July 1885.[101] Then, moving quickly, he liquidated the company in order to avoid lawsuits by shareholders.

THE TECHNOLOGY OF PLACER MINING

It was partly because the obstacles to deep-reef mining seemed so intractable that many of the early Wassa companies gave exaggerated attention to the chances for quick profits from alluvial deposits. The classic rushes at Sutters Mill in California and Ballarat, Victoria Colony, in Australia, which had occurred within the recent memory of most of the leading Wassa promoters, had conjured up images of mounds of gold dust and overnight fortunes that were difficult to expunge. Despite the fact that panning all day for a few grains of river gold also could be a laborious and disappointing process, placer mining rather than reef mining invariably looked more appealing to the uninitiated. Besides, it appeared at the time that technology had moved forward much more rapidly in alluvial mining than in reef mining since the early days of the Sacramento sourdoughs: by the 1870s gold seekers were using steam dredges to dig up the ore, and larger sluices—"rockers," "cradles," and "long toms"—to separate the sand from the gold.[102] To the unfledged, successful mining seemed to depend as much on the efficiency of moving vast amounts of earth quickly as on the intrinsic value of a particular claim. And for men like Bonnat, Burton, and Cameron, the fancy hydraulic gear recently developed in North America seemed to offer a quick way around the supposedly insurmountable West African labor problem.[103] Burton and Cameron became ardent publicists for gold sluicing at places like the Apatim concession of the West African Goldfields, Ltd., on whose board they sat. But they were easily carried away by sensational pictures and diagrams of great sluicing nozzles and hydrostatic suction devices,[104] which were not used with great success, even in North America, until the 1890s. At this point such machines still contained numerous flaws; and considering their bulk and logistical problems of installation, their introduction to West Africa at this juncture was wholly unrealistic.

Paulus Dahse and the Effuenta Mining Company

One of the few promising ventures associated with James Irvine's name was the Effuenta Mining Company, which emerged from collaboration between Irvine, Ferdinand Fitzgerald, and Paulus Dahse, a German-born West African trader whose sole claim to mining experience had been a brief trip to Sutter's Mill at the time of the California rush of 1849. But he had become familiar with the Wassa country and chiefs, having served as traveling agent for the Bremen Mission trading factory based in the eastern Gold Coast since the 1860s.

Dahse was as shrewd as any concessions dealer who worked the Ankobra-Wassa gold districts in this period.[105] Journeying overland to Wassa in May 1879, after hearing of the Anglo-French company's activities, he had purchased a fifty-year lease to a 2,000-by-400-yard tract that lay just south of the Paris-Liverpool firm's Tarkwa property (see map 4.2).[106] The compensation given the local stool authority was paltry in comparison with the lucrative transfer fee, which Dahse skimmed off for himself. The lease provided that Chief Ango of Apinto would receive a mere £200 per year, plus 3 percent of net profits. Five months later in England Dahse sold the lease to Irvine and Fitzgerald, who then formed the Effuenta Company. Other directors and major shareholders were Solomon Hecht, a London stockbroker, who served as chairman, Samuel Cearns, and Edward Berman.[107] Through the connections of the Hecht brothers in the City of London, the Effuenta was more successful than most of its Wassa competitors of the 1880s in marketing its shares. Out of a nominal capital of £60,000, £57,000 was paid up by 1882.[108] But this was not translated into productive mining. An artful manipulator, Dahse cajoled the directors into paying him £3,000 in cash plus the outrageous sum of £30,000 in installments over several years for mere transfer of the lease.[109] As if this were not stupid enough, the directors in turn appointed Dahse (with his meager prior experience in California) as local comanager of the mine at a salary of £300 per year. An addendum allowed Dahse 20 percent of future mines profits, not to exceed £1,000 per year.

Despite this unpropitious start, the Effuenta became one of the handful of thirty-seven paper companies to advance beyond the ground-clearing stage to active crushing operations. The coresident manager was E. T. McCarthy, a mining engineer and son of the famous Sir Charles McCarthy, early governor of the Gold Coast forts, killed in the Asante War of 1824.[110] On reaching the site in January 1880, McCarthy and three European confederates employed some 200 imported Kru laborers from Liberia to hack away brush from the hillside and start the tunneling into the side of the gold reef. Afterward, they built a road with a 300-foot bridge and erected some twenty-five outbuildings and houses for a crushing plant, storage facilities, machine shops, and quarters for staff. Such apparently mundane works, repeated by all the other operating companies should not be forgotten when, in the final chapter, I point out the linkages between the gold boom and a budding building construction industry in towns like Axim, Tarkwa, and Prestea. Even when a first generation company failed, such buildings might be used as a base and extended by later companies on the same sites. Through the wages paid out to workers, such activities as land clearing, timber cutting, and house building, like regular mining, pumped money into the general economy. Within two years the Effuenta had driven three tunnels into the face of the hill (the longest was 240 feet) and had sunk three shafts from those tunnels.[111] By the summer of 1882 two gravitation batteries (with six heads each) were in place and the extraction of ore had begun.

Even so, the Effuenta mine was plagued by setbacks, traceable to the difficult local working conditions, to the inexperience of the promoter-managers, and to the primitive state of the European technology then available. The rudimentary pumping system—which tapped into a nearly stream—was unable to supply sufficient water for steady operation of the steam engines that drove the stamps. Of the total of twelve heads of stamps ultimately installed, only six ever worked.[112] And while the miners were said to be capable of bringing 100 tons of ore a day to the surface, the stamps proved incapable of crushing more than one-tenth of this amount. The use of mercury-coated copper amalgamation plates to entrap the gold particles was botched.[113] The extraction rate never reached the one and a half to two ounces of gold per ton that the directors had predicted, and the company was forced into liquidation in 1883.[114]

The Abontiakoon Mines

There has been no attempt here to summarize in detail the history of every minor mining company, but several showed promise for the future. One of the many claims originally staked out by Swanzy Essien for the Horton-Fitzgerald interest was the Abontiakoon Concession (see map 4.2), located just north of Tarkwa. In 1880, Horton sold the concession for £37,000 to the Gold Coast Mining Company, whose list of major shareholders had a familiar ring—Ferdinand Fitzgerald, company secretary; Horton himself; James Irvine; George Pencockes, a retired shipowner; and the London Mercantile Association, a trading group linked to Fitzgerald's London agency. African entrepreneurs played a prominent role in the founding and early direction of this company. "The Abontiakoon Company" had a nominal capital of £65,000 and an initial paid-up capital of £40,349. For his recompense, Chief Ango of Apinto received a payment of £300, half of which was to be paid only after work commenced, and an annual royalty of 3 percent after the mine became a paying operation.[115]

Once again, it is important to stress, in the face of all the puffery and profligacy, that not every mining venture associated with the Anglo-African group was a speculative romp. The Abontiakoon enterprise recorded fair success in marketing its initial stock issue to the public, and by 1881 it boasted 295 shareholders. To supervise development Horton and Irvine appointed two qualified engineers Louis Gowans and his brother, David, who managed a staff of five Europeans and over eighty-five Kru and Bassa men from Liberia. At the time of the colonial government's earliest mines report in 1882, four vertical shafts (two over 90 feet) and three tunnels of 95 to 110 feet had been gouged out, but no pulverization or treatment of ore had taken place.

The Abontiakoon Company was more innovative than most of its rivals in attacking the problem of the local roads. To overcome the difficulties of transporting sectionalized machinery overland by porters using muddy bush tracks, the Gowanses brought in crushing machinery and the component parts and materials for their treatment plant on small hand-drawn carts, or "trucks" (resembling gun carriages), the first wheeled conveyances run between Tumento and Tarkwa.[116] This method seemed to support Louis Gowans's contention that stamping machinery could be compartmentalized in larger blocks, but this did not necessarily mean that the machines would be installed in good working order. Furthermore, the cost of employing fifty-seven men to lay down logs over swampy places (the so-called corduroy technique of road building) and of hauling the trucks over a seventeen-mile journey that took two weeks was obviously prohibitive.[117] As with nearly every other company launched in this period, the Abontiakoon's directors published grandiose prophecies concerning proportions of fine gold to batches of crushed ore that far exceeded practical realities in the prerailway and precyanide age.[118] They increased their nominal capital stock to £80,000 in 1884. But the peak of the boom was now over and the stockholders were so drained that the company, like most of the others described here, found it impossible to attract a second wave of investment. The fact that it was nearly impossible for the Abontiakoon's light-weight (300-lb.) stamps to crush the hard and unweathered banket ores found at the deeper shaft levels certainly underscores the difficulties and achievements of the independent African peasant miners, who continued to labor on using traditional methods. It is noteworthy that the Gowans brothers sent home one or two shipments of gold bars.[119] But the combination of high labor and transport charges coupled with the exhaustion of capital stock in the purchase of leases forced the directors to dissolve in 1886. As we shall see in chapter 6, the Gowans brothers used the experience gained with this company to good effect in shifting their employment to the better-organized Swanzy mines several miles north.

THE IMMEDIATE EFFECTS OF
THE CONCESSIONS BOOM

In attempting to understand the checkered and controversial record of so many Wassa mines in the early phase, one must separate the handful of solidly based mining firms that cleared ground, installed machinery, and started operations from the horde of minor entities that had no greater goal than to profit from the sale of worthless leases and dubious shares at inflated prices. At the same time it is well to keep in mind that this phase of extravagant and wasteful share pushing was nothing unique in the mining world. Speculative euphoria was typical in the history of nearly every renowned gold rush of the Victorian Age. The same tortuous game played out in the Gold Coast had close parallels in the epic rushes at Victoria in Australia, Dawson Creek in Canada and at Leadville in Colorado, and the Yukon.[120] Success in mining is a hard thing to judge. It would appear, however, that the Gold Coast, even in this early period, had a success rate equal to the average at other goldfields of the world at this time. Thus, if we correlate the rough total of the thirty-seven paper companies in table 4.2 (below) with the ten or more reputable working companies summarized partly in this chapter (and in chap. 7) it is a fair estimate that 27 percent of the registered limited companies engaged in some mining activity, while only 10 percent were producing mines over a sustained period of time.

It says something for the integrity of some members of the contemporary London mining press that even in the unregulated atmosphere 1870s and 1880s, one or two newspapers shot up warning flares about the dangers of overspeculation in unknown West African companies, so that by 1882 enthusiasm for Gold Coast shares was waning, and in 1883 the boom fever subsided. Even so, the records of the Essaman mine, the Abontiakoon (summarized here), together with and the "big three" producing companies—the Tarkwa and Aboso, the Wassa (Gold Coast) Mining Company, and Gie Appanto Mines (summarized in chap. 7)—illustrate an important truth about gold mining that may be forgotten amid the stories of bogus claims that were never worked. Even for the richest of goldfields, owing to the complexity of imponderable factors, it is the conventional wisdom is that it generally takes eight or nine failed enterprises for just one to succeed. As in science, so too in mining, the testing and refutation of hypotheticals is not necessarily a wasted effort, since this process prepares better footholds for those who follow. As we have seen, even Burton, Cameron and their cohorts attempted some serious mining along the valley of the Lower Ankobra River, and by their failures proved once and for all that the gold strata and alluvial sites of that district were not worth the heavy investment required for mechanized development. When the Irvine group moved northeast to Tarkwa, it scored some modest successes with the Essaman property. The Abontiakoon mine as well proved to lie in an especially valuable strike zone; and its early management under the Gowans brothers was more effective than most. Of course all these mines experienced problems. It took far stronger organization and capital input than any of these firms had at their disposal in the 1880s to survive the disheartening long periods of "dead work" through "country rock" that were a precondition for profitable production. Few companies in mining are ever so fortunate as to reap a profit on their first spurt of effort. Several of the most competent prospectors and engineers of the period—such as the Sams, McCarthy, Louis Wyatt, and the Gowans brothers—put their experience in the 1870s to good use as technical advisors for more effective companies in the 1890s.

With the onset of the gold rush we can see also the incipient eroding effects of the rapid multiplication of mining leases upon traditional Akan land law pertaining to the profitable use of stool lands and also on the relations and obligations between paramount rulers (amanhene), and subordinate chiefs (ahenfo) governing the grant of concessionaire rights. What the inflow of European money to the interior African states tended to change—in the case at hand mainly in Wassa Fiase, but also in Wassa Amenfi, Nzema, and surrounding states—were the demands of subordinate chiefs or stool holders, such as the rulers of Apinto and Aboso, to retain greater if not total control over the incomes derived from the purchase prices and rents paid for the new mining leases by foreigners. This trend ran into direct conflict, of course, with the traditional three-tiered abusa share system for the distribution of proceeds from gold mining or the extraction of other forest products—one-third to stranger miner, one third to the immediate or local stool authority, and one-third to the king or paramount stool. The fact that successive kings of Wassa Fiase, during the greater part of the period under review, lacked strong personal leadership qualities (see succeeding chapters) tended to contribute to the fragmentation and erosion of their centralized authority with respect both to the approval of leases to concessionaires and to participation in the incomes derived from annual rents. By the end of the period under study what began as small examples of growing friction between kings and subordinate stools would erupt into a plethora of litigation in both the African and colonial law courts over control and rights to proceeds from land leases and concessions.

Table 4.2
European Mining Companies Registered to Do Business on the Gold Coast, 1878–1895

Company and Date of Registration	Nominal Capital (£)
Abontiakoon Mining Co. (1880)	65,000
Aboso Mining Co. (1880)	30,000
African Concessions Trust (1891)	10,000
African Consolidated Mines (1882)	20,000
African Gold Coast Co. (Anglo-French Co.) (1878)	50,000
African Gold Coast Syndicate (1882)	28,420
Akankoo Mining Co. (1881)	150,000
Ankobra River Syndicate (1891)	25,000
Ankobra Valley Syndicate (1888)	50,000
Appolonia Gold Mining Syndicate (1882)	18,000
Axim (Gold Coast) Mining Co.	2,000
Cankin Bamoo Gold Mines (1882)	100,000
Cinnamon Bippo Gold Mines Co. (1889)	75,000
Effuenta Gold Mines Syndicate (1885)	2,000
Effuenta Mining Co. (1879)	60,000
Egwira Mines (1882)	120,000
Essaman Gold Mining Co. (1885)	50,000
Gie Appanto Gold Mining Co. (1888)	110,000
Gold Coast Development Syndicate (1895)	n.a.
Gold Coast Mining and Exploration Co. (1890)	80,000
Gold Coast Native Concessions Purchasing Co. (1882)	25,000
Gold Fields of Appolonia (1887)	60,000
Guinea Coast Gold Mining Co.	125,000
Kitfia Mines (1883)	20,000
New Akankoo Gold Mining Co. (1888)	150,000
North Akankoo (Gold Coast) Mining Co. (1881)	2,000
Sefwi Gold Mining Pioneer (1892)	2,500
South Akankoo Gold Mining Co.	2,000
South Gold Coast Mining Co. (1882)	75,000
Swanzy Estates and Gold Mining Company (1881)	25,000
Tacquah (Tamsu) Gold Mines Co.	85,000
Tamsoo and Menosoo Syndicate (1891)	6,000
Tarkwa and Aboso Gold Mining Co. (1888)	100,000
Wassa and Ahanta Gold Mines Syndicate (1880)	10,000
Wassa (Gold Coast) Mining Company	100,000
West African Gold Fields (1882)	100,000
West African Gold Mining Co. (1882)	50,000
Total	1,982,920

Sources: Stock Exchange Yearbook for 1887, p. 330; and for 1890, pp. 443, 464, 488; Walter Skinner, *The Mining Manual for 1887* (London 1887), 3, 5–6, 21, 140, 165–69, 170–72, 183, 432, 464–65, 468; *Mining Journal*, 1 July 1882, 783; *Mining Journal*, 9 January 1886, 54.

Some Leading Gold Mining Entrepreneurs from the African Business Community of Cape Coast

James Africanus Horton, medical doctor; leader of the Fante Confederation; owner of 31 mining concessions.

William Edward "Tarkwa Sam," Mining Engineer and Manager of the Wassa(G.C.) Companys Mines. (Known as the "Mining King of West Africa.") Courtesy Ahani National Archives.

John Sarbah, Cape Coast merchant and
Managing Director of the Gold Coast
Native Concessions Purchasing Company.
Courtesy Ghana National Archives.

Joseph Peter Brown, African nationalist. Director
of Ashanti Concessions Ltd. (1891) and co-developer
of the Obuasi Concession in Asante---site of the
later Ashanti Goldfields Corporation. Courtesy
Ghana National Archives.

Transporting Supplies and Equipment to the Interior

A mining company agent recruiting transport workers on the coast (c. 1890s)

Typical 16th century Akan village in the heart of the forest zone. Photo from "Ashanti, Kingdom of Gold Exhibit." American Museum of Natural History (Enid Schildknout and M.D. MacLeo coordinators).

Porters (including women) transporting supplies to Wassa.

Women porters, working for an expatriate company, headloading gold ore to crushing mills. Courtesy Ashanti Goldfields Corp. (Mr. Tommy Rowe).

Road builders (1874 Anglo-Asante War) using logs over streams and swampy areas

Caravan of porters carrying supplies to the Interior. (Note European reclining on hammock.)

5

Barriers to Gold Production in the 1880s

Capitalization, Technology, Labor Recruitment, and Transportation

While it is tempting in analyzing the Wassa mines of the 1880s to focus on one or two simple explanations for failure, such as corporate greed or mismanagement, one needs to comprehend a multiplicity of variable causal factors. With full allowance for the inexperience of many company directors and their underlings, it is also important to place these early decades in broad comparative perspective by understanding the slow and often ineffective application of modern ore extraction technology coupled with the high risks of reef gold mining in almost every part of the world. Critics in professional mining associations and distraught shareholders of the 1880s and 1890s, faced with meager yields, were apt to lash out at a single cause for their troubles—be it African labor, poor prospecting, or the colonial government—in the same way that late-twentieth-century revisionist critics may view the amorphous leviathan international capitalism as the prime culprit behind the inadequacies of mining-led programs for economic development in Africa and other continents.[1]

The reality was far more complex. Radical interpretations contained part of the truth, but were often Eurocentric and reflected limited analysis of practical organizational and technical requirements, including high capital, transportation, and operating costs of mining in northern wilderness areas as well as tropical regions. Given the presumed advantages made available to the expatriate companies in terms of rich resource endowments, low-interest capital, and cheap labor, the opportunities for "super profits," according to this line of argument, should have been enormous.[2] In fact, seasoned veterans of mining in Australia, the United States, and Europe stated that the adverse conditions in the Gold Coast were more formidable than those encountered in other mining regions of the world. Perhaps it was all the more remarkable that the West African gold-mining ventures fared as well as they did. Building on the last chapter and my estimate of the number of producing mines on the Gold Coast in relation to all the companies registered, it is worth repeating that the average success rate for pioneering mining ventures throughout the world at this time was only one in ten.[3] This was practically equivalent to the rate for the Wassa companies. But there was another, more technical standard of measurement: the cost of extracting one ounce of gold from its parent ore. As James H. Batty, the agent for the Swanzy trading firm and later prominent in mining circles, informed a Gold Coast governor, gold mining in West Africa, owing mainly to the formidable physical obstacles, was at least "three times more expensive than anywhere else."[4] This, better than any other professional comment, puts the present story in perspective.

COMPANY ORGANIZATION AND CAPITALIZATION

In the history of any stock market craze it is difficult to disentangle genuine investments from paper capitalization. To quantify investments in any mine accurately, one would need to know what was spent on such inputs as machinery, building materials, tools, labor, and supplies in West Africa, as opposed to the mere recording of funds raised in Europe.[5] Table 4.2 in the previous chapter shows that total nominal capital for thirty-seven registered companies was close to two million pounds sterling. But this reveals next to nothing about actual investment. One has to distinguish between authorized, or "nominal," capital and fully "paid-up" capital. My own estimate for the nominal capital of *working* mining companies in Wassa between 1878 and 1897 is £1,150,000. This is slightly higher than one official estimate made at the time.[6] Yet when we probe company records we find that the amount of capital actually raised was, at a conservative estimate, only about £450,000.

There is insufficient information on the entire batch of thirty-seven companies floated from 1877 through 1895 to estimate the percentage of capital investment dissipated on the leasing of real estate concessions and the subsequent sale of these same leases (at a high markup) to the parent companies.[7] Taking ten of the major companies for which we have

Table 5.1
Apportionment of Capital by Three Companies

Companies	Initial Capital	Amount Paid to Vendors for Purchase of Site		Working Capital	Annual Rental Fees
		Cash	Shares		
Akankoo	100,000	17,000	33,000	50,000	121.10.0
Guinea Coast	100,000	41,607	33,333	25,000	100. 0.0
Tarkwa Mining Co.	85,000	27,500	27,500	30,000	100. 0.0

Source: Supplement to the Mining Journal, 18 Mar., 1882, 330.

data on prices paid for mining leases, I find that the average was as high as 45 to 60 percent. If we were to include the host of minor paper companies (also listed in table 4.2), many of which were involved only in real estate transactions and not mining, then the percentage of nominal capital squandered in this manner undoubtedly would be far higher.

Who purchased shares? How much money flowed in from the general public? There were two main classes of shareholders in these companies: first, the company promoters themselves; and second, a myriad of small investors—clerks, shopkeepers, city merchants, a few lawyers, and numerous stock brokers—a majority of whom purchased shares in small blocks. There was not necessarily any correlation between the success of a company and the number of shareholders it attracted. Often the better managed and more successful firms kept major blocks of shares within a relatively small circle, whereas a purely speculative venture might find many small buyers.[8] After enticing numerous small speculators to purchase shares on margin in the initial euphoric wave, most of the companies experienced difficulty in getting such subscribers to remit the full balance owed once the boom subsided. It appears that the public heeded (though somewhat late in the game) the advice of editorials in the London mining press for buyers to beware,[9] and we see that the prices of "West Africans" fell far short of the listings for South African gold-mining shares a few years later. Despite desperate appeals to well-heeled country gentlemen and industrialists to subscribe to new issues, it was the company directors and their business associates who put up the bulk of the capital. There is no doubt that the dissipation of capital stock on concessions and the difficulty in raising capital from later stock issues were prime factors in accounting for a large percentage of company failures. Among the most successful ventures, the Wassa (G.C.) Mining Company probably could not have survived early losses except for advances and bailouts from its parent, the F. and A. Swanzy Trading Firm.

Boards of Directors

Recent studies of twentieth century mining enterprise place a heavy emphasis on organizational structures and rational managerial techniques as keys to success.[10] Such analyses, applying the theory of the firm to what became giant amalgamations and multinational conglomerates, bear little resemblance to the rough-hewn, small-scale bourgeois capitalism that existed on the West African mining frontier a hundred or more years ago. Taking the ten to fifteen working companies of Wassa, from 1880 through 1898, one must picture a single London office off Leadenhall Street, Cheapside, or Austin Friars with a chairman and board of directors, a secretary-treasurer (who did most of the work), and perhaps a single office assistant or clerk. Boards of directors might meet once a month; meetings of shareholders were held at a city hotel or restaurant twice a year. For many companies it was the task of the office staff to keep shareholders largely in the dark about current mining strategies and the true rate of progress. Not that size of offices or numbers of filing cabinets and office furniture were the criteria for successful mining. Several of the firms listed here had conscientious and hard-working managers who exhibited remarkable energy and resilience in driving hillside adits, erecting headgear for shafts, and installing extraction plants in the heart of the wilderness. These ventures will be examined in chapter 7. At the same time a majority of companies stacked the cards against their own effectiveness because they lacked the disciplined leadership and competent subordinates necessary to manage the meager working capital at their disposal. How could boards of directors made up mainly of minor stock brokers, old-time palm oil dealers, one or two celebrated explorers, plus a few scattered lawyers, baronets, and bewhiskered army officers with practically no training in mining, be expected to oversee technical operations in a distant tropical country? In conjuring up extravagant fantasies of quick bonanzas, few of them had the slightest appreciation of the tremendous capital reserves necessary to sustain a young company through an initial period of ore discovery and development. In addition to appropriating huge sums in both cash and shares for concessions purchased at low prices from Gold Coast chiefs, the promoters also awarded themselves substantial annual director's fees out of companies that were earning little or no profit. Plainly put, a majority of these firms were top-heavy, with do-nothing directors whose prime purpose was to lend status to projects whose productive worth had yet to be demonstrated. In the view of one critic from the Royal School of Mines, the "effrontery" of the original prospectors and promoters who asked such outlandish prices for unproven claims was equaled only by the "utter recklessness" of the incompetent directors and managers who squandered the funds of their shareholders.[11]

Capitalization, however, was not the only difficulty.

TECHNOLOGICAL PROBLEMS

Fundamentally, the success of any mining operation depends on two basic factors: the richness of the ore body and the effectiveness of science and technology in extracting sufficient quantities of marketable minerals to offset high operating costs. The popular impression, derived in part from the writings of certain classical as well as Marxist economists, [12] that minerals—whether coal, iron, copper, or gold— are basically a "free gift of nature," totally sidesteps the tremendously high costs, including technical skills and effort, required for geological research and ore valuation. At many concessions of the southwestern Gold Coast the gold did exist, but the early field managers lacked the equipment and scientific knowledge to test for it.[13] While it is true that many of the early prospectors and promoters could have saved themselves much grief by obtaining more effective assays, it is also true that the Gold Coast, and particularly Wassa geological formations, presented unusual testing problems. Not all "bankct" formation was ore. And, as noted in chapter 2, the banket gold of Tarkwa was generally so fine and so highly dispersed that it was often invisible to the naked eye. How were miners to know which large chunks were representative enough to ship to Britain for assay? There were no trained assayers on the coast; and not even the most reputable London assay houses could make reliable estimates of the projected gold yield from a large concession based on a single chunk or parcel of ore.[14] For accurate results, ore samplings taken from a wide area of a given concession were necessary. And in order to sustain a profitable enterprise, ore had to contain gold in sufficient quantities to more than offset the costs of production. None of the nineteenth-century companies had the knowledge or capability to make such forecasts.

Prospecting in Wassa was doubly difficult until the early 1900s because of the hilly topography and the thick forest, which made discovery of outcrops difficult. Even when company agents were perceptive enough to acquire a gold-laden property and pursue ancient African shafts through to a workable vein, they had no way of ascertaining its depth, thickness, or line of strike. One independent mining engineer sent to the Gold Coast to advise the investing public in the late 1880s ascertained that in most of the Wassa mines early drives and cross-cuts were not well designed to attack the richest parts of the lode.[15] In one of the most persistent comments on official indifference to the needs of the companies, critics contended that a broad government mineralogical survey would have helped alleviate many of these geological and location problems—thus saving the companies much time, money, and effort.

Drilling and Blasting

Mining technology at Tarkwa, Aboso, and Prestea in the 1880s and 1890s was crude even by the rudimentary standards then in use throughout much of the world. Excavation of drives and stopes at Wassa was accomplished entirely by hand tools, followed by blasting. There were as yet no steam-powered or compressed-air drills, which later miners would regard as indispensable for the deep rock penetration required for setting up explosive charges in a scientific manner. We are apt to forget that dynamite had only recently come into general use in the mining industry (having replaced black powder and guncotton in most countries).[16] During the opening years (1879–83) of mechanized mining in the Gold Coast, black powder was still used for blasting. But a decade later most of the companies had moved to using dynamite, and even traditional Akan miners, having quickly perceived the value of this innovation, were attempting to purchase it for their *nkron*.[17] The holes for the charges were pounded out by hammer and chisel, or, in some cases, bored by primitive hand-powered augers known as field drills; after blasting, excavation, and dumping was done by pick, shovel, and wheelbarrow. We have seen that in traditional African mining it may have sometimes required two able-bodied men a full day to dig out one cubic foot of ore. The rate of progress by pioneering European miners using slightly more efficient techniques was not much greater. In nearly every instance there was a significant time lapse between the patenting of a new mining device and its use in West Africa. Thus, advertisement of the first compressed-air rock drills (called percussion drills) began to appear in British mining journals in the 1880s. Their use at one of the important Gold Coast mines was first recorded in 1897;[18] but Jacob Eduam-Baiden, a retired Ghanaian company employee from the early days, stated that they were not used in large numbers at major mines in Asante until well after 1910.[19]

Timbering and Stoping

Yet another weakness lay in the inadequacy of timbering needed to shore up adits and drives so as to protect against collapse of the "hanging walls," or ceilings. The dangers to miners working underground in this period were awesome, and the fear of suffocation or being crushed by cave-in has been insufficiently emphasized in most previous studies of Ghananian mining (see section on labor, below). Admittedly, the art of square-set timbering and strengthening underground galleries by "filling in the stopes" with waste rock after extracting ore had been perfected in Europe and North America only since mid-century; and much further testing needed to be done. Still, independent experts sent to the Gold Coast by the Royal Institute of Mining Engineers in the 1890s observed that the companies had critically scrimped on underground timber work (in most cases it was almost nonexistent) and that in many passageways the buntons (beams that divide veins into "stopes," or working compartments) and headtrees were shaky and vulnerable to breakdown under the weight of the rock.[20] Part of the fault lay with the inability of companies to attract experienced timbermen from Europe, as well as with their desire to cut labor costs. True, several representatives of modern mining companies have countered this charge by pointing out that in the earliest days of European mining in Africa "open stoping" (without much timbering) was quite common. Since miners mined only the richest parts of reefs— usually only the "contacts" between the footwalls and the hanging walls—it was common, they say, to have left great blocks of rock standing between the stopes. In hard-rock areas—including the Tarkwaian banket—these natural pillars, they say, could have provided, the necessary support.[21] Against this, other professional critics argued at the time that most of the Wassa companies had relied on excessively thin rock pillars, and that, by failing to fill in the open stopes with waste rocks, diggers had abandoned mined-out galleries that were dangerously vulnerable to later collapse. This was born out when twentieth-century work crews had to devote far too much attention to damage repair in order to recommence operations.[22]

Groundwater and Flooding

If there was one physical and technological problem above all others that barred both precolonial and colonial miners from penetrating to the deepest reaches of the Tarkwaian banket, it was the aggravating presence of water. Capitalist companies of the 1880s had somewhat better techniques than local methods of hand bailing by bucket or calabash bowl. But flooding from groundwater and rainwater remained constant problems for European miners, as they had been for Akan farmer-miners. Most of the early pumps were of the "Cornish," or "beam" type, powered by steam engines that differed but little from the double-acting pistons of James Watt's time. Companies lacked the heavy-duty differential steam pumps with tremendous lifting power of later years. One of the most successful of the Wassa mines, the Tarkwa and Aboso, reported in 1897 that it was forced to pump out 30,000 gallons of underground water per day during the dry season; during the rainy months the average was 150,000 gallons per day.[23] Such pumping efficiency was, indeed, a primary reason for this firm's relative success compared to other companies. By contrast the Gie Appantoo Mining Company had to stop all mining frequently owing to pump breakdowns and their inability to get spare parts.[24] High operating costs also governed company decisions in this sector. Unless high gold content per ton of ore could be sustained over many thousands of feet of tunnels, it did not pay to keep pumps going at the lower depths. In the twentieth century some of the worst mining disasters (with heavy loss of life) resulted from the mistake of boring into rock walls adjacent to long-forgotten but flooded galleries.

Crushing and Chemical Treatment

Once the ore was brought to the surface, further impediments arose in the intermediate crushing and pulverization stages. Gold ore in the form of crushed rock was raised from the deep-level pits by steam-powered cable elevators run by winches and transported from the pitheads to the extraction plant in ore carts or in some instances in buckets on aerial ropeways. This was the classic age of gold separation by gravitation, where extraction plants were built on the side of hills or valleys, with each stage of extraction occupying a lower tier in the wooden structure. At the top stood the ore bins. From there the fragments of rock were run through the grizzly rods (a screening process): the smaller pieces of ore fell through the openings between the rods, while the

larger chunks were pushed into the jaw crusher for further pulverization before being dropped into the chutes leading to the stamp mills
(see fig. 5.1 and photos of stamp mill). The workhorses of the gold-
mining industry throughout most of the thirty-five to forty years surveyed here were the huge crushing pestles known as steam navvies or
stamps. Ordinarily driven by a 25- to 100-horsepower steam engine
and grouped in batteries of five to ten, the 750- to 1,000-pound iron
weights were lifted several feet and dropped into a framed iron die or
"mortorbox," which contained a mixture of cut ore and water. But the
stamping machines also were plagued by persistent mechanical problems during the early decades. Often the mortar boxes were so poorly
constructed that the hammers or pestles broke through the wooden
frames. Power sources were usually weak: the small donkey engines
that powered the stamp frequently broke down and, with a shortage
of skilled mechanics, repairs were slow. As a consequence, many of the
mines had to be content with lightweight stamps of the 250-pound
variety. And most of the companies listed in the last chapter did not
have a sufficient number of heavy stamp batteries to sustain effective
large-scale crushing operations over the long haul. After crushing by
the stamps, gold ore at most mines throughout the industrialized world
was sent by conveyer belts to the next stage, secondary grinding with
pulverization by heavy steel weights rotated in cylinders known as tube
or ball mills. If a mine had a secondary ball mill, the gold could be
pounded still further into a fine powder and mixed with water to form
a pulp, or "slime." However, in 1885, the *Mining Journal* reported that
there were no large ball mills in use in the Gold Coast.[25] To compensate,
production bosses simply improvised by running the crushed rock a
number of times through the stamps. But the method was less than
effective.

For the chemical separation of fine gold from the dross, the only
technique available in West Africa at this time was by "mercury amalgamation," wherein the gold-containing pulp was coated with a solution of mercury on the tilted copper amalgamation plates. Afterward,
the mercury-coated dross would be drawn off by contact with the
copper, leaving free gold. Most, but not all of the free gold would be
"caught" on the amalgamating tables. In the last stage an attempt
would be made to draw off more free gold from the sandy solution by
running it over the "concentrators" (or Wilfley tables). These were
slanted vibrating tables that contained grooves and raised portions
called riffle bars or strakes. As the table vibrated and the gold-laden

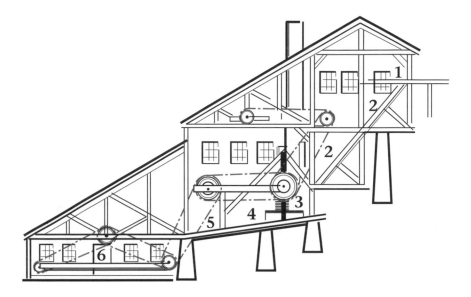

1. *At top right crude ore was dumped through the grizzly rods or screen.*

2. *Finer lumps and particles would fall through the screen down the chute to the stamps.*

3. *Steam-powered stamps crush the large ore chunks into fine particles.*

4. *Finely crushed particles of gold-laden ore mixed with water to form a muddy paste called pulp.*

5. *Pulp was passed over the amalgamation plates, where the sandy ore was combined with mercury to make an amalgam. Some of the gold freed bypassing the amalgam over copper plates.*

6. *At the bottom level were the vibration concentrating tables where the dross was drawn off, leaving the pure gold because of its higher specific gravity on ridges or strakes.*

Fig. 5.1. Cross-sectional sketch of gravitational stamp mill (of the type built in the Gold Coast and at gold mines worldwide).

sandy solution moved across the table, the heavier gold was caught by the ridges or bars and sank into the grooves, while the waste water and mud fell by gravity into a trough (see photos). But this method as implemented by most mines of Gold Coast in the 1880s was said to be extremely inefficient as too much of the gold was lost.[26]

It was only with the introduction of the newly patented MacArthur-Forrest cyanide process that Gold Coast companies gained the potential to recover a higher percentage of gold from their ore. Cyanide would bring a revolution to gold mining because it became possible for the first time to expand previous "selective mining," which had concentrated only on rich "pay streaks," by first mixing these streaks with lower-grade ores and then adding previously rejected gold from the tailings, so that the companies could rely on an average gold content. Timely introduction of cyaniding in the 1890s helped to rescue the faltering South African gold-mining industry, which was becoming heavily dependent on deep-level low-grade ores; but it was not adopted in time to save these Gold Coast companies of the first generation. Under the mercury amalgamation method, which continued at some mines into the twentieth century, it was estimated that no more than one-third to one-half of the gold actually present in a body of crushed rock could be recovered; all the rest was lost.[27]

Machine Corrosion and Disrepair

The study of technology transfer and its relationship to the twin phenomena of colonialism and economic development in the humid tropics has become an important field for scholarship in recent years. While it may be true, as A. G. Hopkins suggests, that the constraints of geography and environment have been exaggerated in some studies of economic underdevelopment in Africa,[28] I contend that climate and environment have received insufficient attention by historians in analyzing serious problems in the adaptation of machine technology to mining in tropical regions. A major factor largely ignored in recent historical studies on technology and imperial expansion[29] concerns the rates for rusting and corrosion on pistons, gears, rods, and other moveable parts—processes that proceed far more rapidly in the high rainfall and humidity regions of the equatorial zone than in dry savanna and temperate climates. Modern research in materials engineering verifies that iron, copper, zinc, and other metals corrode rapidly in relative humidities of more than 50 percent.[30]

In those parts of the southwestern forest zone of Ghana where the mines of Wassa and Asante were situated, the average annual rainfall runs over 50 inches per year, while relative humidity may run as high as 90 to 100 percent (with averages at around 75 percent) during mid-day in the rainy season. Miners' accounts of the Gold Coast are filled with complaints about rusted-out or cracked machines that failed to function after several months of hard pounding and grinding. Moreover, the wooden sheds designed to shield the machines from rains may not have helped, since modern studies have shown that sheltering machines from the high humidity of the atmosphere tends to slow down evaporation.[31] Only through the greatest care in drying and constant lubrication of machine parts could this process have been arrested. Of course, the problems of breakage, rusting, and malfunction have to be viewed from the perspective of transportation difficulties, discussed later in this chapter. The quality of know-how required for the breakdown and reassembling of machines, let alone for constant maintenance, repair, and protection against corrosion, was extremely low among expatriate mine managers in the 1880s. Summing up the condition of technology at Tarkwa in 1882, a traveling official reported that at one mine there were more than one hundred tons of machinery and equipment in place, but that none of it was working owing to various defects—most of it related to wetness and corrosion.[32] Fifteen years later, the manager of the Wassa (G.C.) Mining Company continued to lament:

> Jones is overhauling some of the piles of all kinds of machinery lying about here. He reports that some of it is really utterly ruined with rust and exposure, but he is keeping the 25 Elmina boys working . . . generally soaking the stuff in paraffin.[33]

EARLY FIELD MANAGEMENT

The old adage, repeated in many engineering textbooks, that the transition from ad hoc to systematic mining was epitomized by the shift from the independent prospector to the professional engineer,[34] has to be qualified when applied to West Africa. A number of the pioneering Wassa companies did, in fact, appoint mining or civil engineers, qualified by institutional training or service in the goldfields of Australia or North America, to serve as their first resident managers. A more serious missing ingredient was the lack of a substantial support group of intermediate-level supervisors and specialists (foremen, blastmen, timbermen, and fitters) with experience in the tropical world. Among immigrant skilled workers, Cornish miners were valued for their toughness, but even they sometimes wilted under local conditions. Given the physical obstacles and machine malfunctions just described, there was often little that one or two competent field managers could do unless assisted by a corps of skilled miners and mechanics. It was both a weakness and a strength that every resident engineer had to be a jack of all trades at this stage of development. More than two decades would elapse before scientific engineering by specialists would reach maturity in Gold Coast mining.

One or two of the more proficient companies, examined in the next chapter, allowed their resident engineers considerable freedom in managing local affairs according to their best judgment and professional expertise. But resilient yet flexible engineers, with experience in Africa—such as Louis Wyatt, the Gowan brothers, W. H. Swift, and the three members of the Gold Coast Sam family (see also chap. 7)—were rare. Most of the deskbound company founders lacked the common sense to delegate authority to the few men on the spot who really knew their trade. We read instead that "officious, intermeddling directors attempted to dictate to experienced mining engineers how the works at the mines should be conducted, and as to what machinery, goods, material, etc., should be procured."[35] Such blundering interference demoralized the field managers and impeded development. Furthermore the quality of bookkeeping both at the mines and in London was generally uneven and sometimes atrocious. Shareholders rarely received accurate, up-to-date reports on machines in operation, costs of production, the amount of ore in sight, the gold yields of ore bodies, or rates of return. Under these circumstances, it was no surprise that a majority of European staff (if they retained their health) resigned after a short time on the job.

Health And Sanitary Conditions

The major environmental problem, which cannot be swept aside as inconsequential, was disease. Because the health problem on the West African Coast was so often viewed in Victorian times from the Eurocentric standpoint of the White Man's Grave, there has been a tendency in recent studies to downplay its seriousness as an important element among others in the demise of the early mining companies.[36] But the dangers of physical enervation, invaliding, and death from malaria were real enough for expatriates in the 1870s through the 1890s. Moreover, malaria and a wide variety of other parasitic diseases affected the work performance of Africans as well as Europeans to an extent we are only beginning to understand.[37] I shall deal with African health more fully in the next chapter. But it was a sad fact that neither the mining companies nor the colonial government began to collect information on health statistics and mortality rates among their indigenous workers—the backbone of the industry—until far into the twentieth century.[38] Of course, a fair amount of European irritability about the "health problem" can be ascribed to the heat and humidity and to simple boredom with the monotonous round of work and discomforts of camp life. To give credit where it is due, a number of the tougher bushbeaters among the supervisory staff at the early mines were willing to sustain heavy work loads despite the complications of fever, and they often poked fun at tenderfeet who confined themselves to their tents at the drop of a hat. The fact remains that Europeans were particularly susceptible to death and invaliding from malaria (whose causes were not yet understood) and its close relatives, the insidious cerebral malaria and blackwater fever. No statistical data on either European or African mortality at the gold mines are available for the nineteenth century. However, the death rate for government officials on the Gold Coast was an excruciating 75.8 per thousand, and the mortality rate for expatriate miners was said to be even higher than that[39] One correspondent for the *Mining Journal* who had served in Wassa wrote that "the disadvantage under which all the Gold Coast mines labor [was] first and foremost a most unhealthy climate, which prevents Europeans from working there for any length of time, and much reduces their working efficiency while there. . . ."[40]

Impact of Disease on the Efficiency of Expatriate Staff

Benefits from the prophylactic uses of quinine were beginning to be recognized, but European travelers were still ignorant of the connections between open drains, stagnant breeding pools, and the transmission of the malaria parasite by the *Anopheles* mosquito.[41] Considering the relative ease of fieldwork in most parts of Africa at the present time, it is easy enough to scoff at the stories of "death and disease" by Europeans of a century ago as mere legend or romantic hyperbole. But many of the miners were a resilient lot who took their miseries and even death with a matter-of-fact shrug that would be difficult today. In the compendious literature of official health reports it was common enough to read:

> Mr. Criswick, manager of the Gold Coast Company, went home sick on the 25th of March. The doctor of the French Company died this month. Another European belonging to the same Company was sent down, and died on board steamer.[42]

or again

The Staff of the Tarkwa Company, consisting of Mr. Graham, manager, and two white men, arrived on the 5th instant. A week afterwards one of the latter was sent home sick, and on the 29th instant the other man died.[43]

William Bradford Griffith, lieutenant governor and later governor (1886–95) attributed the abandonment of the Guinea Coast Mining Company's (James Irvine's) largest mine to the deaths of three successive managers and two other supervisors all in the early 1880s. Henry Louis estimated that about one out of every four prospectors who went to Wassa up to 1885 either died or were invalided home, and those who remained were "laid up" by ill health about 15 percent of the time.[44]

Quite apart from the aura of heavy risk and feelings of anxiety that enveloped life the Wassa mines, the frequent steamship passages for recuperation to England plus shorter rest leaves at the coast towns drained company finances. Observers at Tarkwa spoke of the enormous frittering of time caused by the constant "comings and goings" of European staff between the mines and the coast. In addition, the health question has to be judged in conjunction with two allied problems generally passed over by modern writers: European "laziness" plus psychological depression, then labeled tropical neurasthenia.[45] Heavy drinking during the long tropical evenings, which became an accepted practice in the expatriate staff social circle, often aggravated depression, led to alcoholism, and retarded work efficiency.[46] Sickness was an impediment not only because of its debilitating effect on both Europeans and Africans who worked at the mine, but because the fear factor made it difficult to recruit the best engineers and managers from abroad. Only one or two stopgap solutions were tried in this period. E. T. McCarthy, who worked for both the Effluenta and later the Gie Appantoo companies, lamented that three of his early associates at Tarkwa paid with their lives, and he recommended that the only way for a new mine to have a ghost of a chance was to employ two constantly rotating managers—one on leave in London while the other remained on site.[47] Although the table below covers too brief a period for an adequate sampling of staff at all the mines over time, it is revealing that the most successful of all the Wassa mines—the Wassa (G.C.) Company—was also the one that had the best health record for expatriates and the one mine that also had the good sense to use Africans in important supervisory posts.

RECRUITMENT AND TREATMENT OF
AFRICAN LABOR IN THE 1880S AND 1890S

Contemporary Attitudes and Realities

No topic received more attention in contemporary commercial reports on the Gold Coast than the so-called "native labor problem," a colonial euphemism for the alleged incompetence and resistance of local Africans to disciplined wage labor. What are we to make of these largely negative verbal effusions that were absolutely central to the ideology of late-nineteenth-century imperialism? Many people today are uncomfortable about even addressing this topic. A common approach in modern works of African economic history has been to offer a brief explanation from the standpoint of economic or anthropological theory and then to skip on to other subjects. But European attitudes toward indigenous labor were so fundamental and pervasive in reports on frontier mining—not only in Africa but elsewhere in the world—and so intrusive in company management strategies that they deserve detailed scrutiny. The most commonly expressed views about the Gold Coast mines "labor problem" were that the Akan people either "would not work" or "could not work efficiently" at the Wassa mines.[48] This opinion was repeated so often that many Europeans believed it as a matter of popular wisdom with or without direct evidence. For this reason field bosses, impatient over delays and unwilling to analyze the problem in depth, argued that the bulk of the unskilled labor force would have to be recruited from outside the colony, in such neighboring areas as Sierra Leone or, most commonly, from the Kru Coast of southeastern Liberia. All told, during the first twenty-five years of mechanized mining in Wassa, the European companies drew nearly 70 percent of their labor force from the Kru and Bassa men of the Liberian coast (see table 5.2).

What were the realities of local Akan labor? How do we separate fact from fiction? It is revealing that some of the most blatantly biased and superficial views against African miners were voiced by those Europeans and North Americans with the least experience in Africa.[49] On occasion there might be a softening or transformation of ethnocentric attitudes among expatriate miners who remained on the Coast for any length of time and who learned more about the many variables and complex facets of the problem. Indeed a number of European traders and miners who recorded their views, came to appreciate the Akan region and its people

Table 5.2
Average Terms of Service for European Miners at Several Wassa Mining Companies, 1882

	Name of Mine	Number of Eurps. employed	Average length of Service
1	Gold Coast Mining Co. (Abbontiakoon)	5	9 months
2	Effuenta Gold Mines Co. (Tarkwa)	4	6½ months
3	Tarkwa Gold Mines Co. (Tamsu)	1	2 months
4	African Gold Coast Co.	7	12 months
5	Abosso Gold Mines Co.	3	9 months
6	Wassa (G.C.) Mining Co. (Swanzy Mines)	3	21½ months

Source: Return from Tarkwa Mines (6 July 1882) encl. 3, in no. 10, Moloney to Kimberly "Further Corres," etc. *PP* (1883) 48 [C.3687], 34–35.}

very well. A few attempted to cut through the clouds of myth and to understand African attitudes and actions on their own terms. One participant in the gold rush of 1879 declared that he had seen

> very large numbers of [local] natives, as well as several hundreds of Krumen, who worked regularly both day and night at the mines and in transporting heavy machinery and other goods. I slept in native huts without doors or fastenings . . . yet the whole extent of any loss by theft during six months was one plated table fork stolen on board the steam launch. Surely this does not look as though the "native cannot be induced to work" or that "the people are debased beyond conception."[50]

While it is true that other knowledgeable Europeans and some educated Africans expressed more serious reservations about chances for the success of expatriate-controlled wage labor recruitment schemes among the indigenous rural population, they tried to analyze the reasons for this alleged reluctance in a balanced manner. Their explanations were often based on talks with local people and on occasion contained more than a measure of empathy and insight. Such explanations ranged from the fact that underground mining was dark and associated with unfriendly spirits to the perception that mines labor of any kind (whether for wages or not) was viewed among some individuals and groups as a degrading, low-status pursuit associated with the "work of slaves."[51] W. F. Hutchinson, a leading Eurafrican merchant and promoter of commercial agriculture for his farms near Cape Coast (1875-95), added that the special responsibilities of family and kinship, including frequent requests for loans or gifts and the obligation to share in the costs of expensive funerals, could deprive young men of the incentive to work hard and to accumulate savings by steady labor.[52]

Equally if not more pertinent were the health and medical problems suffered by the African population. The debilitating effects of chronic sickness and poor nutrition were heavily underscored by, among others, the respected African physician of the 1880s Dr. James Farrel Easmon.[53] In a conversation with the writer, Dr. Charles Easmon of Korle Bu Hospital Accra (J. F.'s grandson) stated, "there is much greater recognition today that malaria and its complications are a primary cause of alleged African malingering on the job, or what used to be called laziness."[54] Thus the combination of barriers emanating from the tropical environment and traditional sociocultural ethos that militated against rural Africans "working for the white man" were not wholly a figment of the colonial imagination. But the key point is that there were an infinite range of variations in the responses of individuals to requests for wage labor, so that it is impossible to make a blanket generalization as to the single most important underlying reason for negative attitudes toward underground mine labor across the entire Akan region.

Some scholars contend that the constraints against regimented unskilled wage labor were perhaps initially strongest in centralized military states, such as Asante or Denkyera, where there was also a sizable population of captives or ex-captives, subordinated groups who had traditionally performed a substantial portion of the physical labor.[55] But the issue was more complex than this. Nothing better underscores the cultural differences between the Westernized capitalistic economic sector of the Coast and the transitional economy of Asante and other interior states than R. S. Rattray's comment that the notion of payment according to a set wage per unit of time was nonexistent in traditional Asante society, and that the Asante Twi vocabulary had no words that were equivalent to "pay wages."[56] Though the system was obviously undergoing change, throughout the greater part of traditional village economies of interior regions at this time, the characteristic form of compensation for labor was still invariably by a share of the proceeds from the product. As the monetized market exchange economy widened, most rural Gold Coastans still preferred payment by the job rather than payment according to a set time period.

Generalized objections to long-term regimented wage labor applied even more strongly to industrialized mining labor. The key points were surely these. First, some of the local resistance against mining for white men on sacred gold-laden ground rested on age-old sociocultural constraints and taboos (see chaps. 3 and 4). Second, many of these objections were equally understandable in European as well as African terms and sprang from a highly realistic understanding of the physical dangers associated with working underground derived from traditional mining. Third, decisions not to work at the mines often also had a highly rational economic foundation. What appeared to many contemporary observers as clear-cut differences in worker responses to labor opportunities based on ethnicity could be seen on closer examination as the product of a complex interaction between environmental, demographic, historical, and economic factors. For example, company recruiters continually complained that relatively few men from the two Wassa states (except for tributors) signed up for work at the European mines. This was hardly surprising. We saw in chapter 3 that not even a majority of the traditional Akan "diggers" around Tarkwa came from the local area, but rather from Nzema, the coastal state west of Wassa. Again, one reason for this was that Wassa was a very sparsely populated forest region, whereas the population of Nzema was more densely concentrated on the coast and, therefore, more expansionistic.

A related point, commonly acknowledged by African as well as by outside observers, was that since most people of the forest zone could maintain themselves and their families reasonably well by cultivation of traditional food crops (yams, cocoyams, cassava, bananas, plantains, and green vegetables), supplemented by hunting, fishing and occasional gold mining, there was no need for them to give up a large measure of their freedom in order to acquire additional earning power by moving to cramped quarters in an alien and overcrowded mining town and selling their labor to Europeans.[57] This widely observed phenomenon bears sharply on Hopkins's point that shortages of labor in West Africa can be explained in large part by low population densities, sufficient food supplies, and, hence, limited population pressures on agricultural production and on the land.[58] This did not mean that the Akan, Ga-Adangeme, and Ewe peoples of the time were immune to the lure of wage incentives. It simply meant that this factor was sometimes offset by other equally rational considerations—including the obligation of tending the family farm, hunting and fishing, and the desire for leisure time. When acerbic mine managers complained that certain local groups "would not work at all," what they often meant was that they could not get many men to stay fixed to one job with scarcely a break for two to three years. But this very notion of continuous employment for one organization was a foreign one, totally inimical to the traditional rural economic cycle. In one of his more insightful comments, V. L. Cameron noted that the main reason why rural Akan men did not flock in droves to work for wages at Tarkwa is that they trusted their own kin-based method of extracting gold from shallow pits and trenches and that they believed they could make more money from crushing and washing gold in their old ways (assuming a good deposit) than by working for European wages (which averaged from 1s. to 1s.6d. per day). Indeed, as we shall see in later chapters, some Wassaws and other southwestern Akan peoples tried working for the companies for a while, found that it did not pay to undergo the added risks and discomforts, and reverted to traditional mining.[59]

Literacy and familiarity with "town life" constituted another variable that could act as a constraint against the acceptance of heavy mining labor. Remi Clignet, in his study of wage labor in Cameroun, helps to undercut the modern myth that there is a "single labor market," even in contemporary African countries. He demonstrates that varying responses to offers for employment in manual labor, sometimes ascribed to ethnicity, are most commonly a function of differing levels of schooling, with the better-educated preferring government and business jobs over blue-collar positions.[60] So too on the Gold Coast it proved difficult to enroll members of the literate, "scholar class" from coastal towns such as Cape Coast, Saltpond, and Elmina for manual labor of any kind, whether as porters or underground workers at the mines; but they often proved dependable employees of the companies in skilled and in clerical positions. This was related to the common British mine managers' prejudice against "Fante" men from the central coastal states, who, it was said, came to Tarkwa or Prestea not to work hard for a week's wage but only to make money by trading with those who had some ready gold dust or cash to spare. As J. W. S. Hammond, a retired African mines supervisor living at Tarkwa, explained it to me:

> The coastal Fante people felt that mining was low in prestige—very manual. The Fantes are very proud and, through previous associations with Europeans, wanted clerical jobs. Thus, most of the Fante men who came north to [Tarkwa] found jobs as storekeepers."[61]

Carrier Labor and the Role of Women

No aspect of the colonial labor issue aroused more controversy than that of raising large levies of unskilled workers to serve as porters and bearers of supplies from the coastal ports to hinterland mining sites. And it was little wonder. The exhausting toil of carrying backbreaking loads over narrow bush tracks, often dense with underbrush and sometimes flooded by rains and swollen streams for forty to sixty miles—and sometimes longer—into the interior made this the most despised form of physical labor in the entire country. This low repute was also related to the fact that in times past in some African states long-distance porterage service had been the work of slaves.[62] Coupled with this aversion was the fact that most coastal people had a shrewd capacity for bargaining, which many colonialists did not like or understand. Frequently, prospective porters or other laborers would play off one company against another or a company recruiter against a government agent for the best wage. Mining company agents became easily exasperated when their "generous" wage incentives were not readily taken up by prospective carrier labor.

> The usual difficulties were met with. Half-a-dozen men would present themselves and agree to our terms, which as we were anxious to get off, ere the rains set in, were liberal. In a few hours they would return and say that they would not accept our offers, and the palaver had to be gone over from the very beginning. A shilling a day wages and 3 d. per day subsistence were offered, accepted and declined half-a-dozen times a day. Now a man educated in the mission house would present himself and state he could obtain us as many carriers as we required in a very short time if we would engage his services. This would be done. The terms would be stated to the man, and he would be instructed to engage men on those terms and no others. After some delay, perhaps a third of the number of carriers we required would be marshaled before us.[63]

We have already seen that in traditional peasant gold mining, women had always played a substantial part in a variety of roles, including transport. One of the great untold stories of the early years of European mining enterprise is the heavy use made of women as porters and carriers. During the peak years of plant installation at Tarkwa and Aboso, there was a steady stream of traffic from river junction to the mines. Not only were women used for the lighter tasks of carrying sacks of gold ore from mine shafts to crushing plant before the advent of aerial ropeways and railed tramways, they also headloaded the most phenomenal burdens of crated heavy machine parts and other equipment to Tarkwa prior to the advent of the railway. Often these loads weighed well over a hundred pounds, even though the standard weight was supposed to be about sixty. Because both governmental and company reports were understandably loath to refer to this fact at all, we have practically no details on the numbers of women involved in porterage at any given time. But the accompanying photographs tell us a great deal. Even with labor from this vital source the Wassa mining companies could not have sustained themselves with the necessary food, equipment, and supplies without the additional recruitment of overland transport teams, along with boatmen for river transport from the male populations of such coastal towns as Elmina, Cape Coast, and Axim. What should have been one of the most humiliating features—for all parties—of carrier labor was the transport of many Europeans through the bush entirely on hammocks carried by four men on poles (see photos). This was, of course, accepted practice. Its importance is seen in the large number of transport workers for every mining company designated as hammockmen. That Fante men from the coast might occasionally sign on for these tasks, but not accept underground mining is explainable by the lack of danger and shorter duration of carrier jobs: men could take their money and leave without making a long-term commitment. The problem of human porterage continued to be a thorny issue for all parties who were involved in it. Europeans wanted a steady stream of tied laborers; but Gold Coastans detested this kind of work. In 1883 the Gold Coast Legislative Council passed a Public Labor Ordinance; but the ordinance was never used on behalf of the mining companies. The law empowered government agents to go into villages (presumably with the permission of chiefs) and order up labor levies primarily for public works and other "public emergencies," which—augmented by other ordinances—subsequently included carrying provisions for overland military expeditions.[64] Though workers were paid, this amounted to a kind of corvée. Such episodes demonstrate that the colonial state was far more willing to use interventionist methods on its own behalf than to assist private enterprise—let alone mining.

Migrant Labor: Kru, Bassa, and Grebo Men from Liberia

Varying combinations of most of these constraints help to explain why a majority of the mining companies, during the first two decades covered here, preferred to recruit their unskilled, and especially underground, workers primarily from Liberia. When needed these strong all-purpose workers—the navvies of West Africa—might also serve as porters in addition to a wide spectrum of other jobs. First, Kru, Grebo, and Bassa men had long experience (knowledge of which had been passed down through generations) in a variety of skilled and physically arduous jobs, not only as boatmen and navigators, for which they were most famous, but also as warehousemen, sanitary workers, road build-ers, chain pullers, loaders, as well as porters on caravans.[65] They were said to take a fierce pride in their work, based partly on tradition and partly on the fact that they were by recruited through their own local headmen, who often accompanied the Kru men on a twelve-month tour of duty abroad. Most important, from the standpoint of mining capi-talism, a company could pay Kru men below the average rate for unskilled workers on the Gold Coast.[66]

To place these various observations in perspective, it is important to underscore that I am talking about dissonances in the initial adaptation to wage labor that are not uniquely African but that have impinged upon nearly every preindustrial society that has attempted to move quickly to mechanized or industrial forms of production. Comparative analysis of primary sources in English and European history attests to the unusual harshness of the miners' life and the jarring transitions from the older rural culture, where even landless workers had possessed some freedom to rest on the job and to move about on their own volition.[67] For the first time in their lives men had their day dictated by the clock or the whistle. Miners had to work an extended work week with long daily shifts and they were subjected to an hour-by-hour pressure to produce in a way that they had never known before. Likewise, retired African underground workers and European supervi-sors presently on the job emphasized to the writer that underground working conditions at the gold mines were indeed hot, humid, dark, claustrophobic, and depressing.[68] Miners soon found that to meet con-struction deadlines and production quotas they would be required to work at night, overtime, and on weekends. With the increased use of dynamite and gelignite in the 1890s, there was also the danger of being blown up or suffering from bone fractures or death from falling rock. We cannot stress often enough that one of the main reasons why local Wassa people resisted service in the white man's labor cadres so reso-lutely is that they knew of the risks of death in deep-pit mining first-hand from long prior knowledge and experience. Clearly they preferred to continue mining in the old ways rather than work underground for the colonialists in ways that presented new dangers. Added to this is the fact that various forms of intimidation, including physical punishment by shift bosses for lateness or lagging on the job, became commonplace. Among the number of expatriate managers and foremen who held to the distortion that Africans were incapable of working hard for long hours, except under older conditions of slavery, the conclusion gained acceptance that only the toughest forms of coercion, enforced by fear of flogging, would be effective.[69] Until well into the third decade of the twentieth century flogging with a stick was the most common punishment for minor infractions.

Against this dominant drill sergeant mentality among mine bosses, isolated voices of dissent occasionally could be heard, even within the paternalistic colonial ideology of the age.

> . . . I am fast coming round to the opinion that well-treated and well looked after, the average native may yet prove a good laborer, whose diligence and intelligence may be depended upon: the fault may sometimes be in the employer [rather] than in the employed.[70]

As we shall see in chapter 7, the latter part of this observation contained more than a grain of truth when applied to the actions of a number of the Wassa mining companies, who were sometimes so strapped for funds that they delayed and deliberately defaulted in paying workers the back wages that were owed them. There is no doubt that the "mines labor problem" was engendered in part by the attitudes and actions of mine owners and managers.

Adaptations between Peasant and Industrial Capitalist Relations of Production

Whatever the exact combination of inhibiting factors in each instance, it is clear that mechanized mining could upset the rhythm of ordinary rural village life and that it placed considerable stress and feelings of disturbance on individual peasant farmers, who harbored a severe dislike of regimentation. In these circumstances most mine managers were willing (or forced) to allow a good deal of flexibility and to fall back on devices that would ease the strain. We have seen that many local farmer-miners were willing to take on periodic wage labor or even piecework during the four to five months of the dry season; but they insisted on adhering to the traditional cycle by returning to their homes for planting once the rainy season began. Recognizing these proclivities, two or three of the European firms were willing to allow periodic leaves of absence. Some of the workers returned to the mines after the rainy and planting season and many more did not. An ancillary problem for the companies was the constant need to train new workers.

The principal technique utilized time and again by a number of the Wassa companies was to hire Akan "tributors" based on the traditional *abusa* share system. Keep in mind that private ownership of mineral rights had been unknown in traditional Akan land law. The people of the stool were the ultimate owners of the land, with the stool holder as trustee of the land on behalf of the people. Thus when the first French and English concession holders moved into Wassa, the initial reaction of a majority of peasant miners was either to continue to mine according to their old ways on the fringes of the new company properties or to depart altogether in search of new outcrops. At Aboso the Anglo-French Company quickly came to the realization that, until their crushing and reduction gear was ready, it would be practicable to allow the Wassans and Nzemans to remain on the property to dig their trenches and pits for surface gold as in the past and, indeed, to exploit this practice for company advantage. Instead of wage payments, the miners were allowed to keep one-third of their winnings while turning over two-thirds to the company,[71] rather than to the local chief or stool holder, as in times past. In some instances the proportion was divided in half with fifty percent to the miner and fifty percent to the company. There were two sides to the use of this technique. On the one hand it suited the companies: they did not have to pay out any of their limited supply of cash; tributors did not require housing, food, or administrative paperwork The companies did not have to recruit individual workers but could turn over responsibilities for mining certain sections to chiefs and headmen. Some argued that the system favored the African peasant miners, since under most previous arrangements, they had kept only one-third of the proceeds, whereas now they might retain one-half or even more. Burton and Cameron, arguing from the owners' perspective, took a dim view of this arrangement, saying that it gave the traditional African miners the freedom to steal from their new employers in the same way that they had from the chiefs in the past—by failing to pay their full shares.[72]

In the immediate instance, reliance on this transitional device suited Chief Enemil Kuma, who ruled over the mines of Aboso. The traditional pit mines of Aboso had been rendered useless by repeated flooding from the rains and groundwater. In order to revive any kind of production he realized that European pumping machines were indispensable. In return for the use of several company pumps at his own private mines, the chief turned over a portion of his gold production system (including workers) to the companies. Thus, perpetuation of African tributary mining appeared to work to the reasonable satisfaction of all parties. For some of the companies that used it, tributing was viewed as a temporary or stopgap mechanism on the pathway to mobilizing a permanent wage-labor force. Their overly optimistic hope was that as more and more workers saw the advantage of a steady income based on their daily labor output, they would give up piecework and share work and accept steady employment on the terms offered by the companies. It is interesting to note, however, that even though they tried to introduce wages, the Anglo-French Company felt constrained at various times by lack of cash to revert back to the "tributing" relationship.[73] And as I shall note in chapter 7, the Wassa (G. C.) Mining Company continued to utilize this quasi-feudal, or "sharecropping" technique as the central platform of its production system until the mid-1890s.

THE TRANSPORTATION PROBLEM

Despite contrary arguments by some revisionist historians, transportation continued as the most serious barrier to mining success in the prerailway age. So long as heavy machinery had to be lifted on to canoes or surfboats for river transport and then headloaded in pieces by porters over narrow, circuitous woodland trails to the mines, there was no way that complex extraction machines could be emplaced in effective working order. That most Gold Coastans so strenuously objected to and resisted this form of labor only exacerbated the problem.

Traditionally, there were four possible routes from the Wassa gold-mining districts to the coast,[74] but one of these came to be used predominantly for heavy machinery during the years under survey. This was the combined river and overland route from the port of Axim up the River Ankobra to its confluence with the River Bonsa, a distance of about forty miles, and then directly east along narrow bushtracks for another twenty-two miles to Tarkwa and Aboso. Shipment inland required that Kru mariners first unload the building materials, heavy machinery, and other equipment from offshore freighters by surfboat, then cross the sandbar west of Axim and ascend the River Ankobra by canoe as far as Tomento (near its junction with the Bonsa). Every part of this journey was plagued by dangers and obstructions (see accompanying photos of the River Ankobra). It was common for surfboats to flip over in the pounding breakers or while crossing the bar of the Ankobra, with total loss of cargoes.[75] Many of the smaller mining companies resented that the Swanzy trading firm, under its local agent, had a monopoly on the surfboats, which transported all freight across the bar of the Ankobra. Swanzy charged the high rate of ten shillings for every ton so loaded and landed; and since a single shipment of mining machinery and supplies might require up to ten trips from shore to anchored steamer and back, the governor agreed with the companies that this monopoly enabled Swanzy to reap an inordinate profit while adding greatly to general transport costs.[76] This also explains why the Swanzy firm's agents were not initially among the ardent supporters of a colonial railway from the port of Sekondi to Tarkwa, since it would have cut out their lucrative franchise at Axim.

The River Journey

The journey by surfboat or canoe, over forty miles upstream and against the current, might be done in one day or could take as long as three, allowing for rests and portages around rocks and rapids. The Ankobra was effectively navigable only during the five months of the rainy season, and even then boats could easily strike a rock or capsize in the swift and flooding torrents. During the dry, or low, season of the year (November through March) the river was so choked by submerged logs and snags and blocked by outcrops and sandy shallows that continuous passage upstream was impossible.[77] The need for frequent detours around rocks greatly lengthened the basic journey and the physical demands of lifting, paddling, and portaging on the canoemen can scarcely be grasped. Even J. J. Price, a reasonably resilient Methodist missionary who made the journey up river on numerous occasions, described the journey by water to the Gie Appanto mine near Prestea as horrendous.

> After spending Sunday at Akanku [the Akankoo mines] where I did two services, I did the rest of the river journey by surfboat. The river is very bad, and for a day and a half the boys had to get out of the boat about every half hour and drag us over the rocks and shags. We went up about eighty or ninety miles and then I tried to walk the other eighteen to the mines. I got half way and then broke down completely. Fever came on and I was strengthless.[78]

At the Tomento junction company foremen for the Tarkwa mines still had to transfer the heavy crates of machinery to teams of porters who carried them on parallel poles or headloaded them the remainder of the journey overland to Tarkwa or Aboso, another seven to nine hours of backbreaking effort. Seasonal conditions on the narrow bushtrack between the Bonsa junction and the Tarkwa mining locations were the reverse of those on the river. Passage was reasonably smooth during the dry season, but for the five peak months of the rainy season foot transport required a Herculean effort because the incessant downpours and overflows from nearby brooks turned the paths to quagmires and caused the carriers to sink under their heavy loads. Louis Wyatt, onetime district commissioner at Axim and later a miner, was one of the first British officials to report on Tarkwa at the time of the first gold rush.

> . . . it is impossible to move, in most places, a yard from the path and in parts huge fallen trees encumber and block the way. . . . A stream has to be waded through thirteen times, knee deep [in water] in the dry season and from five to six feet in the rains. In some places the ground is very swampy.[79]

We should keep in mind that few if any African porters left a record of how they felt about these stupefying working conditions. And most of the Europeans who complained so much about travel never had to undergo the backbreaking tasks of carrying crated machinery, supplies, and even people on their shoulders on arduous journeys "up-country." In many of the travelers' accounts, used as one source of evidence here, the storyteller was invariably an Englishman of the managerial class, who may have tramped by foot over part of the territory described, but who also enjoyed the privilege of being transported over the bulk of the mileage from coast to interior while reclining in a hammock suspended from poles carried on the shoulders of four porters (see photos).

The Role of the Government and Improved Road Transport

The quality of construction of roads and bridges was a constant focal point of attack by both European and African critics of the colonial government. Company spokesmen estimated that a passable permanent road from the Bonsa junction to the Tarkwa mines, involving straightening, widening, and the use of logs over rough spots, might have been built by the government for about £1,200. But the proposal was shelved by the Accra government as "useless," since "for seven months of the year the land is flooded, and even in the dry season it is swampy through lack of drainage. . . ."[80] This attitude is interesting in view of the Public Labor Ordinance (noted above), which the government had passed in part for road construction in the Gold Coast Colony.

In the reminiscences of the times one runs across extremely high estimates on the costs of breaking down heavy loads of machinery and transporting them up-country to the Wassa mines, but not all of these are reliable.[81] A report containing one of the lower calculations of the time (£7.0.0 to £9.0.0 per ton) stated that this cost from Axim to the mines was three times that for shipping the same weight by sea from Britain to the Gold Coast. Most company and government spokesmen agreed that the high cost of river and overland human porterage increased the up-country prices of itemized provisions and equipment by at least 33 percent over what they would have been with railway transport.[82] But even these estimates failed to include the tremendous losses sustained by most of the companies through breakage and abandonment of loads en route. The major impediment was the need to "sectionalize" machinery. Heavy stamps, steam engines, hoists, and pumps had to be broken down into manageable head loads of no more than 100 to 150 pounds for porters. But this process was dysfunctional.[83] Loss of small parts in packing or along the way meant that machines frequently failed to function on reassembly at the mines. As if these problems were not enough, teams of tired porters sometimes dropped their cargoes in the bush and deserted. This was not a rare occurrence. Reports by later travelers are replete with comments about the misshapen black hulks of rusting, moss-covered equipment that littered both sides of the trail from Bonsa to Tarkwa (see photo of derelict equipment). Nor was river transport, even by the largest surf-boats, all that effective.

> Frequently, on voyages up or down the Ankobra river cumbersome pieces of machinery are seen embedded among the rocks, or half buried in the muddy banks, while at one spot is the wreck of a once fine steam launch which came to grief on the return voyage of her first trip.[84]

Historiographic Reinterpretation

Despite this evidence, revisionist historians have belittled the need for Gold Coast inland railways from 1877 to 1905, suggesting that this was a pure myth conjured up by Victorian geographers and imperial publicists in order to add technological respectability to "opening the

Dark Continent" and to attract government support for capitalistic investment. In 1973, Paul Rosenblum ventured the thesis that nineteenth-century spokesmen for the mining industry had exaggerated the hardships and costs of river and bushtrack transport and concluded that construction of a railway was not really necessary for successful mining enterprise.[85]

This hypothesis cannot be sustained. Rosenblum argues, for example, that had more companies made use of large ocean-going surfboats (with a normal capacity of two long tons, or 4,480 lbs.) on the River Ankobra plus trained teams of carriers, they could have installed more machinery in good working order than with canoes, which was the common practice. This neglects the fact that the Ankobra was seldom, except perhaps at the highest water (which posed its own problems), navigable for its entire length to the Bonsa junction. Portage around rocks and rapids was almost always necessary. In such instances the canoes would have had to be unloaded and reloaded and either dragged over the ground or carried on the shoulders of porters. How would larger and heavier boats have made this easier? It is true that two companies were able to achieve fair success in installing their heavy stamp mills, through a combination of larger boats and more effectively managed human portage. Yet we shall see in chapter 7 that the Gie Appanto Mining Company at Prestea was unusually well favored, since its mine shafts were within walking distance of Ankobra. In addition the Swanzy firm's Wassa (G.C.) Company, using boats and a combination of wooden spars and wheeled "dollies" on the muddy roads, was able to get its machinery to Tarkwa with a minimum of loss and breakage. But these instances were exceptional. One assistant surveyor of roads underscored the fact that it was "almost incredible considering the state of the roads and the enormous difficulties of the situation" that a few companies had been able to get segments of their heavy machinery into even partial working order.[86]

Some of the data presented by the revisionist historians themselves (showing numerous wrecks and overturns of surfboats on the Ankobra)[87] militates against the supposition that a majority of companies could have made a success of mining without railway transport. Equally significant, Rosenblum and Silver neglect the crucial fact that few of the companies of the 1880s and early 1890s were able to install regulation-sized stamping machines (of the larger, 750- to 1,000-lb. type) using mere human portage. Given the intractable routes by river and undulating bush tracks through the rain forest, the only way such companies could make any progress at all was to carry special lightweight stamps of 240 to 250 lbs., which as several contemporary experts noted were at best "mere prospecting" or ore-sampling batteries.

Revisionist scholars do make an accurate point in saying that spokesmen for British mining and commercial interests, when badgering the Colonial Office, sometimes exaggerated the average costs for transporting a ton of equipment from Axim to Tarkwa over the normal land and water route. It was not a uniform £26 to £29 per ton mile as some promoters stated, although it may have risen close to this for some companies.[88] Still, after making a more conservative estimate of cost per mile, based on the cheapest methods available, I still come up with prices far in excess of the service railways would ultimately provide more cheaply and effectively. Average total costs were £11 to £15 per ton for the combined upriver boat journey of over forty miles and the eighteen- to twenty-two-mile overland trek by human porterage.[89] Again, Rosenblum's estimates fail to account for the incalculable and, in many cases, ruinous financial losses that the corporations incurred from machines that would not work at all because they had been "sectionalized" prior to the journey, or from machines that never reached their destination owing to loss or destruction en route. Will Swift, one of the most capable mine managers of the period, reported that some companies had lost £5,000, £7,000, or even £10,000 worth of machinery at a single throw when heavily laden surfboats overturned trying to cross the bar of the Ankobra. As for sectionalized machinery, another engineer affirmed that "it is only a few degrees better than no machinery at all."[90]

Typical Nineteenth Century Gold Mining Machinery

A 19th Century Cornish Steam Pumping Engine. Photo by the

A Crushing Mill in the midst of the rain forest. Courtesy Ashanti Goldfields Corp.

A hillside gravitational crushing mill under construction. Note workers next to a battery of steam-powered stamps. Courtesy Ashanti Goldfield Corp.

The battery of a ten head stamping machine for ore crushing. Photo by the author.

Inside early mechanized gravitational crushing mill. (Crushed ore pulp combined with mercury amalgam and washed over copper plates.) Photo by the author.

Concentrating (or vibrating) tables—the final stage for separating pure gold from amalgam. Photo by the author.

6

The Colonial Government and the Expanding Miners' Frontier

Pressures for Mining District Administration, Health Services, and Transport Improvements

At this point it is necessary to grapple with two or three ongoing questions: what were the connections between gold mining and colonialism between 1875 and 1890, and how did the British government view mining and related activities within the larger context of West African economic and social change? After the brief expansionist exuberance that accompanied the 1873-74 Asante war, when the British Colonial Office had demonstrated concern for the welfare of Africans, extension of law and order, infrastructure projects, and the general development of the country,[1] the ruling authorities had reverted to their early Victorian stance of confining formal Gold Coast administration to the port towns and nearby coastal districts. That mechanized gold extraction could be turned into an engine for economic development with backing from the colonial state was an idea whose acceptance lay in the future.

While the Secretary of State for Colonies received numerous requests from expatriate and coastal African entrepreneurs for assistance in both mining and trading enterprise in the interior, these disparate interests had not coalesced into a strong enough force for sustained colonial expansion—and, indeed, the individual mining companies of Wassa, as well as the miners and traders, were often at loggerheads with one another.[2] Based on ample precedents from gold rushes in other parts of the Empire (Australia, India, Canada), there were, in fact, a number of wider social issues—adjudication of conflicting claims over gold-bearing tracts, assurance that chiefs and their larger African communities should receive just compensation for leases, plus regulation and taxation of companies—that cried out for immediate attention by the Gold Coast government. Even more fundamental were questions pertaining to law and justice and fair treatment for African workers in those areas where economic change threatened the traditional political order. The Colonial Office staff made only fleeting attempts to investigate the causes of mining district tensions. It failed utterly to investigate miners' living conditions or suggest administrative procedures that would benefit either the European companies or African workers in this period. Although a majority of the mine managers, had they been polled, probably would have balked at the idea of government regulations on behalf of Africans, they nonetheless believed that the Crown's indifference to their own long-range needs, especially in the area of transportation improvements, had a detrimental effect on their operational success.

COMPANY PLEAS AND PROTESTS

From the first days of European prospecting in 1877, leaders among both Gold Coast African and expatriate business communities had argued that the volume of sustained investment required for the survival of the mining industry would never flow to the Coast without expenditure on more effective communications with the interior, plus police protection and other administrative services that only the colonial government could provide. Ferdinand Fitzgerald, the ardent African promoter, had recommended three areas for immediate and direct assistance: to build government roads and clear inland waterways to the mines; to conduct a mineralogical survey that could assist the companies in their quest for the most valuable gold veins; and, most radically, for the colonial government to set aside certain so-called "unoccupied"[3] Akan mineral lands for a favored number of "efficient" working companies. That such broad designs implied intervention and control of the interior by imperial interests had never troubled Fitzgerald, despite his belief in progress toward greater African self-government. If Africans wanted assistance in the development of their homelands, he argued, then they had to face the practical need for close collaboration with European companies and the colonial powers.[4] Such proposals were seconded in early letters to the Colonial Office by General E. Wray of the Paris- and Liverpool-based African Gold Coast Company; by Louis Wyatt, sometime government official and later mines manager; and by the explorers Burton and Cameron, representing the James Irvine block of interests. Taken together their early petitions called for an even broader range of government services, including: (1) a professional survey of the geology of Wassa; (2) more precise demarcation of the boundaries of mining leases to prevent disputes; (3) compulsory registration of concessions with high leasing fees to curtail endless resales and speculations; (4) institution of formal safety and sanitary regulations at the mines; (5) government inspection of mining towns and villages; and (6) extension of colonial liquor licensing laws to the mining districts in order to curb small crimes of violence, smuggling, and drunkenness.[5]

Ultimately, the miners' overarching demand would be for a railway constructed at some point on the coast to the Wassa mining region. But recognizing the probable intransigence of the imperial bureaucracy toward requests for any kind of heavy expenditure, they were willing to settle for less in this first decade. Louis Wyatt, who knew the Tarkwa district well, thought that the government's minimal immediate goal ought to be construction of a short road from the confluence of the Ankobra and Bonsa Rivers to the mines at Tarkwa—a distance of eighteen to twenty-two miles.[6] To this list Wray and Burton added more grandiose proposals, including annexation of all unused "waste" land by the British Crown to be held in reserve, partly for mineral development, for construction of schools and medical facilities, for the establishment of a government department of mines and, perhaps most controversial, a proposal for the direct taxation of mining companies in order to sustain the many services for Eastern Wassa enumerated in their plans.[7] On one preliminary point nearly all the early mining and railway petitioners were agreed. There was an absolute need to establish law and order in the mining towns of Tarkwa, Tamsu, Aboso, and Prestea; and this could only be secured through authorization of a full-fledged permanent district commissioner's court at Wassa with a detachment of constabulary.

GRUDGING COLONIAL RULE

The View from Whitehall

That the Colonial Office turned a deaf ear to nearly all such proposals for more than a decade can be traced to four main constraints: (1) fear of frontier turbulence and the renewal of armed hostilities with the

Asante Kingdom if British interior administration were overextended; (2) constricted colonial budgets, which were a function of the Gold Coast's meager annual revenues; (3) over-frequent changes in the governorship and numerous minor posts, which destroyed continuity of policy; (4) bureaucratic indifference to the needs of both the mining companies and their African employees. Furthermore, there was as yet no strongly perceived threat by foreign imperial expansion to the wealth of the Gold Coast hinterland. (It is interesting in this light that officials in Whitehall gave no thought whatever to a possible French colonial interest in the Anglo-French Tarkwa and Aboso Gold Mining Company. This company was, after all, simply a joint venture by the nationals of two countries.) By 1877 even Lord Carnarvon, the Secretary of State for Colonies, who had worn the mantle of an imperial expansionist in the aftermath of the Asante War, had retreated to the more acceptable Cobdenite stance of balanced budgets and restrictive coastal administration. His axiom that "everything as regards good government and the Progress of the Colony" depended on defense and a tightly controlled financial system[8] put a damper on taking risks with untested programs that might lead to further "expansion." The Gladstonian credo that "revenue determined policy" was no myth and carried special force with reference to tropical Crown colonies.[9] During the late 1870s and into the next decade, the Gold Coast government was primarily committed to staying put and ensuring its own survival. Coupled with this was Downing Street's innate reserve toward most mining company directors and their agents as men on the make and wheeler-dealers of doubtful scruples—a judgment not far off the mark in many instances.

Activity of Pressure Groups: The Growth of a West African Mining Interest

As an important secondary theme of this story, scattered groups of London, Liverpool, and Manchester businessmen interested in West Africa—including representatives of the mining companies and the chief trading firms—began to coalesce into a nascent pressure group in the 1880s. The trick was to develop a permanent organization of a type that would induce Whitehall mandarins to take serious notice. Early petitions engineered by F. Fitzgerald and the Swanzy interests in London anticipated formation of two organizations at the turn of the century—the West African mine managers association and the Anglo–West African railway lobby. This would be a slow, crablike process. As is well known, a central pillar of mid-Victorian informal empire was that the home government should assist private enterprise only to the extent of ensuring equal access and opportunities for British merchants in colonial and foreign markets as against competition from the businessmen of foreign nations. But this was a bland formula for doing next to nothing. In contrast to the 1890s, when the ideologies of protectionism and monopolistic power converged in the imperial administration of Joseph Chamberlain, there was at this time no strong predisposition in Whitehall to provide assistance to a single block of British companies—whether traders or miners—for special advantages over its competitors.[10] Setting aside the protestations of Fitzgerald and the other West African propagandists, the three main working mining companies of Wassa—the Tarkwa and Aboso, the Wassa (G.C.) Mining Company, and the Gie Appanto Mining Company—lacked a strong enough foothold, between 1880 and 1895 to impress the top echelons at the Colonial Office. Sporadically, individual company directors peppered both the governors and the C.O. with letters and petitions on behalf of harbor improvements, road construction, and public sanitary works, but few carried much weight at this juncture. Even less significant in terms of its financial base and numbers, but more potent in the political clout it carried among the general public and at Westminster, was the London-based Aborigines Protection Society—the natural heir of the Buxtonite Anti-Slavery Society—which, because it could claim to speak for a variety of Christian humanitarian interests and because it had significant allies in the House of Commons, could stir up heated debate from time to time on West African issues in the press and in Parliament.[11] Criticism of the imperial government's go-slow antislavery policy in West Africa, its weak protection of "native" interests, the debate over the liquor and firearms trades, criticism of "exorbitant" customs duties on imports, plus pinchpenny public expenditure—all these were issues on which the humanitarian lobby and one or two of the major British chambers of commerce occasionally might join forces in the transitional "prescramble" period of informal colonialism and reluctant empire.

Although this study concentrates on the local parameters of policy formation as it affected expatriate business enterprise and economic development, some of the formulations presented here run parallel to and find confirmation in broader surveys of mid-Victorian imperialism presented by John Hargreaves, Peter Cain and A. G. Hopkins, John Cell, W, David McIntyre, and other writers.[12] Apart from the central common theme of parsimony and retrenchment, the constant rotation of personnel in the Gold Coast governorship, along with frequent changes in the post of Secretary of State for Colonies (then a second-rate cabinet office) also militated against comprehensive long-range planning and continuity of policy on colonial spending programs for infrastructure. Even in the case of routine approvals for municipal works projects, positive declarations issued under one administration were often shelved and had to be reaffirmed innumerable times by successors before implementation could be guaranteed.[13] We should keep in mind too that except in critical situations—decisions on wars and peacemaking, the ending of slavery, international boundary crises, or major votes on appropriations—West African colonial problems only rarely received high ranking on the agendas of the prime minister and cabinet. Against such structural constraints it was inevitable that laissez-faire and nonintervention should continue as the policy norms. Within the corridors of power, Liberal principles of free and open access to markets, a reluctance to countenance state intervention, and, above all, fiscal retrenchment continued as the understood assumptions among a succession of undersecretaries of state and a majority of clerks at the Colonial Office as well as in the Imperial Treasury. Direct Treasury review of colonial budgets or routine policy statements was rare, except in the case of major grants or subventions—particularly those for war. A hard core of the Colonial Office's permanent staff, led by Assistant Under-Secretary Robert Meade, who supervised West Africa, could be expected to veto any policy departures that called for annexation of new territory, undue elaboration of administrative services, or costly imperial appropriations on behalf of development.[14]

The Inadequacies of Colonial Administration

To place the conflict between the Gold Coast government and the "mining interest" in proper perspective, I should perhaps modify the concept of the "colonial state," which has gained wide usage in recent formulations.[15] This label, with its connotations of broad territorial sovereignty, organizational hierarchy, and specialized bureaucratic functions, geared to serving the needs of capitalism, is more applicable to the formal colonial governments, departmental functions, staff specialization, and economic relations of the twentieth century and less to the ad hoc, or "custom house," administrations of the nineteenth, which were only slowly expanding beyond the confines of "informal empire." For the Gold Coast, I would reserve introduction of this concept to the early 1890s and the systematic overhaul and expansion of Gold Coast administrative agencies under Governor William Bradford Griffith (see chap. 7). Throughout most of the period surveyed here, the Gold Coast "colonial establishment" slowly increased its numbers, but the administration worked within a narrow compass of action. Improvisation was the key: there was no concept of the state holding "sovereignty" over vast interior tracts of territory (which were largely undemarcated); the administration operated within extremely stringent budgets; and the functions of government were strictly limited. It is more appropriate, therefore, to speak of an embryonic or "inchoate colonial state" until at least 1900.

If we exclude clerks and interpreters (who were increasingly recruited from the local African population), the number of salaried European officers remained fairly constant at a meager forty-two between 1872 and 1885.[16] This included district officers, who were expected to handle court cases in outlying towns and provinces. But even these figures are deceiving since the ever-present menace of malaria and other health problems continually reduced the available working staff owing to death, hospitalization, and the necessity for frequent furloughs to England. I have already mentioned and shall talk again about sickness and mortality rates among miners. But the same diseases were also a bar to effective colonial administration. Between 1878 and 1884 there were no less than seven changes in the governorship—five for extended rest and invalidating leaves and two resulting from death in office.[17] In 1877, out of a total of ten district magistrate's posts (including the coastal towns), only two were filled by qualified Europeans with the requisite legal backgrounds, two were filled by qualified Africans, two were vacant, and the remaining four were filled by European policemen of the Gold Coast Constabulary on a part time basis. The Colonial Office's A. W. L. Hemming estimated that the invalidating rate (those so sick they had to be sent home) for Gold Coast officials was an extremely high 13 percent, or 130 per thousand (this did not include ordinary leaves) per annum.[18]

The consequent breakdown in government routine was shown in the tremendous backlog of partially completed and totally untouched work. In 1879 the newly appointed governor learned that sixty-three civil disputes were awaiting trial at the Cape Coast district court alone. At Accra he found that no record had been kept on the number of arrest warrants for two years. In other instances he discovered that district officers had exceeded their legal power or had been guilty of misappropriation of funds or dishonesty in office.[19] The development of a colonial road-building and maintenance program for the colony was a standing joke among mercantile and trading classes. At the same time there was considerable myth making about the necessity for European-style roads. Many would argue from a more Afrocentric perspective that the traditional bushtracks and footpaths were perfectly adequate for ordinary interior travel and trade. Later a debate would develop between the backers of more colonial trade roads and those who believed that state monies would be better directed toward railway construction. For the moment, however, a majority of the coastal Africa entrepreneurs joined with their European colleagues in arguing that the colonial government ought to put more money into coastal roads, which were commonly in a state of disrepair. It was generally agreed that the government's 1883 Public Labor Ordinance, discussed earlier, had been a failure, since (despite its coercive provisions for mobilizing village labor) chiefs had not responded to the government's inducement to pay them ten shillings a mile for the upkeep of roads within their districts. Once again, it is important to understand that it was not only the European representatives of the mining companies who complained about the retarding effects of government inaction with respect to internal improvements. Some of the loudest critical outcries continued to come from the protonationalist "educated community" of African lawyers, merchants, teachers, and clergymen from Cape Coast, Accra, and other coastal towns. They denounced the wasteful expenditure on rest leaves for expatriates to England under the "short service system," money that could have been better spent on salaries for a higher grade of officials; and they ridiculed the government's shortsighted policy on internal transportation projects and "opening up" the hinterland. In a blistering attack, the *Gold Coast Times* questioned:

> What has the governing body done for us on the Gold Coast after being in our midst for two or three centuries? Look, wherever you may, and what do you see? Not a single town which is not a disgrace to the government. . . . Streets, where are they? Roads, where can you see one? . . . The importance of public works, railways, and improved sanitary arrangements to the Gold Coast cannot be overrated. . . .[20]

Contradictions in the Official Mind

Most of this fell on deaf ears in Whitehall. In rejecting proposals for government regulation of the concessions companies and protection of African mine workers in the mining hinterland of Wassa, the C.O.'s

African and Mediterranean Department adhered to an idealized Smithian vision of limited expenditure and noninterference in the hinterland that was hypocritical and defied reality. For Robert Meade, simply to believe in a state of equilibrium between contending forces—coastal traders, African kings and chiefs, indigenous farmers, and expatriate miners and companies—was sufficient to ensure the status quo. Extravagant talk of greater government responsibilities, he feared, might encourage a further stampede of miners into Wassa and bring chaos. Again the possibility of aggravating major frontier conflicts between contending Akan kingdoms loomed as a very real bogey in the official mind. Throughout the late 1870s and 1880s the Colonial Office continued to withhold support and recognition of miners' claims out of a fear that the onrush of unruly concession hunters might ignite another war with Asante or disturb relations with other interior states.[21]

The reality was that the Gold Coast hinterland was already destabilized. The educated Africans and Eurafricans from the coastal towns (some of whom had served with British forces in the 1873-74 Asante war) understood the hinterland issue very clearly, and they did not want to let the government out of its responsibilities so easily. What about the facts that the British had entered the war, defeated Asante armies, and supposedly taken on new responsibilities for the protection of the coastal Akan states and for governance of the nearer hinterland? The contradictions in Meade's laissez-faire assumptions in relation to the myth of the Pax Britannica were exposed, not only by the rough dealings of wildcat miners, concession brokers, and so-called bush magistrates who infested the Wassa mineral districts, but also in the Accra government's direct military actions, which had undermined the traditional authority structures and balance of power in both Wassa and Asante. In short, the disruptive effects of the gold rush were already too far advanced in the early 1880s to be wished away.

Another pro forma rationalization for government inaction, brought out of the bag whenever the Colonial Office became caught in its own contradictions, was its narrow and restricted definition of the word *protectorate* when referring to the Gold Coast Colony and adjacent African states in the hinterland. Although HMG had supposedly "annexed" the adjacent "protected states" to the colony by orders in council in 1874, it subsequently decided against publishing a draft royal proclamation that spelled out a broad range of the Queen's powers (including preservation of peace, powers of legislation, administration of justice, abolition of slavery and the slave trade, promotion of public health, and the raising of revenue) on the grounds that it would be best to leave such matters deliberately vague.[22] Several reasons were advanced for this loose definition. The embryonic colonial state did not want to confine the boundaries of the protectorate so tightly that it could not extend them at some time in the future. At the same time the secretary of state did not want to risk arousing the antipathies of Asante and other interior African kingdoms, nor did he want to raise unnecessary disputes with the French and Germans, who were just beginning to expand their own protectorates northward from the adjacent Ivory Coast and Togoland.[23] But the Gold Coast government reserved the right to exercise its theoretically unlimited powers in the protectorate for certain states on a selected basis. A key example where extended colonial powers might be applied to a specific problem in the mining districts came with the new anti-slave dealing ordinances. In fact the extension of full-fledged district administration within certain parts of the protectorate was also possible—even without formal absorption into the Crown Colony—by the proclamation of district status under the Supreme Court Ordinance of 1876. In 1882 a single temporary commissioner was appointed to the Wassa region but with less than full district magistrates powers and status. The Accra government did not consider it a permanent appointment, and after two years the post was allowed to lapse in favor of occasional visits by roving commissioners.

DISRUPTION AND DISCONTENT ON
THE MINERS' FRONTIER

The Colonial Office's indifference to mining company requests and its rigid adherence to the rubrics of minimalist government included: (1) the refusal to extend all the ordinances of the colony to inland areas; (2) limits on appropriations for inland roads, bridge construction, and river dredging that would serve the mining companies; (3) denial of a geological survey; and (4) refusal to validate leasing arrangements (whether on behalf of local chiefs or the mining companies). Interestingly enough, this reticence even extended to the issuance of gold-mining permits or licenses as a rationale for taxation. At the very least, one would have thought that the revenue-earning potential of a royalty on the producing mines, an idea broached by one lieutenant governor,[24] would have appealed to the advocates of the pinchpenny colonial administration in Whitehall. But no, the contradictions between the imperatives of maintaining political and fiscal stability while promoting the commercial prosperity of the colony were laid bare in verbal exchanges between the C.O.'s Meade and his principal clerk, Augustus Hemming. The latter contended that the Gold Coast government had consolidated its position in the hinterland sufficiently to justify some encouragement to British business enterprise. He insisted that the mining companies "were doing good work for the Colony in introducing capital into the country."[25] Meade, on the other hand, saw no need to establish formal district administration in the mining areas until the companies had proved themselves, and concluded in a puzzling non sequitur that "we have little control over their proceedings, and they may be using forced labor or otherwise misconducting themselves."[26] Here was the head-in-the-sand formula for indifferent colonial administration. The Colonial Office enjoyed the prestige of having imposed a quasi-protectorate status over the interior Akan states, yet abuses or infractions by companies or individual Europeans in the region were apparently none of its concern. Both the imperial and colonial governments were oblivious to the insidious and intrusive aspects of "ruggedly individualistic" capitalism. They ignored not only cases of misconduct by coastal miners and traders but also the fact that local African leaders were complaining quite vigorously about a slowly spreading erosion of their political and judicial power among their own kinsmen and villagers. Some chiefs actually requested the presence of colonial magistrates courts as the only way of maintaining justice and order in their stool districts.[27]

The Case of Enemil Kuow and the Diminished Power of Kings and Chiefs

What points up the contradictions and the unreality of the Colonial Office's proclaimed limited presence at Tarkwa and Aboso at this juncture is that the Accra government had already intervened directly in the internal affairs of Wassa Fiase and had overthrown the legitimate ruler at a time when the gold rush had barely commenced. This episode underscored the unpredictable course that characterized British West African colonial administration. It demonstrated that Cobenite precepts of nonintervention were not iron-clad. For example, the so-called humanitarian factor could occasionally be raised to upset and override it. The events of the 1870s and 1880s also demonstrate that the man on the spot could easily undermine policy consistency by impetuous actions.

Despite the deliberately vague interpretation of its legislative and executive powers in the protectorate, the Accra government had taken its 1874 antislavery and anti–slave dealing ordinances fairly seriously and had tried to enforce the latter law strictly at several key points in the interior.[28] Even so, given low staff levels for traveling commissioners and officers of constabulary, there was considerable capriciousness in the methods and regions selected for antislavery law enforcement. A few Cassandras in London and at the new seat of the colonial government at Accra had predicted social turbulence and a radical disruption of the interior gold and palm oil trades as a consequence of abolition because, in their view, rural production units were so dependent on slave labor. Recent research shows that these dire forecasts were excessive. Most traditional slaves chose to remain with their old masters and families. There was no mass exodus of slaves from particular interior states to the coast. Those slaves who chose to take advantage of the new law did so quietly in small numbers or as individuals: some sought temporary refuge at Christian mission stations; others joined the free labor market of the coastal towns.[29]

But the government could act obstreperously in certain instances. In 1875 the judiciary charged King Enemil Kuow in his capital at Manso, Wassa Fiase, with purchasing seven young slaves from Asante for his personal retinue, in direct defiance of the new ordinance. Determined to make an object lesson of Enemil, the government tried and convicted him ignominiously in the Judicial Assessor's Court at Cape Coast, and subsequently sentenced him to the extremely harsh punishment of payment of 100 ounces in gold and three years in prison. Considering the recency of the antislavery legislation plus the facts that the colonial regime (despite moral pronouncements against it) had long looked the other way on interfering with traditional forms of servitude and pawning,[30] and that other equally culpable chiefs had not been treated in the same manner, the punishment could only be viewed as unjust and heavy-handed. The exile and imprisonment of Enemil Kuow for nearly fifteen years (from 1875 to 1889) amounted to outright "destoolment," an arbitrary usurpation of Akan state authority not included in the narrow powers that the government had allowed itself in the Annexation Orders in Council of 1874. Then, as if to pour salt in the wound, the colonial government replaced Enemil with another king of their own choosing, Kwamena Impira, a man of inferior qualifications with little or no support from a majority of the Wassa chiefs and people.[31] This led to protracted discontent and intermittent protest by the people of Wassa Fiase against the Gold Coast government, all of which made a mockery of imperial government claims to nonintervention with respect to the Gold Coast hinterland.

If any two factors predominated in this apparent deviation from mid-Victorian norms of nonintervention, it was, therefore, not mineral development nor the desire to protect the mining interest, but continued agitation by the antislavery lobby in London[32] and, more important, the arrogance and impetuosity of a single colonial governor who felt the need to bend a recalcitrant "native ruler" to his will.[33] This and later instances where a Wassa chief was destooled by force—and where mining imperialism, indeed, became a factor, demonstrated that the Accra government could easily interfere with up-country "tribal" governance when it had a mind to.

In sum, three converging forces—(1) slowly diminishing respect for coastal chiefs as a long-term aspect of colonial rule and Westernization; (2) further fragmentation of chiefly power in the interior amid the lure of payoffs by European prospectors and African middlemen as a consequence of concessions leasing; and, finally, (3) arbitrary actions by the colonial government—served to erode traditional authority structures in Wassa state. By a strange irony some chiefs and headmen lost power directly because they had delegated all control over stool lands to grasping middlemen and concessions dealers from the coast, while others suffered from the diminished respect of their kinsmen because they were growing too wealthy from concessions down payments and rents. Several Wassa chiefs declared that the antislavery laws and the destoolment of King Enemil served more than any other single event to undermine the respect of their peoples for traditional authority. By the mid-1880s the government desperately needed to cooperate with kings and chiefs in order to maintain law and order, to clear and repair roads, and to develop guidelines for town sanitation and for assistance in labor recruitment. None of this took place; instead there was turmoil and upheaval.

> The Chiefs seem to have little or no power over their people now. They complain that when they order the people to clear the roads, or clean the towns, they invariably get the answer that everyone is free now, and that they do what work they please and what suits themselves.[34]

Life in the Mining Towns: African Resilience in the Face of an Advancing Capitalism

Conflicting views over the appropriate role of colonial administration in the protection of interior trade and mineral development came to a boil in discussions about the maintenance of a permanent district commissioner at Wassa in the early 1880s. The potential dangers from an expanding and boisterous miners' frontier became all too apparent in the sprawling shanty towns of Tarkwa, Aboso, Tamsu, and Prestea. From a tiny village, Tarkwa alone had grown into a mining camp of 600 by 1880, and by 1882, at the peak of the first Gold Coast boom, its population had mushroomed to between 1,600 and 2,000.[35] The town of Aboso was nearly as large. Some observers pointed out that figures for the two towns reached as high as 6,000 with the ingress of traditional peasant miners as well as wage-earning miners and traders during the dry season.

As in the North American West the sudden influx of people into the new mining centers created serious problems of housing, sanitation, and law and order. Almost overnight they became poles for socioeconomic change—and not always for the better. One major difference between these West African gold-mining centers and their counterparts in the United States or Canada was, of course, the much greater participation in both mining operations and in the commercial life of the town by the indigenous population. On the other hand, a majority of the African populations at the mining towns were strangers: traders and hangers-on from the coastal towns, Nzemans, and a very large segment of Kru men from Liberia, who were the bulwark of the wage-earning labor force for most of the companies. There is no doubt that the Wassa mining camps had a definite attraction for roustabouts who wanted to turn a quick profit from activities other then mining. Still, when we consider the diverse ethnic groups represented and the natural tendency among migrant mine workers around the world toward rootlessness, aggressiveness, and vice, we must conclude that the people who lived at Tarkwa, Aboso, and Prestea during these years exhibited a remarkable ability to live together in relative peace and order.

Contemporary reporters described scenes of freewheeling hustle and tension resulting from the myriads of human interactions that made Tarkwa and Aboso centers for economic and social change. Hundreds of new people not only from the central coastal or Akan states, but also from more distant areas, such as Nigeria and Sierra Leone, were seen trickling into Wassa. This type of cosmopolitan enclave was described by literate coastal Africans as a new phenomenon to the Gold Coast. "Hundreds of Europeans and foreigners are constantly pouring in, and all the town is now hardly known by the natives."[36]

It was no wonder that both African and expatriate-owned newspapers and trading establishments at Cape Coast and Axim stirred up the idea of a continuing gold rush in the 1880s and 1890s in order to maintain a steady stream of wide-eyed prospectors and miners who would boost consumer demand for food and supplies and so keep retail prices and profits at high levels.[37] Apart from the concession hunters and claim jumpers, it was reported that scores of petty traders and hawkers, plus assorted debtors, thieves, prostitutes, con artists, and other "renegades" had sought to avoid the short arm of the colonial law in the anonymity of the mining towns. Indeed, one late report guessed that more than half the population of the towns was composed of "hangers-on," who were not employed by the companies but hoped to profit from the work of others. It was said almost every house along certain Tarkwa streets contained either a small retail stall, a gold-weighing station, a palm wine bar, or a "chop house" on its premises. Brightly colored bolts of cloth and silk handkerchiefs festooned lines strung across doorways. Brass pans, hardware, toiletries, soap, candles, and tinned provisions—not to mention liquor, tobacco, and women— were readily available. Gold dust and coins were "conjured from pouch to pocket" in exchange for "pipes and tobacco, needles and thread, beads, knives and other notions."[38]

When viewed against the constant movement and jostle at close quarters between diverse individuals and groups, with so little government regulation, it was a credit to the mining town populations in the early days that a far greater number of serious disputes and crimes did not break out. That certain ethnic groups (Fantes from Cape Coast and Sierra Leoneans, for example) did not get on particularly well, made it inevitable that minor squabbles over rights to gold winnings, titles to property, and charges of fraud or thievery would occur. On the other hand, much natural order derived from the fact that some ethno-linguistic or tribal groups preferred to live in their own separate ward, or "zongo," under their own leaders or elected headmen. One roving government official assessed conditions at Tarkwa and Aboso as probably better than the average among rowdy mining towns of the world, as indicated by the fact that he made on the average only about four arrests per week. The majority of complaints lodged by Africans, he said, were for assault with a deadly weapon.[39] Of course, it might be argued that the small number of arrests were also a function of a colonial outpost that was seriously understaffed and could not perform its duties fully and effectively. Some officials concluded more harshly that the "law-and-order" problem stemmed mainly from the fact that so many of the new inhabitants at Tarkwa and Aboso did not work at the mines at all: they owed allegiance to no local chief or ethnic subgroup, but represented "about the worst class of natives [from the coast] and the most difficult to manage."[40] Others traced an increasing climate of unruliness to the heavy importation of spirituous liquors: "The liquor traffic, particularly, is carried on there with remarkable briskness, gallons of American rum and gin being consumed."[41]

Mining Freebooters, Abuse of African Workers, and Government Nonintervention

Overarching every dimension of the law-and-order problem was the intrusion and expansion of an alien capitalism. Throughout the entire world in the nineteenth century it was proverbial that capitalistic mining engendered cutthroat competition, unscrupulous methods of crowding out a rival's claims, and avoiding the law. This was seen most flagrantly in the sale and indiscriminate purchase of ill-defined and overlapping leases to mining lands that often deprived local farmers and hunters of their traditional use rights. A mechanism for government registration of leases should have been set up at Tarkwa under a magistrate at an early date. The related question was how to protect farmer-miners who wanted the freedom to mine for surface gold in the old ways, without interference or takeover by the companies. Here again, the basic problem was lack of a permanent and formal district commissioner with an adequate staff who had the power to enforce the law by holding regular colonial district courts and who could keep close watch on relations between the companies and the local people. What existed at Tarkwa was a temporary government commissioner, assisted by a handful of African constabulary, who tried to keep a modicum of order at the goldfields during the peak two to three years of the boom. After 1882, as the rush subsided, this temporary official was removed, and the mining towns had to be content with an occasional traveling commissioner (with frequent turnovers in the position) who had to cover the whole of the two Wassa states. Any criminals apprehended had to be taken to the nearest magistrate's court at Axim on the coast, forty miles away, or, even further, to Cape Coast. Under such lax conditions, it was said that there was a continuing atmosphere of lawlessness, coupled with bullying and oppression of the weaker by the stronger.

We are hampered in efforts to reconstruct the early labor and urban histories of the mining towns owing to the glaring inattention given in government and company reports to what should have been basic questions on the health and physical treatment of African workers. There is little detail in extant African records (oral or written) for the nineteenth century on such questions. Since two or three traveling officials from the coast did sporadically visit the mining towns during the 1880s, the neglect in record keeping can be explained only in part by the lack of a permanent district commissioner's court at Tarkwa. The colonial bureaucracy paid somewhat greater attention to calls for increased expenditure on public works and emphasis on sanitary regulation in the coastal towns, not only because of the sizable number of official and unofficial European residents there, but also owing to the relatively greater importance of the palm oil, rubber, and merchandise import trades to the total economy of the colony, coupled with the rise of embryonic lobbying associations among Cape Coast, Saltpond, and Accra merchants.[42]

Still, there was no unified group or elected mouthpiece promoting mining company interests at this time to compare with the coastal commercial associations, which became a genuine force for garnering government favors in the early twentieth century. For those few British mine managers on the spot, the logic of the job was more often simply to keep government inspectors off the premises than to ask for state assistance. Not even local missionary organizations, such as the Wesleyan Methodist Church, showed much interest in broader miner safety and welfare problems when they sent their first preachers and teachers to the mining districts.[43] In those few cases where a former mining engineer or supervisor jotted down his reminiscences, it was uncommon for such a writer to spell out in detail the prevailing methods of labor control. For the bare outlines of what took place in the minds of African workers, one must rely on the rare information supplied from twentieth-century oral interviews, by letters from humanitarian groups in London or occasional reports in local African newspapers.

Just as we should not exaggerate the harshness of conditions at Tarkwa, Aboso, and Prestea, neither should we gloss over what took place, as most contemporary accounts and general economic and social histories of the Gold Coast/Ghana have tended to do. First, engineers and foremen paid scant attention to the health or physical well-being of African workers placed under them. This was the most basic abuse and one that continued into the twentieth century. To have shown such concern for individuals would have jeopardized the core of the labor system, which was to keep men working as fast as possible and for as long as possible, regardless of their condition, at the lowest cost. Second, what today would constitute physical abuse and racial slurs were regarded as run-of-the-mill or the "order of the day" in most sectors of the colonial order in West Africa.[44] And it is probable the rougher aspects of "labor discipline" used at Wassa were also typical of European mechanized mining nearly everywhere in the world at this time. Even today seasoned miners are at pains to remind outsiders that the rigors and hazards of hard-rock mining demand tough, military-type discipline.[45] A century ago, floggings, beatings, cuffs about the head and body, not to mention verbal abuse, were administered as a matter of course for "slow work," tardiness, malingering, or failure to carry out assigned tasks.[46]

Further reports channeled to the Colonial Office by the Aborigines Protection Society in 1883 revealed even worse coercion and intimidation of workers, on and off the job, both directly by the companies and indirectly through generous payoffs to local chiefs and their advisers, who were sometimes drawn from the coastal "scholar class."[47] What we see is a stage of "freebooter" imperialism in which the smaller, less well capitalized mines were the worst offenders. Because many of these wildcat companies declared bankruptcy after only limited gold production, they left the coast bag and baggage, without paying their workers at all. The numbers of workers subjected to fraud and injustice can never be known. Even though it operated only spasmodically, this kind of ill-defined withholding of a man's just wages certainly added up to a type of forced labor (defined as labor for which no payment is given). A bit of rare detail on these tactics and conditions at Tarkwa, ignored in the government reports of the time, was printed in the African-edited and -published *Gold Coast Times*.

> Certain of the scum of European society have, as was to be expected, found their way out there and these do everything in their power to render uncomfortable the lot of the blacks who are working under them, and oppression is becoming prevalent. The slightest attempt of the black "employee" to contend against fraud or oppression is met with ill-treatment of the grossest kind and very often with threats of the revolver.[48]

If the widely proclaimed "paternalist" ingredient in British imperialism meant anything at all, such practices and conditions at the mines called for thoroughgoing government investigation and regulation.

Governor H. T. Ussher's Vision for Direct Administration

One governor who refused to be intimidated by Colonial Office strictures against the expansion of administrative services to interior districts was Governor H. T. Ussher. His prior experience in West Africa had not been altogether agreeable. Having served as administrator of the Gold Coast Settlements between 1867 and 1872, he was targeted for criticism by educated Africans and traditional chiefs for turning aside the latent Gold Coast nationalism, expressed in the Fante Confederation of 1868-73.[49] A tough-minded consolidationist, Ussher proposed extension of "direct rule" by the colonial government to the interior Akan states. He also favored direct taxation—a proposal for augmenting the normal customs revenue that had never worked in the past, even in the coastal states. Despite these imperious plans, he earned grudging respect from several members of the African and European business and professional communities, including Ferdinand Fitzgerald, for greater conscientiousness than his predecessors in attempting to improve colonial administration.[50] Ussher thought it deplorable that so little had been done for Africans in town health and medical improvements and in education. That the British Government of the Gold Coast should "remain a sort of military. . . occupation on a strip of coastline" should "no longer be condoned."[51] "Why," he said in a scathing indictment, "nine-tenths of the people who contribute[d] to [the revenue] surplus . . . receive[d] no benefit from it. . . ." An unabashed annexationist, Ussher would have been an apt agent for Joseph Chamberlain's "developmental imperialism," fifteen years later. Criticizing the countertrend toward a type of incipient indirect rule (then known as native administration) in the interior, he advocated direct government controls in the mining districts and other commercially valuable parts of the hinterland. To him the spread of a capitalist exchange economy and Westernizing influences (which appeared to be inevitable) demanded formal colonial rule. Surely, he argued, slave raiding, forced labor, banditry, and other forms of oppression—whether by whites or blacks—were a blight that called for direct and formal district administration. Ussher believed it was a serious mistake for the British to attempt to rule through kings and chiefs and traditional "native courts" at a time when such institutions were rapidly deteriorating in the face of radical economic and social change.[52] As an "improving administrator" he was more astute than most of his predecessors in framing his requests in ways that would appeal to the budget trimmers in London. He justified his proposals for formal control in

Wassa by underscoring the need for an official supervisor of road construction and by conjuring up dark images of the instability and turbulence that might result if the government failed to act. His opposition to "native jurisdiction" or "indirect rule" in the hinterland in no way precluded his support for a greater number of educated African personnel, as district commissioners and even in higher posts of the colonial administration. "There can be no doubt," he wrote, "that a really reliable African is far more preferable to a European."[53] Equally important, considering the heavy Colonial Office emphasis on balanced accounts, he argued that direct government control along the western (or Ivory Coast) frontier and also at the town of Akuse, on the River Volta, might strengthen revenue collection and check smuggling of firearms and liquor from the French zone of influence and from the Ewe region east of the Volta.

With the influx of miners into Wassa approaching a peak in the mid-1880s, the need to replace rough-hewn frontier justice with a formal colonial police and court system became especially urgent. Eyewitness accounts of kings, chiefs, and their courts being manipulated by European company agents and by "bush magistrates" from the coast reached a crescendo.[54] Again, the nearest D.C.'s court was at Axim, many miles to the south, on the coast. Could immigrant African miners from Nzema, the Fante states, or the Kru Coast and Sierra Leone get justice under such a system? There was also a great need for a mining claims court located, not at Cape Coast, fifty miles away, but on the spot in Wassa. Given the rising capitalistic currents of the time, Ussher's requests do not appear today far off the mark. Boundaries between leases had never been clearly laid down, and there was a growing problem of overlapping claims. Ussher reported that one dispute over a new gold mine in the western districts had led to violence between two rival chiefs. "As fresh gold mines are discovered," he warned, "fresh quarrels and squabbles will arise."[55] Though a supporter of free enterprise in "opening up" the hinterland, he did not believe in unbridled European capitalism.

> The only road to improvement is to bring the European into immediate contact with the native of the interior. A certain number of district commissioners should be appointed . . . to rule certain districts hereafter to be formed, in nearly the same manner as . . . the coast stations.[56]

It is interesting that soon after this the Colonial Office did uphold Ussher's request for two permanent district commissionerships for the palm oil—and rubber-producing states of Akuapem and Krobo in the eastern Gold Coast; but they did not approve a permanent commissioner for the mines of Wassa.[57]

Still, Ussher's penchant for state intervention ran well ahead of the prevailing mood of political and fiscal restraint by the "gentlemanly" bureaucracy in Whitehall. His long-term plans (never fully implemented) envisaged a pyramidal structure of regional commissioners (in Eastern, Central and Western regions) under whom cadres of fully qualified district commissioners would serve. But his unilateral action in extending British coastal and customs control over the Agbosome and Aflao countries east of the River Volta (adjacent to the future German Togoland) drew strong rebuke from the Secretary of State for Colonies, Sir Michael Hicks Beach, in London.[58] Ultimately, the Colonial Office allowed Ussher's extensions of direct colonial jurisdiction in the eastern districts, but only on grounds of more effective smuggling prevention and customs duties collections, which would help balance the colonial budget.[59]

As I have noted, provision for a "temporary" commissioner for the Tarkwa mining area had been approved, but at less than full district status;[60] the official so appointed had no formal standing and hence little law enforcement power. One of his few responsibilities was to "inculcate a healthy interest in roads among the Chiefs."[61] When the officer so assigned was transferred to another British colony after ten months, no replacement was appointed. Governor Ussher died of complications from several ailments before he could bring his program of centrally coordinated regional commissionerships and district subheads to fruition.

Samuel Rowe and "Native Jurisdiction"

The next governor of the Gold Coast, Sir Samuel Rowe, reverted to a more passive stance with respect to territorial expansion and direct control over hinterland districts. Incredibly, considering what had happened in the interim, officials continued to debate the question of whether Wassa Fiase was officially inside the Gold Coast Protectorate. Rowe believed that it had been unconstitutional for his predecessor to attempt to appoint a permanent district commissioner at Tarkwa since Wassa Fiase had no precise boundaries under the terms of the Supreme Court Ordinance.[62] An early advocate of "native administration," Rowe seems to have believed that the mining districts would be an ideal place for implementing methods of indirect government along lines then in force in parts of India and Natal, in South Africa. With the full compliance of the Colonial Office he drew up a Native Jurisdiction Ordinance, whereby the hinterland of the Gold Coast Protectorate would be entrusted to the semi-self-governance of chiefs and their traditional councils. Rowe actually imposed his ordinance on parts of Eastern and Western Wassa in 1883, together with special bylaws designed to protect traditional African cultivating and mining rights against infringement by the companies; but these rules lacked teeth for enforcement.[63] Despite several surface similarities, the Gold Coast Native Jurisdiction Ordinance had little in common with classic Indirect Rule theory later articulated in Northern Nigeria under Lugard and his disciples. Too many of the essential preconditions that had existed in Northern Nigeria (a system of adjudication based on written law codes, a centralized hierarchy of court officials and tiers of subordinates, plus a system of "native treasuries") were lacking in most of the hinterland states of the Akan region. Most flagrantly, the Rowe scheme totally ignored the fact that in Wassa Fiase, more than anywhere else, as a consequence of the inroads of concessionaire capitalism, traditional rulers had already lost too much power and respect of their own people for the ordinance to work. Also missing was the strong dose of "direct rule" under British resident advisers that would facilitate the system in Northern Nigeria. Even African middle-class leaders from the coast were calling on the governor to intervene directly in those states where kings and chiefs were losing their authority and were increasingly unable to adjudicate complex disputes between their kinsmen and between kinsmen and strangers.[64]

Roads Improvement Schemes and Compulsory Labor Legislation

The superficiality of Rowe's analysis was nowhere better seen than in the government's miserable record in organizing local chiefs and villagers for road construction in the mining hinterland and elsewhere. Here was the one practical area, above all others, where "native jurisdiction" was supposed to work by aiding trade and development. With railway construction still years away, the government presumably could work through chiefs and villagers to widen roads and build bridges as a means of reducing transport costs and time between the coast and Tarkwa-Aboso. Under the Native Jurisdiction Ordinance, in conjunction with the Public Labor Ordinance (1883), every able-bodied villager was liable for three days compulsory service in repairing the roads of his or her district every year.[65] The scheme adhered admirably to the overriding rubrics of colonial fiscal orthodoxy, since the ordinance supposedly plugged into traditional Akan forms of "communal" labor. It was thought sufficient incentive for the government to pay each man a mere 3d per day of road work. Upon completion, chiefs were to receive 10s. every three months for each mile of road kept up in their stool areas. Chiefs could be fined up to £50 or confiscation of stool property for nonperformance.[66] After ten years of experimentation, the colonial roads maintenance system proved a flop, especially in the Wassa mining region. One impediment was the lack of direct supervision by government commissioners. Moreover, the ten shillings per mile offered to chiefs was a negligible incentive, and there was nothing to ensure remuneration to male workers once chiefs were paid by the government.[67] The issue of gender also cropped up in these discussions. Later reports noted that where village roads maintenance, using corvée, was carried on at all, the main instruments were women and children because they were more easily controlled by the chiefs.[68]

Until completion of the Gold Coasts first railway, between 1901 and 1903, "road building" continued as a central shibboleth of colonial administration in the Gold Coast. Here, one cannot help recalling the symbolic obsession with construction of "the great road" in Joyce Cary's classic tale of colonial administration in twentieth-century Nigeria, *Mr. Johnson* (London, 1934). The difference, of course, is that in Cary's novel the road was actually built; whereas in the Gold Coast during this period, a great government-built road to the mining districts remained—despite all the talk—a total delusion.

Over the years, the Gold Coast Legislative Council passed into law a series of instruments that appeared to justify coercion in enlisting the services of able-bodied young men on various public works projects, including road and bridge building. Though widely condemned in the African nationalist press of the time as being tantamount to "forced labor," these "public labor" ordinances merely allowed colonial government officials to recruit workers through their chiefs, in a manner that differed little from traditional African communal labor or community service. (It is true that a request from a king or a chief could be intimidating, and radical critics resented the fact that the colonial government seemed bent on usurping this power for its own uses.) Against the view that this was forced labor were the facts that workers were, after all, paid a wage—albeit at a low rate—and they could leave these public works jobs at any time—which they did in droves. (Ways in which nonpayment of mine workers by some derelict companies did constitute forced labor will be discussed below.) In practice none of the so-called public labor ordinances were very effective in raising large levies of workers. What is more interesting for the analysis here is that, in direct contrast to the later labor policies of French, Belgian, and Portuguese colonial Africa, no one in the Gold Coast at this time even suggested, ways of using colonial laws and government personnel to recruit workers directly for private business ventures, such as the mining companies. (On the other hand, a harsher form of "compulsory labor," designed to recruit porters for military expeditions to Asante and the northern region, was instituted by the colonial state in connection with the aggressive imperialism at the end of the century.)[69]

Closer investigation by the Colonial Office of comparable schemes for native administration or "indirect rule" throughout the empire at the earlier juncture might have alerted Gold Coast officials to the need for much more direct government involvement by the state in local works projects, greater disbursements of monies, and larger powers of supervision over building projects by district commissioners.[70] Even Meade, prime apostle of minimal government expenditure and involvement in Wassa and the hinterland, grew cynical about indirect rule through "native jurisdiction."

> I have often heard that the mining cos. get their own way by heavily feeing [sic] the native Kings. If so, the ordinary people will not get much justice under the Native Jurisdiction Ordinance.[71]

CONCERN ABOUT THE ASANTE THREAT

Another nagging problem on the Gold Coast miners' frontier throughout the decades covered here was the threatened repeat outbreak of hostilities between Britain (together with her Fante allies on the coast) and the Asante Union to the north. The complex history of Anglo-Asante relations between 1875 and 1900 has been recounted at length elsewhere,[72] and the brief present summary relates only to contemporary government perceptions and an incident that affected the mining companies. Britain's Asante policy was not only confused but ran at cross-purposes. For even though the British administration on the coast had attempted to maintain a delicate equilibrium with that great kingdom since 1874, it was clear that the Colonial Office did not want a strong, unified Asante,[73] and that the secession of two Asante sub-

states—Adanse and Dwaben, which the British encouraged and facilitated with promises of protection—had sparked a resurgence of the
"war party' in the court of the new Asantehene.[74] But, the serious war
scare of 1881, associated with the episode of the "Golden Axe," was
traceable almost entirely to the blundering diplomacy of Governor
Rowe. In this dispute, one Awusu, a prince of Gyaman previously held
captive in Kumasi, had escaped to the coast, seeking the protection of
the Gold Coast government. Incensed over such interference, the Asantehene had sent a messenger, bearing the Golden Axe, calling for the
return to Kumasi of this important political prisoner. But, because
Rowe mistakenly believed that the Golden Axe constituted an ultima-
tum of war instead of a symbol of negotiation,[75] he aggravated the
tension by mobilizing colonial troops, even after the Asantehene,
Mensa Bonsu, had clarified his peaceful intentions.[76]

During the protracted crisis the mere rumor of an imminent Asante
invasion sent tremors through the various Wassa mining installations.
Indeed, the entire work force of nearly 200 men at the Effuenta Mine
deserted to the coast, forcing a shutdown of operations. Against this
background several company heads called on the governor and Secretary
of State for Colonies to clarify the Gold Coast government's obligations
to the mines and whether it included a guarantee to defend European
properties against attack.[77] This, combined with demands from both the
European and African trading communities in Cape Coast and Accra that
Asante ought to "be dealt a blow from which it will never recover,"[78]
anticipated a more aggressive alliance between government and business
interests with respect to policy toward the great inland African empire
after 1895. Fifteen years later, under the aegis of the "new imperialism,"
the colonial state would consider the protection of interior mining installations as a vital strategic element in a West African Pax Britannica. But
not in the 1880s. In reply to a question put in Parliament on whether Her
Majestys Government had, in fact, taken any steps to protect the mines
against rumored attack by the Asantes, Mountstuart Grant Duff, the
Parliamentary Under-Secretary for Colonies, summed up the essence of
mid-Victorian noninterventionist policy toward concessionaire enterprise
in West African territories:

> These mines are . . . far inland, and the company to which they belong
> was warned in the most distinct manner by the Secretary of State that
> Her Majesty's Government could assume no responsibility for the pro-
> tection of its interests or of the persons employed in its service.[79]

VIOLENCE IN THE MINING CAMPS

Because the Native Jurisdiction Ordinance was never effectively applied, and since there was no permanent district magistrate holding court in Tarkwa, law and punishments were increasingly hedged and manipulated both by the European mine managers and local African and coastal Eurafrican "bush magistrates" (outsiders who gained influence over kings and chiefs), without much fear of criticism or intervention by the colonial government.[80] Despite their increased wealth from concessions leasing, a majority of the traditional rulers, such as Ango of Apinto and Enemil Kuma of Aboso, had lost control over the maintenance of law and order in their stool districts. Again, the Colonial Office made no effort to press Gold Coast authorities to impose full-scale or district status in Wassa Fiase: middle-echelon officials appeared indifferent to sporadic reports about the rough-and-tumble frontier justice being meted out in Wassa Fiase. They rejected the notion that Britain held responsibility for the protection of either African or European employees at the mines, and they were quite willing to let the companies sink or swim without either government regulation or protection. But the Accra government was jolted out of its complacency by the murder of a mine supervisor in 1883. Four African workers were found guilty of homicide in the act of robbing the company safe and were subsequently tried and convicted.[81] The case became something of a cause célèbre, less for the crime itself than for what critics said it reflected about the harsh working and living conditions then prevailing at Tarkwa and Aboso. F. W. Chesson, secretary of the London-based Aborigines Protection Society, enlarged the discussion beyond the limits that officials would have preferred by presenting new evidence that African mine laborers had for some time "been brutally mistreated";[82] and he traced aggravated misconduct by white overseers to the Gold Coast government's "false economy" in failing to support systematic district administration and the policing of the mining camps.

As is often the case in mining history, occurrences of violence can be interpreted in more than one way. Jeff Crisp has interpreted this event as one link in a longer "pattern of resistance" by African proletarians, who were frequently mistreated by the mine owners.[83] On the other hand, field managers for the mining company, including some African supervisors, evaluated this event quite differently, seeing it as an exceptional act of violence, and placing primary onus for the crime on the four Africans and not on company labor policy or working conditions.[84] Once again, it seems to me, Crisp has read too much into his data: there was no "working-class consciousness," nor even organized worker resistance against capitalist authority at this early juncture. After all, the crime in question had occurred at one of the best-staffed and most efficient of all early Wassa ventures, the Swanzy-owned Aboso Company, where, under the direction of W. D. Sam, Africans were said to be relatively well treated. From one standpoint the felony was a straightforward and untypical act by four criminals; and that was that. A third interpretation, and one supported by the evidence here, is that the crime was also the predictable result of the Accra government's lackadaisical policies regarding law enforcement and the climate of permissiveness that had developed unchecked around Tarkwa and Aboso. Various parties involved in the ensuing controversy—including educated African nationalists from the coast and spokesmen for the companies—believed the crime could have been prevented, and they blamed it on the absence of good government and police protection in the region.

Under pressure from Parliament and both the humanitarian lobby and the mining firms, the Colonial Office urged Governor Rowe to appoint a full-time district commissioner with complete magistrate's powers at Tarkwa in 1883.[85] Illustrating the power of the man on the spot, Rowe stubbornly refused to comply with the recommendation,[86] explaining that he was content to rely on his own system of "traveling" and "temporary" civil commissioners ruling through chiefs. The C.O.'s request was totally at odds with Rowe's misconceived indirect rule strategy. Regular administration under a formal district commissioner was not established at Tarkwa on a permanent basis until the early 1890s, under Governor William Brandford Griffith (see chap. 8).

OFFICIAL INDIFFERENCE TO HOUSING AND SANITARY CONDITIONS

Many of the original African houses at Tarkwa and Aboso had been reasonably well built in the traditional Akan fashion of bamboo thatch or swish. But by 1881, the quick fabrication of hoards of makeshift shanties and lean-tos to make room for the influx of non-Wassa wage laborers, plus coastal traders and a substantial floating population, had given the town and outlying villages a run-down, squalid appearance.

Bathing facilities, refuse pickup, and sanitary amenities were deplorable for the rapidly growing population. We should not imagine that the domiciles at Tarkwa and Aboso were neatly laid out in compact fashion, row on row, in the manner of twentieth-century whitewashed company quarters. Instead, the huts and shanties were spread out in small clusters or camps over a wide area. These tended to be arranged according to ethnic affiliation: the Krus from Liberia occupied the western base of the main Tarkwa ridge plus two other hamlets near the Tarkwa stream, at the valley floor. Accra and Sierra Leonean workers set up their own hamlets between the Krus and the main stamp batteries.[87] Reports by roving commissioners, appointed temporarily to report on the mining centers, had described Tarkwa as a floating population composed of Wassas, Fantes, Appolonians (Nzemans), and Asantes.[88] Other mining agglomerations were Essaman and Tamsu, also located in the river valley, and Heman-Prestea, twelve miles to the northwest. We should not forget that a large portion of the so-called floating population on the outskirts of Tarkwa and Aboso was made up of traditional African traveling miners. And just as the grubstake miners of the North American Old West had lived in tents and moved further into the hills at the slightest rumor of a new gold strike, so too many of the African diggers at Wassa had moved away from their original domiciles to makeshift bamboo-and-palm-leaf rain shelters, hastily built near the latest strikes along Tarkwa Ridge and elsewhere. These traditional peasant miners moved with the tide whenever a new part of the reef was opened up.

Inadequate housing and nonexistent town planning led to severe public health and medical problems. If living conditions for Europeans at Tarkwa and Aboso were hazardous, those for the hundreds of African unskilled laborers who worked as underground pick-and-shovel men or as occasional transport workers and wood fuel gatherers were wretched beyond belief. More than one observer described the hastily put-together mining camps as sinkholes unfit for human habitation. Open water receptacles in the streets and near houses were obvious collecting points for the spread of malaria—though the connections between stagnant water and the breeding grounds of the anopheles mosquito, carrier of the parasitic malaria plasmodium, had not yet been identified. Fresh water supplies for the chain of small mining encampments stretched out along the Tarkwa ridge were satisfactory at first, being obtained from the hundreds of small rivulets that flowed from the hillsides down into the valley where they joined the larger river.[89] But as housing on the hillsides and on the valley floor became more congested (see modern photograph of Tarkwa town at the end of this chapter), drainage and wastewater entered the main flows used for both drinking and cooking water for villages further downstream.[90] Miners' thatch lean-tos, were stacked extremely close to one another without adequate space for ventilation. Fleas and lice proliferated. Roads (such as they were) and pathways turned to mud after a heavy rainfall. Public latrine ordinances implemented by the government for the coastal towns were not enforced in any consistent way at the mining towns in this period. Thus, malnutrition and sickness—always serious problems in the coastal areas—were more of a danger in the mining district owing to the constant influx and outflow of migrant workers, many of whom carried disease pathogens. And because facilities for sewage disposal were practically nonexistent, these shantytowns became the natural dissemination grounds for the insidious air-borne and water-borne respiratory and fecal tract diseases spread by contaminated water, food, and soil.[91] A firefighting capability was also needed at Tarkwa since instances were recorded where congeries of worker houses had been wiped out by accidental fire. Nor was much done to improve underground mining safety. Largely meaningless inspection tours of miners' living and working areas were carried out on an irregular basis by some mine managers. The colonial government had launched some of the earliest medical and sanitary surveys of the coastal towns (see reference to the work of Dr. Easmon, chap. 5, esp. notes 45, 53, 54) in the mid-1880s,[92] but the administration took no similar responsibility for reporting in detail on conditions—let alone acting on recommendations—in the mining districts. A Police and Public Health Ordinance imposed in the coastal towns was not applied to Tarkwa or Aboso. A report delivered by a company engineer at the end of the period covered in the present study not only underscored the hard facts of workers' lives, but revealed unintentionally much about shortsighted and arrogant European attitudes toward the realities of living standards in the African quarters of the mining towns. The reports recommendations focused entirely on the health needs of expatriates. This meant that destruction of noisome dwelling places was never viewed as a preliminary toward company construction of decent houses for their African workers, but rather in the context of protecting European staff by a process of "wholesale removals." The report's reference to improving the supply of fresh vegetables for the town community was intended only for the benefit of expatriate supervisory personnel.

> At present one great reason why the general health of the camp has
> been so bad is the want of proper sanitation. Their native village ad-
> joins the white man's quarters. I went through it with your doctor, and
> found such a shocking state of filth, that I requested to have all the
> huts within a certain limit burnt down. A good deal could also be done
> by the company to provide fresh vegetables and fruit. . . .[93]

It is impossible to estimate African miners' mortality rates for these
early decades. Although one or two of the larger mines, such as the
Tarkwa and Aboso, the Wassa (G.C.) Mining Company, and the Gie
Appanto, might employ a single doctor, there were as yet no hospitals.
And these M.D.s complained that they were overworked merely looking after the aliments of European staff plus those Africans who suffered physical injuries on the job. They contended that they had no time
even to count "native" deaths traceable to illness, since many of these
took place off the premises after miners returned to their home villages.
I have explained in another publication some of the deeper reasons why
both the companies and the colonial state refrained from tabulating
African deaths due to disease until well into the third decade of the
twentieth century.[94] Based on descriptive evidence for the pre-1900
period and statistical data I have collected for the twentieth century, a
conservative guess for the 1880s and 1890s would place the mortality
rate of African miners at 80 to 90 per 1,000. The rude fact was that
most mine managers preferred not to know the true state of their
workers' health, since it was recognized that most underground men
were probably working sick. Evidence for the 1920s and 1930s would
show that the major causes of African miners' deaths were the respiratory diseases: pneumonia and tuberculosis—with silicosis often a complicating factor.[95] Other causes of miners' mortality were dysentery and
fatal injuries from mining accidents (falls down shafts, explosions,
falling rock, underground flooding, and suffocation.) Calls for state
assistance in dealing with these complex health problems did not elicit
a strong response from Whitehall until a hue and cry was raised by a
courageous physician, Joseph Simpson, as late as the mid-1920s. It
would take a combination of disasters (in the form of contagious
disease epidemics) plus dogged perseverance by reformers from the
London School of Tropical Medicine to institute government statistical
surveys of African miners' deaths on a regular basis. But this lay far in
the future.

TRANSPORTATION: EARLY REQUESTS FOR GOVERNMENT ASSISTANCE

From about 1883 onward, the potentialities of a Gold Coast railway became the great focus of mining company and Anglo-West African merchants' discontent over government lethargy and ineptitude across a wide spectrum of interrelated problems: these included the colony's poor revenue base and overdependence on import duties; the weak administrative establishment at Accra, with a disproportion of expenditure spent on salaries for the highest officials; and unrealistically low disbursements on public works and infrastructure projects, including roads, schools, medical dispensaries, and sanitary amenities. To simplify and synthesize their long list of grievances the companies contended that cheap and effective movement of goods and machinery, preferably by railway, was the one essential technical element that would enable them to turn a profit. At the same time, some of the mine managers might have been placated had the government spent a modicum of funds on effective road construction between Axim and Wassa, or even between the Ankobra-Bonsa junction and the Tarkwa and Aboso mines.

The First Railway Petitioners

All these transport schemes had an earlier genesis. A glance at the record shows that leadership for many of the earliest proposals for a Gold Coast railway had come from Ferdinand Fitzgerald and his trading allies, who had envisioned steam locomotion as the ultimate solution not only for gold mining but also for greatly expanded exportation of forest products (palm oil, rubber, timber) from the Gold Coast. Characteristically bold, his initial plan for a private, government-subsidized railway system called for three separate lines: one running fifty miles from the port of Shama to the Tarkwa mines; a second along the central coastline from Mankessim to Elmina; and a third from Accra to Kpong on the River Volta, where the eastern district palm oil and northern River Volta trades could be tapped. Fitzgerald and his business partner, William Mercer, should be remembered in another way for being the first to organize the prototype for a colonial "commercial association," which would expand its influence and power in the mid-1890s as the West African mining and railways deputation.[96] Though it was too early to speak of a formal Anglo-West African business lobby

Table 6.1.

London Businessmen, Professionals, and Politicians Concerned about West African Railways, 1879

Thos. Bazely	Geo. Osborn, D.D.	Horsley, Palmer, Starling
Wm. McArthur	John Kilner	& Co.
Wm. Ingram	M. C. Osborn	J. Stewart & Sons
Robt. Ferguson	E. E. Jenkins	W. Fleming
John Rattenbury	R. A. W. Hanbury, M.P.	African Steamship Co.
Gervase Smith	Evelyn Ashley, M.P.	(Fred W. Bond, Chmn.)
Wm. Morely Pushong,	Frederick Young	Rylands & Sons, Ltd. (R.
L.L.D.	A. McArthur, M.P.	B. Hoggan, Dir.) Mgr.,
Solomon A. Hecht &	G. W. Gatcleng, Aitken,	City Bank, Ludgate
Chas. Hecht Trading	Jessup & Co.	Hill
Firm		

Source: Petition encl. 2 in Mercer and Fitzgerald to CO, 11 August 1879; CO Conf. Print 451, no. 3, p. 36).

or railway pressure group in the late 1870s, this was for its time an impressive ad hoc collection of "gentlemanly capitalists" interested in Gold Coast development. Largely centered in London, these enthusiasts included over twenty civic leaders whose ranks ranged from steamship company agents and overseas export merchants to doctors and lawyers and key members of Parliament (see table 6.1).

The next major step would come in the mid-1880s with the formation of specialized African Trade Sections by each of the three major chambers of commerce of the United Kingdom at London, Manchester, and Liverpool. This coincided with the Berlin West Africa Conference and the first stages in the Scramble for Africa in 1884 and 1885.[97] As a consequence of the leadership of Francis Swanzy and the concentration of a majority of the other Wassa mining companies in London at this time, the West African Trade Section of the London Chamber of Commerce would remain at center stage in future Anglo-West African mining and railway lobbying activities.[98] From these early stirrings to the laying of the first rails would require twenty years of effort. The shifts in Fitzgerald's promotional efforts away from heavy emphasis on political representation in colonial legislative councils toward government-assisted transport improvements and general development was reflected in the change in the title of his newspaper to the *African Times Railway and Commercial Gazette* just before his death in 1884.

By no means all proposals for inland rail transport came from representatives of the mining companies. Many of the earliest schemes were put forward by self-styled railroad technical experts (a few with genuine engineering credentials) who formed their own concessionaire companies for which they hoped to lure private investors after a promise of government subsidization. While a majority of such promoters hoped to cash in on the mining mania, two or three sought state approval for rail lines to the palm oil zones of the central and eastern states. New technology, embodied in a type of light railway perfected in France and known as the larigue system, found its way into plans by Arthur Brun, merchant and later Dutch consul at Elmina, for a railway from the port of Elmina to Kumasi via the River Pra, which attracted the notice of William Bradford Griffith, then serving as lieutenant governor. Offering a foreglimpse of the comprehensive railway strategies of the Chamberlain period, Brun argued with some depth and conviction that a number of lightweight, narrow-gauge railways would have a fivefold benefit. First, they were much cheaper than standard wide-gauge lines. Second, they would strengthen the revenue base of the colony. Third, in the view of promoters they would bring Westernization: thus Fitzgerald went so far as to declare that "railways alone will civilize Africa." Fourth, "troops could be quickly sent to Coomassie." Fifth, a line to the central forests would help to develop additional rubber and timber products that were at present unexportable.[99] Griffith, a step and a half ahead of his contemporaries on a number of development issues, tended to agree. Without a railway, he wrote, the quantities of raw materials and the distance from which they could be shipped to the coast would always be limited.[100] But the lieutenant governor still found no support from his colleagues at this juncture. Such projects obviously challenged the prevailing parsimony and underlying contradiction between the venture capitalism and restrained colonialism of the time. Another quixotic scheme by Frederick Barry for a coastal railway in 1881 was quickly shot down by Governor Rowe.

> The scheme seems to me to be far in advance of the general condition of the Colony. Ordinary roads, improved water supply, and better dwellings for officers, all appear to be of a more pressing moment than the railway, and though I should be glad to see it introduced, I don't think the prospect of its proving a paying scheme is enough at present to justify the guarantee which Barry asks for.[101]

The Gladstonian View on Colonial Works Projects

All the old arguments and defenses that had been used to delay the formulation of a general minerals development policy in the past—geographic barriers, health problems, difficulties of labor recruitment, lack of trained personnel, the shaky credentials of entrepreneurs, and, above all, lack of funds—were brought forward once again to delay a decision on railway construction. When the first request for a private Gold Coast railway reached the desk of Sir Michael Hicks Beach, secretary of state in the last two years of Disraeli's administration, he quickly quashed the idea on grounds that the British government lacked the authority under the existing theory of the "Protectorate" to appropriate African lands for such use.[102] In any case, the promoters—including Fitzgerald—had shown no evidence of sufficient capital or professional capacity for undertaking private construction. A slightly more optimistic tone came from Hicks Beach's liberal successor, the Earl of Kimberley, who conceded that a Gold Coast railway "would be a great public advantage" and might be considered at some time in the future provided that basic financial conditions were fulfilled.[103] But it was Robert Meade, basing his findings on research in the India Office files, who steered the imperial government away from all further serious consideration of private railway projects:

> . . . bitter experience with privately constructed railways shows that the Colonial Government always has to buy it off anyway at enormous cost. The days of guarantees are gone . . . the Colony with a precarious revenue cannot undertake to pay £30,000 a year.[104]

There is seems little doubt that further pricks and prods from the mining companies—as when a civil engineer hired by James Irvine arrived unannounced on the coast to conduct his own railway survey,[105] coupled with growing complaints by Anglo-West African traders about government inaction across a broad spectrum of public works[106]—actuated a very slow and subtle shift toward official acceptance of a railway policy for British West Africa. From Kimberley's attitude that a Gold Coast railway *might* be considered, conditions being favorable, the Earl of Derby, Colonial Secretary in Salisbury's first Conservative government, moved to a further position—that any requests for government guarantees of interest on private railway investment still would be denied, but that "if satisfied that [a] railway would pay, the colonial government would itself construct and work it."[107]

Even without a railway, less expensive forms of state assistance might have assisted some of the early companies to push beyond the first difficult stages of pioneering and development. For example, a mineralogical survey lay well beyond the financial capabilities of most of the mining firms, but if begun by the government, even on a modest scale (with the sampling instruments then available), it might have saved some companies and unwary investors from the exhaustion of funds on worthless claims.[108] Less excusable was the Accra government's failure to authorize a surface survey of land titles in order to clarify the rights and royalties owed to chiefs and to prevent needless litigation in disputes between Africans and Europeans and between contending Europeans over overlapping concessions. Under pressure from the mine managers and from Manchester and Liverpool export-import firms, the Colonial Office did grudgingly approve a schedule of customs duty rebates on imported mining machinery. This was a small upward blip on the graph of pressure group activity. But the decision was motivated less out of a desire to develop the mining industry than to avert unpleasant political repercussions at home. The gesture was, in any case, too insignificant to be of any great benefit. Lord Derby's note to Rowe betrayed the government's essential cynicism: "If these co[mpanie]s are going to breakup as I expect, we shall have to be careful not to give the engineers who work for them the opportunity of saying that their failure is due to the action of this office."[109] Here indeed was the essence of the mid-Victorian policy stance toward government assistance to colonial business—particularly mining—enterprise in Africa. Derby had also urged Rowe to draw up a general plan for roads improvement in the Gold Coast Colony and Protectorate; but the Accra government's plans to implement a large-scale and systematic road-building scheme through "native labor levies" imposed on chiefs had been a disaster so far as the Wassa mining district was concerned. Large quantities of sectionalized mining machinery continued to be left abandoned and rusting on the bush tracks as before. It is my argument that the failure of a majority of the first wave of gold-mining companies was traceable to multiple causes. It would be an exaggeration to suggest that intervention by the soft and inchoate colonial state of the late 1880s would have altered the outcome greatly. Still, several knowledgeable spokesmen for the British mining profession argued that there had been a contributory responsibility: "The failure does not reflect entirely on the companies themselves, but much on the want of spirit, if not indifference on the part of the government."[110]

Tarkwa Town and Surroundings, Wassa Fiase, Ghana

Market stalls and traders of the type seen in Tarkwa at the time of the gold rush

Steven Marfoh and view of Tarkwa town from Tarkwa Ridge (c. 1975). Photo by the author.

Crushing mill, chemical treatment plant, and offices for the Essaman Mine at Heman-Prestea (c. 1890). (Photo of the Essamon Mine from J.T.F. Halligey, "A Vistil to the West Africa Gold Mines," *Work and Workers in the Missionary Field* Vol II (1893).)

Early steel headgear for cable hoist and ore lift for pioneering mining company on Tarkwa Ridge

Early photo at Tarkwa, showing how pioneering expatriate company agents often used traditional Akan pit mines as leads for their own excavations

Abandoned mine shaft and headgear for lift. Site of an old Abontiakoon mine, Tarkwa Ridge. Photo by the author.

British freighter anchored off Cape Coast ready to take on cargo (1890).
Scene of Cape Coast from G. MacDonald, *The Gold Coast Past and Present*
(Longman, London, 1898).

Will Swift, British
mining engineer, who
worked for the Tarkwa
& Aboso and the Gie
Appanto companies.
From Francis Hart, *The
Gold Coast: Its Wealth
and Health* (1904)
(London: Erecksons,
Effingham House,
Arundel St. Strand).

William Brandford Griffith, Governor of the Gold Coast, 1886–1895. From Francis Hart, *The Gold Coast: Its Wealth and Health* (1904) (London: Erecksons, Effingham House, Arundel St. Strand).

Verney L. Cameron, explorer of Central Africa and promoter and surveyor of Gold Coast mines. From Michael Hastings, *Sir Richard Burton* (Coward, McCann, & Geohagen, New York, 1978).

7

Overcoming the Odds

Labor,[1] *Technology, Management,*
and Production at the Big Three
Wassa Mining Companies, 1883-1897

The story of nineteenth-century mining in the Gold Coast cannot be summed up in the short spurt of the concessions rush, from 1878 to 1883. Not all the early mining companies were operational failures or mere paper entities spawned solely to make a killing from inflated share prices on the London Stock Exchange. Despite the formidable odds against them, a handful of reputable ventures were able to sustain investment for ten or more years and to progress from prospecting and concessions leasing, to underground development, and finally to the ore production stage. At least three mines extracted substantial gold for export, although their capacity to distribute dividends on a sustained basis fell short of projections. These were the Tarkwa and Aboso, the Gie Appanto, and the Wassa (G.C.) Mining companies. Newcomers to gold mining often wondered why it took so long to turn a profit from mining enterprise in West Africa. But the profusion of company failures was no shock to old mining hands with experience in Australia and the American West, who had searched for years, often in vain, for the one lucky strike. Even when gold was found, they recognized that the development phase might take half a decade or longer, especially in remote wilderness areas, where supporting railways, harbors, and road systems were rudimentary or nonexistent.[2]

To focus in this chapter on the three main ventures that survived into the 1890s is not to set aside our argument that railway transport would be the ultimate essential element for launching a successful mining industry in the twentieth century. The three companies examined here strained against immense odds and continued in business only very tenuously without locomotive transport. All of their managers complained of the impossibility of conducting efficient mining over time with the sectionalized and reassembled machinery then in use. Even though many other companies succeeded in producing some gold for export, they were forced to slow down or halt operations on the very brink of success (1897–1900) because they had exhausted their capital surpluses on improvident concessions deals, expensive machinery, and high and inefficient transport labor costs. All of them subsequently joined forces in demanding a state-built mining railroad. Intractable environmental and physical obstacles, namely rainfall and drainage, were also a part of the equation. Considering the very real technological barriers, it is remarkable that any of the Wassa companies reaped even a modicum of success in the prerailway age.

THE MINES OF THE AFRICAN GOLD COAST COMPANY AND ITS SUCCESSOR, THE TARKWA AND ABOSO GOLD MINING COMPANY

In chapter 4 we saw that the first modern corporation to attempt gold mining in Wassa was the Anglo-French Compagnie Minière de la Côte d'Or Afrique (CMCOA), the African Gold Coast Mining Company. A totally independent entity, it was one of the few that had no organizational ties with either the Swanzy trading firm's London-based interests nor with the tangled speculative ventures of the Irvine-Dahse and the Fitzgerald-Horton promotional empires. With both Parisian and Liverpool entrepreneurs on its board of directors, the CMCOA had begun operations with a reasonably solid working capital of £30,000.[3] We noted that despite its early start mainly in alluvial mining, this company made scant headway at its Tarkwa banket mine during the first four years of existence. By 1882 the traveling commissioner, Murray Rumsey, had reported that their stamping machinery was in disrepair. Four tunnels or adits had been driven into the side of Tarkwa Ridge, but only one had touched the lode.[4]

The Aboso Mine

There were two connected Anglo-French ventures working in Wassa (see map 7.1). The group's second claim, "the Aboso," was situated on Aboso Hill, about one mile northwest of the village by that name and seven miles northeast of Tarkwa (see also chap. 4, map 4.3). Bonnat

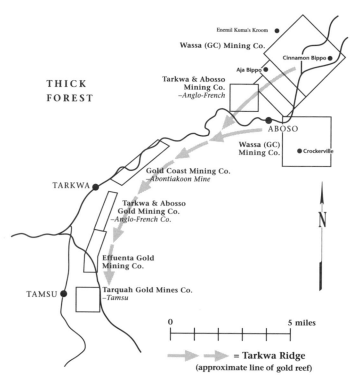

Map 7.1. Sketch map of the major producing mines of Tarkwa, Aboso, and Tamsu (1878–1900)

had leased it from chief Enemil Kuma of Aboso; and the concession was endorsed by that chief's superiors, Ango of Apinto and King Enemil of Wassa Fiase. Thus, in 1880 an offshoot venture, the Compagnie des Mines d'Or Aboso (with many of the same directors as the parent group) took over Bonnat's Aboso claim for £30,000 and set up operations.[5] This firm also took control of the Frenchman's riverbank concessions on the Ankobra but with no great success. And work at Aboso reef over the first two years was equally desultory and unrewarding. During the Asante war scare of 1881, most of its European staff had fled to the port of Axim.[6]

By August 1882, however, the local managers had reactivated the Aboso mines with a staff of two Europeans, twenty Fantes (mainly surface workers), and fifty-six Kru men. The resident manager, Will Swift, started with a "pioneering"-type lightweight twelve-head battery of stamps, which (despite flaws) served its initial purpose in demonstrating that a fair proportion of gold could be obtained from almost every ton of ore treated. Swift, an able and experienced mining engineer of whom we'll hear more later, had a hard time making headway against the natural barriers of hard country rock and groundwater with the crude technology of this period. One new horizontal adit was driven 170 feet and a second one started. Again, I must emphasize that the venture could have made but little headway without the remnants of ancient African mines to guide them. Assisted by these leads, Swift sank five small vertical shafts, following the crest of the ridge, along the line of reef. But the staff waited anxiously for the arrival of the heavier stamping machinery essential for more efficient crushing.[7] The Aboso Company did not endure for long as a separate entity.

Early Labor Policy

So long as they remained under management of the original Anglo-French combine, neither the Tarkwa nor the Aboso mines registered good productivity. With their reputation for toughness, two or three managers and foremen recruited from Australia and the Cornish tin mines often got more work and respect from their African underground men than did the unseasoned greenhorns initially brought in from London white-collar jobs to manage a mine. To illustrate this point, an early resident manager at Tarkwa, Albert Bowden (an ex-palm oil broker),[8] who followed Bonnat and Moulton, drew fire from the London mining press for absenteeism, for failing to pay local chiefs the mining rents due them under their leases, for neglecting to maintain machinery in working order, and for an overly harsh labor policy that alienated his workers.[9] Summing up progress at the Tarkwa property in 1882, Rumsey reported that thousands of tons of rough-hewn rock had piled up outside the bins, and that crushing had taken place only at irregular intervals, owing to constant steam engine breakdowns. The firm's labor policy was certainly a crude one. V. L. Cameron thought it extremely "unwise that the managers had imposed a rigid minimum standard for sustained labor of over 20 [consecutive] working days, in dereliction of which wages would be docked proportionately."[10] This inhumane rule endangered workers' health by forcing them to show up at the pit head even when they were ill. As a consequence, the company was further weakened by high sickness and mortality rates. A related problem was the Aboso's "rotating" field management, the inevitable result of illness, frequent rest leaves, and convalescences in Europe, which saddled the firm with heavy operating costs and destroyed continuity of administration.

Extraction Technology

As with staffs at every other mine, the Aboso field bosses agonized over the inefficient, expensive, and wasteful overland and river transport, with consequent malfunctioning of machinery for crushing, pumping, and chemical treatment. Before the advent of cyanidization, the Anglo-French group experimented with several transitional chemical extraction techniques, none of which were very effective. In the early 1880s the production flow chart called for three Behanzin amalgamators to force the crushed pulp from the stamps into a mercury solution bath. But the system did not work as prescribed, and skilled ore treatment specialists who knew how to run it were scarce. During the intensive early phase of the 1882–83 "gold rush" the company had 1,000 tons of quartz backlogged for crushing, but could do nothing about it. None of the primitive stampers were working because their wooden foundations had fallen apart (see photos of pioneering stamping machines at end of chap. 5).[11] One official noted that it was difficult to determine exactly what was going on at Aboso. "There appeared to be a great want of system in the working of the [Anglo-French] mine. . . ."[12] Only in September 1882 could anyone report that the ten heads of light-weight stamps at the Tarkwa mine were starting to function on a regular basis.[13] Hence, even though the Anglo-French was one of the first companies in the district, it lagged behind other major concessionaires in the production of gold.

The Resilience of Traditional African Mining

Who were the most resourceful and resilient gold miners? Was it the Europeans, with their supposedly modern technology, or the traditional Akan miners, the "born gold seekers," who knew how to locate the richest outcrops and work them efficiently? One leitmotiv of this study has been the continuity in traditional modes of production by peasant miners in tandem with the advance of expatriate-controlled capitalistic mining. Incredible though it may seem, the Akan farmer-miners remained the backbone of the colony's gold-exporting industry until the end of the nineteenth century—and even after—despite the advent of mechanization. For the next six years, with its crushing plant largely inoperative, the Anglo-French company turned their premises back to the local African miners, who paid the company as leaseholder a one-third division of their gold dust according to the traditional *abusa* share system. This technique had a longer life than is commonly supposed. In addition, we should keep in mind that the companies were also surrounded by scores of independent Akan gold diggers, the mainstays of the overland gold trade: "The native miner for a long time to come will be the real prospector of the wealth of the soil of this country. . . . His industry should be protected by ordinance."[14]

The government took limited steps to implement this recommendation when it tried to apply the Native Jurisdiction Ordinance to the two Wassa states along with bylaws for the protection of traditional African mining and farming rights. But, as noted in chapter 6, in Tarkwa and Aboso the Native Jurisdiction Ordinance meant little without greater hands-on support by the colonial law courts and administration. Kings and chiefs in the mining districts were now complaining more loudly than ever about a loss of respect and obedience among their people. In the absence of strong formal district administration, protection of age-old African surface rights under the ordinance depended mainly on the totally unpredictable whims of individual mine managers. The companies might be supportive of such traditional mining rights, but mainly when they continued to utilize the services of local African tributors as their own miners.

Management and Labor at the Tarkwa and Aboso Gold Mining Company

The new Tarkwa and Aboso Gold Mining Company, built on the bones of the defunct Compagnie Minière de la Côte d'Or Afrique's concessions, improved tremendously on the management practices of its predecessor. It was the inability of the French founders to attract sufficient new capital in Paris that forced reconstitution as a British limited company under the more flexible English companies laws in 1886.[15] The new entity controlled twenty-four concessions and now boasted a nominal capital of £100,000 (of which £79,829 was allotted and paid up). Its new board chairman was William F. H. Morecroft, a lawyer with offices in Liverpool. But even though the corporation's headquarters were moved to Merseyside and its capital base widened to bring in more British shareholders, there was considerable continuity with the previous administration. Large blocks of shares were still held by the group's French founders, Albert Verillon, R. E. Illurant, Ernest Begoran, and E. Basset, all of Paris. To these were added substantial holdings by Morecroft, J. S. Banner, L. Gruning, Major General E. Wray, C. Stewart, and Frederick Radcliffe, all of Liverpool.[16] Showing once again the connection between many of the new gold-mining

ventures and the stagnating palm oil trade, it is worth noting that
Radcliffe was the scion of a long-established firm of Anglo-West Afri-
can produce brokers and merchants that traced its connections to the
Gold Coast as far back as the eighteenth century.[17]

In accounting for the reconstructed firm's greater efficiency in the late
1880s and first half of the 1890s, a good deal can be chalked up to
better local management coupled with simple trial-and-error experience. The new directors were confident that their property was a
valuable one, and they were determined to avoid the blunders of the
past. Second, through improved relations with chiefs and workers over
its predecessor, the new entity was better able to cope with the recruitment of transport labor than most of its rivals and could move large
parcels of machinery in better condition to the mining site.[18] Sheer
doggedness in attacking geological obstacles slowly paid off. Underground crews pressed forward with driving and shaft sinking to the
extent that they penetrated the higher gold-bearing sections of the lode.
Plagued by the inevitable problems of machine corrosion and disrepair,
the staff had to redouble their efforts to recruit more skilled machine
operators and fitters, especially since a large percentage of the first
European staff had resigned in the mid-1880s for reasons of poor
health and dissatisfaction.

Though never so effective as its rival, the Wassa Gold Coast Mining
Company, the Tarkwa and Aboso nonetheless revamped its employment techniques, not only in the hope of hiring more European specialists, but also to encourage Africans to apply for higher-grade skilled
positions. By December 1891 the company had just eight Europeans,
three superintendents, three skilled miners, and two machine attendants
left on the job.[19] Severe underground flooding and engine malfunctions
remained constant threats, but superintendents reported that total shutdowns were less frequent than before. As for machinery, the firm had
in place one battery of ten heads of stamps and another of eight,
powered by one twenty-horsepower steam engine, capable of crushing
one ton of quartz per hour, plus about 2,680 feet of light railway, with
steam locomotive, used for the gathering of wood fuel.[20] This, along
with a similar tramway at the neighboring Wassa (G.C.) Mining Company, was the first example of steam transport in the colony. The Aboso
site also maintained a large stonebreaker, a blacksmith's shop, and a
sawmill. My informants pointed out that a sawmill was one of the
important but overlooked early contributions that a gold-mining installation could make toward improving the technological capabilities of

a developing country.[21] Sawmills had both forward and backward linkages: they facilitated building construction in the mining districts and elsewhere; they played a part, along with the expansion of overseas markets, in stimulating the new Gold Coast timber-cutting industry, centered on the River Ankobra; and they helped, along with many other mining company jobs, to provide employment and to train workers in new and useful skills.

Sources of Wage Labor for the Tarkwa and Aboso Company

By the 1890s some 550 men were listed on the company's regular African workers roster, but the figure was misleading. As table 7.3 (below) demonstrates, the number of underground miners on the job at any one time fluctuated greatly with the year and with the season, sometimes rising as high as 600, but in 1891 it averaged just 66.[22] A majority were non-Akan workers recruited from outside the Gold Coast (mainly Bassa and Kru men from Liberia) who returned home after six to twelve months of labor. The reported official figures on mines labor neglect a major dimension of the labor problem. That this mine alone used approximately 400 workers exclusively for carrying equipment and supplies inland underscored better than any other figure the harassing persistence of the transportation problem and the huge money outlays required for human porterage.

Whether the offer of higher entry-level wages would have attracted more coastal Akan people to unskilled wage labor at the Wassa mines remains doubtful. However, this should not blind us to the important and expanding trickle of "Fante" men into skilled surface positions such as office clerks, ore dressers (chemical plant), and drivers of winch engines that ran the cable hoists that raised and lowered the mine shaft cages and ore skips. It is clear that local Africans did respond favorably to the offer of the genuinely higher (at 2s.3d. to 3s. per day, double the rate for unskilled labor) wages for surface-level versus underground jobs. At the same time the Tarkwa and Aboso remained in a quandary over the lackluster response of Fante and Wassa men to offers of ordinary wages at the unskilled and underground positions. Reasons for worker reticence were not hard to find (see chaps. 5 and 8). When in the twentieth century an expanded number of Fante and Asante men were at last drawn to underground labor it was less due to increased wage rates (which remained low) than to greater familiarity with imported manufactured merchandise and the import market exchange system. At its peak of nineteenth-century production (about 1896), this company boasted a labor force of 1,050 (made up almost entirely of Liberians and Sierra Leoneans), more than 50 percent of whom were underground miners, working around the clock in three shifts, twenty-four hours a day, seven days a week.

Technology and Management

In the mid-1890s there were faint hints in West Africa of the worldwide technological revolution in minerals extraction and processing that was just getting underway. For the first time we read of two or three compressed-air percussion rock drills introduced for setting dynamite charges in tunneling and sinking shafts, and there was talk about introducing the newly perfected cyanide separation technique.[23] In the stamping process full-fledged steam-powered pestles, raised and lowered on a rotating shaft using parabolic cams, would eventually replace the older gravitational stampers at most of the major mines. By 1896, forty-three steam stamps of 750 pounds each had replaced most of the lightweight stamps at the Tarkwa and Aboso; and the new system was capable of crushing 1,600 tons of ore per month (see photos at the end of chap. 5). Even under the inefficient mercury amalgamation method of gold separation, gold yields were fluctuating between ten dwt. and two ounces per ton of ore.[24] Here were tangible steps forward. This increasing optimism by miners of the 1890s ran parallel to a more centralized public works program inaugurated by Governor W. B. Griffith and growing optimism about railway construction. Shares of the Tarkwa and Aboso Company, which a short time earlier had sold for four shillings each, were now quoted on the London Stock Exchange at thirty shillings.[25]

No year-by-year financial statements nor extensive folios of business correspondence exist for any of the Wassa mining companies. Company records formerly at the Register of Joint Stock Companies and now at the Public Records Office, London, contain limited data on articles of incorporation and capital stock, as well as the names of directors and shareholders, but there are no complete surviving profit-and-loss statements nor lengthy series on income and expenditures. Modern accounting concepts such as costs per unit of production or returns per man-hour of labor were not applied in the West African mining of the 1880s and 1890s. Hence the story has to be pieced together from small fragments of widely dispersed data in government reports, journal articles, and rare instances where company reports were filed at the Colonial Office. Previous studies have suggested that

Table 7.1
Gold Production by the Tarkwa and Aboso
Gold Mining Company

Year	Ounces	Value (£)
1889	1,851	7,406
1890	1,966	7,007
1891	2,968	10,685
1892	1,012	4,048
1893	1,956	7,041
1894	4,870	19,480
1895	5,212	20,847
1896	6,116	24,462
1897	5,295	19,063
1898	5,935	22,258
1899	2,219	8,788
1900	939	3,386
Totals	37,338 oz	£79,970

Sources: Gold Coast Colonial *Blue Books* for the years.
Gold Coast Customs Office Rept., (Encl. 3 in Govr. Nathan
(66) to C.O., 14 Feb. 1901; C.O. 96/377.

no continuous gold production series for the Tarkwa and Aboso Gold Mining Company (formed in 1886) were available.[26] This is not the case: statistics for the early 1880s are lacking; but after the reconstructed company recommenced operations in 1888-89, annual production for the Tarkwa and Aboso increased sixfold during the four years from 1892 to 1896. These figures show a marked upswing in gold production about the time that the new drilling and crushing equipment was introduced. The company also had good luck in locating new and richer lodes.

Major Costs of Production at the Tarkwa and Aboso

If we exclude 1900, a miserable year for all the Wassa mines, then the average annual gross revenue from the sale of gold by the Tarkwa and Aboso from 1892 to 1896 was £10,940. Did this enable one of the Gold Coast's premier mines to survive? Just barely. One government source, based on hearsay, listed an average annual expenditure for this company at £600 per month, or £7,200 for the year; but this estimate was much too low.[27] Isolated data on expenditure for 1896, a good year, show that at the very time the Tarkwa and Aboso was earning about £24,500 from the shipment of processed gold to Europe, it was paying out £8,200 in miners wages, plus £3,000 for fuel and £4,000 for the transport of supplies between the coast and interior.[28] This adds up to a total expenditure of £15,200 and an apparent profit of £9,300—in a very good year. Such figures confirm once again that heavy transport costs, equal to one-half the bill for labor, lay at the heart of the mines problem, since, as just noted, the company routinely had to employ 400 carriers on the Bonsa to Tarkwa road shouldering loads of sectionalized machinery, equipment, and supplies.[29] Another increasingly expensive item for all the mines, difficult to isolate because it was so bound up with labor charges—was fuel. The high cost of headloading and hauling huge quantities of cut wood (500 to 600 cords were burned each month to heat nine steam boilers) over ever greater distances (as more of the surrounding forests were hacked down) at a cost of ten shillings per cord made up about one-fifth of all annual charges for the Tarkwa and Aboso.

To be sure, these listings of "production costs" leave out a host of other ongoing management charges, such as (1) travel for European personnel between Britain and West Africa; (2) administrative and office expenses in London and Tarkwa; (3) annual interest payments on loans; and (4) shipments of tools, food, and supplies. Whatever the exact totals, it is clear that annual operating expenditures nearly equaled revenues even in the best production years, making it impossible for the company to earn sufficient profits to pay out regular dividends. And when we bear in mind that the troubled Tarkwa and Aboso was considered one of the few success stories, then the far more typical trend for companies to halt operations after three or four years of unrewarding toil becomes understandable.

THE WASSA (GOLD COAST) MINING COMPANY AND THE SWANZY INTEREST

At this point we turn to the main success story in the early "jungle boom." Of the pioneering Tarkwa firms, the Wassa (G.C.) Mining Company (WGCMC), Limited, maintained the most consistent production record and earned the largest profits. This was traceable only in part to the quality of its particular segment of the Tarkwa banket (see map 7.1). A number of the other basic requirements for turning an ore body to account, unavailable to a majority of the other early ventures—adequate capital resources, engineering expertise, solid central direction and local management, effective use of available technology, and fair labor relations—were met to a degree by this company. As a central link in F. and A. Swanzy's chain of trading and mining interests, the WGCMC owed a good deal to the financial backing of its parent group and especially to the technical and management skills of the illustrious Sam family of Cape Coast (see earlier photo of W. E. Sam). We have seen that the company began operations in 1882 with a small nominal capital of £30,000 (in £1 shares), later expanded to £100,000, and then to £150,000, out of which a respectable £120,000 was paid up by 1900. Its properties were extensive; but by concentrating on just two or three sites within the larger concessions, it avoided the squandering of vital capital on a plethora of worthless claims that plagued so many of the first-generation ventures.

Mining Sites and Company Finances

As we have seen, in March 1878 Francis Swanzy had ordered his three main trading agents on the Coast—William Edward Sam, Frederick J. Crocker, and William Cleaver—to buy up gold-bearing properties along the Tarkwa-Aboso road. The first and most valuable was a long rectangular tract, located two miles northwest of Aboso, called Aja Bippo. A second mine, which lay several miles further to the north, had been known to traditional African diggers as Cinnamon Bippo. That the Swanzy firm was able to grab these two sites ahead of competition must be credited to W. E. Sam's negotiating skills with the local Aboso chief, Enemil Kuma (see photo at the end of chap. 8).[30] After registering their concession with the Gold Coast government, Crocker and Sam built a gold extraction plant and a company village at Crockerville, about two and a half miles southeast of Aboso (see map 7.1). By using gangs of Fante labor (first recruited in Cape Coast as carriers)[31] to improve local roads by laying cut logs (the so-called corduroy method) over swampy areas between the River Bonsah and Tarkwa, the two men were able to install crushing mills and extraction plants with considerably less toil and expense than the other mines.

As another advantage the geological structure of the rich Aja Bippo Hill differed from that of other mines in the Tarkwa area. Here the main lode ran nearly straight and perpendicular, with a minimum of folding, plus it had a uniform thickness of about twenty inches. By 1882 work crews had sunk several shafts, from forty to eighty feet deep, along with horizontal adits. During the mid-1880s production by the company picked up noticeably. In 1884 the WGCMC produced

Table 7.2

Ore Crushed and Gold Recovered by the Wassa (G.C.) Mining Company's
Aja Bippo Mine During September and October, 1885

	Ore Crushed (tons)	Gold Retrieved (ounces)	Approximate Gold Yield per Ton of Ore (dwt.)*
Deep adit	87	103.5	24
Refuse headings	120	28	5
No. 4 Tunnel	176	53	6
No. 5 Shaft	6	3	10
No. 6 Shaft (North Level)	146	73	10
No. 6 Shaft (South Level)	86	43	10
No. 7 Shaft (North Level)	18	13.5	15
No. 7 Shaft (South Level)	23	17	15
Totals	662 tons	334 ounces	10 dwt. Ave. (½oz.) per ton

*One dwt. (pennyweight) = 0.05 ounces.

Sources: Report on the Aja Bippo Mine, owned by the Wassa (G.C.) Mining Co., Ltd., Mining Journal, 12 November 1885.

1,363 tons of ore, or 4.24 tons per day; and by 1885 the total figure had grown to 4,276 tons, or a rate of 13.70 tons per day.[32] At one point Crocker boasted to his London office that sixty-eight ounces of gold had been drawn from twenty-five tons of ore—almost three ounces of gold to the ton. This was extraordinarily good; but it was unrealistic to suppose that such a rate could be sustained. Different ore zones along the reef varied considerably in thickness and richness. Even ten to fifteen years later, with better equipment, returns would show that the best average yield that could be expected for all tunnels and shafts was closer to half an ounce of gold per ton of ore (see table 7.1, above).[33] Nonetheless, the Aja Bippo Hill proved to be one of the very best sections of the entire Tarkwa gold banket.

The Swanzy Network of Mines

Although the organizational structure of the Swanzy mining empire was complex, the bare outlines can be summarized quickly. Initially, there were three main companies in the Swanzy portfolio: the Aja Bippo Mines, the Swanzy Estates Mining Company, and the Tamsu Gold Mining Company (based on an original concession and investment by Ferdinand Fitzgerald), located south of Tarkwa town. It was only in 1882 that the Swanzy firm decided to sell shares to the general public, after which just two entities, the Wassa (G.C.) Mining Company and the Swanzy Estates Mining Company, were registered on the stock exchange.[34] Early records of the Swanzy Estates revealed the financial structure of a tightly knit family firm. Its first nominal capital was only £25,000, of which £21,921 was paid and called up. The major share-holders were F. J. Crocker, named managing director of all Swanzy mining interests in the Gold Coast (6,599 shares); Marion Swanzy (879); Francis Swanzy (6,160); and the on-site manager of the WGCMC's Aja Bippo property, William Cleaver (5,720). The remaining paid-up shares, distributed in very small bundles, were held mainly by the wives, friends, and employees of the parent trading firm.[35] The Aja Bippo mine was first placed under the control of Swanzy Estates, but in 1882 Swanzy Estates sold their mining rights in Aja Bippo to the WGCMC for £75,000.[36]

Clearly, this transaction illustrates how the directors of the early companies could skim off a fat profit for themselves by frequent reorganizations and transfers of stock between related companies, often to the detriment of general (noninsider) shareholders. The Swanzy Estates Company had paid the original African owners comparatively little for the Aja Bippo lease. But the original British vendors profited a great deal from the resale of their lease to the new entity. As noted, the Wassa (G.C.) Mining Company boasted at one point that its capital of £100,000 was paid in full.[37] Even this figure is misleading. About 33,000 of the initial 100,000 shares simply reflected a transfer from investors in the old Aja Bippo property to the new company. The question that remains is, What source did the ex-Swanzy Estates shareholders draw on for the remaining £44,000 owed to them in the transaction?

Because its early managers had only the dimmest knowledge of the line of strike or direction of its gold-laden lode, the Wassa (G.C.) Company like its competitors had no systematic plan of how to hit the reef, other than to follow the abandoned pits and hillside adits of African miners. But they achieved some success owing to the relative straightness of the reef along key sections and by developing their properties more methodically than competing firms. Verney Cameron, generally critical of company management throughout the Gold Coast in the eighties, credited Swanzy work crews with building roads made to last through the so-called corduroy process over the Bonsa-Tarkwa road, plus wheeled dollies that were pushed by hand to get the company's heavy machinery in place with minimal dislocation.[38] The Swanzy group's first decade of operations were circumscribed, however, and the results should not be exaggerated. As elsewhere, machines were still small and rudimentary. The twelve stamps in the first battery were of the light-weight type, purchased for easy disassembling, and for the first year or so, only six of those stamps functioned. As with practically every other venture of the time, the Wassa Company also had to face staggering pumping problems. So great were the hazards from underground seep-age and flooding, that expatriate foremen, like the local Akan farmer-miners, had to gear their activities to seasonal climatic variations. Mean-while, the management also had to face the opposite problem, since water pumped in from surrounding streams during the dry season was often insufficient to accommodate the water needs of steam boilers and the chemical reduction process.[39]

It offers some comment on the stupefying range of problems on the mining frontier that even this most successful of all the Wassa compa-nies stumbled many times in the two decades between 1880 and 1900 and at several points appeared on the verge of collapse. The directors were perhaps naive in supposing they could recover more than a small percentage of the gold embedded in the dense rock samples with the unsophisticated crushing and reduction gear then available. Despite acquisition of additional properties at Beniribi and at Tamsu the WGCMC continued to face serious technical and production con-straints. It lent weight to the colonial government's early pessimism about the industry when, in 1883, the plant was able to crush only 516 tons of ore yielding 940 ounces of gold.[40]

New Management: The Gowans Brothers and the Sams, Father and Sons

After a hiatus in local management, the London board of directors appointed two brothers, Louis and David Gowans, as chief engineers to oversee technical operations in April 1886. Their assignments were to raise gold yields on the ore extracted at the Aja Bippo main reef and to reduce production costs. One obvious way was to hire more qualified Africans in place of Europeans for supervisory positions, in the hope of easing the heavy annual expenditures on steamship passage and rest leaves with pay to the British Isles. It was partly for this reason that Swanzy decided to make Thomas Birch Freeman Sam an integral part of his team as deputy manager of the Aja Bippo mine. This was no token African appointment. As the son of W. E. "Tarkwa" Sam, T. B. F. Sam knew the local geology better than any man, and he had recently graduated with distinction as a mining engineer from a reputable technical college in London.[41] We saw earlier that the family name carried great resonance with inland chiefs, partly because the father, William Edward, had served for years as an up-country agent for the Swanzy trading firm and as a skilled negotiator for the colonial government in its dealings with leading African states. As senior men like Crocker, Cleaver, and the two Gowans brothers distinguished themselves more and more by their absence from West Africa, it enabled the Sams—father and two sons—to show their technical skills and managerial abilities. Aja Bippo was the big gun in the Swanzy arsenal. Measured by the personnel who received the lion's share of the accolades for improved local operations in the years ahead, the Aja Bippo and her sister mines under the Sams careful stewardship, can be considered in no small degree as African-managed enterprises. When travelers and inspectors, including Governor Griffith, toured the premises they invariably reported that there was only one European in residence (usually one of the Gowans brothers) and sometimes none at all. In fact, the two technicians most continuously involved in day-to-day operations were William Edward Sam and his son Thomas.[42]

The younger Sam resembled his contemporary, another eminent African professional, the geologist and mapmaker George Ekem Ferguson, in a number of respects. Both men were scientists and theoreticians as well as practitioners in their respective fields. As noted in chapter 3, George Ferguson had taken an interest in and reported on the traditional African gold mines of Akyem and Asante (see drawing in chap. 3). T. B. F. Sam, like Ferguson, contributed papers to scientific symposia and journals and was honored with membership in British learned societies.[43] According to the venerable W. S. Kwesi Johnson, a retired Ghanaian businessman, who recalled in interviews with the writer life at Cape Coast at the turn of the century, "W. E. Sam and his two sons also purchased and developed several of their own private gold mines in the Ankobra region. They were great leaders much admired in the local community."[44]

LABOR

Considering the endless complaints by expatriate foremen, company directors, and colonial officials about the "intractable" mines labor problem, the apparent success of the WGCMC in mobilizing and handling local African labor merits special attention. Francis Swanzy and his senior European advisers, Crocker and Cleaver, no doubt showed great wisdom in turning labor recruitment and control over all local operations mainly to W. E. Sam Sr. and T. B. F. Sam. With their intimate knowledge of Akan culture and fluency in the Twi language, the Sams helped the Swanzy group avoid some of the common language blunders, arrogance, and social crudities that frequently offended Africans. In addition, it did not hurt mining operations that the Swanzy mercantile firm over the years had adhered to reasonably fair standards in trade and had built up considerable good will in their dealings with both African chiefs and ordinary customers and suppliers.[45] On the other hand, we must raise serious questions concerning the reported effectiveness of this company in mobilizing local "Fante" workers as the nucleus for a future "industrial work force" in Ghanaian gold mining.

Continued Use of African Tributors by the Wassa (G.C.) Mining Company

Upon taking control of their leasehold properties, a number of companies had barged in without formalities and had ejected the traditional African miners, even though most of the original leases had provided for protection of surface mining, as well as of farming rights for the local community. As a part of the capitalist penetration of the hinterland, traditional mining rights could be swept aside or curtailed in two ways: (1) as leases were bought and sold several times by middlemen, agents and various companies, the meaning of clauses protecting African rights were easily forgotten or deliberately glossed over; (2) some European managers believed that protection of African surface mining rights pertained only to marginal areas far distant from the major shafts and adits of the new mechanized mining installations.[46] On the other hand, at certain of the European concessions work crews were slow in getting started and groups of Wassa and Nzeman pit miners continued to work their lands in the old way, initially unaware of the exclusivist attitudes of most capitalist companies. From the start, several of the more astute company field managers tried to incorporate this kind of spasmodic farmer mining into a tributing system that the companies could exploit to the fullest extent for their own purposes. As we have just seen, the pioneering Anglo-French (subsequently the Tarkwa and Aboso) Company allowed African pit miners back on to their Tarkwa installation, but only after operations had run down due to machinery malfunction in 1883.

Now, according to the bare face of the colonial reports and statistical records, the Wassa (G.C.) Mining Company supposedly was the one major European venture that made massive use in underground work of indigenous Gold Coast labor, usually labeled Fante. None of the formal reports and tables offer a detailed explanation for use of this term, the mechanisms for recruitment, or a breakdown of employment figures as to subgroups. Given the generally accepted notion that most "Fantes" (men from the central coastal states) preferred surface jobs and were disinclined to work underground for the white man's wages, the reported recruitment of over 200 "Fante" workers in the mid-eighties, rising to a stated 600 in some reports by the mid-nineties, appears not only as a remarkable feat but at odds with reality. If true, it would mean that the Swanzy group was able to recruit vast numbers of a population, known in this period to be steadfastly opposed to any form of underground labor on a wide spectrum of arguments. This conclusion about Swanzy and the hiring of unskilled laborers from Fanteland needs to be carefully dissected.

What emerges from closer investigation is something quite different. First, we learn that underground workers, listed only as "Fantes" in some reports, were in fact mainly "Wassas" and Nzemans from the southwestern states close to the Tarkwa and Aboso mines.[47] *Fante*, for Europeans, often became a catchall term that had nothing to do with the traditional boundaries of the "Fante" territories. Sometimes the word *Fante* was used in mining reports—like the word *Akan* today— simply and broadly to distinguish men from the Gold Coast from migrant mine workers of Liberia, Sierra Leone, and other distant African countries. Second, official surveys of the towns of Tarkwa and Aboso stated that the population was made up of Wassas, Nzemans, and Kru men. Only small numbers of Fantes from the coast were listed mainly as traders and drifters. Third, it is important to note that most of these Akan men did not sign on as regular, let alone permanent, wage earners on the company payrolls. For in contrast to the Tarkwa and Aboso and several other European mines, where *abusa*-share men might be used on an occasional basis to supplement full-time wage earners, it is now apparent that a *majority* of the unskilled workers at the WCGMC's mines remained *abusa* or *abuna* share tributors up to the end of the period under review. Upon visiting the area, one traveling official noted that at Swanzy's Aja Bippo installation, three main shafts had been sunk—the Swanzy, the Cleaver, and Bishop's Shaft—and that at all three the entire underground labor force, with the exception of twenty to thirty Kru men and Sierra Leoneans, was made up of Akan *abusa*-share men working in the traditional way under the partial supervision of their own chiefs and headmen.[48]

In so far as I can make out the details through the haze of meager records, the system worked in the following way. The Sams made agreements with Chief Enemil Kuma of Aboso and the headmen of outlying villages to encourage as many able-bodied men as possible to come to the mines and work for a set number of weeks. European foremen, skilled explosives experts, and timber men continued to manage the blasting and stoping, while the tribute men would handle all the pick and shovel work. Each mine shaft was placed under the control of a different village and headman. At the end of each day a strict accounting would be made of the amount of gold ore or earth turned in by each village team. Crushing and treatment of the ore was turned over to the company's skilled-wage-earning staff at the surface treatment plant. When the rough-hewn rock was extracted from a given shaft, the company kept half for itself and turned over the remaining half to the tributors. Although the sources are silent on key details, it seems that tributors had to extract the pure gold from their share of the ore on their own time in the traditional ways and could not utilize the company's extraction plant for their own purposes. On the face it would appear that opportunities for confusion and unfairness in payment to some individual workers must have existed. But there is no record of any complaint by miners registered against the Sams, the Swanzy organization, or the chiefs on this particular score.

William Cleaver, Swanzy's senior representative, praised the system, contending that all parties had benefited from the arrangement: first, workers at this mine got to keep a larger portion of the ore (up to 50 percent) than they usually had received under the old *abusa* (one-third) system; second, the chief administering the system was relieved of responsibility for checking to see whether his miners were cheating him. The company also was obviously pleased with the results, since by use of the tributing method it was possible to (1) avoid the expense of importing unskilled labor from Liberia, (2) reduce the need to constantly train new migrant workers, (3) eliminate payments for food and subsistence, and for town and street repairs (since workers lived off the premises), (4) curtail the administrative costs of maintaining wage sheets and other records for unskilled workers, and (5) secure at the very least a trade-off, if not an advantage, by paying workers in unassayed ore.

Table 7.3
Labor Employed in Wassa by Major Companies, 1880–1897

	Name of Company	European Staff Average Size in the 1880's	Size of African Work Force[a]		Ethnic Breakdown
			1882–1887	1891–1895	
1	African Gold Coast (Anglo-French) Co.	—	300	—	mainly Kru men and Bassa men from Liberia.
2	Aboso Mining Co. (Anglo-French) Co.	3	76	—	mainly Kru and about 20 Fante and other local laborers.
3	Brumasi Mines (Gold Reefs of West Africa 1897)	7	—	238	no data available
4	Effuenta Mining Co. Gold Coast	5	120	—	mainly Kru men, plus Sierra Leonean blacksmiths and carpenters
5	Essaman Gold Mining Co. (Prestca)	—	215	—	reported as almost entirely Kru and Bassa men
6	Abontiakoon Mine (Gold Coast Mining Co.)	5	85	—	55 Kru and Bassa men; 30 from local Wassa and Fante men
7	Gie Appanto Gold Mining Co. (Prestea)[b]	10–15 (down to 3 in 1890's)	200	190–614[a]	Ninety percent Kru men
8	Swanzy Estates & Gold Mining Co. (Teberibi)	9	175	120	mainly local labor (Fantes, Wassas and Nzemans)
9	Tarkwa & Aboso Gold Mining Company	12–17 (down to 6 in 1890's)	640	50–554[a]	A mixed group: 94 from local Akan (Wassa, Fante) men, majority from Kru Coast of Liberia
10	Wassa (G.C.) Mining Co. (Swanzy interests):	1–2	230	60–626[a]	mainly Wassa, Fante, Nzeman, & other local Gold Coast workers plus 20–30 Kru men

[a] These figures show great variation from month to month in the records, owing to climatic factors and other conditions. The reports are unclear whether the figures'include tributors and occasional 'piece' workers., In 1896 one distinct commissioner estimated a high of 1,200 workers at all the 'big three' mines of Wassa.

[b] This company did not begin active operations until 1887. It took over properties from the Esswnan company in 1890 and reconstructed itself as the Appanto Company in 1893.

Sources: Rept. by Rumsey, encl. In Moloney to Kimberley, 4 Sept. 1882: No. 19 "Further Corres., Re. Affairs of Gold Coast: P.P. (1883), [C. 3687], XLVIII, 53-4., Report on the Mining Co.'s of Wassa, Encl. in Griffith to Knutsford, 25 June 1889; P.P (1889), [C. 5620-24], LIV, 173. Quarterly Dist. Rept. for Wassa, Encl. in Griffith (210) to Knutsford, 25 June 1891, C.O. 96/217., Returns for Quarter ending 31 Dec. 1891, encl. 6 in Griffith (278) to Ripo, 12 Oct 1892; c.o. 96/226., Wassa Dist. Rept., Encl. No. 13 in Maxwell (330) to C.O., 23 Jul. 1897: C.O. 96/297.

In sum, there is little doubt that the WGCMC saved on its operating costs over rival companies mainly through the use of African tributors. It is also evident that this entire system continued to function effectively until well into the 1890s owing, in large part, to the backing of Chief Enemil Kuma of Aboso, who is described in contemporary documents as the most wealthy, powerful, and effective ruler in Wassa in this period.[49] Another interesting feature of this transitional stage between what might be called archaic "seigniorial" mining and modern capitalistic mining is that Chief Enemil simultaneously was allowed to maintain several of his own personal mine shafts, using his personal tributors, inside the boundaries of the WGCM's concession, indeed very close to the above-mentioned main shafts.[50] The chief stored some of this gold in his treasure house and exchanged portions in the usual way for trade goods to traveling goldsmiths and itinerant traders, who transported the gold dust to the coast.

The Attempted Recruitment of Permanent Wage Earners

Pragmatic though this hybrid system may have been for the Wassa Mining Company in the short term, there is no doubt that tributing was a stopgap measure that in the normal flow of historical change ultimately would have to be phased out. The remarkable point is that the technique lasted as long as it did. As for regular unskilled laborers willing to work underground for a daily wage, again the Swanzy managers publicized the fact that they were more effective than their competitors in recruiting miners from among the local (mainly Wassa and Nzeman) population. While something must be credited to the persuasive powers of the Sams with local headmen, it is doubtful that the Swanzy-controlled mines were all that effective in securing the retention of wage-earners and building up a stable or permanent work force, except perhaps in the surface plant. Although some mine managers tried very hard, the powers of coercion by capital to hold Gold Coast workers on the job for any length of time at this juncture were extremely limited.

Nor was the colonial state prone to intervene very strongly on behalf of the mining companies in this sphere of action. Because the Accra governments Master and Servant Ordinance passed in 1877 bore a resemblance to similarly named laws in South Africa designed to hold migrant workers in a kind of semi-bondage to mining companies under the infamous "compound system," some students of labor history have wondered whether the Gold Coast law worked to the same purpose. It is true that the British master-servant legislation had been designed to instill respect for labor contracts by imposing stiff fines and jail sentences against wage laborers who walked off the job in breach of written work agreements.[51] At various times mine managers did try to induce the colonial government to prosecute such cases under the ordinance. Hillard Pouncy, who has studied court cases under the Master and Servant laws in detail, has concluded that these regulations were applied mainly on behalf of merchants in the coastal towns and that ultimately very few arrests and convictions were obtained against workers who absconded from the mining companies.[52] This could be traced in part to the distance of Wassa from the main colonial courts on the coast.

Wassa mine managers came to expect that most laborers would request to return to their home villages at least once every year for planting (April-May) and probably twice, including the harvest season (November-December). Beyond this, company foremen had to be prepared to see workers take temporary leaves for a variety of other reasons, including funerals in their home villages and commands from chiefs for other tasks and observances. One rare on-the-spot tally shows that the number of underground wage earners on the job fell to as low as thirty-five during the rainy season of 1891.[53] Eyewitnesses noted again and again that it was rare for wage-earning miners to remain on a single company payroll for more than one year.[54] The WGCMC's management was plagued by desertions and the need to constantly recruit new workers. Few local people developed any permanent loyalty to the company. The tributing arrangement, coupled with payment from project to project by "contract labor," worked for such a long time because it was convenient and because the village mining groups under headmen and Chief Enemil Kuma retained a commitment to the company, even though individuals might come and go.

The lesson from this is that it is important to avoid overly facile teleological conceptualizations in African labor history. Although the Sams and the Gowans brothers were able to recruit some permanent unskilled wage-earners from local Akan men and also to train a number for skilled positions, it is impossible to demonstrate that these workers served as a pathway for expansion of an indigenous "industrial" mines labor force, let alone the nucleus of a "proletariat" for the twentieth century. Furthermore, we should keep in mind that most of the other companies summarized here made no effort whatever to recruit Gold Coastans for unskilled underground labor, but relied almost entirely on immigrant labor from Liberia (see below). The tributing system did not necessarily or inevitably lead to a "higher," or more advanced, level in the ladder of evolutionary capitalism. What is doubly interesting is the way in which the European companies by employing tributors contributed to the traditional flow of the African-controlled overland trade in gold dust to the coast from pits on their own premises.

Wage Payment and Food Sustenance of Workers

Since financial statements for individual Wassa mines are few and incomplete, there is no way of determining precisely what annual percentage of each company's working costs went to wages and what proportion went to other expenses. Going by the limited data available, I estimate that for all the mines roughly 55 percent of annual expenditure was taken up by underground mines labor. Normally transportation (headloading of supplies) and fuel gathering (also essentially labor expenses) were budgeted separately. Whether the firms could have paid their regular African workers at a more remunerative level will probably forever be debated by mining industry spokesmen and their critics. Several modern critics have argued that the companies should have paid a higher wage, not only on grounds of fairness, but on grounds that this would have been the only way to attract and acclimatize local people to regimented wage labor on more permanent footing.[55] But the rubrics of professional accounting theory and standards for mining firms (often ignored or ridiculed in modern social science tracts centering wholly on labor) underscore the fact that in the nineteenth century gold mining throughout the world was normally a low-yield, high-cost extractive operation wherein most firms could barely break even when they paid at ordinary—or what today would be regarded as low—wage levels. Since gold sells at a nearly fixed price, company managers in most countries over the years have put a high priority on paring all working costs to the bone. And because labor was by far the largest item on the cost sheets—up to 70 percent of underground production costs—the wages bill for unskilled labor was invariably the prime target for parsimonious scrutiny by managers and directors.

Obviously this did not excuse or justify some of the extreme and unjust payment policies, which will be discussed presently. There is certainly good reason to scoff at business accounting theory as purely self-serving and to condemn the mine managers for paying the lowest possible wages that the market would bear in order to enhance their personal profits. Beyond this, it is possible to argue that many of the companies would not have been placed in such dire straits with regard to working capital had they marshaled their financial resources better at the outset. On the other hand, it is important to bear in mind that the three major producing companies under examination here had been relatively careful about spending too much of their initial capital stock on purchase of dubious concessions. The heads of the Tarkwa and Aboso, the Wassa (G.C.), and the Gie Appanto mining companies argued convincingly that if their overhead costs (mainly labor) exceeded profits for too long, they would have no alternative but to suspend operations.

These were the principal justifications for what could be called the standard wages policy implemented not only by the Wassa mining companies, but also by a majority of the British coastal merchants and by the colonial government in various services throughout the period surveyed. Even in the twentieth century more powerful and efficient mining companies, like the Ashanti Goldfields Corporation, would continue to use the argument of high overhead costs to keep wages down, even after income from gold production soared and profits began to mount.

What kind of evaluation can we make of these wage rates? Were they too low, as scholars of a radical persuasion have averred? The usual ways of judging the fairness of wage rates in a particular industry at a particular point in history is to compare those wages with rates paid for similar manual work in other sectors of the economy and to relate wages to prices for food and other basic necessities—in other words, "real wages." A glance at the ordinary scale of wages paid to unskilled Akan mine workers (see table 7.4, below) shows that "starting" pay rates for underground men—average about one shilling per day—was higher than that paid by some coastal merchants for men willing to work as porters, warehousemen, and other unskilled positions at this same period. For example, John Sarbah of Cape Coast was paying young men 7d. per day for picking palm kernels up-country in 1877.[56] At the same time basic food prices had not risen by very much over the previous thirty to forty years; nor were they to rise at a very fast rate in the decades ahead. It is true that some commentators spoke of inflationary prices at Tarkwa during the peak years of the gold boom. But this applied mainly to imported European merchandise (such as liquor, cloth, and tinned goods) rather than to African vegetable crops, which were the staples of the average persons diet. By whose standards should we judge what was a just wage—modern expatriate scholars or Ghanaians who lived at that time? Oral interviews with retired miners and farmers in the 1970s and 1980s, who remembered early-twentieth-

century food prices, confirm what figures in the colonial records suggest: that "everything was much cheaper then." One of my oldest
informants, Nana Akodaa Kwadwo Ofor, who remembered life at the
time of the Yaa Asentewa War (1900), said that in the early days about
three pence worth of fish would last an individual for three or four
meals.[57] Other informants among ex-miners who were active during a
later period said that unskilled workers' wages, which remained at
about 1s.6d. to 2s.6d. per day, were "adequate." "You could buy
sufficient articles of food with your daily wage and have some left over
to save as well," they said. Another retired miner recalled that you
could buy yams, even in the mining towns, for as little as halfpenny
each.[58] Other basic foods like plantains and cassava were even cheaper.
Miners could either buy yams or other food already cooked by market
women or at "chop houses" or stalls in the town, or they could buy
fresh vegetables, meat, or fish and cook it themselves. Some miners even
grew their own food at small plots in the bush outside the mining
towns. If these facts were generally true for the period from 1920 to
1950, they were probably accurate also for the late nineteenth century.
Thus, we would have to conclude that for the indigenous Akan miners
of the late nineteenth century, the relationship of wages to prices was
reasonable for that time. One might question whether these wages were
still sufficient if a miner brought his wife and children into his mining
village. However, to bring wives to Tarkwa was not a common practice
in the 1880s and 1890s, and informants did not mention this as a
problem, even for the twentieth century.

Given the relative economic stagnation, it is hardly shocking that the
mining companies, like most other businesses in a similar predicament,
took advantage of local conditions by continuing to pay African miners
at as low a rate as the traffic would bear. To get the additional unskilled
African workers, which might be required at critical points, individual
companies and promoters might provide very small short-term wage
inducements and raises; but these were offered mainly on an occasional
and ad hoc basis and then reduced or rolled back altogether with later
recruits. Over time the wages paid to local unskilled underground
shovel boys were seldom sustained at more than 1s.4d. per day. Of
course the lack of any significant class consciousness or collective
feelings of group oppression (let alone trade union organization) also
militated against mine workers petitioning for pay increases. If a man
disliked working conditions under European supervision at the mines,
he had the recourse of walking off the job.

Skilled Workers

Many West Africans qualified for skilled positions, such as carpenters and blacksmiths or as machine operators, at rates from 2s.3d. to 3s. per day, or about £3.10 to £4.10 per month. Again, these rates varied slightly with each company. A majority of these skilled workers came from outside the southwestern gold-mining districts. Along with Sierra Leoneans from Freetown, some of the best carpenters, stone masons, and blacksmiths were recruited from Accra and Akuapem, a fact traceable in part to the special training in skilled crafts available at the schools of the Swiss Basel mission that were concentrated in the southeastern region. Men from central coastal towns like Cape Coast, Saltpond, and Elmina (with their dislike of working underground) gradually moved into positions as machine operators, office clerks, and chemical treatment men.[59] Small numbers of immigrant Cornish miners from Britain, renowned for their skills as timbermen and blastmen, were still recruited for skilled underground positions. But skilled European miners dwindled in number in this period. Concerned about the high costs and high invaliding and death rates traceable to malaria, some mine managers had the sense to recognize the practical necessity of hiring greater numbers of Africans to replace the much higher paid expatriates as skilled workers and technicians.

The Migrant Workers from the Kru Coast of Liberia

We must not forget, however, that outside the boundaries of the F. and A. Swanzy-owned Aja Bippo, Cinnamon Bippo, and Swanzy Estates mines, the bulk of the Wassa mines labor force was made up of the migrant Kru men from Liberia. Based on the available data for 1886 (shown in table 7.3), these hardy workers from the Kru Coast, together with their close neighbors the Bassa and Grebo men, made up from 67 to 70 percent of the total labor forces, including skilled and unskilled, at all the mines. Clearly they were the backbone of both the underground labor force and of the surface unskilled work force at most of the mines. If we exclude the Wassa (G.C.) Mining Company and the other Swanzy-owned ventures where, as just noted, there was a greater effort to recruit indigenous labor (whether as wage earners, day-to-day contract workers, or tributors) then the proportion of the Liberian contingent in the overall mines labor force was even higher, namely about 81 percent.

Map 7.2. Republic of Liberia, including the Bassa, Kru, and Grebo areas.

The "Exploitation" Question

In this study I have been careful to avoid ideologically loaded words, such as *subjugation* or *exploitation*, often applied haphazardly in some labor histories, without any specification or comparative criteria. These terms by their very usage tend to convey an assumption about labor relationships under colonial capitalism without comparative standards of measurement and the backing of solid evidence. If, however, we follow David Landes and take as our definition the acquisition of products or of labor services at prices well under the going market rate,[60] then there may be a factual basis for a charge of exploitation in the case of the Kru (including Bassa and Grebo) miners in the Gold

Coast in this period. Taking the lowest wage levels for ordinary Gold Coastans employed as unskilled underground workers at the mines from 1877 to 1900 at 12d. per day or £1.10.0 per month, and the equivalent for the ordinary imported Kru unskilled worker at 8d. per day or £1.0.0 per month, then we see that even the lowest category Gold Coast unskilled mines worker received half again as much pay as his Kru or Bassa counterpart. (This assumes a seven-day work week and a thirty-day month, which was the norm in this period.) True, the Kru and Bassa men received subsistence from the companies in the form of one cup of rice daily and 6d. per week for fish money. This did not amount to much; and close examination shows that the rice ra-tion—which had to be imported—was not always delivered on time, or even provided according to agreement. Furthermore, Gold Coastans occasionally could advance up the labor ladder to skilled positions, so that the averages of 12d. per day and £1.0.0 per month, quoted above for Akan men, errs on the low side and were not immutable. There is no record of any Kru worker ever having achieved a pay raise from a company simply as a consequence of good work or seniority—any such notion would have undermined the entire group migrant labor system. The Liberians continued as unskilled laborers, either above or below ground. Undoubtedly, the most exploited group in terms of pay were the Kru surface unskilled laborers (fuel gatherers, loaders, porters, clean-up men, etc.), working at a paltry 3½ to 4d. per day plus subsistence. This was one-half, sometimes even one-quarter, the rate paid to Gold Coastans for the same heavy above-ground work (see table 7.4).

In response, the mining companies contended that no one had forced the Kru and Bassa men to take on this foreign employment (still, one would like to know more about recruiting conditions under headmen in Liberia), that they were used to a lower standard of living in their homelands, and that management had incurred additional burdens and responsibilities as well. The Kru and Bassa men received free steamship passage to the Gold Coast from Liberia and return, paid for by each contracting company. In addition the mining firms had to pay both an official tax and an agency fee to the government of the Republic of Liberia for assisting with recruitment. At the same time, the distance from the southeastern Kru Coast—main embarkation point, Grand Sess. (see map 7.2) to Axim or Cape Coast was not that far; and the mining companies got a low rate for shipping sizable blocks of people in steerage on a regular basis. Kru men were normally engaged in gangs of a dozen to sixteen. On the average, the governmental tax and agency fee imposed by the Liberian Government, coupled with the shipping fees, cost the mining companies about £2 per person. However, one knowledgeable miner added that it was common and perfectly legal for the companies to deduct the Liberian government tax from each Kru man's wages after he reached the Gold Coast.[61] Furthermore, we can safely conclude that mining companies would never have continued to use Kru and Bassa men unless there had been demonstrable savings on labor costs over the long run that easily absorbed the costs of steamship passage. Besides, the transport of large blocks of workers by ship from such a nearby country brought numerous ancillary advantages, including ease of recruitment in Liberia; continuity of flow, coupled with malleability and the maintenance of discipline on and off the job through use of Kru headmen. Companies could further reduce their shipping costs by inducing a few Kru men to stay on for a second year. If a Kru man decided to leave the job (desertion) before the end of his contract period, and a fair number did, then companies were exempted from paying for return steamship passage altogether (see photos of Kru men at the end of this chapter).

More than this, there were cases where certain mine managers deliberately and dishonestly reneged on their promises to repay the return passage of Kru men to Liberia, leaving the poor men stranded on the beach. As if this were not enough, it was reported that "a very considerable portion of the pay of each 'Krooboy' finds its way into the pouch of the headman."[62] One wonders whether the expatriate mine managers could not have exercised greater oversight to prevent such infractions? In the absence of regular inspection tours and close knowledge of mining company personnel by permanently stationed government district officers at Tarkwa, this was unlikely. Set aside in their own squalid wards on the edges of towns, the Kru men had even less guarantee of minimum standards of housing, health, and sanitation than were available to other African unskilled labor. During the period covered here, Kru and Bassa men had no protection or redress for grievances at English law against European employers for infractions on the job or breach of contract. Since agreements were normally arranged through their headmen, there was seldom any absolute proof that labor recruits even understood clearly the terms of their work agreements. At a time when the Gold Coast government was passing legislation insisting that Gold Coastans employed by foreign colonial governments or companies abroad should have all work contracts read and explained to them by British officials,[63] there was nothing commensurate to protect the interests of foreign labor traveling for work to the Gold Coast. In the records I found few instances of pleas presented or damages awarded in British colonial courts on behalf of Kru or Bassa workers as aggrieved parties in suits for breach of contract against a European employer. So greatly did British mining and commercial interests covet the services of these hardworking West Africans that as the compass of imperialism widened in the 1890s, there was talk of state action to establish permanent Kru labor settlements in the Gold Coast.[64] All the above data contrasted tremendously, of course, with the pay of Europeans in the Gold Coast, which ran from £10 to £15 per month for ordinary miners to £15 to £20 for skilled craftsmen.

General Treatment of Workers

Even for locally recruited labor these early decades were not without worker discontent over company delays on wage payment, use of physical punishment, and other forms of coercion. Most harsh acts in the name of discipline occurred randomly, depending on the type of worker infraction complained of and the attitudes and inclinations of particular shift bosses. One government report stated that "fining" was the most common method by which the mining companies disciplined their workers, even though strictly speaking this was illegal under English law. Given the lack of any group consciousness, the most difficult task for the mining historian is the attempt to guess what went on in the minds of the thousands of African underground mine workers, who were mainly illiterate and who left almost no record of their feelings about working conditions or their responses to tough expatriate supervision. It may be, in comparison with the twentieth century—when more rapid machine crushing and chemical extraction meant extremely exacting discipline in meeting precise timetables—that working conditions between 1877 and 1895 were somewhat more relaxed.[65] On the other hand, it can be argued that because so many indigenous people were totally unfamiliar with corporate regimentation, the mere barking of orders and threat of physical force were all the more jarring and intimidating to them. And, I would contend that the frequency of such acts increased as work crews on shifts became more regimented and impersonal in the decades ahead. At a majority of mines in the first half of the twentieth century, flogging with a birch rod across the backside was still the usual punishment for laxity on the job.[66] In the absence of any strong action by government commissioners to prosecute deserting mine workers under the master and servant laws, most companies continued to justify docking wages as a legitimate method of forcing miners to complete their terms of contract. Furthermore, failure of individual workers to meet quotas for a set number of working days per month might be followed by corresponding deductions from pay. Even if a worker was absent due to genuine illness, his wages might be forfeited. The effect of this was to induce African underground men to exert themselves even when they were ill or unfit for service. Other examples of delayed or canceled pay were, as we shall see, the result of downright dishonest dealings by unprofitable or bankrupt companies. The weaker the company's capitalization, and the more marginal its productive operations, the greater the temptation to cut corners by trumping up excuses for total default in payment of just wages.

This by no means exhausts the present effort to reconstruct the realities of working conditions at the Wassa mines in the 1880s and 1890s. There were many other abuses that received less notice at the time—mainly because they were commonly accepted practices at mines throughout the tropical world and partly because there were few social reform groups in West Africa alert to the needs of mine workers and in a position to gather information on working conditions. Hardships included the following. (1) Workers were forced to work underground barefooted, thus increasing their vulnerability to foot and leg injuries. (2) Miners had to buy their own carbide lamps. (3) At most mines African laborers worked at least six days per week on long shifts and often on Sundays as well; there were no days off during the year except at Christmas. (4) As noted earlier, there were no hospital beds for sick African workers in the early days. (5) Good housing for African workers was still lacking. (6) Sanitary conveniences were totally inadequate. (7) Quite apart from designated punishments with a stick, workers might receive random cuffs about the head and other body blows, coupled with racist slurs from shift bosses for alleged slow work.[67]

MANAGEMENT AT THE WGCMC

Stock Manipulations by Insiders: The Cinnamon Bippo Mines and the Aja Bippo Mines

Despite its reputation for sound management, the Swanzy group, like every other Wassa mining enterprise, also sought profit through "share pushing" and market manipulations; and their involvement with James

Table 7.4
Average Pay Scales for Workers in Wassa in the 1880s

Category	Avg. Daily Wage (or Equivalent)	Monthly Wage
1 European Skilled Surface Workers (Carpenters, blacksmiths, fitters, etc.)	£3. to £5. per week	£15 to £20 per month
2 European Skilled Underground Workers (timber men, blasting men, etc.)	£2.10 to £3.10 s per week	£10 to £15 per month
3 African Skilled Surface Workers (carpenters, blacksmiths, etc.)	2s.3d to 3s per day	
4 African Unskilled Underground Workers (hammer boys, shovel boys, etc.)	1s to 1s4d per day	
Akan Miners[a]	1s to 1s4d per day	
Kru headmen		£2 per month
Kru underground miners	8d. per day plus subsistence	
5 Unskilled Surface Workers (loaders, fuel gatherers, etc.)[b]		
Fante surface workers	8d to 1s per day plus subsistence	
Kru surface laborers	3 1/2 d. to 4 1/2 d. per day plus subsistence	

[a] Akan miners: includes Wassas, Nzemans, Fantes and others

[b] Thes could also be paid accoding to 'piece work.'

Sources: Same as under Table 7.3 (above).

Irvine in several questionable speculative schemes revealed a network of alliances between practically all the British Wassa concessionaires, whatever their claims to proprietorial independence. Most of my comments on productive mining by the WGCMC have focused on the Aja Bippo main reef. But in the mid-1880s the company also tried to turn to account the 4,000-square-yard Cinnamon Bippo property, which William Crocker had purchased directly from Chief Enemil Kuma in 1884 (see map 7.1, above). As we have seen, Swanzy group kept a tighter rein over its mining operations than most of the other London-based companies. For example, they did not proceed through independent concessions brokers or agents on the coast, but rented their mining lands directly from the chiefs. As a result they avoided exorbitant prices for purchase of their leases; and they protected themselves against paying a substantial rent until after proof of a paying yield. The original contract for Cinnamon Bippo provided that Chief Enemil would receive a measly £21 12s. per year, to be increased to £180 per year only upon commencement of operations. Meanwhile Crocker died, and his executors, William Cleaver and the ubiquitous Irvine, sold the Cinnamon Bippo lease to the Swanzy-controlled Cinnamon Bippo Gold Mining Company in January 1888 for a preposterous £65,000 worth of shares in the new company.[68] This appears to have been mere paper shuffling; there is no indication whatsoever that any new capital was invested in the property. It may well be that the Swanzy firm hoped to turn Cinnamon Bippo into a producing mine that could stand immediately on its own. At the same time it is clear that by forming a new company, Irvine and Cleaver wanted to profit by the unloading of overpriced new shares in a venture they hoped would be associated in the public's mind with other more successful Swanzy ventures.

Despite appointment of the Sam brothers as superintendents, the Cinnamon Bippo mine never got off the ground. Between 1890 and 1892 the Cinnamon Bippo garnered £6,150 in gold while expenses exceeded £8,000. In 1893 production sank to £3,000, and the next year still lower.[69] Though not a total failure, the Cinnamon Bippo proved to be a drag on the Swanzy firm's mining interests. Nothing better illustrates the bursting of the hot-air balloon than the fact that its properties were sold off to the parent Wassa (G.C.) Mining Company in March 1895 for a trifling £153.[70]

By contrast the Aja Bippo Mine, also placed under the stewardship of the Gowans brothers and the day-to-day supervision of the Sams, proved to be a long-run success. These teams of engineering brothers were tough taskmasters. We have talked at length about their schedule of wages for unskilled African labor. At the same time the company continued to reduce costs by trimming its European staff to the bone. By 1889 there was only one European on the job at any of the Swanzy firm's four operating mines: the Aja Bippo, the Cinnamon Bippo, Crockerville, and the Swanzy Estates. Again, we should keep in mind that the firm's effective use of tributors drawn from the local Wassa population also helped greatly in keeping working costs down. An average of about 240 African laborers, including 33 skilled machine attendants, were employed at Aja Bippo (out of which only 30 were imported Kru men), and the management reported that expenses were held down to about £350 per month.

Technological Improvements at the Wassa
(G.C.) Mining Company, 1885–1898

The Wassa Company's extraction plant was reliable for the precyanide age; and the staff was able to handle machine breakdowns better than most of its rivals. In contrast to engineers at many of the surrounding mines, who often lost sight of their sharply angled and twisting reefs or who found that the gold content of ore petered out the further operations were extended, the fortunate managers at the WGCMC found that "the ore improved the deeper down they went." By the mid-1890s the enlarged crushing mill consisted of twenty-two heads of stamps, with a primary battery of ten 750-pound crushers and a second twelve-head battery of 550 pounds each. The two were driven by a single seventy-six-horsepower steam engine, while the recovery plant, using the mercury amalgamation process, was powered by a light-weight eight-horsepower Belleville engine.[71] Under the Sams' direction this firm, like its rival, the Tarkwa and Aboso, also built a tramway with a steam locomotive and a train of wagons for transporting wood fuel to its boilers from the surrounding bush. Even more important at this juncture was the installation's relative effectiveness in dealing with flooding problems at the lower levels. During the early 1880s the company had proceeded only a bit deeper than old-time African hard-rock miners before being stymied by groundwater. But by 1886 introduction of compact "sinking type" pumping machines (see photo) enabled the company to open up 586 yards of rock or an additional 1,170 tons of ore for extraction at a tunnel previously submerged.[72] That the WGCMC had installed the most effective precyanide reduction gear and treatment plant of any of the companies was reflected in its capacity to glean gold from a large backlog of tailings (residue from previous gold extraction), which most rival mines could not handle at this stage.

Whereas some Tarkwa firms tried to gouge out the richest sections of veins straightaway in order to impress shareholders with early revenues, the WGCMC continued to proceed scientifically and methodically by following a set plan and sampling a variety of outcrops before commencing new drives. By 1889 four shafts (the Swanzy, the Cleaver, the Bishop, and, subsequently, the Sam Shaft) plus four adit levels were in regular use at Aja Bippo, and the Gold Coast governor reported that "much stoping has been done." As a consequence, the Aja Bippo plant crushed some

18,000 tons of ore, yielding about £25,000 in the four years between 1885 and the beginning of 1889.[73] The company's investment in the best available machinery had clearly paid off. Though getting rid of ground-water remained a constant bugbear, overall performance improved steadily from 1892 to 1897, in terms of first-rate development work, monthly volume of ore crushed, and yields of gold per ton of ore. As a direct result of the installation of an air compressor and the company's first pneumatic percussion rock drills in 1897, all the main shafts reached 200 feet or more in depth by the turn of the century. At the end of the period covered in this book, the weight of gold extracted in one month was in some cases double that garnered during two-month segments in 1885. At the same time the recovery rate of about $1\frac{1}{4}$ to $1\frac{1}{3}$ ounces of gold per ton of ore mined was more than double the average rate (about $\frac{1}{2}$ oz. per ton) of twelve years earlier.

General Assessment: The Wassa (G.C.) Mining Company

No company accomplished more at this early stage in the history of Gold Coast mechanized mining. It is certainly true for each of the mines covered here that in the absence of cyanide treatment, a sizable portion of the fine gold in the tailings remained unrecoverable. Still, this company had been extremely lucky in getting its hands on the richest segment of gold reef in the entire Tarkwa-Aboso district. Though they were less confident about the Tarkwa district as a whole, experts from South Africa said that the banket ore on the WGCMC's properties was equivalent to the average, if not the best, on the Rand. Modest about British prospecting accomplishments, Swanzy and his managers were quick to acknowledge that the most valuable segment of the entire Aja Bippo lode lay directly under the old African workings. With further deepening of the Swanzy main shaft to the 250-foot level by the end of the 1890s, assayists were confident that more than 20,000 tons of gold ore, worth up to £160,000, would become accessible.[74] By a combination of reasonably good long-range planning and a workable, if archaic, system of labor relations, plus the buffer of sustained financial support from the London-based Swanzy mercantile firm, the Wassa Company appeared to have surmounted some of the transportation, technical, and budgetary difficulties that brought so many of its competitors to grief.

As already noted, the Wassa Mining Company was also the first to move slowly from crude ad hoc, decision making to systematic management involving surveys of workable reefs; applications of up-to-date engineering techniques to underground excavations, long-range develop-

Table 7.5

Crushing Schedule and Gold Yields for the Wassa (G.C.) Mining Company
January–June 1897

Month	Ore Tonnage	Gold Weight (oz.)	Avg. Yield of Gold per Ton of Ore (oz.)	Yields Value (£)
January	491 tons	751.25 oz.	1.53	2,930.13.1
February	539.5 tons	7425 oz.	1.36	2,897.8.3
March	537 tons	643.75 oz.	1.20	2,513.12.6
April	448.5 tons	547.75 oz.	1.22	2,139.19.8
May	466 tons	645.67 oz.	1.39	2,521.12.11
June	394 tons	530.9 oz.	1.35	2,073.17.9
Totals	2,876 tons	3,861.817 oz.	1.34	15,077.42

Source: R. A. Freeman, *Travels and Life in Ashanti and Gyaman* (London, 1898, 1967), 535.

ment for layout of ore reserves, and use of improved pulverization and reduction technology to obtain a better return per ton of ore. Part of this was traceable to careful direction by the London Managing Director, Frederick Crocker. Not content with the usual stock market machinations and grandiose boardroom proclamations, he spent three months on the Gold Coast studying the underground works and recovery techniques of various mines in order to better understand local operations. At the same time Crocker was never overbearing or over demanding; and he continued to delegate maximum authority to the men on the spot.

Crocker was also a responsible company accountant, untypical for that day in his commitment to full financial disclosures in semiannual meetings with all the members. For the benefit of shareholders he drew up an itemized list of the depths and distances excavated in the Aja Bippo's main shafts, the estimated gold-yielding value of exposed ore ready for excavation, and the predictable financial returns on ore crushed up to a given date. The Swanzy interest was also one of the first to make frequent and effective use of telegraphic communications after the West African cable was completed to Cape Coast and Accra from Madeira in 1886.[75] Cable messages to and from London enabled the field managers to report emergency supply needs and helped directors to diagnose weaknesses in company operations in the incipient stages. There is no doubt that cablegrams on gold shipments also affected the prices of company stock on the open market, as seen in the rising value of WGCMC shares in this period.[76] Between 1882 and 1898 the mine produced 45,648 ounces of gold valued at £177,819. These totals were described at the end of the century as "a better result than had been obtained from any of the other mines in the Tarkwa district up to this time."[77] What needs to be born in mind is that every year the company directors had to make huge outlays for new and up-to-date machinery (£1,000 to £2,000 at a single order was common) in order to maintain production levels. Crocker tried to compensate for these outlays by further cuts in administrative and office costs, but he could do no better than average cuts of around £100 per year. Under these circumstances any company considered it a great success when they could break even. From the date of its incorporation through 1896 revenues for the Wassa (G.C.) Mining Company totaled £181,433, as against a total outlay of £163,243.[78] The role of local African entrepreneurship in opening up the Akan region's resources to capitalism, though seldom adequately credited in the London financial press or history books of the day, did not pass unnoticed in the company's printed reports. At the close of one general meeting we read of the terse but inspiring comment: "The Chairman proposed, and Mr. Swanzy seconded, a hearty vote of thanks to Mr. Sam, the manager, and the staff for their untiring zeal. The motion was carried."[79]

Despite these accolades, there were still serious problems to be worked out. A turn-of-the-century report in the *Mining Journal, Railway and Commercial Gazette,* praised the work of the Wassa Mining Company, but with reservations. That the company had survived a period of heavy indebtedness was due entirely to a hefty and timely loan bailout by the parent F. and A. Swanzy trading firm with minimal interest charges. Much has been made of the fact that this was the only mining company of the period to pay a dividend,[80] but the records show that only one dividend of 5 percent was paid to shareholders between 1882 and 1900.[81] Inspectors later raised questions about the solidity of development work (including timbering) in the mine shafts, and they expressed concern about the quantity and value of staked-out ore reserves that would be readily available in the years ahead.[82] If such criticisms touched raw nerves with the managers of this successful company, one can surmise their even greater pertinence to the less well endowed mines of the district. Again, judgments about the sophistication of development work and mining techniques have to be placed in the perspective of what was attainable in the humid tropics at this juncture in history. Without a doubt work at Aja Bippo was superior

Table 7.6

Gold Production of the Wassa (G.C.) Mining Company's Aja Bippo
Mine,[a] 1882-1898

Year	Ore Crushed tons	Bar Gold oz.	Standard Gold oz.	Gold Yield per ton oz.	Value per Account Sales[b] £	s.	d
1882	120	147.18	155.52	1.32	604	13	5
1883	516	463.32	477.05	.90	1,855	3	10
1884	1,363	898.39	931.20	.73	3,622	4	2
1885	4,276	1,468.20	1,409.13	.44	5,478	7	5
1886	2,320	1,470.69	1,419.10	.67	5,517	8	0
1887	2,716	1,927.09	1,901.75	.70	7,397	15	10
1888	3,410	1,990.15	1,760.06	.55	6,802	1	10
1889	4,137	1,928.48	1,902.13	.48	7,407	11	5
1890	2,515	1,159.02	1,175.23	.40	4,570	17	8
1891	2,747	1,555.70	1,618.43	.60	6,300	2	5
1892	2,190	2,011.62	2,051.85	.90	7,989	7	7
1893	2,753	4,178.99	4,386.45	1.58	17,105	17	5
1894	3,384	3,569.05	3,747.82	1.107	14,604	4	9
1895	3,848	3,726.45	3,872.60	1.22	15,090	5	11
1896	4,027	6,581.80	6,959.17	1.728	27,096	19	7
1897	5,799	6,967.95	7,255.00	1.251	28,300	15	8
1898	4,162	4,433.50	4,625.94	1.11	18,045	3	9
Totals	50,285	44,477.58	45,648.43	.907	177,819	0	8

[a] These figures exclude returns from the company's Cinnamon Bippo and other mines.

[b] At the rate of £3-10.72s per oz.

Sources: Rept. on the Wassa (C.G.) Mining Co. Ltd. in The Mining Journal Railway and Commercial Gazette, 16 June, 1894, 650. Also Rept. by Stanley Clay, "Progress of the Company," Encl. in Wassa (G.C.) Mining Co. to C.O., 9 Mar. 1900; above.

to any other Gold Coast mine of the prerailway age; but the twentieth century would bring more mining engineers with extensive underground experience from South Africa, Australia, and the United States who would judge Gold Coast mining by even stricter standards.

THE ESSAMAN AND GIE APPANTO MINES OF THE HEMAN (PRESTEA) DISTRICT

One other significant set of gold mines that received major attention in the period from 1885 to 1898 lay near the villages of Essaman and Prestea in the Heman district of the Upper Ankobra River, about twenty-two miles northwest of the main Tarkwa excavations (see map 7.3). I noted in chapter 2 that the Heman district constituted a separate mineralogical subzone whose hard quartzitic formations differed totally from the Tarkwa banket. That the strata of the Prestea-Brumasi gold belt over eons had been subjected to severe faulting with numerous overthrusts and shears into which gold and other elements had intruded meant that miners experienced great difficulty in following the line of strike. Though well known to traditional African miners and to the Dutch (who had built a small gold-trading station there), Prestea (also listed as Essaman on some early maps) had escaped the infestation of claim jumpers descending on the Tarkwa area in 1877 through 1882, partly because the location of the richest mines had been kept under tight wraps of secrecy by Chief Kofi Kyei. Twentieth-century geological surveys confirmed that the thickness and persistence of gold ore channels between the strata were unusually promising at both the Prestea and nearby Brumasi sites.[83]

In chapter 4 we saw that the first capitalist miner to sense the importance of this district was an African, Swanzy Essien, a Fante from Cape Coast, in the employ of Dr. Africanus Horton, whose initial tunnel, called the Essien Adit, laid a base for future operations. Horton subsequently sold the concession to the London-based Wassa and Ahanta Syndicate — directed by James Labouchere, Henry Tolputt, and Thomas Gillespie — which delegated control to its subsidiary, the Essaman Mining Company. Attempting to avoid the heavy expenditures and workload required for deep-shaft work, Labouchere determined that all the early reef penetrations at these mines would be by hillside adits. In 1888 the Essaman directors placed management in competent hands of a trained British mining engineer, George MacDuff. Employing nine Europeans and 215 Africans (the bulk of whom were Kru and Bassa men), he drove a second tunnel 490 feet into the lode. Twelve stamps were set in operation and places for another twelve constructed. At this time the Essaman Company also controlled the neighboring Brumasi and Kwa Badu concessions, but did not develop them (see map 7.3).[84]

Capital and Concessions

Lacking the capital for sustained underground development, the Essaman Company then made a number of ill-advised expenditures that drained its liquid capital and forced it to sell out to the better-capitalized Gie Appanto Mining Company in 1890. The Gie Appanto paid off all the older firm's debts (£5,000) and Essaman shareholders re-

Map 7.3. Heman-Prestea mining subdistrict of Wassa-Fiase on the River
Ankobra. During the period surveyed in the book this district contained the
sites of the Essaman, Gie Appanto, the Prestea, and Brumasi mines. From
Gold Coast Government, Geological Survey.

ceived (as a group) 25,000 shares in the better-rated Gie Appanto at a
ratio of three to five. The three top directors of the Essaman venture,
Labouchere, Tolputt, and Gillespie, retained positions on the board of
the second company. Essaman stockholders expressed disdain over
their compensation for loss of ownership in the older company, a
decision in which they had no voice, because, they argued, the Gie
Appanto had gained a tremendous advantage from the Essaman's richer
and more extensive properties.[85] Their tune changed when they saw the
market price of the new Gie Appanto shares rise markedly and learned
of the far greater borrowing leverage that this better organized company could command in the City of London.

The Gie Appanto Company had arrived late in the game, having
been chartered in 1886 to take up an earlier concession leased from
Chief Kyei of Heman by Louis Wyatt, the former Gold Coast government official. One key point about African-European relations deserves
special mention here. From the record this appears to have been one of
the few transactions of the time in Wassa where a traditional ruler
received anything even remotely approaching fair compensation for
mineral rights from a European entrepreneur. For the fifty-year lease of
a moderately sized mining property, the young Chief Kyei (see photo
at the end of chap. 8) was to receive £200 per month or £2,400 per
year (not high enough of course, but far better than the rents many
companies paid for even larger and richer mines).[86] Beginning with an
investment of £35,000, the Gie Appanto, after its takeover of the
Essaman properties, steadily increased its share capital to £110,000 by
1891, of which 80,000 shares eventually were called up. Not all these
shares were paid for in full, of course, and, in an ominous sign for the
future, the company expanded its plant and machinery largely by
borrowing through the issue of debentures, which stood as a first
mortgage on future profits.[87]

Without a doubt, the driving force behind the early development of
Heman-Prestea as a mining center was Louis Wyatt, the first manager of
the Gie Appanto, who had made many trips to the middle and upper
Ankobra, while serving as Gold Coast Commissioner for the Axim district. Here was a small example of a bridge between the "gentlemanly
capitalist" cliques of the City of London and overseas business expansion
through the assistance of an aggressive "civil servant-on-the-spot" in
West Africa. Wyatt had been a well-informed and hard-working district
magistrate. Note, however, that the connection was less between mining
capitalists and civil service elites in Whitehall than between mining cap-

italists and officials in West Africa. Wyatt had seen no point in allowing his familiarity with the Akan peoples and hands-on experience in the Wassa goldfields to go to waste while newcomers turned a profit. Moreover, like Ferdinand, Fitzgerald, Horton, and others, he had been an active promoter and agent of strengthened colonial administrative control in the hinterland for purposes of economic development. Sometime in the mid-1880s he got in touch with prospective mining investors in London about floating the new company.

While there is no evidence of impropriety or a direct conflict of interest (Wyatt resigned from the colonial service before undertaking his duties with the Gie Appanto), there is no doubt that he maximized his prior knowledge of the country as well as contacts with government personnel to further the company's advantage. More than a mere factotum, he became the leading entrepreneur at Prestea. As a trained engineer, he received 7,250 shares and the managing directorship in the new Gie Appanto Company, and he and took the lead in organizing the sale of Kofi Kyei's lease to the new venture. Chief Kyei undoubtedly trusted Wyatt who next surrounded himself with a board of directors that included well-heeled stockbrokers and bankers of some prominence in the City of London. These included Sir Samuel Cawston (chairman), 7,633 shares by 1893; George Edward Burnett (stockbroker) 4,782 shares; and John and F. Baker, 6,250 shares. Minor shareholders included the familiar names of E. T. McCarthy and the African founder, Swanzy Essien.[88] As noted earlier, only the top-producing Wassa companies attracted a thin veneer of those higher-rung British investors that P. J. Cain and A. G. Hopkins have dubbed the "gentleman capitalists." The plutocratic mien of this and other company directorships at this stage was still as nothing compared to the assemblages of worthies that would be drawn to Gold Coast colonial mining directorates of the post-1900 period.

Operations at Gie Appanto/Prestea

The series of companies that dug for gold in the Prestea district had one singular advantage over every other producing company of 1880s and 1890s, namely, ease of transportation based on canoe transport and close proximity to landings on the River Ankobra. For these the poor quality of Wassa roads did not matter so much: the main Gie Appanto installations lay less than a mile (a mere twenty-minute walk) from the river's edge. Wyatt had traveled up the river scores of times and understood the rhythms of its flow. We have seen how river journeys, particularly at low water, could be tough and dangerous. But during the rainy season, when water levels were high, steam launches and large canoes could carry machinery all the way from Axim to Prestea in about sixteen hours. Wyatt's experience had positive effects on the emplacement of stamp batteries in fair working order and thus on the operating efficiency during the first several years.[89] He had the good sense to hire an able assistant in Will Swift, mentioned earlier in this chapter, as deputy manager. A trained mining engineer, well seasoned to West African conditions, Swift had worked for both the African Gold Coast Company and Swanzy's Aja Bippo Mine before joining the Gie Appanto in 1887. The two men ensured that machinery of the latest and most effective type was installed at their mine. Use of some of the first steam percussion drills in boring holes for dynamite blasting enabled them, like the WGCMC, to sink deep shafts. Of course, all this saddled the company with heavy costs. The Gie Appanto was one of the first to employ a full-time physician on its premises, a Dr. Martin of Edinburgh, to look after the medical needs of the mining population.

Swift, whose wiry appearance matched a tough constitution, had a reputation as an indefatigable worker (see photo at the end of this chapter). Though constantly plagued by malaria, he shunned all talk of rest leaves and, according to reports, never allowed the disease to affect his work. Moving quickly, he helped to construct a sawmill, erected a large thirty-foot steam boiler and set up a second battery of ten heads of heavy-weight 750-lb. stamps. Next he gouged out another new adit parallel to the old Swanzy Essien drive 459 feet into the heart of the gold lode. And whereas earlier the "Mono," or main shaft, at the Appanto mine had descended to just forty feet, Swift in two years work bored down to the 160 ft. level. On his first tour of all the Wassa mines in 1889, W. B. Griffith, the new governor, was especially impressed with the rapid work at this mine during its first two years of development. He descended the main shaft by steam-powered cable lift and noted that the gold reef had a nearly uniform thickness of five feet, bulging to twelve feet in some places.[90] On its face this gold site, like the WGCMC, was taking on many of the features of a twentieth-century mining installation. But two essential devices for a truly modern plant were missing: cyanide treatment vats for high-percentage gold extraction and differential steam pumps for sucking up deep-level groundwater. The last of these two missing elements proved fateful for the company's survival.

Technical Problems and Financial Structures

Without any doubt the combined Gie Appanto-Prestea-Brumasi properties comprised one of the most valuable mineral subzones of Ghana; but the early promises of sustained productivity and development could not be maintained in the prerailway age. Two thousand tons of ore were crushed in 1889, and from this the first gold was extracted and exported. Unfortunately, by the time the Gie Appanto began to move to the high production stage in 1891 and 1892, the lurking bogeys of effective mining—bad weather, rusting machinery, heavy groundwater seepage, flooding, incapacitation of miners from illness and injury, labor desertions, and above all, heavy expenditures—ominously began to close in. To make matters worse, Swift, by now broken in health, was ordered to leave for England. Almost immediately, his successors, who were neither so resilient nor so reliable, began to encounter problems. Some of these were no doubt personal and managerial, but the majority of obstacles were still geological and environmental. As noted earlier the Prestea deposits were hard-quartz "reef gold," not Tarkwa banket. Early gold winnings were mainly in surface deposits. Once the above-surface adit levels and shallow underground levels were mined out, deep underground work became frustrated by dips in the reef, which were unpredictable and difficult to follow, and expenses shot up. There is considerable variation in the scattered data on annual gold returns for the Gie Appanto Company culled from different sources (see table 7.7 for a synthesis). If we take average production figures for the eight years from 1889 through 1896, we get an annual yield of approximately £1,050 worth of fine gold per month. Yet at the same time, monthly expenses at the Gie Appanto's mines were running about £1,200 to £1,500 per month.[91] This meant that the firm was operating at considerable loss, since not even those figures took account of all administrative charges.

Details on the Gie Appanto's flagging production by 1899 were a mirror of the struggles faced by all other companies on the West African mining frontier in the pre-railing age. The lion's share of expenditures went for underground development work and repairs, not for ordinary operating costs. With each turn of the wheel there appeared a recrudescence of old hardships and frustrations. Thus in 1892 the Gie Appanto suffered a tremendous setback when the collapse of hanging walls (or ceilings) on one of its main tunnels (poorly reinforced by the antecedent Essaman Company) necessitated a huge expense for retimbering.[92] Over

Table 7.7
Gold Output of the Gie Appanto
Mining Company, 1889-1899

Year	Weight (oz.)	Value (£)
1889	1,974	7,106
1890	n.a.	16,363
1891	1,455	5,238
1892	4,388[a]	17,552[a]
1893	4,388	15,798
1894	2,603	10,086
1895	4,371	16,944
1896	2,865	11,458
1897	425[b]	2,041[b]
1898	4,433	15,680
1899	203	733

[a] Returns of Gie Appanto after 1891 combined
with Essaman Company.

[b] Covers production at the Prestea Mine only.

Sources: G.C. Blue Books for the Years. Also
Trade Repts. Encl. in Hodgson (175) to C.O., 4
May 1895; C.O. 96/257. M.J. 23 July 1892, 817.

the next several years this mine, like most of the others, suffered from
intermittent shutdowns owing to protracted flooding during the long
seasonal rains.[93] Machinery faltered under the stress, and the staff was
unable to make repairs without spare parts. To shareholders who questioned why the company could not pay out a dividend, the chairman,
Sir Samuel Cawston, pointed out that not only did ordinary operating
expenditures exceed revenues, but the company also had incurred a huge
general debt of £48,000, plus an extra loan of £16,550 to meet development and capital costs (including new machinery).[94] Interest payments
to debenture holders, therefore, would have to be met before any returns
on gold sales could be considered a profit. In an effort to solve these
problems the board of directors once again restructured the company.
In 1893, calling themselves simply the Appanto Company, they increased their capital stock to £150,000 (see chap. 4, table 4.1).[95] But the
cosmetic surgery did little good. The abrupt halt of nearly all mining in
1897 through 1899 was due primarily to the incapacity of the primitive

pumping systems then available and also to the fact that (as the upper levels became mined out) engineers working ever deeper underground lost sight of the main reef.[96] This third successor firm, the Appanto, also failed, and was in turn bought out in 1903 by a fourth entity on the same properties, the Prestea Mining Company.

Labor Problems at Gie Appanto and Elsewhere: The Failure of Government Regulation and Intervention

The history of the Gie Appanto and numerous other companies also illustrates how the so-called mines labor problem was inextricably bound up with mismanagement and budgetary bedlam. Although geological and climatic problems were formidable, it was the early company directors and field managers who, after all, were responsible for the financial and strategic decisions that sent their companies into early arrears. Some of these decisions might have been avoided, others not. For example, the Gie Appanto, with a larger European staff complement than most of its competitors, had to set aside an inordinate sum every year to pay for steamship passage to and from England for ordinary rest leaves and recuperation from illnesses. Since, as we have seen, African unskilled labor was invariably the largest expenditure under Operating Account, this was the first item which the Gie Appanto directors targeted for belt-tightening. In these circumstances the Gie Appanto, even more than its closest rivals continued to depend heavily on the use of cheap Kru and Bassa men from Liberia to fill its 400- to 500-man roster. And because the company had borrowed heavily to finance new machinery and plants, it took advantage of the amiability and pliability of its Kru workers in the imposition of severe financial stringencies that would help amortize its debt.

Worker discontent and resistance toward industrialized labor extended beyond the sociocultural impediments, such as the need to return home for farming, enumerated in earlier chapters. Ill feeling arose also from unusually heavy workloads and harsh treatment meted out by some managers and foremen. Again, data on such incidences are sparse in this period, not only because of the destruction of company correspondence and the colonial regime's inattention, but because few companies had the candor of the Gie Appanto in admitting any embarrassing facts or mistakes on labor practices in a public forum. But when one of the directors, J. R. Knight, toured the premises at Prestea in 1892 he found "that great dissatisfaction existed among native workmen at the mines who number[ed] between 400 and 500."[97] After extended discussion with Kru headmen over such grievances as diminished quantities of rice in food rations and a failure to provide money for return steamship passage to the Kru Coast (as per contract), Knight determined that the local manager, Tinney, would have to be sacked.

Such prompt action by London directors on behalf of African workers, as against local management, was indeed rare. In numerous other instances workers had received no redress for complaints about unfair treatment, including the withholding of wages; and we can only speculate on the pent-up feelings of injustice that went unreported and lay hidden in the recesses of workers' minds. Most of the criticisms concerning poor housing, public health, and corporal punishment, noted in chapter 6, were also applicable here. Without any doubt the most unconscionable infraction was the total nonpayment of a worker's back wages, which (because so many fly-by-night companies fled without a paper trace) probably occurred more frequently than anyone cared to admit.

As just noted a majority of firms held to the practice of either delaying or docking a portion of a miner's pay in order to deter absences from the job, or what shift bosses criticized as loafing and malingering. This was done even when miners showed obvious signs of illness.[98] But in an increasing number of cases, especially as mines failed to earn a profit, it was common to renege on paying workers altogether. One egregious example was the Gold Coast Company's Abontiakoon Mine (another in James Irvine's stable of ventures), which stinted on wages even while shipping gold dust to England and recording profits in order to please investors. Even its European staff displayed anger over a batch of unpaid wages and salaries. And the company's Kru workers, thoroughly distraught when they failed to get the wages due them at the end of their one-year stint, had to delay their departures for Liberia because they lacked funds for return steamship passage.[99] Similar practices by defunct or bankrupt companies occurred well into the next century.

Though trade union organization was unheard of in British West Africa at this early stage, the accumulation of incidences where workers were in a position to complain—not simply about low wages and wretched working conditions (which were a recognized part of the miners' way of life) but about dishonest practices by owners, provided the genesis for some of the first organized African miners' protests and strikes in the early twentieth century.[100]

It was a scathing indictment against the colonial regime's minimalist and passive regulatory stance toward the emerging goldmining industry, and especially toward the needs and just grievances of African workers, that throughout the period surveyed here officials rarely intervened against the companies in order to help workers recover defaults of pay. It was indeed hypocritical that although the Gold Coast Master and Servant Ordinance of 1877 in theory was to have been applicable to either party (employer or employee) who broke a contract, only a handful of complaints lodged by Africans against Europeans for damages were adjudicated in the colonial courts. (The odds were even lower that cases involving Kru men would be heard.) Even if the Gold Coast governor's hands were tied in launching a local (colonial) legal action against a defaulting expatriate company, articulate African critics thought that the British imperial government should have brought charges against the offending corporate directors in London under English law. It was not until fifteen or twenty years later that the Colonial Office seriously investigated the possibility of bringing charges against West African mining firms for defaulting on wage payments. In the event they decided against legal action on grounds that a majority of the companies had gone into liquidation, so there was no hope of recovery.[101]

MOUNTING PRESSURES FOR RAILWAY CONSTRUCTION: THE GOVERNORSHIP OF W. B. GRIFFITH

With the evidence of sustained productivity by the "big three" mining companies in the first half of the 1890s, the demand for government authorization for of a line of rail to the gold districts became more heated. For some years, as we have seen, a number of engineering firms and assorted promoters (many with scant capital or professional credentials) had continued to pester the Colonial Office with requests for a government guarantee of future profits on any line they might construct. All such offers had been set aside.[102] It was increasingly recognized that no private contracting firm could meet official conditions for a first-rate railway and that the British government itself would have to undertake full responsibility for construction. Of course the vehicle for mobilizing the necessary men, equipment, and matériel existed in the Crown Agents for the Colonies. The vital question was, When, if ever, would the go-ahead signal be given? In this initial phase the mining firms had to curry favor and convince local officials before they could hope to win the backing of the imperial government. Important preliminary groundwork was laid during the effective governorship of William Brandford Griffith (1886–1895).

Though well into his sixties at the time of his appointment as governor (see photo at the end of this chapter), Griffith proved to be a serious-minded and hardworking executive who took an interest in the welfare of the total population of the country and who altered the course of Gold Coast colonial administration.[103] Faced at the outset with a demoralized staff, a backlog of untried court cases, and a mountain of undigested paperwork, Griffith threw himself into the task of expanding and revitalizing the colonial bureaucracy. At the heart of his reforms was a keen appreciation of the fundamental importance of stable colonial government finances: he greatly augmented customs revenues based on prosperous trade and a new ten-percent customs import duty; and he developed a definite program of focused priorities for reorganization of the government. Between 1889 and 1895 the colony's annual revenues more than doubled, from £111,388 to £232,075. After greatly expanding the size of the civil service and adding to the number of specialized departments, Griffith launched what was for the time an ambitious program of public works for the coastal districts, including new public buildings, new roads, street drainage, and public latrines in the towns, the reclamation of swamplands and pestiferous pools, the establishment of forty-eight public cemeteries, and street lighting by oil lamps in Accra and Cape Coast.[104] Scores of outlying villages, as well the main coastal towns, were brought under a new Towns Police and Public Health Ordinance (1892). And expanded medical services were provided for Africans, as well as expatriates at one new hospital and scores of smaller dispensaries under the leadership of the African physician, Dr. James F. Easmon. Though government support for public education was still minimal and pinchpenny, being based on voluntary religious associations, Griffith increased government subsidies to mission schools; and he intensified government research and extension with respect to both cocoa and coffee cultivation at the Aburi horticultural research station.[105] With Brandford Griffith we can say the basic structure for the colonial state begins to take shape on the Gold Coast; and that numbers of programs later formalized in Chamberlain's "tropical estates" doctrine were quietly implemented at the local level in this period.

More than any previous executive, Griffith placed a strong emphasis on the mechanized gold-mining industry in his plans for the general development of the colony, and he became the first Gold Coast governor to visit the Wassa mining districts. Journeying up the River Ankobra in 1889 he toured the underground and surface works at Aboso, Tarkwa, and Prestea and talked with mine managers about their most pressing problems. Several of his thorough reports on living conditions and mines productivity provide important evidence for the present study. He took special note of the professional leadership of Gold Coastans, such as Swanzy Essien at the Gie Appanto mines and especially the Sam Family at the Wassa (G.C.) Mining Company.[106] Concerned about the extension of more effective colonial district administration into the hinterland, Griffith formalized permanent district status at Wassa-Fiase in 1891 and appointed the first full-time commissioner in Henrik Vroom, a prominent member of the Eurafrican community.[107] After further meetings with the local leaders of the mining industry at the port of Axim, he pledged government cooperation with the companies in several spheres, most notably transportation improvements, new roads, clearance of the River Ankobra for more efficient boat transport, and, finally, planning for a government railway.[108]

From this time until his retirement in 1895, Griffith became one of the most vocal and consistent advocates of railroad construction among all British officials in West Africa. Since "mines appear to be coming more remunerative and are likely to attract more capital," urged one Accra subordinate, "this question may at any moment be pressed forward on the attention of the [imperial] government. . . ."[109] An editorial in the African-owned *Gold Coast Chronicle* in the early 1890s sensed that the prospects for a Gold Coast railway were never brighter, but the paper chastised the British home government for its indecision and obstructionism on major expenditures for colonial advancement. A hinterland railway, the newspaper argued, was "an indispensable prerequisite for the material elevation of the colony." It urged officials not to be led astray by the delusion that the addition of numerous improved roads alone could serve as a substitute for rail transport. A "few lines of rail to the interior would do the country more good than an infinite number of roads which cost large sums of money to keep in good condition."[110]

Meanwhile, the buildup of pressures from trading and shipping as well as mining interests in the United Kingdom helped to jostle the lethargic, status quo mood in the Colonial Office and contributed, along with Griffith's own achievements, to a slowly gathering groundswell for expansionistic change, the early rumbles of the "developmental imperialism," during the waning years of the Gladstone-Rosebery Liberal Ministry of 1891–95.[111] In a steady stream of letters and memorials over a ten-year span, the African sections of the London, Liverpool, and Manchester chambers of commerce were joined by the representatives of other British chambers—including Glasgow, Birmingham, Sheffield, Leeds, and Bristol—plus the recently formed congress of the combined chambers of commerce of the United Kingdom in reminding both the Colonial and Foreign Offices that African hinterland railways would be absolutely vital, not only for tapping new hinterland markets and raw material supplies, but also for ensuring, in conjunction with military expeditions and boundary delimitations, that distant hinterlands should not fall by default into the hands of the rival imperial powers, France and Germany.[112] With fervid rhetoric the real and imagined threats posed by powerful African states and empires—most notably Asante—both to the political stability of the forest zone and the flow of trade to the coast was highlighted by the mining and railway lobby in their barrage of appeals for imperial intervention across a wide front.[113] Responding in their usual methodical way, members of the C.O.'s West African Department began to gather all pertinent data on railway building programs in French West Africa, the Leopoldian Congo, Portuguese Africa, and throughout the British Empire.[114] "There is no doubt," wrote Augustus Hemming, "that we ought to undertake the making of railways in our West Coast colonies. The French are doing it in theirs. The Congo is building a very expensive line and even poverty-stricken Portugal has made over 100 miles at Loanda."[115]

For the gold industry the culminating achievement of the Griffith administration was to gain acceptance from the Crown Agents for a preliminary railway route survey in order to narrow the choice of routes for a future line of rail in the event a project were to be approved. Did this mean that by the mid-1890s the mining companies and their allies could rest confidently in the belief that construction of a mining railway from the coast to Tarkwa was a foregone conclusion? Not at all. There was still an encrusted thicket of bureaucratic obfuscation and ideological resistance in the New Public Offices at Whitehall, which weighed heavily against risk-laden colonial works expenditures. The indirect, as well as the direct controls exercised by the retrenchment-oriented establishment in Westminster were still far too daunting for colonial governors like Griffith or even the British chambers of commerce to pierce or overcome. Insiders knew that without the stamp of approval from an unusually strong secretary of state for colonies, all such proposals would continue to be shot down by senior staff within the Colonial Office itself, led by R. H. Meade, long before they reached the inner bastions of the Imperial Exchequer.[116] Complicating the decision making in London was the realization that once funds were approved for a Gold Coast railway, the imperial government would have to entertain parallel proposals for hinterland railways from the governors and merchants of Sierra Leone and Lagos as well. In each area extensive preliminary surveys for the best choice of routes would have to be conducted by the Crown Agents. In the final analysis the categories of outsized imperial loan authorizations required for railway and harbor construction throughout British West Africa would necessitate nothing less than the full backing of the prime minister and cabinet and several acts of Parliament. Caught between the aggressive new forces for imperial expansion and the powerful counterweight of conformity to Gladstonian fiscal tradition, the Liberal Secretary of State for Colonies, Lord Ripon, appeared to pull back even from the cautious optimism of his predecessor, Lord Knutsford. Petitioners were told that

Lord Ripon fully appreciates the probable advantages that would result from the construction of railways in the West African Colonies, but he could not hold out any hope that the Treasury or Parliament would consent to an Imperial guarantee of interest on the cost, the provision of funds for which is undoubtedly the main difficulty in carrying out the work. . . .[117]

African Laborers Working for the Mechanized Companies
(Note the roles of women, expecially in transport and porterage)

African skilled surface workers and early company sawmill, important for building construction. Ashanti Goldfields Corp.

African 'shovel men' at entrance to the adit level of a mechanized mine. Ashanti Goldfields Corp.

Women—working for an expatriate company—headloading sacks of gold ore to crushing mills. Ashanti Goldfields Corp.

Workers clearing ground for construction of a hillside gravitational crushing mill. Ashanti Goldfields Corp.

Mining company hammockmen with hammock for transporting expatriate personnel (late 19th cent. photo). (Note African store in background.) Ashanti Goldfields Corp.

A woman carrying her child plus a 100 lb. load of mining equipment or provisions to the mining site. Ashanti Goldfields Corp.

Kru men from Liberia, Important for the Unskilled Mines Labor Force at the Wassa Mines, 1879–1900.

Kru mariners manning surfboat between steamship and shore. Photo from the collection of George Brooks, Indiana University.

Contemporary sketch of Kru men in Liberia. Photo from the Collection of George Brooks.

Kru and Akan unskilled laborers on the Gold Coast (c. 1895–1905)

8

Retrospect and Aftermath

Mining Frontiers, Capitalism, Labor, and the Colonial State

Throughout this study I have stressed the resilience and effectiveness of African farmer-gold miners in the face of expatriate-controlled mechanized enterprise. Indeed, we have suggested that there were two simultaneously expanding mining frontiers. The most dramatic and visible was the expatriate-controlled capitalistic mining frontier that centered on the three mining towns of Tarkwa, Aboso, and Heman-Prestea in Wassa. This colonial mining frontier was potent because it brought new technology, capital, jobs, and the clash of economic systems. It generated considerable wealth through the wages and salaries paid to workers—both Africans and Europeans—the money from which had a multiplier effect on trade from the coast through the increasing demand for food, drink, clothing, tools, and other necessities and luxuries. Informants attested that, even for temporary and part-time workers, the availability of coined money from wages enabled them to make a host of sundry purchases they never could have considered before. Thus mining capitalism, often criticized for limited linkages to general economic development, nonetheless in the Gold Coast, exhibited a fair number of spread effects outside the immediate mining enclave. Earlier chapters emphasized that far greater numbers of both women and men became involved in more trading and service activities in the informal sector as a result of the boom—including the sale of mining leases, porterage, boat traffic up the River Ankobra, fuel gathering, cooking, retail store sales, prostitution, hawking, the making of palm wine, the selling of beer and spirits—than ever could have been employed directly by the mining companies. More basically, the mining centers became magnets for external investment, and expenditure on mining machinery—steam engines, boilers pumps, winding engines for lifts, stamp crushers, chemical treatment plants, and small tramways—plus supplies—cement, coal, hardware, and lumber—all of which added greatly to the colony's volume of fixed capital.

THE TWO MINING FRONTIERS AND
THE GOLD BOOM

Historians and economists will continue to debate the benefits and detriments of a short-term inflationary mining boom economy to a region's economic growth. All exploited minerals are a wasting asset; and gold rushes, in particular, are known for their short life. Yet mining industries may experience numerous cycles of decline and resurgence— as a consequence of deeper penetration and new discoveries—before they inevitably exhaust themselves. Thus the gold boom analyzed in these pages was followed by another in the early 1900s, which I will examine in a later publication. No one doubts that the concept of El Dorado is bound up with exaggerated claims, deep-seated psychological needs and illusions. As noted in the opening chapter, the very notion conjures up Eurocentric fantasies of untold wealth in exotic lands brought within the reach of intrepid adventurers willing to risk danger and try their luck. From at least the time of Columbus, the El Dorado myth has been one of the pillars of the European imperialist mystique, which (as modern colonial discourse theory reminds us) was itself founded on a welter of self-centered delusions. It is true that West Africas first modern mechanized gold rush, examined here, never brought the great returns that the prophets and promoters had foretold. Indeed, one of the supreme ironies of the Akan region's first expatriate-led gold boom is that the mining companies—even allowing for diversion of funds by fraud and wastage (another prominent feature of El Dorados)—probably pumped more into the country in the form of fees paid for the purchase of concessions, building and plant construction, purchase of machinery and supplies, and the payment of labor than they ever took out of it in direct profits. At the same time it is worth recalling that in classic definitions, myths and legends mirrored historical substance as well as dreams and fantasy. (The archetypal story of Jason and the Golden Fleece is a clear case in point.)[1] The gold rush examined here scores on both criteria. Though gold production in Ghana never approached the levels of the top world producers, such as South Africa. Canada, Russia, or Australia, the West African metal was respected by gold dealers in London and it attained a high rank on world export lists in the early 1900s.

As for the impact of the gold boom on the general economy, there is no effective way of giving numerical expression to the complex integers. No one would go so far as to suggest that mining generated as much employment or had as many linkages to broad based development as the famous cocoa-growing revolution which began in eastern Ghana during these same decades. (Not that cocoa brought uniform and ceaseless prosperity to farmers: even the country's premier industry experienced fluctuations, depressions, and serious blight over the long haul). It can be argued, nonetheless, that even prior to the Gold Coasts first railway (1901–3), the initial stage of mechanized gold mining had greater positive impact on the general economy than used to be believed. First of all, the main western and central port towns, especially Axim and Cape Coast, became feeder ports and stopover points for steamships that regularly unloaded supplies and personnel en route to the mines—personnel who in turn had to be fed and lodged at various intermediate posts along the way. The outskirts of these same towns became beehives of activity as shipping agents supervised the transfer of expensive cargoes from ocean-going liners to river canoes for the journey up the Ankobra, or recruited scores of porters into caravans for the arduous overland journey to Wassa. Market traders in fish, poultry, meat, and vegetables also did a brisk business at Axim, Cape Coast, and intermediate points along the route to the hinterland. It even can be argued that the extravagant speculative expenditure on mineral leases—which was certainly wasteful and injurious from several perspectives—nonetheless injected money into the local economy through the hands of kings, chiefs, and their retainers, as well as through the numerous middlemen and lawyers who made money from lands transactions and disputes.

In the midst of this frenetic expansion a building industry also flourished—both at the mining camps, with numerous workers huts, warehouses, outbuildings, and the housings for machinery and crushing plants—and at the coastal towns—chiefly Axim and Cape Coast—in the form of new stores, warehouses, hotels, and chop houses. We saw earlier that the introduction of sawmills by each of the major gold companies was a significant innovation. Backward linkages were created between building construction, with its demands for raw materials, and such local production as stone quarrying, gravel crushing, and the new timber-cutting industry of the Lower Ankobra. Finally, the mechanized mines also provided instruction and experience to numbers of African skilled workers. Carpenters, wheelwrights, stonemasons, mechanics, welders, office clerks, and engine drivers got their start at the mines, and after leaving company employment, they contributed to the general development of the colony during future decades.[2]

THE SURVIVAL AND EXPANSION OF TRADITIONAL GOLD MINING

The second mining frontier was less commonly recognized both at the time and afterward. The African-controlled indigenous miners frontier had been expanding slowly and imperceptibly with the gentle penetration of remote hinterland areas over the centuries; but, as noted in chapter 4, traditional family-based mining experienced a resurgence in tandem with the European gold rush from the mid-1870s onward. This indigenous farmer-miners frontier had its own dynamic; and, though its impact on individuals cannot be calculated, it absorbed the activities of far more Akan men, women, and young people than the European mining enclave, with its heavy reliance on foreign labor. Territorially, this was the more pervasive and far-reaching of the two frontiers: it intruded into the environs of villages and hamlets close to the main roads, and also into isolated gold-laden river valleys and remote, heavily forested regions where human habitation was extremely sparse. Its pulsations and directions were constantly changing, depending on the discoveries of valuable new lodes and the variable actions of thousands of individuals and family groups (see map 8.1). As in earlier centuries of the precolonial gold trade, the peripatetic Nzeman (or Apollonian) gold entrepreneurs continued to take a leading role in opening up new mining areas and in expanding the arc of the overland gold trade into the most distant western and northern mining areas. But British officials also observed that many more people from other southwestern states near the coast, such as Ahanta and Gwira, were now also venturing further inland to earn money from gold mining and the gold trade.

Statistics on Gold Exports

We can never know the exact amount of gold actually produced either by the African farmer-miners miners or by all the European companies. Many of the expatriate firms never published annual reports. Table 8.1 lists the annual gold exports for the entire Gold Coast Colony, from 1889 through 1900; here I distinguish the gold produced and exported

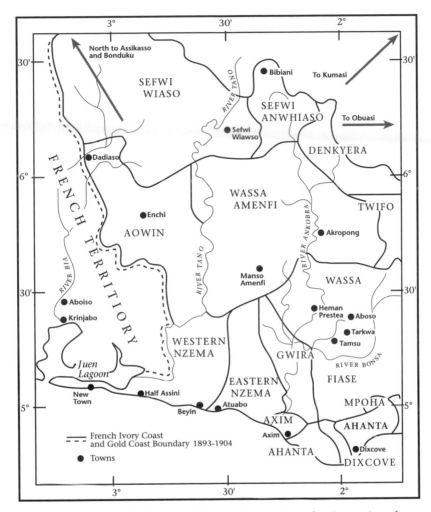

Map 8.1. Western Gold Coast and Eastern Ivory Coast showing regions for expansion of indigenous gold mining by miner's from Nzewa.

by all the mechanized companies from overall gold exports, which includes trade gold from indigenous suppliers. The absolutely remarkable phenomenon revealed in this table is the continuing high importance of ordinary trade gold dust produced from African traditional sources by the time-tested methods of surface pit mining, deep-level reef gold mining, and washing for river gold at the same time that the Europeans were engaging in mechanized production.

These figures do not purport to include all the gold that was mined, nor do they mean that every ounce of peasant-produced gold was exported the same year that it was extracted. As noted in chapter 3, rural people in the Akan states were generally thrift conscious. Every year incalculable amounts of gold dust and nuggets were set aside for savings or melted down into jewelry. We should keep in mind, moreover, that the portions of gold dust that would have been appropriated for state surplus in the form of tribute, taxes, or special tithes and stored in royal treasuries can never be estimated. It is also vital to remember that gold dust was still the main currency among interior peoples, so that the largest amount of gold mined by farmer-miners every year probably remained in circulation and that which was brought to the coast for shipment by African gold-smiths and traders probably had changed hands many times. Throughout the greater part of the period surveyed in this study, it is improbable that African petty traders and goldsmiths sold vast quantities of gold dust in bulk directly to coastal merchants for cash prior to shipment overseas. (It is true that European and American minted coins were slowly gaining acceptance among coastal Africans as a favored form of currency; but in the interior gold dust and nuggets retained pride of place as the favored forms of doing business, of saving, and of demonstrating wealth.) For the most part exportable gold dust reached the major expatriate mercantile houses (F. and A. Swanzy, Alexander Miller Brothers, Pickering and Berthoud) and the leading African firms (Sarbah, Grant, and Ocansey and others) indirectly, having changed hands hundreds of times as pay-ment for imported European merchandise or to pay off debts in a myriad of transactions. These coastal merchants and traders then shipped the gold dust, along with other African bulk commodities—such as palm oil, palm kernels, and rubber—to London, Liverpool, and Hamburg in order to balance their own merchandise debit accounts.[3]

The significant continuing role of traditional gold production and the indigenous gold trade is better understood when we examine the de-tailed breakdown for 1889 through 1898 in table 8.1. By this period the three major companies of the Tarkwa and Aboso, the Wassa (Gold Coast), and the Gie Appanto companies, examined in chapter 7, were making a major contribution to the colonys gold export bill. Yet, even for this late ten-year span, African indigenous miners continued to contribute an average of 13,723 ounces to gold exports every year. For the twelve years covered in the table, African production added up to 141,346 ounces, or over 53 percent of the total gold exports for the colony. Gold exports derived from the European mines, on the other hand, averaged 10,276 ounces per year from 1889 through 1898. For the twelve-year period, European mechanized mines produced a total

Table 8.1

Gold Exports of the Gold Coast Colony Showing Trade Gold Exports in Relation to Production by the Mining Companies, 1889-1900

Year	Gold Exports by European Mining Companies Weight (Ounces)	Value (£)	Trade Gold Exports Weight (Ounces)	Value (£)	Total Gold Exports Weight (Ounces)	Value (£)
1889	5,423	20,220	23,244	82,980	28,667	103,200
1890	3,174	11,429	22,286	80,228	25,460	91,657
1891	6,066	21,875	18,409	66,237	24,475	8,112
1892	7,182	35,810	20,264	62,996	27,446	8,806
1893	11,401	40,974	10,571	38,125	21,972	79,099
1894	11,381	43,028	9,951	33,768	21,332	76,796
1895	13,355	52,583	12,061	38,914	25,416	91,497
1896	15,538	62,149	8,403	32,440	23,941	86,186
1897	14,515	52,685	9,040	32,112	23,555	84,797
1898	14,729	54,583	3,003	9,295	17,732	63,878
1899	11,122	42,433	3,128	8,867	14,250	51,300
1900	9,551	34,383	986	3,624	10,537	38,007
Total	123,437	472,152	141,346	489,586	264,783	953,335

Source: Gold Coast Blue Books for 1889 through 1900. In cases of conflict over data, this source ruled. Also, G.C. Annual Colonial Reports, 1894–1900; Returns on Gold Exports, encl. in Griffith (75) to Ripon, 15 March 1893, CO 96/232; Trade Reports, encl. in G.C. (175) to CO, 4 May 1895, CO 96/257.

[a]According to the Gold Coast Annual Colonial Reports, the export figures were exclusive of specie shipped by the colonial government.

of 123,437 ounces, or just 46.6 percent of the total overseas gold trade. Again, it is important to emphasize that the annual amounts of gold mined by rural producers in the greater Akan region can never be known from the British colonial overseas export figures; and it may well be that the largest proportion of locally produced gold dust was retained in the communities or diverted to overland trade elsewhere.

Explanations for the Survival and Expansion of Peasant Gold Mining into the 1890s

What are the explanations for this surprising persistence and expansion of indigenous small-scale mining during the 1880s and greater part of

the 1890s? Of first importance was the deep entrenchment over generations of the basic mining skills among the people. The Akan people had
been dubbed born gold finders for good reason. An age-old talent passed
down over the centuries could not be set aside or forgotten. Second, the
seasonal cycle of family-based economic activity— harvesting yams and
other crops in November, gold mining during the dry season, and
planting crops plus alluvial gold mining during the rainy season—was
perpetuated year after year. It was a necessary part of a familys livelihood. In chapter 4 we noted that the resurgence in indigenous gold
mining in the late 1870s was influenced to no small extent by arousal
and competitiveness against the unprecedented mania of European concessionaire activity. Clear evidence of the resurgence of traditional gold
mining by Akan people of both the coastal and interior states vitiates
the notion put forward by one prominent government official at the time
and repeated by historians more recently, that (1) the greater part of
traditional gold mining was carried on by indigenous slave labor, so that
when the government ended the legal recognition of African slavery by
ordinance in 1874, it therefore (2) ended or destroyed the traditional
production of gold by rural communities in many areas.[4] All the documentation presented here on continuous up-country gold production
militates against this supposition. Mining continued to flourish as an
occasional and seasonal economic activity, even in those areas where the
extraction of new forest products—especially rubber—was taking hold.[5]
At a time when the survivors among the first wave of European companies were becoming uncertain about their future and wondering if they
would ever get their much needed railway, small-scale family miners
were as optimistic and as active as ever. In 1891, Henrik Vroom, a man
of African parentage and newly appointed permanent district commissioner for Wassa, wrote, "Latterly native prospectors have discovered
fresh mines." And they also "give attention to alluvial mining. In the
rainy season of 1891 two nuggets, weighing 23 ounces and 11 ounces,
were found near the Tarkwa-Dixcove road."[6]

This burgeoning was also evinced by the presence of greater numbers
of traveling goldsmiths in the more distant up-country regions. And
African farmer-miners continued to be innovative, some making use of
new devices and experience they had gained while working for six-
month stints at the European mines. These new methods included
tunneling, timbering, the increased use of explosives, and even the use
of steam-powered drills.[7] Even in the Lower Ankobra Valley, where the
new West African timber industry was beginning to take hold, and in

the eastern auriferous states, namely Akyem-Abuakwa, where the major economic revolution based on cocoa growing was just getting underway, many rural people continued to engage in part-time gold mining. Thus, it was said that people in the vicinity of Kyebi meandered when it suited them to outlying villages such as Asiakwa and Tano in the Birim Valley to mine for subsurface gold or pan for river gold on an occasional basis right up to the First World War and after.[8] In Asante too, gold mining experienced a resurgence in the early 1890s, owing at least in part to strong attempts by the new Asantehene, Prempeh II, to stabilize the country politically and revive commerce to the coast through the assertion of a strong central administration at Kumasi.[9] What people were witnessing was the real "hey-day" of the indigenous gold-mining frontier.

MINING LABOR

The analysis of labor presented in this study differs from some others in recent historiography in that I have found no inevitable, evolutionary pathway toward the molding of an industrial proletariat through mining, even though gold production has been a mainstay of the country's modern economy. Although Fante and other coastal Akan people comprised a growing proportion of the office clerks and crushing plant staff at many of the mines, the ratio of these surface workers to the total labor force was never large. Therefore my earlier conclusion concerning the disproportionate number—on average, 67 to 70 percent—of the total work force for the mines being made up of migrant Kru and Bassa men from Liberia remains hard and fast (see chaps. 4, 5, and 7). They remained the bulwark of the unskilled labor force during the period under review. In the opening decades of the next century imported Kru labor would continue to play a role, but increasingly, for a variety of unskilled tasks, they would be augmented by ever larger numbers of migrant workers from Nigeria, French-speaking West African territories, and especially the northern savanna region of Ghana.

Though attractive as an idea for theoretical debate, there is little or no evidence from the Gold Coast between 1875 and 1900 for the interpretation, advanced quite accurately by some scholars for other parts of colonial Africa, that expatriate mining companies deliberately perpetuated a system of nonpermanent migrant labor because it served as a better method of labor control and allowed them to keep their wages bill down.[10] Rather, they relied on it because it was the only alternative. There is no doubt that several of the companies—especially the WGCMC—stayed with the tributing system; but most of the European firms remained frustrated over their inability to recruit and maintain a permanent force of underground workers because it cost them far too much money in lost time and skills and the continuous training of new workers. One official reported that just as soon as workers became useful to employers, "they go away," so that there was no assurance whatever of developing a long-lasting force of experienced workers.[11] It is important to emphasize that—even into the twentieth century, when a variety of new market forces and conditions would gradually alter the composition of the mining labor force—a majority of the unskilled, underground work force enlisted for a short term at the mines and remained closely tied to their traditional rural home economies.

A striking related phenomenon, completely unnoticed in all the previous literature, is the way that many Akan men, having gained experience as wage earners with new methods and new technology at the European mechanized mines, later reverted to traditional gold mining. The colonial and company archives are all too silent on the names and personalities of their African workers. But an interesting and rare document of the 1880s shows that indigenous Akan miners might reside in the Tarkwa and Aboso district for a number of years, moving several times in and out of expatriate-company employment, and then return to informal traditional mining when it suited them. A miner named Kofi Accra, whose case may have been representative, was originally purchased as a slave and then taken to live with a family in Gwira state, west of Wassa. In a pattern of assimilation that was common among the Akan, he later married into his adopted family and, after gaining his freedom, succeeded his former master as head of the household. In the early 1880s he followed the gold boom to Tarkwa and succeeded in getting a job at one of the Wassa companies, where he earned a reputation as a hard worker. Having grown tired of the routine, he continued to work both as a tributor for a one-third to one-half share of all the ore he produced, and subsequently as an occasional contract, or pieceworker for several companies. The record suggests that he enjoyed the freedom of mining on his own. After this, having accumulated sufficient wages for the purchase of a few luxuries and some savings, Kofi Accra returned to village life in his home country with time for periodic small-scale mining.[12] Another document shows that some Akan men worked for brief periods for the expatriate companies, and then turned to rubber tapping or rubber transport to the coast.[13] Such vignettes, however small and unimportant, help cast light on what was taking place among the people at the grassroots level.

There were other crossovers and interactions between the expatriate and the indigenous mining frontiers. Former wage earners for the mechanized companies who returned to traditional African pit mining, often brought with them knowledge of new and improved techniques, such as timbering and use of explosives. Henrik Vroom noted in the 1890s that some of the *sikadifo*, through emulation, were for the first time making use of black powder and dynamite to speed up the cracking of hard rock.[14] In later company reports, thefts of sticks of dynamite and detonation caps by employees and ex-employees became a frequent complaint of mine managers and shift bosses.[15] Some independent African miners also pestered European acquaintances to help them obtain pumping machinery.

What the records clearly demonstrate is that most men from the Akan forest states valued their freedom and independence too much to stay on the payroll of the mining companies for any length of time. As we have seen throughout this study, the strongest motivating factors for miners removing themselves from the capitalistic wage sector were: (1) the basic need to return to one's home and kinship group (the strong pull from family, friends, and chiefs to participate in food production and contribute to various village and stool activities); (2) the desire to escape the drudgery and dangers of regimented labor underground, which could lead to serious illness, discomfort, and physical injury; (3) the simple desire for independence and the freedom to move in order to escape the monotony of routine; and, finally, (4) the strong incentive to work for wages up to a given point in order to satisfy an essential need or specific set of goals. Though the term had not yet been coined, there is little doubt that Gold Coast mine workers in these years were operating implicitly according to a rationale very much akin to the modern concept of target incomes.[16] We noted in chapter 7 that the cost of living in those days was quite low and that after working for wages for six months, or a year at most, a man could easily meet his daily subsistence requirements and earn sufficient surplus for savings and a few major purchases besides.[17]

On top of this some rural people in the major gold-producing states—Denkyera, Asante, and Akyem-Abuakwa, as well as the two Wassas—believed that, with an ordinary amount of good luck, they could earn more from a given amount of labor under traditional kin-based gold mining than at prevailing entry-level wages for underground labor at the European installations.[18] One of the classic tests for the development of a genuine working class in a country is that it must *reproduce* itself. Another is that there should be some kind of developing class consciousness concerning present feelings of exploitation or subjugation, coupled with strategies for amelioration or radical social change. Both differences in the ethnic backgrounds of workers and ties to the traditional village and family economic units militated against the development of this kind of working-class continuity and solidarity in the mechanized gold-mining industry of the Gold Coast until at least the second half of the twentieth century.[19] Instead, as we have seen in this study, cadres of unskilled underground laborers constantly had to be *re-created* by the companies.

THE COMMERCIALIZATION OF
LANDHOLDING AND LAND TRANSFERS

By far the most disruptive dimension to the encroachment of Western capitalism on the traditional economy and society of southwestern Ghana at this juncture could be seen, not in the mobilization of a modern capitalistic labor force, but in the movement toward the commercialization and individualization of land. The trend began slowly, commencing with the leasing of stool lands to Europeans and to coastal African entrepreneurs in the immediate vicinity of Tarkwa Ridge in the late 1870s. It then spread slowly outward, until by century's end, it embraced much of Wassa Fiase, parts of adjacent states, such as Wassa Amenfi, and much of the lower and middle Ankobra River Basin. After 1900 it also advanced into southern Asante. Starting with the activities of prospectors, company agents, and concessions middlemen in their transactions with chiefs, it was not long before many others—the paramount rulers, subchiefs, and village headmen learned to attach money values to lands believed to contain gold-bearing soil or other marketable products. Somewhat later a British parliamentary commission on the Gold Coast lands question would report that the extent of land leased to foreign concessionaires was not that great in relation to total lands available for human habitation and farming in the southwestern region. However, it can be argued that the square mileage of lands leased to strangers in proportion to known mineral-bearing lands was indeed high.[20] In fact, concessions leasing was a major spearhead of the expanding capitalistic mining frontier.

One of the first to react angrily to the new atmosphere of profit making from land transfers had been the paramount ruler of Wassa Fiase in the 1880s, Kwamena Enemil Kwow.[21] Some of the tension between kings and chiefs had gone back a long way in Wassa history; but this was nothing compared to the fractiousness generated by the handling of proceeds from concessions as a consequence of the gold rush. We have seen that under Akan land law the leasing or mineral lands fell mainly under the powers of chiefs or *ahenfo;* in fact, the paramount rulers, or *amanhene,* felt that their roles in decision making had been reduced or bypassed; and they complained that they saw far too few of the returns from concessions leasing. Recognizing all too clearly the significance of the money being siphoned off by subordinates under the aegis of his own stool authority, Enemil Kwow, before his destoolment, had persuaded his chiefs, especially Kwabena Ango of Apinto and Enemil Kuma of Aboso, to enter into agreements whereby in lieu of the long-established *abusa* share system, they should pay him a flat 10 percent of the monies they received as rent every year from their expatriate mining leaseholders. Here certainly was one indicator of the adjustments being made in the traditional system in the face of inroads by an alien capitalism. As time wore on other *ohene* and village chiefs would try to introduce the notion of money rents into the grant of farming and timber cutting as well as mining rents to strangers who became tenants on lands under their authority.

It is important to keep in mind that in ancient or basic Akan land law there was nothing approximating individual freehold proprietorship or ownership in the sense of the English land law.[22] Similarly, the outright sale for a fee and the long-term lease of stool lands by written agreement had been largely unknown in the interior of the southwestern Akan region prior to the 1870s. Although families and individuals did enjoy "use" rights over parcels of stool land (generally called family lands) in perpetuity, and though chiefs could easily grant a parcel of land to strangers to work on an individual basis for an indefinite period upon payment of a nominal fee, the "alienation," or "devising," of parcels of land by such holders, whether by will or by outright sale, would have contradicted the concept of ownership vested in the total community with the chiefs as custodians under Akan land law. When some scholars write as if the commercialization of land had existed in Akan societies since time immemorial, they are minimizing the impact of changes that were the product of Westernization and intrusive capitalism.[23] Obviously, the notion of freehold proprietorship over houses and lands had been developing in the environs of the major coastal towns, such as Cape Coast and Accra, since at the least the early 1800s and undoubtedly before that. I am speaking of the commercialization of land in the interior. By the early 1890s, the erosion of traditional rules and constraints governing the conveying of lands by long-term lease and by sale was becoming much more widespread in the valley of the Ankobro, Wassa Fiase, and adjacent districts in the southwest. It is worth adding that the proliferation of capitalistic concessionaire activity derived not only from the impetus of gold mining at Tarkwa, Aboso, and Prestea, but, secondarily, from the burgeoning commercial timber industry—one of the great untold stories in Ghanaian economic history—which was centered on the Lower Ankobra and the port of Axim, in which both African and European merchants plus the ever-present Nzeman workers took a leading part.[24]

Proliferation of Lands Disputes and Litigation

This acceleration of concessions-mongering had a deep economic impact, and it was accompanied by sociopolitical confusion and upheaval. Disputes frequently resulted because chiefs were not used to dealing with tracts of land whose dimensions and areas were measured according to European standards (such as square feet or acres); and their notions of dividing lines between lands belonging to one stool or between families, if they existed at all, usually rested on general landmarks, such as the bank of a stream or the crest of a particular ridge. This may have been sufficient in the context of traditional landholding relations between Africans, but not in the maelstrom of leasing and subleasing that was now taking place between rural people, aggressive company agents, and concessions middlemen. Make no mistake, a substantial number of coastal Africans as well as Europeans made good sums of money from the negotiation and resale of leases. At the same time, it became common for chiefs to mistakenly grant leases to properties that overlapped one another, or even to lease out the same property twice.[25] Subchiefs and stool elders complained that they had not been consulted, as per custom, in approving the grant of such concessions in the first place. Another transformation and violation of traditional norms was the tendency of expatriate concessions holders to treat their properties as if they had exclusive or monopolistic rights to them which (because they were mere leaseholds) they manifestly did not. As we have seen, such attitudes sometimes led to the ejection of African peasant miners and cultivators whose traditional surface rights were supposed to have been protected by codicils in the written leases. If European leaseholders were able to take over staked-out parcels of land in the mining districts as if they owned them, then, men reasoned, what was to prevent ordinary Akan people from asserting that they too had a long-term, vested family interest—approaching legal title—in the very lineage or family lands that they now saw being leased in such a reckless way by profit-conscious chiefs? This certainly was one of the logical pathways along which ideas about the individualization of land could take root.

Intrusive Capitalism and the Authority of Chiefs

One of the complex paradoxes surrounding the commercialization and individualization of land transfers in the southwestern Gold Coast was that just as some chiefs—such as Ango of Apinto, Eniemil Kuma of Aboso, and Kofi Kyei of Heman-Prestea (see photo at the end of this chapter)—gained in wealth and power as a result of the mining boom, other traditional rulers in the southwest spoke of a long-term loss of respect for the kingly office among their people. It appears to have been more the paramount kings, or *amanhene*, of Wassa Fiase and Wassa Amenfi, who suffered from a loss of authority. Because the power of making concessions leases fell increasingly under the control of the *ahenfo*, there was a gravitation of authority down to the local level. Enemil Kuow of Wassa Fiase and his successors complained to colonial government officials that they could no longer get young men to obey their orders in such matters as the maintenance of public roads and other communal obligations.[26] Some observers declared that it was the capitalistic companies who had become the real dispensers of wealth and fonts of authority in the region; others blamed the African coastal concessions middlemen—like Joseph Dawson—who sometimes doubled as advisers to the kings and chiefs; still others traced the diminution in respect for traditional rulers on the chiefs themselves.[27] The question was whether any of these poles of power served the interests of the ordinary people of the districts? Complaints brought first in the traditional stool courts and later in the colonial courts that chiefs had granted leases to strangers, without prior consultation with subchiefs and *odikro*,[28] as per customary law, were an accurate reflection of the concessions muddle and also a manifestation of simmering popular resentment. An equally serious problem of governance and eroding authority stemmed from the fact that the populations of the three main company mining centers—Tarkwa, Aboso, and Prestea—were made up, not of Wassa people loyal to their stool authorities, but dominantly of strangers: traders and drifters from the Akan coastal states; traveling miners from Nzema; and most important, the migrant mine workers from Liberia. How were the traditional rulers of Wassa to manage these diverse peoples and subgroups?

As a consequence, beleaguered stool holders called upon the governors of the Gold Coast and district commissioners at Axim or Cape Coast to bail them out of their difficulties by endowing them with the supposedly stronger powers of kings and chiefs enunciated in the ambiguous 1883 Native Jurisdiction Ordinance. I discussed the provisions of this ordinance in chapter 6. Here indeed is one of the ironies of colonial policy and "native administration" during these decades. It points up the pitfall of attempting to divide the leaders and advocates of that time into two simplified categories: one group (mainly expatriate) supposedly supportive of colonial laws, and another (primarily African and pro-nationalist) necessarily critical of all colonial laws. Interestingly, the rulers of the two Wassas and some other states favored the Native Jurisdiction Ordinance (NJO), not because they believed it would allow them greater independence of action, but because they believed it would involve the colonial state much more directly and supportively in their state administrations. In other words, rulers hoped that the NJO would shore up their declining powers. As noted earlier this ordinance was a dubious blueprint for stable interior African government. Over the next several decades colonial district officers in the southwest would hear a crescendo of charges filed in the courts by subchiefs and commoners against their *ahenfo* for alleged abuse of traditional powers, not only in connection with the misuse of proceeds from lands deals with foreigners, but also for excessive use and abuse of their authority under the recently accepted and highly touted Native Jurisdiction Ordinance.[29]

In a related problem, a growing number of able and aggressive coastal lawyers both instigated and profited from a plethora of court cases in which individual chiefs and often their entire stools were plunged deeply into debt as a consequence of claims lodged against them by "the people" in the colonial district courts of the southwest. Some of these law suits were legitimate, but, as the lawyers drummed up more and more business, a growing number of cases seemed to rest on very shaky grounds. *Ahenfo* now complained to colonial administrators that the spate of land disputes were not only draining their personal wealth but also subtracting from their traditional judicial authority by removing disputes from the Akan stool courts to the colonial courts.[30] As if this were not enough, traveling commissioners also took note of a growing number of internal political disputes by rival factions over the succession to the Wassa kingship and to various chieftaincies in the mining region following the deaths of incumbents.[31] Following in the wake of the gold rush and the concessions boom, an age of litigiousness seemed to have dawned in the coastal law courts.

It is difficult to imagine many more wrenching examples in colonial Ghana of the destabilizing impact of Western capitalistic individualism and materialism. The chaos of hastily drawn up, vaguely defined, and largely unregistered leases of traditional stool lands to Europeans and coastal Africans would lead to a series of flawed attempts by the colonial state to frame concessions legislation for state regulation of mineral and forest lands development in the years ahead.[32]

THE ROLE OF THE COLONIAL STATE

On the question of the relationship of the colonial state toward mineral development, I have referred to a government policy (more rather a nonpolicy) riddled with vacillation and half measures that were a mirror of the contradictions in general colonial political economy and administration in British West Africa from 1875 to 1897. At the heart of the imperial government's dilemma on gold mining lay two or three fundamental paradoxes—perhaps best described as indifferent imperialism. First, as educated African critics and even one or two government officials had the temerity to suggest, the very idea of a colony implied some sense of commitment to the welfare of the people and to general economic advancement; and they argued that this could be achieved only through the expansion of governmental services and territorial control. But we have seen that officialdom in Whitehall throughout the period surveyed here—at least until the governorship of W.B. Griffith—by and large rejected the idea that the Gold Coast government had any genuine responsibility for the administration, let alone the development, of interior districts. Until the mid-1890s the Colonial Office staff stoutly resisted grand programs for revenue-supported education and public health measures on behalf of hinterland Africans and, equally, major public works improvements in aid of the mining companies, on the grounds that such expenditures would saddle the colonial treasury with huge debts, which could in turn prompt outcries by radicals in Parliament about extensions of empire.

The Colonial Office Staff and the Railway Question

A second and related set of contradictions stemmed from considerations of Smithian political economy combined with civil service elitism. Both senior and junior clerks at the Colonial Office, led by the assistant undersecretary, Robert Meade, were unbending in their beliefs in balanced colonial budgets and minimalist government. Well known as an ardent Gladstonian in fiscal policy and strongly Cobdenite with respect to extensions of state power, Meade, who numbered senior treasury officials among his closest friends, remained steadfastly opposed to practically all forms of direct colonial government assistance to private enterprise and the use of British taxpayers money for extensions of imperial control.[33] That the British imperial government, like most leading industrial powers of the day, might favor overseas mineral development in principle for its contributions to national income did not mean that the fastidious Oxonian senior civil servants who commanded the C.O., Foreign Office, and treasury in the 1870s and 1880s had any affinity for miners or desired any interchange with the directors of the Anglo-West African mining companies, even if many of the latter could boast addresses in the City of London. Quite the contrary: it is difficult to imagine a wider chasm separating two groups.[34] Until very late in the period surveyed here, when the movement for railway construction at last gained momentum and a new secretary of state, Joseph Chamberlain, found a way of squaring the circle between questionable methods and desired ends, the Colonial Office staff, under Meades leadership, was quite successful in keeping the "ungentlemanly capitalists" of the West African mining lobby at arms length.[35] Transportation projects remained the major problem and bone of contention between the Anglo-West African mining lobby and the imperial government and also—especially during the governorship of Griffith—between Gold Coast officials and the Colonial Office. Throughout the greater part of the period surveyed here the Secretary of State for Colonies and his senior staff felt no sense of urgency on the railway question nor did they, from all appearances, perceive the vacuity in their responses to requests for guarantees by promoters of private railways to the gold mines—summed up in the Dickensian circumlocution that if such railways were to be built, then they would have to be built with government funds, which were not likely to be forthcoming.

The Colonial State and Compulsory Labor

Yet another set of issues focused on the ambivalence in the governments position with regard to the recruitment and treatment of African wage laborers by the companies. On the one hand the colonial state often expressed a vague rhetorical concern for African miners wages and conditions on the job. But we noted in chapter 6 that the Accra government did little or nothing to regulate housing or health conditions for Africans at the mines. While some officials were sensitive to mining company problems with labor recruitment and retention, they were also aware that company managers bristled at the slightest hint of a government inspection, let alone criticism of conditions for labor at the mines. The result was a general inertia and an unwillingness by the government to probe very deeply into the mines labor issue, whether from the position of the companies, or from the standpoint of African unskilled labor. Though various ideas were tossed about, the Colonial Office refused to countenance in this period most of the stringent proposals for labor control, notably the concept of a hut tax (used elsewhere in British Africa both to raise revenues and to stimulate labor exertion),[36] a restrictive compound system on the South African model, or a strict system of arrests, fines, or imprisonment for leaving the job without permission—which spokesmen for the mining interest advocated as essential to prevent absenteeism and desertion. The closest that the colonial state came to adopting the latter idea was seen in the set of Master and Servant Ordinances that the legislative council passed over a twenty-five year period.[37] But we have seen that, despite much spilled ink, practically all the governments efforts in the compulsory labor area in these years simply bypassed the mining industry. That such laws were seldom implemented in a way that met the standards of extreme imperialists must be traced to the long tradition of laissez-faire indifference on the coast, as well as to possible fear of arousing hostile opinion among the educated African elite and humanitarian critics in Westminster.[38] In a policy stance that ran counter to master and servant laws later applied in South Africa, the Gold Coast labor laws were rarely used by the colonial courts on behalf of the Wassa mining companies in restraining workers who had walked off the job in defiance of agreements. Instead, the government simply looked the other way when the mining companies in quasi-judicial fashion punished their own workers by fines and docking wages. By the same token, however, the Accra government never actively encouraged district commissioners to seek out cases of infractions or abuses by management against workers under the terms of these same ordinances. The fact of the matter was that in comparison with other colonies of the British Empire very few arrests of any kind were prosecuted by the Gold Coast government under these laws.[39]

The governments basic indifference on the labor question showed up most egregiously in its inattention to the frayed relations between a number of mining companies and the migrant workers from the Kru Coast of Liberia who, as we have seen, were the backbone of the mines underground labor force. Interestingly, the colonial state would later claim that the regulatory provisions of some of its labor laws were specifically designed towards protecting Kru workers in a strange foreign country.[40] In fact, in ways that I have described, the Kru men were, arguably, the worst treated of all the mine workers in this period. Only on rare occasions in the twentieth century would the colonial government take the trouble to investigate cases where individual workers had been punished cruelly for minor infractions or where—in breach of contract—they had been denied return steamship passage or justly due back wages by irresponsible companies.[41] And it must be emphasized that these few instances were due to courageous actions by one or two dedicated officials, not to general policy. Unless a blatant felony were committed, it was next to impossible to bring the colonial courts into action against a European for an infraction or for exercising "excessive zeal" against African workers.

AFRICAN ENTREPRENEURS AND THE FOUNDATIONS
OF THE ASHANTI GOLDFIELDS CORPORATION

By examining the foundations of the Ashanti Goldfields Corporation, we can catch a last glimpse of the activities of the African middle-class mining promoters of the central coastal states, who figured strongly in earlier chapters, and at the same time, gain some insight into the shift from the pioneering stage of mines development to a new twentieth-century order dominated by two or three well-capitalized syndicates and one behemoth corporation under state-backed concessionaire-imperialism. The indigenous merchant-promoters of Cape Coast had certainly contributed to the Wassa gold rush; and a second group of prosperous Gold Coastans also played a crucial preliminary role in opening up the Kingdom of Asante to industrialized gold mining. The three trailblazers were Joseph Etruson Ellis, Joseph Peter Brown, and Joseph Edward Biney. Each of these men stood close to the center of the educated bourgeois class that had grown up in the western and central coastal towns since the 1830s and 1840s. Brown was born at Dixcove in the western Gold Coast, where his father had been a Wesleyan minister; the other two men came from villages near the port of Saltpond. All three were educated at the Cape Coast Wesleyan elementary school.[42] Two of the three obtained secondary education at Freetown, Sierra Leone; and Brown started his professional life as a teacher at Cape Coast before working his way up to chief accountant for the Swanzy trading firm. Ellis began his career as a tailor, but later became an independent trading agent and produce broker, working closely with the British firm of Alexander Miller Brothers. Biney earned a good living from a retail store at Saltpond, which according to his nephew, specialized in haberdashery and jewelry.[43] All three—particularly Brown—would become active in African nationalistic pressure group activity and ardent critics of the colonial government. Brown (see photo) became one of two nominated African members of the Gold Coast Legislative Council.

In the early 1890s Ellis and Biney formed the Ashanti Exploration Company (1891), designed to prospect and open up the goldfields at Obuasi in Asante. Soon afterward Brown joined them as a major shareholder and director; among other early subscribers were Dr. Ernest Hayford, headmaster at the new Wesleyan Secondary School (founded in 1876); J. W. Sey, first president of the Gold Coast Aborigines Rights Protection Society (1897); and J. M. Sarbah. The firm was registered on the London Stock Exchange but was never very successful in raising substantial sums of European capital. The three men had the advantage of close personal contacts with the paramount rulers of both Adanse and Bekwae, important states in the Asante Union, who sold them the leases for mining rights at Obuasi.[44] Ellis was the main dynamic force in sparking the commencement of mining operations and he spent a good deal of time at the Asante installation. Benefiting from old-time African deep probes, he was credited with opening Ellis's Shaft. The production of ore was steady; but the company had to extract gold from a single small stamping machine and mercury amalgamation table. Still, observers reported that in 1894 the company employed more than 200 laborers working on four shafts.[45] This allows the restatement of another point: The educated African businessmen who take up one of the important themes in this story were not only company promoters and land concessionaires, a number—Swanzy Essien at Heman Prestea, the three Sams for the Wassa (G.C.) Company, and Brown, Ellis, and Biney at Obuasi—qualified as bona fide capitalist miners and hard-working managers of producing mines.

No doubt the last three venture capitalists would have preferred to remain in command of the first totally African-owned producing company. Extremely sagacious, they realized that they had possession of a true bonanza property; but they also had to face the intimidating nature of the task ahead of them. Their predicament was illustrative of other able African businessmen of the time who sought to bridge the gap from commercial to industrial entrepreneurship in a ruthlessly competitive mining world. The plain fact is that they dug deep shafts and carried on underground development work for three years without the large-scale machine production and economies of scale that would have been necessary to turn a substantial profit. The cyanide separation process was just coming into use, but the equipment was too expensive. They recognized that huge capital reserves, a railway, batteries of modern machinery, and a corps of skilled mining engineers and technicians would be necessary to turn their properties to account. As a second and fallback choice they hoped to make good money from their arduous groundbreaking efforts. To determine the worth of their concession they sent ore samples for evaluation to a British contact they believed they could trust in the City of London.

This was the little-known mercantile firm of Smith and Cade, which had been one of Biney's chief merchandise suppliers from the United Kingdom. Having determined that the ore samples were indeed valuable, this firm established the Côte d'Or Company (parent of the Ashanti Goldfields Corporation) to survey the properties and to negotiate purchase of the Obuasi lease from Ellis, Brown, and Biney. The ultimate concession was a tremendous one, covering 100 square miles of territory for ninety-nine years. Considering the ultimate value of gold produced from this fabulously rich property, Brown, Ellis, and Biney did not receive just compensation from Côte d'Or, and Cade admitted with some compunction that had driven an extremely hard (and probably unfair) bargain.[46] On the other hand, Jacob Eduam-Baiden, Biney's nephew told the writer that three men became relatively wealthy by West African standards as a result of the transaction.[47] It was the rulers and people of Bekwae and Adanse who were cheated. To cover itself, in the event of future controversy over land rights, the corporation also signed agreements with the kings of Bekwae and Adanse (representatives of the people who were the true owners of the lands in question), paying one the paltry sum of £66 per year and the other £100 to £133 per year in rents.[48]

It would carry us too far afield to summarize the complete early history of the Ashanti Goldfields Corporation here. From the vantage point of hindsight, it is easy to speculate on what might have happened had Ellis, Brown, and Biney tried to work through other London investors or management consultants. It was difficult enough in this age of flamboyant scheming for unknown European mining firms to obtain credibility and backing on the London Stock Exchange—let alone companies managed by Africans. Racism aside, it was also a question of experience in the City and pipelines to capital resources. In fact, at least one other expatriate company with an interest in the Obuasi concession had approached Ellis, Brown and Biney about a contract;[49] but they turned it down. Apparently, though, the three Africans did not have many contacts that they believed they could trust in London;[50] and with their own money running out, they probably felt constrained to make an early decision with a firm they had dealt with in the past. The African and Eurafrican mining capitalists, like their expatriate counterparts deserved credit for their trailblazing efforts, which paved the way for the next developmental phase in Gold Coast and Asante mining. As might have been expected in an age of growing imperialism, the three men did not receive a full and just return for their great efforts and sagacity. It may be that they received what their own Ghanaian heirs viewed as an acceptable overall consideration: in addition to cash they also became shareholders in the Ashanti Goldfields Corporation (AGC).

Because the working of the huge tract ultimately required imperial intervention in a territory outside of formal Gold Coast colonial control, it was of tremendous benefit to the directors and shareholders of the Ashanti Goldfields that their leasing arrangement in 1897 coincided with the more aggressive administration of Joseph Chamberlain, Secretary of State for Colonies. As part of his program for imperial aggrandizement and development, Chamberlain had praised the staking out of large "tropical estates" for mines and forest products. Even then, approval of the unprecedented AGCs Obuasi concession did not come easy: the directors had to enlist the support of members of the City of Londons financial elite, who invested heavily in the corporation and brought substantial pressure to bear on the Colonial Office before Chamberlain proved willing to gave his imprimatur to the monopolistic concession.[51] The commencement of operations at Obuasi was closely bound up with two other spearheads of the new imperialism: massive investment in railway and harbor construction and the British military conquest and annexation of Asante. These complex episodes, completed after 1900, will be dealt with in detail in a future publication.

THE EXPANDING ARC OF THE
INDIGENOUS MINERS' FRONTIER

The story of the two mining frontiers—traditional as well as modern—expanding side by side continued through the first decade and into the second decade of the twentieth century. Even in the 1890s, the indigenous miners frontier seemed to get a new breath of life as it pierced new geographic regions far outside the perimeters of what had been recognized as the British zone of commercial influence. In other publications I have discussed how the absorption of more distant markets and sources of supply into the commercial orbits of the ports of Axim and Cape Coast was also partly a function of the simultaneously expanding trade in wild rubber.[52] This is not to say that trading linkages between such Akan states as Wassa, Denkyera, Asante, and Twifo and the more distant gold-mining regions of the north had not existed earlier; but under the influence of the dynamic gold trade and the new rubber trade there was a tremendous revival and *intensification* of economic activity by thousands of new people on the older trade routes from the late 1880s onward. In other words, a greater number of peripatetic hunter-trader-miners stopped, set up camp, and began to probe and penetrate more deeply into potential gold regions and districts that they had probably traveled through very quickly before. Informants from Atuabo in southwestern Ghana stated that one of the most important new mining centers for Nzeman gold seekers in the early twentieth century was in the area around Bibianiha in the heavily forested and somewhat inaccessible (for Europeans) western state of Sefwi, about 115 miles northwest of Tarkwa.[53] This conforms exactly to what the Gold Coast government geologist Junner observed and later described in his detailed report.

> A good example of the [African] open-cut type of workings can be seen near Ntubia, Sefwi district . . . on the south bank of the Bensupata stream about 1908. Immediately there was a rush to the workings, and in 1909 it was estimated that fully 2,000 people from all parts of the Sefwi district were actively engaged in winning gold from the rer [reef] which was opened for a length of about 1/4 mile and from 10 to 60 feet in depth. . . . Open-cut workings and trenches were mainly used by the coastal tribes, e.g. Apollonians [Nzemans], Ahantas, Gwiras and Wassas. . . .[54]

Regard for the gold potential of Sefwi spread so rapidly that it became an additional new site for large-scale European deep-level mining, under the powerful Bibiani Company, organized under the leadership of the British millionaire Alfred Strauss in the 1910s and 1920s.[55]

Even before the turn of the century there had been a simultaneous stretching of this Axim-centered gold-trading frontier far to the north-west, into the hinterland of the French-controlled Ivory Coast—the region of the Comoé and Manzan Rivers (see map 8.1). This was partly because immediately after the British military "pacification" of Asante in 1896 (not so violent as the 1900 Anglo Asante war), travel by both coastal Akan and Asante traders and middlemen to the north and northwest was said to have picked up considerably.

One of the richest targets for reactivated indigenous gold mining and the overland gold trade in the late nineteenth and early twentieth centuries lay in Gyaman, a Brong state, which in times past had been tributary to Asante. To a considerable extent this expanding trade was import-generated. For years the Nzemans had been active middlemen in the Anyi states north of the Ivory Coast lagoons—Morenou was one district often mentioned— "exacting," one report said, "high prices in gold" from the local people for the sale of European merchandise that was much in demand—guns, gunpowder, cotton cloth, knives, and salt.[56] Having once traded in a new area, the Nzemans often found it easy to settle in—not always to the liking of the inhabitants—as resident miners. What is more, the rich Brong-Ahafo region between Asante and the River Comoé in the west also became an extremely lucrative new center for rubber tapping as well as the resurgent gold-mining industry.[57] If we look at the expanded map of the eastern Ivory Coast hinterland and the western Gold Coast, we see that the entire river valley region from Dadiaso on the River Bakakora, south of Bonduku, down to Bettié on the Lower Comoé River was one continuously rich gold-mining zone—especially for alluvial and shallow subsurface gold.

Perhaps the most famous of these northwestern centers was "Assikasso" (both a town and a larger district)—the name of which means "place of gold." The celebrated French explorer and anthropologist Louis Binger noted that there were many small tributaries flowing into the Manzan, Ba, and Comoé valleys, which contained countless small pit mines, and he especially stressed that these mines were "worked mainly by Apollonians" (i.e., Nzemans).[58] Two other gold-mining centers of this rich frontier zone, which continued to be worked by Gold Coast migrant miners until as late as 1914, were at Wam, in Ahafo and

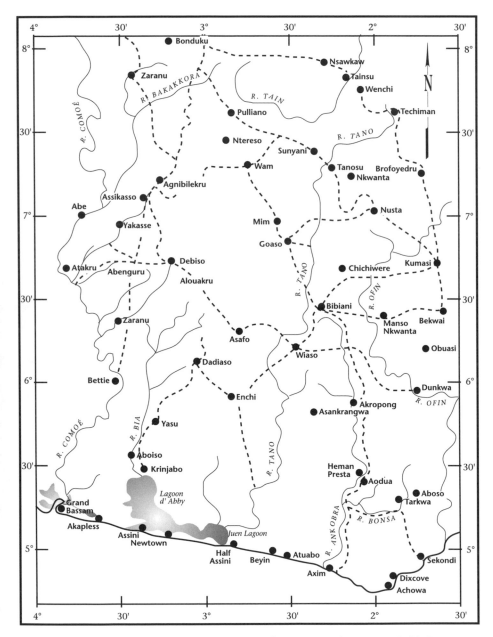

Map 8.2. Expansion of the African gold-mining frontier into the greater Gold Coast–Ivory Coast hinterland (sketch map, ca. 1895). Dotted lines indicate trade roads taken by indigenous gold miners.

the gold-bearing hills north of Pulliano in southeastern Gyaman.[59] In emphasizing the vital opening-up role of the indefatigable and ubiquitous Nzemans, however, it is important not to oversimplify what were really very complex and alternating patterns of interregional trade in which different ethnic groups and trade flows crisscrossed one another many times. Abron and Anyi traders traveled southeast all the way from the Ivory Coast hinterland to Axim and other Gold coast ports, and Fante traders from Cape Coast and Saltpond as well as Nzemans from Axim moved into French-claimed territory west of Aowin and Sefwi. Despite journeys exceeding thirty days, traders from the mid northern Ivory Coast hinterland sometimes preferred to travel southeast to the British ports, where there was said to be a wider selection of imported European manufactured goods and more competitive prices than in the French-controlled seacoast towns of Assini and Grand Bassam.[60] A parallel economic phenomenon of significance, which had been brewing slowly and surely for many years, was the increased sale of gold dust and rubber by the actual producers, as well as by middlemen, on the coast for *cash*. This also casts light on the West African currency revolution, in which the major European powers sought to establish their own uniform coinage systems in their respective colonies. Again, it is important not to exaggerate the suddenness of this currency transition; but by the beginning of the new century it had become a highly visible phenomenon to both the African and European merchants of the coastal towns.[61]

DECLINE, CONTINUITIES, AND REBIRTH

The exportation of gold derived from traditional African production far outstripped exports from the European mechanized sector until 1893. Even afterward, gold mining by African farmer-miners held firm, averaging 9,864 ounces, or £34,300 worth, in exports per annum over the next four years—though exports from the European mines gradually gained the lead. African gold dust movements from the interior of the forest zone dropped precipitously in 1898, an abrupt change that the Accra government could not immediately explain. Some sources attributed the turn-of-the-century drop in the indigenous overland gold trade to British Governor F. M. Hodgson's ill-advised, forceful seizure of the sacred Asante Golden Stool and the resulting Yaa Asantewa War (the eighth Anglo-Asante war), which totally disrupted the internal economy of Asante and surrounding territories in 1900.[62] However, this collapse was temporary and the hinterland trade resumed. Examination of district records suggests that the more serious long-term decline in the indigenous gold trade was traceable, at least in part, to the larger and easier profits per unit of labor that many men could obtain from rubber tapping, especially in Asante, Sefwi, Gyaman, and Brong-Ahafo, where the richest *funtumia* rubber forests were being opened up.[63] Still, this was not a wholesale shift or displacement of economic energies: the indigenous gold and rubber trades continued to exist in tandem for a number of years and many African producer-traders engaged in both simultaneously.

Meanwhile, the expatriate-controlled companies experienced their own set of crises—the conjuncture of twenty years of accumulated problems—partly natural and environmental and partly man-made. The peak year for the "big three" companies was 1896, when the Tarkwa and Aboso and the Wassa (G.C.) Mining companies, together with the Gie Appanto, employed a total of 1,200 workers and produced 15,538 ounces of gold, valued at £62,149. But the cracks were beginning to show. To the absence of railway transport for introducing effective heavy extractive machinery were added problems with timbering and the construction of drives and adits. External critics observed that a majority of company directors fixation on early production had been at the expense of long-range development. Compounding the recurring problems of machine malfunction was the incapacity of existing pumping machinery to cope with disastrous and morale-breaking underground flooding in 1897 and 1898, following two years of extremely heavy rainy seasons, which led to a severe curtailment, if not a shutdown of most of the producing mines. It is well to keep in mind that in most mining regions of the world drainage has traditionally constituted one of the most burdensome charges on mining operations, leading to the undoing of many companies. In the instances at hand, the mining engineer Louis Gowans reported that during the height of one particularly bad summer rain, the floodwaters around Tarkwa had risen as high as twenty-three inches in a single night. Overland transport of heavy loads of supplies and machinery from the banks of the River Ankobra to Tarkwa and Aboso had always been a daunting task during the quagmires of an ordinary rainy season, now eyewitnesses wrote that existing footpaths were totally submerged and rendered impassable by the torrential downpours.[64] All this lent heavy weight to the Anglo-West African mercantile and mining lobby's continuing outcry for a government built railway. In 1896, Francis Swanzy and James Irvine noted that the three major mines were still producing—but on a shoestring—and they blamed the closure of many of the other mines on the lack of a railway, which had made it impossible to install the best-working machinery—including pumps.[65] By 1900 total Gold Coast gold production had fallen to its lowest ebb in forty years. The Tarkwa and Aboso mines were down to 939 ounces, valued at £3,886, which was 86 percent below its best year in 1896. Production at the WGCMCs Aja Bippo mine reached its nadir at a mere 203 ounces of gold, valued at £733. This, potentially the richest installation in the whole of Wassa, had gone heavily into debt and was unable to keep up interest payments on its debentures. There was one bright augury for the future. In the whole of the expatriate mining sector the only entity to export substantial gold at the turn of the century was the newly formed Ashanti Goldfields Corporation. By this time all the old Wassa companies had exhausted their capital and had nothing left for the kind of radical overhaul that would be necessary to put their mines back on the road to recovery.[66] None of the three major producing companies of the 1890s—the WGCMC, the Tarkwa and Aboso, and the Gie Appanto—were able to resume operations in their original form: all had to undergo reconstructions under new directors in the twentieth century. But the mines and their surface works would remain intact, ready for rehabilitation, through infusions of new capital that would allow for the installation of more efficient pumping machinery, heavier stone breakers, electric dynamos, and the latest cyanide treatment apparatus in the years ahead.

By the turn of the century the presence of several crucial elements, hitherto absent from the equation on mining imperialism, would totally transform the configuration of structures, forces, men, and events on the Coast. First, the major mining companies would become better capitalized, better managed, and would organize more potent pressure groups to represent them in the United Kingdom and on the Gold Coast. Second, by that time the modern colonial state would take shape under a series of able governors—Mathew Nathan, William Rodger, and Hugh Clifford—advised by larger staffs, who were prepared to identify more closely with the mechanized mining industry as a major vehicle for development. Third, there developed a radically altered global exchange rate configuration, which heightened the international demand for gold. This was accompanied by the severe reduction in supplies of the yellow metal from the Rand during the Anglo-Boer War, which would greatly accelerate the pressures to bring secondary gold-producing regions, like the Gold Coast, into full production. Fourth, the new age would witness a far more aggressive and expansionistic imperial power emanating from Downing Street and Whitehall under a Secretary of State for Colonies, willing to work closely with mining company executives and other concessionaires, and who was capable of bringing the muscle of the British government behind railway construction, harbor works, and many other benefits on behalf of large-scale economic development. It was only through the Gold Coast—Asante Railway that installation of the more up-to-date heavy crushing and pumping machinery, together with the components necessary for construction of cyanide separation plants, became possible. By making mining more efficient and economical these innovations boosted the Ghana gold industry on its modern trajectory.

Expansion of the Akan Gold Miners and Traders Frontier in the Late Nineteenth and Early Twentieth Centuries

Nana Efoa Tenkroman, Queen Mother of Konongo, Asante, an inestimable source of oral history. Photo by the author, 1987.

Chief Kofi Kyei of Heman-Prestea, Wassa-Fiase improtant during the gold boom of 1879–1895. Photo courtesy of Dr. David Killingray, Goldsmiths College, University of London.

A Nzeman traditional gold
miner, John Ansah Quinoo
of Awiebo, E. Nzema, exhib-
iting the tools of his trade
Photo by the author, 1987

Entrance to advanced African pit mine worked by the African-owned
Ashanti Concessions Ltd., noted in this chapter. (Note innovations: bamboo
lagging, rope windlass with sling for raising and lowering men as well as
gold ore, plus swish roof and ladder.) Ashanti Goldfields Corp.

Akan Goldsmiths and Gold Traders Who Played a Part in the Expansion of the Indigenous Gold Mining Frontier

Traditional African goldsmith and gold trader with villagers preparing to weigh gold dust. Photo courtesy of David Killingray, Goldsmith College, University of London.

Traditional Akan goldsmith and helper with small furnace and bellows for melting gold dust into ingots or jewelry

GLOSSARY OF TWI TERMS

This list of Twi terms pertinent to mining takes as its standard the Akyem Twi dialect rather than Asante Twi. Although many of the terms are used in both dialects, in case of differences the Akyem Twi version is preferred here. I am grateful to Robert Addo-Fening and Edward Reynolds for their review of this list.

Aboso. A small mining town about six miles northeast of Tarkwa. (See maps in this volume.)

abosom. Lesser spirits or deities among the Akan people.

abusa. A traditional Akan method of dividing the returns from cooperative productive activity (gold mining, farming, hunting, fishing, etc.) by thirds. One-third would normally be reserved for the producing individual or group, with the remaining two-thirds being divided by various levels of ruling authority. There were variations on this concept. An *abuna* share meant dividing the proceeds into halves.

abusua. The Akan matriclan. A system of family and wider social organization based on matrilineal inheritance, or descent through females.

afua (pl.: **mfua**). A farm. More often used in the plural form, which denotes fallow land or farm land left to regenerate itself after exhaustion. (Sources: Robert Addo-Fening; Ivor Wilks.)

afunaba. A client or subordinate.

Akan. The Akan are the dominant ethno-linguistic group of modern Ghana (and the former Gold Coast). The language of the Akan is called Twi. The Akan region includes many sub-groups, states and kingdoms, including the Fante, Asante, the two Wassas, Denkyira, Akuapem, Akyem and many more.

Akani (or **Accany**). According to some traditions, Akani was the heartland for the spread of the Akan culture, and the mother region for all later

Akan states. Dutch maps of the seventeenth century sometimes show a Great Akani; but it is difficult to know if this was a state, a league of city-states, or simply a geographical expression. (Sources: Ray Kea and A. A. Boahen.)

Akanist. Early term for a person from Akani. However, the term appears to have stood more for a profession than a nationality. In the seventeenth century Akanists were known on the coast as skilled traders from the interior, particularly in the overland gold trade. After 1700 the sources refer more and more to traders from particular central forest states, especially Adansi, Assin, and Twifo. (Source: Albert Van Dantzig.)

Akani sika. Regarded in earlier centuries as the purest form of Akan gold.

akorow (sing.: **korow**). The largest bowls for washing river gold. Large bowls were normally used at the start of panning. Smaller bowls, used at intermediate stages or toward the end of the process, were called *korowa*. In Asante Twi the equivalent word was *kodoo* (Sources: R. Addo-Fening; T. Garrard.)

amenapeaa. Deep-level or hard-rock mines. (Source: Kwame Arhin.)

Ankobra. The major river that flows through southwestern Ghana. Named by the Portuguese because its course resembled the coils of a snake.

Aodua (also **Awodua, Awudua**). The capital of the Apinto substate of Wassa Fiase.

Apinto. A substate of the kingdom of Wassa Fiase that contained a number of important gold mining sites, including Tarkwa, Aboso, and Prestea. The ruler of Apinto was called the Apintohene. (Sources: oral traditions, Wassa.)

apoa. A river bottom or streambed.

Apuntea (or **Apontua**). the patron deity of the earth and of gold mining in Konongo, Dwaben, and Asante. (Source: Kononogo oral tradition.)

asafo. The "companies" or groups of men in cities, towns, and villages that were organized originally for military purposes.

asafohene. In the two Wassa states emphasized in this study, this term was often used to emphasize the military functions of chiefs, otherwise called **ohene.** (Source: F. G. Crowther.)

Asante. The greatest of the Akan states, it emerged after the battle of Feyiase in 1701 as a confederation of lesser states. Under a series of powerful rulers, Asante in the eighteenth century greatly increased both its territorial and centralized bureaucratic powers, becoming a union, a kingdom, and ultimately an empire.

Asantehene. The king and paramount ruler of all the Asante substates (head of the Asante Union).

aso (or **soso**). The short hoe or adzelike tool used by the Akan people in cultivating the soil and also in gold mining.

awowa (pl. **nnwowa**). A pawn; a person or persons given over to a creditor as surety for a debt.

bokiti. A wooden or metal bucket. Often used to haul gold-laden rock or earth to the surface from a mine. (Source: oral data, Wassa.)

bondo. The name in Nzemaland for wooden or calabash bowls used for sifting gold-laden sand. (Source: oral data, Eastern Nzema.)

epo. A gold nugget (cf. *mpkowa*, small nuggets). (Source: George F. Ferguson and oral tradition.)

fetish. Magic A material object or place associated with religious or magical powers. This could be a grove in the forest, a waterfall, or a cave. Fetish powers (both positive and negative) were associated with gold mining. *Fetish* derives from the French *fétiche*, and Portuguese *feitiço*, "charm, sorcery; artificial."

Heman-Prestea. See **Tarkwa.**

kenkey. The meal, made by crushing maize, that was one of the basic foods of the Akan people. Originally adapted from the Ga people of the Accra area. (Source: Edward Reynolds.)

krodze. Sources in Wassa stated that the wood from this particular tree, owing to its slow-burning properties was used in the fire setting method of cracking gold ore. (Source: oral data, Wassa.)

kroom. Small village or hamlet. The word is a European corruption of the phrase *kuro-mu*, "in the village." See **kuro.**

kuro (pl.: **nkuro**). The correct Twi term for a town or village. In normal useage a *kuro* was a large settlement, often a town; *akuraa* referred to a small village or hamlet, perhaps only half a dozen houses. (Source: Robert Addo-Fening.)

Mankouma. The most important earth deity in the Wassa region, associated with earning a livelihood from the earth, whether by farming, hunting, or gold mining. It functioned as a patron deity of gold miners. There was also a major African traditional mine in Apinto substate, known as the Mankouma mine. In Akyem the people invoked the river deity, Birem, to assist them in mining. (Sources: oral tradition, Wassa; for Akyem, Robert Addo-Fening.)

mobaa (sing.: **ohoba**). The rolling stones used for the crushing of corn for the making of **kenkey.** These stones were easily adapted to the final pulverizing of gold-laden crushed rock in order to extract gold dust. (Source: oral tradition, Wassa.)

mpanyimfo. Stool elders; also the characteristic Akan council of elders that was replicated at the village, the stool, and the state levels. (Source: Edward Reynolds.)

mutua. Ropes made from tree bark or raffia to hoist buckets into mine shafts and for other purposes. (Source: Oral tradition, Wassa.)

Nana. A term of respect prefixed to the names of kings, chiefs, officials, and elders (e.g., *Nana Akodaa* Kwadwo Ofor).

nduke. In Nzemaland, the name for gold. (Source: oral tradition, Eastern Nzema.)

nkoa (sing.: **akoa**). Subjects of a traditional king or chief. Nearly everyone in the Akan region was the subject of some ruling authority.

nkron. The general word for any gold mine. A hole in the ground or a wider hollowed-out underground mining chamber.

nkron nkomena (or **nkromena**). A deep mine.

obirempon (pl.: **abirempon**). A "big man"; a powerful individual, based on wealth or the number of subordinates he controlled (or both).

odikro. A village headman.

odonko (pl.: **nnonko**). Originally, a foreigner, a northerner. Because northerners were among the most common captives taken in war, *odonko* also came to be the word for "slave" par excellence.

ohene (pl.: **ahenfo**). A chief.

oman (pl.: **aman**). A polity; an Akan stool authority. It can also mean a state, a town, or a kingdom.

omanhene (pl.: **amanhene**). A king or paramount ruler; a stool holder. Examples are the Asantehene (Asante), the Okyenhene (Akyem), the Denkyerahene (Denkyera), the Wassa Fiasehene (Wassa Fiase).

owura (pl.: **awuranom**). An overlord or master in the *awura-akoa* (master-subject) relationship.

peredwan. A gold weight that in Asante was equivalent to $1\frac{1}{4}$ troy ounces. (Source: T. Garrard)

opanin. A title of respect for any senior person or elder.

sika. Gold or wealth. Cf. **sikani**, "man of wealth"; a rich person.

sikadie (**asikadie**). The work of digging or washing for gold.

sikadini (pl.: **sikadifo**). A gold miner. (Sources: Edward Reynolds; R. Addo-Fening.)

sika dwumfo (pl.). Goldsmiths.

sika futuro. Gold dust currency; money.

sika kuduo. The earthenware pot where gold dust might be stored.

soso toa. A long-handled tool with a narrow metal blade at the end, used in hard-rock mining. (Source: George E. Ferguson.)

soso tupre. A shovel. (Source: George E. Ferguson.)

Tarkwa, Aboso, and **Heman-Prestea.** Three of the leading mining centers of Wassa examined in this study.

tikororo. "Saturday earth." A term used in certain Akan states when people would mine for gold solely on behalf of a king or a chief. Various states and ethnic subgroups might designate special days when the whole of that day's mining might be turned over to the state as a kind of tax or royalty. (Source: J. M. Sarbah.)

Wassa. The major gold-mining region that is the focus of the present study. Located in the interior of southwestern Ghana, it was divided into two main kingdoms, Wassa Amenfi and Wassa Fiase.

GLOSSARY OF MINING TERMS

adit. A passage driven into the side of a hill to extract minerals from a reef.

alluvial. Deposited by flowing water. See **alluvium.**

alluvium. Unconsolidated material deposited by a river or stream.

amalgam. An alloy of mercury with one or more other metals. Also, the pasty combination of gold and mercury obtained from the milling of gold ore. See **milling.**

amalgamation. A method by which, prior to the invention of the cyanide process in the 1880s, gold (or silver) was extracted by mixing pulverized ore with a solution of mercury. The gold and silver combined very easily with the mercury and thus were drawn off, leaving the sand and other waste materials. Afterward the mercury was drawn off by contact with copper plates, leaving pure gold or silver.

auriferous. Containing or yielding gold.

ball mill. See **tube mill.**

banket. Pebbles of quartz embedded in a matrix of compressed gravel and clay; a type of gold ore found in parts of Ghana (especially Wassa state) and also South Africa.

battery. An ore-crushing plant made up of a number of steam-powered stamps arranged in a line and held together in a frame.

Birimian. A type of Precambrian Rock (probably over 2,000,000,000 years old) first observed near the Birim River in Akyem and special to the Gold Coast/Ghana. The deepest geological stratum that is the fundamental source of gold in the country.

concentrate. A pastelike mass of ore in which the gold has been concentrated by the reduction process.

concentrating table. A device consisting of a riffled or straked deck, usually inclined in two directions, to which a differential vibrating motion is imparted. When the gold-containing amalgam is poured over the table the heavier portions (containing the gold) are collected in the grooves between the riffle bars or ridges, while the lighter portions (water, sand, base metals and waste are carried by the current off the table and into troughs or drains. (see also **strakes.**)

conglomerate. A type of natural concrete consisting of closely packed quartz pebbles and rock fragments cemented together by the action of water and the pressure of overlaying rock formations. Sometimes grouped with the breccias and quartzites.

Cornish pump. A single-action steam engine used in the early days of mining in which the power for pumping operations was transmitted through the action of a cumbersome beam.

crosscut. A short drive cut at right angles across a reef or vein of gold from either a perpendicular mine shaft or from a long horizontal tunnel. A crosscut may connect two parallel drives or tunnels. See **drive.**

cyanide process. A method of dissolving gold from its parent ore by dissolving the matrix in a solution or of potassium cyanide. Afterward the gold is precipitated by the use zinc or by electrolysis.

dead rock (dead ground). Barren rock that surrounds a gold reef.

dead work. Essential development operations—including the sinking of shafts and the driving of tunnels and crosscuts—that precedes the removal of ore.

dress. To pulverize, sort, and wash gold ore in preparation for reduction by mercury amalgamation or cyanide process.

drive. A level horizontal tunnel that follows the line of a reef or vein. Also called a drift. Drifts and drives are distinguished from crosscuts, which are driven through barren ground to intersect with a vein.

dwt. A pennyweight. Equal to 24 grains, or 1.555 grams; a unit of measurement. Gold was generally measured by the dwt. Twenty pennyweights equal one troy ounce.

dyke. An intrusion of igneous rock (sometimes containing gold) into geological strata. See **igneous rock, stratum.**

eluvial. Describes a mineral, such as gold, associated with the debris of rock produced by weathering or the random action of water (e.g., rainfall), rather than by the constant flow of streams or rivers.

fault. A break or dislocation in a geological system.

fire setting. An ancient method of cracking open the country rock surrounding a mineral by first heating by fire to a high temperature and then dousing the hot rock with cold water.

footwall. The lower side of an exposed gold reef.

gangue. The minerals that enclose metallic ores, such as gold, in a reef or vein.

gold. A yellow metal that is highly malleable, ductile, and free from susceptibility to rust. Chemical symbol: Au. *Fine gold* is almost pure gold.

Standard gold contains twenty-two parts of gold and two parts of another metal, most commonly silver or copper. See **auriferous.**

granite. An igneous rock made up of quartz, feldspar, and mica.

grit. A coarse sandstone or quartzite.

grizzly. A device for the coarse screening of bulk ore; used early in the milling process. It can comprise either fixed or moving bars, rods, or rollers. See **milling.**

hanging wall. the upper side of an exposed reef.

headtree. A horizontal beam supported by vertical posts used to shore up weak ground. See **timbering.**

hydraulic mining. A type of ore extraction used to break up gravels, washing them out for gold or tin. The use of water to get at alluvial minerals.

igneous rock. Volcanic plutonic rock.

lagging. Boards or small timbers used to support either the sides of a mine shaft or roof of a mine. Miners of the Akan region described in this study sometimes used thin bamboo poles for this purpose.

lens. A lens-shaped vein or gold ore formation.

level. One of a system of horizontal passages in a mine, normally arranged at 100-foot intervals, where the work of mining is done. Reached by skips and cages, levels are numbered successively from the surface.

line of strike. Geographical direction of a reef or lode. (Also called run of strike.) See also **strike.**

loaming. A process of discerning subsurface ore by examining and analyzing the surface soil of a region.

lode. A deposit of ore with more or less definite boundaries, located between bodies of nonmetalliferous rock.

milling. The process whereby metallic ores are pulverized, separated, concentrated, and otherwise prepared for the smelter.

mining development. The arduous process of excavating shafts and gouging out tunnels, adits, and crosscuts, as well as timbering and a host of other tasks, before ore can be extracted.

mother lode. A main lode. See **lode.**

nugget. A sizable granular substance of gold, alluvial in origin.

ore reserve. At a working mine, the estimated volume of ore that has been blocked out and developed for future extraction.

outcrop. A portion of a lode or reef that is exposed on the surface of the land.

pillar. After extensive mining, the ore that is left standing to support the roof of a gallery.

pithead gear. Surface structure, including elevators and winding machinery, at the top of a mine shaft. Also called headgear.

porphyry. A term used colloquially for almost any kind of igneous rock occurring in sheets or dykes, particularly if it is spotted or light in color.

prospect. (v.) To search for gold or other minerals. (n.) An area of rock that has been marked out as suitable for mining; a claim.

pyrite. A common mineral composed of iron disulfide (FeS_2). Because it had a brass-yellow luster, it was sometimes mistaken for gold. Often called fool's gold.

quartz. A crystallized silicon dioxide (SiO_2). Colloquially, any hard gold or silver ore, as distinguished from gravel or earth. Thus, we speak of quartz (hard-rock) mining, as opposed to alluvial mining.

quartzite. A coarse sandstone, composed largely of grains of quartz.

raise. A slanting connecting tunnel (looking upward) between mine levels.

reduction. The process of extracting metal from ore.

reef. An intrusive formation. A narrow ridge of rock. A vein of rock.

refine. To withdraw impurities from metal, most commonly by smelting.

riffle. A groove or channel at the bottom of an inclined trough or sluice for catching the gold contained in sand or gravel. See sluice.

roast. The heating of metal-containing ore, sufficiently to make it brittle, in order to ease the pulverization process. Roasting furnaces were an important part of modern mining installations.

schist. A crystalline rock that can be easily split or cleaved owing to its laminated structure.

shaft. Mine entrance by way of a vertical excavation.

shear zone. The area of a geological fault. The ragged edge of a broken rock strata.

silicosis. A miner's lung disease caused by prolonged inhalation of silica dust.

sink. To excavate in a downward direction. To dig a shaft.

slime. Ore reduced to a very fine powder and held in suspension in water so as to form a thin mud. A product of wet crushing.

sludge. Mud that contains gold.

sluice. An elongated trough for washing auriferous earth or gravel.

smelt. To remove impurities from a metal, or to extract metal from its parent ore, by a process of fusion.

stope. (n.) Any intermediate excavation to remove ore that has been made accessible by drifts, drives, and crosscuts. Stopes were the main working areas for underground miners. (v.) To blast out a large niche—often in the form of large steps—for gouging out ore between two levels.

strakes. Also known as riffles. These are a combination of ridges and grooves that stretch horizontally across the vibrating or concentrating tables. As the gold-containing amalgam or pulp is washed across these slanted tables, the gold, because of its higher specific gravity, is caught on the ridges and sinks into the grooves, whereas the lighter sand, mud and base metal grains are washed over the ridges and into gutters at the bottom and sides of the table.

stratum (pl.: **strata**). A sheetlike layer of rock lying between beds of other kinds of rock. A formation belonging to a distinct geological period.

strike. The direction or bearing of an inclined bed of ore in relation to a level surface.

sulfide ore. The union of a metal with sulfur. Experts say that the gold embedded in sulfide ore is more difficult to extract than that found in oxide ores.

tailings. Waste material from a processing or reduction plant after metal extraction.

Tarkwaian. In the Gold Coast/Ghana, a Precambrian geological formation consisting of quartzites, grits, and conglomerates. Named after the town of Tarkwa.

timbering. The supporting of drives, crosscuts, and stopes with wooden pillars and crossbeams to prevent collapse (cave-ins).

tributor. A miner working on the property of another and paying tribute based on a percentage of returns.

tube mill. Large steel cylinders filled partly with flint for fine grinding of ore after the stamping process. Ball mills are filled with iron balls for the same purpose.

vein. A narrow lode or reef.

Voltaian. In the Gold Coast/Ghana, a formation named after the Volta River, consisting of sandstones and limestones.

winze. A slanting connecting passage (looking downward) between mine levels.

workings. Mine excavations, such as shafts, levels, adits, winzes, raises, crosscuts, and stopes.

NOTES

CHAPTER 1

1. Throughout this book I mainly use the historically accurate terms *Gold Coast, Asante* and *northern region* in preference to *Ghana*, the modern nation that today encompasses these regions. This is to avoid confusion with the medieval Sudanic state of Ghana (ca. 770–1087). In addition, I use other terms such as *the Akan region* or *forest zone* to refer to culturally, linguistically, and topographically related areas, such as Wassa, Akyem, Denkyera, and Asante, before the consolidation of formal colonial rule. Occasionally I also use the term *Ghana* when referring to the territories encompassed by the modern (post-1957) nation-state. For justification on these points of terminology, see Kwame Y. Daaku, *Trade and Politics on the Gold Coast, 1600–1720* (London, 1970), xvi.

2. For a long time debate and uncertainty have hovered over the question of whether Muslim "Wangara" traders from the Western Sudan had actually penetrated the Akan forest zone and whether they had traveled as far South as the lower Guinea coast prior to the Portuguese contact. In one of his many scholarly studies, Ivor Wilks presents convincing evidence in the affirmative. See Wilks, "Wangara, Akan and Portuguese in the Fifteenth and Sixteenth Centuries," part 1, "The Matter of Bitu," *Journal of African History,* 23.3 (1982): 337–42. See also Philip D. Curtin, "Africa and the Wider Monetary World, 1250–1850," in John F. Richards, ed., *Silver and Gold Flows in the Medieval and Early Modern Worlds* (Durham, N.C., 1981), 238. Outside these works the consensus among scholars is that the goldfields of the Akan probably were the last (after Bure and Bambuhu) to be opened up by Wangara traders.

3. Seminal research on this subject was completed by Ronald Messier, who used radiochemical data to show that most of the gold coins minted by

the Almoravids and Almohads of North Africa contained an almost identical
proportion of copper to the gold transported northward by camel caravan
from the Sahara. R. Messier, "The Almoravids, West African Gold and the
Gold Currency of the Mediterranean Basin," *Journal of the Economic and
Social History of the Orient* 17.1 (1974), 33-38; Wilks, "Matter of Bitu."

4. For a detailed analysis of the radiochemical techniques that have
been employed to determine the origin of the gold found in ancient and medieval coins, see articles by Adon A. Gordus in *Archaeochemistry* 10 (1967);
and *Numismatic Circular* 76 (March 1968). For use of African gold in Medieval Europe, see J. H. A. Munro, *Wool, Cloth and Gold: The Struggle for
Bullion in the Anglo-Burgundian Trade, 1340-1478* (Toronto, 1972), 12-15,
31-32.

5. Duarte Pacheco Pereira, *Esmeraldo de situ orbis* (Lisbon, 1505-8);
reprint, trans. and ed. G. H. T. Kimble, Hakluyt Society (London), ser. 2,
vol. 79 (1937): 114-21; and J. de Barros, *Da Asie de Joao de Barros e de
Diogo de Couto*, 13 vols. (Lisbon 1552-88); reprint, trans. and ed.
G. R. Crone, Hakluyt Society (London), 2d ser., 80 (1937); reprinted in
F. Wolfson, *Pageant of Ghana* (London, 1958), 39-44.

6. These became, of course, notorious at a later date for their use as
slave dungeons. See A. Van Dantzig and B. Priddy, *A Short History of the
Forts and Castles of Ghana* (Legon, 1971), 6-13.

7. Average annual Portuguese gold purchases on the Gold Coast were
188 kilograms in the 1550s and 1560s. See A. Teixeira Da Mota and P. E.
H. Hair, *East of Mina: Afro-European Relations on the Gold Coast in the
1550s and 1560s*, University of Wisconsin, Studies in African Sources, 3.
(Madison, 1988), 26-33.

8. Walter Rodney, "Gold and Slaves on the Gold Coast," *Transactions
of the Historical Society of Ghana* 10 (1969): 16; Richard Bean, "A Note on
the Relative Importance of Slaves and Gold in West African Exports," *Journal of African History* 14, (1977), 351-56.

9. N. R. Junner, *Gold in the Gold Coast* (London, 1935), 13-14;
G. Keith Allen, "Gold Mining in Ghana," *African Affairs* 57, no. 228 (July,
1958): 221-40.

10. Timothy F. Garrard, *Akan Weights and the Gold Trade* (London,
1980), 149-60.

11. V. Magalhaes Godinho, *Léconomie de lempire portugais aux xv, xvi
siècles* (Paris, 1969), 218.

12. Curtin, "Africa and the Wider Monetary World," 231-68. In his section on West Africa, Curtin notes, "We know [that the record] represents
part of the whole, but not how much" (238). And later, he adds, "No conclusion is possible" (261). Among the many methodological problems that
block definitive answers (some raised by Curtin, others by the present writer)
are: (1) that most gold trade statistics reflect imports into Europe rather than

exports from West Africa; (2) that such statistics emphasize imports by major state-controlled monopolies (Portuguese, Dutch, and English) and fail to include gold imports by small traders and smugglers from these and many other countries; (3) that yearly averages mean little owing to wide fluctuations from year to year based on a variety of factors; (4) that there are large gaps during certain decades where we have practically no gold export or import statistics; and (5) that reliable statistics for the all-important overland gold trade and for domestic uses of gold in trade, savings, and ornamentation in West Africa are nonexistent.

13. Daaku, *Trade and Politics*, 12.

14. M. D. McLeod, *The Asante* (London, 1981), 14, 17, 52, 72; Ivor Wilks, *Asante in the Nineteenth Century* (Cambridge, 1975), 106-12.

15. General histories that deal to a limited extent with gold mining are: W. Walton Claridge, *A History of the Gold Coast and Ashanti*, 2 vols. (London, 1915, 1964), 1:39, 161; 2:203, 246-47, 574; W. E. F. Ward, *A History of Ghana* (London, 1958), 17, 60, 70, 159, 349-50; David Kimble, *A Political History of Ghana* (Oxford, 1963), 15-25, 39-43.

16. Ray A. Kea, *Settlements, Trade and Politics in the Seventeenth-Century Gold Coast* (Baltimore, 1982), 24, 33, 74, 78-79, 81, 118, 202-3. Daaku, *Trade and Politics*, 8-9, 15, 21-23, 27, 36, 65, 68, 76, 158, 160, 171-79.

17. See T. F. Garrard, *Akan Weights*. See also K. Arhin, "Succession and Gold Mining at Manso-Nkwanta, 1850-1910," *Sankofa: Journal of the Legon Archaeological Society* 2:33-39; R. E. Dumett, "Precolonial Gold Mining and the State in the Akan Region with a Critique of the Terray Hypothesis" in G. Dalton, ed., *Research in Economic Anthropology* 2:37-68; Dumett, "Precolonial Gold Mining in Wassa: Innovation, Specialization, Linkages to the Economy and to the State," in Enid Schildkrout, ed., *The Golden Stool: Studies of the Asante Center and Periphery,* Anthropological Papers of the American Museum of Natural History (New York) 65, part 1 (1987): 209-44. Special notice should be given to the numerous works on the Akan by Ivor Wilks, including "The Golden Stool and the Elephant Tail: An Essay on Wealth in Asante," in George Dalton, ed., *Research in Economic Anthropology* 2 (1979): 1-36; also Wilks, *Asante in the Nineteenth Century.*

18. Among recent general works of African economic history that do stress the importance of gold mining are A. G. Hopkins, *An Economic History of West Africa* (London, 1973); and Ralph Austen, *An Economic History of Africa* (London, 1987).

19. The following is but the briefest listing of recent works on mining labor history for southern Africa: Patrick Harries, *Work, Culture, and Identity: Migrant Laborers in Mozambique and South Africa, c. 1860-1910*; M. R. Mwendapole, *A History of the Trader Union Movement in Zambia up*

to 1968 (Lusaka, 1977); Randall Packard, *White Plague, Black Labor: Tuberculosis and the Political Economy of Health and Disease in South Africa* (Berkeley, 1989); Ian Phimister, *Studies in the History of African Mine Labour in Colonial Zimbabwe* (Gwelo, Zambia, 1978); Peter Richardson, *Chinese Mine Labour in the Transvaal* (London, 1982); William Worger, *South Africa's City of Diamonds: Mine Workers and Monopoly Capitalism in Kimberley, 1867-1895* (New Haven, 1987).

20. For information on the folk myths of German miners, see the classic of early modern mineral technology and science, Georg Agricola (né Bauer), *Georgius Agricola de re metallica* (1556), trans. H. Hoover; new ed., (New York, 1950); also *Lebewesen inter Tage* (1556; reprint, Munich, 1977).

21. D. Fetherling, *The Gold Crusades* (Toronto, 1988); W. P. Morrell, *The Gold Rushes* (London, 1940); T. A. Rickard, *The Romance of Mining* (Toronto, 1944); Duane A. Smith, *Colorado Mining* (Albuquerque, 1977); Pierre Burton, *The Klondike Fever* (New York, 1958; 1985); G. Blainey, *The Rush That Never Ended: A History of Australian Mining* (Melbourne, 1978); B. Kennedy, *Silver, Sin and Sixpenny Ale: A Social History of Broken Hill* (Melbourne, 1978).

22. Herman Francis Reinhart, *The Golden Frontier: Recollections of H. F. Reinhart, 1851-69,* ed. N. B. Cunningham and D. B. Nunis (Austin, Tex., 1962); A. O. Todd, *The Cornish Miner in America* (Truro, Cornwall, 1967).

23. "The Outbreak of Speculation in the Mining Market," *Economist* 43 (19 December 1885), 1537-38; "A Mining Promotion Boom," *Economist* (21 May 1887), 650-51.

24. The classic statement is by J. A. Hobson, *Imperialism: A Study* (London, 1902; Ann Arbor, Mich., 1965), 82-83. For appraisals of the theory of surplus capital, see L. H. Gann and Peter Duignan, *Burden of Empire* (New York, 1967), 3-54; A. G. Ford, "British Economic Fluctuations, 1870-1914," in D. H. Aldcroft, *British Economic Fluctuations, 1790-1939* (London, 1972), 131-59; Michael Edelstein, "Rigidity and Bias in the British Capital Market, 1870-1913," D. M. McCloskey, ed., *Essays on a Mature Economy after 1840* (London, 1971), 83-111.

25. The big intangible questions at this point are, of course, who were the investors? Did certain economic and professional classes predominate? Were they well-to-do rentiers and chairmen of boards of directors in the City of London? Or were they middle-income salaried people? What might have been their motivations for investing in gold shares? The general parameters of these questions are discussed in Peter J. Cain, "Financial Capitalism and Imperialism in Late Victorian and Edwardian England," in A. N. Porter and R. F. Holland, eds., *Money, Finance and Empire, 1790-1860* (London, 1985), 12-14.

26. Harvey and Press have drawn attention to the presence of a growing number of mining, engineering, and consultation firms in the City of London

as potent forces in the expansion of British-based and -financed global mining enterprise. In the present history, the professional engineering group did
not play so substantial a role in Gold Coast mining in this period. Charles
Harvey and Jon Press, "Overseas Investment and the Professional Advance
of British Metal Mining Engineers, 1851-1914." *Economic History Review,*
2nd ser., 42.1 (1989): 64, 66-67.

27. F. H. Hamilton, "Gold Mining and the Pound Sterling," *Mining
Magazine* 14 (March 1916): 3, 147-49.

28. Companies Archives, BT/series, formerly held at the Registry of Joint
Stock Companies, London, now at PRO, Kew, England.

29. Harvey and Press, "Overseas Investment."

30. See Lance Davis and Robert Huttenback, *Mammon and the Pursuit
of Empire: The Political Economy of British Imperialism, 1860-1912* (Cambridge, 1987), 53, 64-65 (tables 2.5, 2.9).

31. See John C. Hudson, "Theory and Methodology in Comparative
Frontier Studies," in David O. Miller and J. O. Steffen, eds., *The Frontier:
Comparative Studies* (Norman, Okla., 1977), 11-31; Marvin Mickssell,
"Comparative Studies in Frontier History," *Annals of the Association of
American Geographers* 51 (1961): 62-74. I recognize that there are more
complex concepts of frontiers than that used here, including "the interstices
between two cultural systems." But these other definitions are not applicable
to the evidence presented here.

32. For one of the most influential promotional tracts of the time, see
Horace Greeley, *Mineral Resources of the West* (New York, 1867). See also
Donald B. Chidsey, *The California Gold Rush* (New York, 1968); Parker
Watson, *Gold in the Black Hills* (Norman, Okla., 1960).

33. Clark S. Spence, *British Investments and the American Mining Frontier* (Ithaca, N.Y., 1958), 11-12, 51, 79.

34. Diane Newell, Technology on the Frontier (Vancouver, 1986), 78-
85; Bennett H. Brough, "The Nature and Yield of Metalliferous Deposits,"
Journal of the Society of Arts 48 (20 July 1900), 685. Harold Barger and
Sam H. Schurr, *The Mining Industries, 1899-1939* (New York, 1972), 100-
108, 150-53.

35. W. H. Merritt, "The Goldfields of British Columbia and the Klondike," *Journal of the Society of Arts* 46 (June 1898), 656-59. J. J. Curle,
The Gold Mines of the World (London, 1905), 34.

36. By law, in 1866 the United States government took ownership of all
western lands, including minerals. In theory most of the early European miners were trespassers on the lands of the U.S. government. The prior rights of
the Native Americans were ignored by both miners and government. Later
the miners got most of their claims recognized by the new territorial and
state administrations. Duane A. Smith, "Gold, Silver and the Red Man,"
Journal of the West (January 1966): 114-21. See also Robert Spude, "Native

Americans and the Gold Rushes" in Klaus Tenfelde, ed., *Sozialgeschichte des Bergbaus* (Munich, 1922), 213-41.

37. Ian R. Phimister, "Alluvial Gold Mining and Trade in Nineteenth Century South Central Africa," *Journal of African History* 15.3 (1974): 445-56. See also Roger Summers, *Ancient Mining in Rhodesia* (Salisbury, 1969), 143-47, 175-217.

38. For just a few examples of a wider literature on ancient, peasant gold mining, see T. A. Rickard, *Men and Metals: A History of Mining in Relation to the Development of Civilization* (New York, 1932). For the mines of ancient Greece, see E. Ardaillon, *Les mines du Laurion dans l'antiquité* (Paris, 1897); for England, see G. R. Lewis, *The Stanneries: A Study of the Medieval Tin Miners of Cornwall and Devon* (Truro, Cornwall, 1908; 1968), 178-91.

39. Dumett, "Precolonial Gold Mining and the State" and "Precolonial Gold Mining in Wassa."

40. Ricardo Godoy, "Technical and Economic Efficiency of Peasant Miners in Bolivia," *Economic Development and Cultural Change* 34.1 (October 1985): 103-20. The best book on this subject for West Africa is Bill Freund, *Capital and Labor in the Nigerian Tin Mines* (Atlantic Highlands, N.J., 1981), 48-51, 77-78, 91-92. See also Timothy Keegan, "The Dynamics of Rural Accumulation in South Africa: Comparative and Historical Perspectives," *Comparative Studies in History and Society,* 28:4 (1986), 628-50.

41. See for example, Ian Phimister, *An Economic and Social History of Zimbabwe, 1890-1948* (London, 1988), 1-2. Also see John Weeks, "Epochs of Capitalism and the Progressiveness of Capitals Expansion." *Science and Society* 49.4 (Winter 1985-86), 414-36.

42. Jeff Crisp finds the inception of working-class consciousness and solidarity in acts of resistance by Gold Coast mine workers even as early as the late nineteenth century. Crisp, *The Story of an African Working Class* (London, 1984), 19. Other scholars, including the present writer, have doubted whether one can speak of a working class in Ghana even by the mid-twentieth century. For a discussion of the literature, see V. L. Allen, "The Meaning of the Working Class in Africa," *Journal of Modern African Studies* 10.2 (1972), 169-89.

43. Godoy, "Peasant Miners in Bolivia."

44. Carola Lentz and Veit Erlmann, "A Working Class in Formation: Economic Crisis and Strategies of Survival among Dagara Mine Workers in Ghana," *Cahiers d'études africaines,* 113 (1989): 69-111.

45. Too much should not be made of the palm oil trade volumes of British West Africa, and of the Gold Coast, in particular, as if they were a wholly successful substitute for the slave trade. In the 1830s and 1840s, when the oil palm trade of the Niger Delta already was in a reasonably prosperous state, that of the Gold Coast was just getting going and lagged far be-

hind. Hopkins and others have shown that palm oil production and slave labor existed side by side in many regions, and also that the external slave trade persisted in to the era of so-called legitimate trade. Hopkins, *Economic History*, 128–39.

46. A. McPhee, *The Economic Revolution in British West Africa* (London, 1926), 71–73, 95–100.

47. Prices for Gold Coast palm oil fell from 2s.3d. per gallon in 1872, to 1s.9d. by 1880, to 11d. in 1888, and returned to a still low 1s.2d. in 1894. Reference to depressed and stagnant oil prices in *African Times*, 1 February 1886, 14; see also letters from C. Rottman (Hamburg), 2 and 16 February 1887; Ocansey Trading papers; Sc. 8/64ff., GNA. Survey histories have generalized all too facilely concerning annual price trends for palm oil. Annual averages tell us little about the frequent and multiplex daily, weekly, and monthly price swings within the longer series. The figures in the series quoted are from *Gold Coast Blue Book* statistics and contemporary trade newspapers, such as the *Liverpool Journal of Commerce*.

48. In geographic terminology, a bight is a gulf or large indentation on a seacoast. The Bight of Benin (to the west) and the Bight of Biafra (in the east) lie on either side of the great promontory that contains the delta of the River Niger. All three of these sections contain numerous riverine trading towns that were active and prosperous during the periods of either the slave trade or the nineteenth-century trade in palm oil and palm kernels.

49. In a number of writings, Hopkins shows the close connections between the crisis of adaptation in West African commerce and "the new imperialism." A. G. Hopkins, "Economic Imperialism in West Africa: Lagos, 1880–92," *Economic History Review* 21, (1968): 580–606; also *Economic History of West Africa*, 135–40, 160–66.

50. For comment on "tonnage hunting" and the need to pay extra "dashes" to palm oil producers, see the *African Times*, 23 March 1871, 100; Josiah Mills (trading agent, Winneba Dist.) to John Sarbah, 10 December 1876; Sarbah Trading Papers, Sc. 6/4, GNA.

51. "The great drawback to the trade with the interior has been the existence of the Ashanti State. . . . All goods passing through Ashanti were charged a 100% transit duty, besides being detained a month at Coomasie en route." Quoted in the African-owned newspaper the *African Times*, 1 July 1884, 94; see also the *Gold Coast Chronicle*, 21 March 1892, 2.

52. Weekly unit prices were given in the regular James Irvine palm oil price reports in the *Liverpool Journal of Commerce* and reprinted in the *African Times*. Irvine was extremely worried about his business prospects as a consequence of the general depression in trade.

53. For an overview, see Raymond E. Dumett, "African Merchants of the Gold Coast, 1860–1905: Dynamics of Indigenous Entrepreneurship," *Comparative Studies in Society and History* 25 (October 1983): 661–93.

54. The rise of the independent African entrepreneurs is discussed in the *Gold Coast Report* on the *Blue Book* for 1849, *PP* (1850) 36 [C. 1232]: 95. For a good account of the first generation of indigenous African merchants during the era of legitimate trade see Edward Reynolds, *Trade and Economic Change on the Gold Coast*, 1807-1874 (London, 1974), 53-63.

55. Interview with W. S. Kwesi Johnson, retired businessman, Cape Coast, Ghana, May 1967 and December 1971, Dumett Collection.

56. Memorandum of Observations from Ferdinand Fitzgerald sent to Earl Carnarvon (Sec. of State for Colonies), encl. in Fitzgerald to Carnarvon, 13 April 1874, CO 96/114. See also editorials in the *African Times*, 23 November 1864, 62 and 1 November 1879, 127.

57. Horace Bell, "Recent Railway Policy in India," *Journal of the Society of Arts*, 29 April 1898, 529-48. See also chap. 10 of P. J. Cain and A. G. Hopkins, *British Imperialism*, 2 vols. (London, 1993), 1:316-50.

58. In an illogical and Eurocentric, yet revealing statement on this subject, Michael Hicks Beach, Secretary of State for Colonies in the late 1870s, declared that because legitimate commerce on the Gold Coast was primarily "carried on by Europeans who had no intention of settling it, [there was] no desire to sink money in permanent improvement." The Gold Coast, he concluded would continue to be ignored by the government "until public opinion [was] brought into play." Speech by Sir M. Hicks Beach on British Commerce in Africa (n.d.), quoted in the *African Times*, 1 February 1879.

CHAPTER 2

1. This was not saying much about values, since practically all banket gold tends to exist in minute grains (invisible to the naked eye) and scattered with great variation in frequency of occurrence throughout a given zone. In the Gold Coast banket, as in South Africa, large amounts of crushed rock had to be treated for relatively small returns of gold. The banket strata of the Transvaal was much wider than that of the Gold Coast. And it was said that separation was more difficult in South Africa because the gold matrix below the decomposition line was composed more of iron sulfide, whereas in the Gold Coast the matrix was mainly iron oxide. O. A. L. Whitelaw, "The Geological and Mining Features of the Tarkwa-Aboso Goldfield," *Gold Coast Geological Survey*, Bulletin no. 1 (Colchester, 1929), 11-14.

2. Junner, *Gold in the Gold Coast*, 17-18.

3. Eluvial gold is that derived from the debris of rock produced by weathering or random water action (rainfall) unrelated to the constant flows of rivers. Ross Ellis, Geologist, personal communication, Western Washington University, August 1987.

4. J. A. Skertchly, "A Visit to the Goldfields of Wassa, West Africa," *Journal of the Royal Geographic Society* 47 (September 1879): 274-83.

5. William Bosman, *A New and Accurate Description of the Coast of Guinea* (Dutch ed. 1704; 1st English ed., 1705; new ed., London, 1967), 80-87; R. Clarke, *Remarks on the Topography and Diseases of the Gold Coast* (London, 1860), 10.

6. G. V. Hobson and A. M. Robinson, "The Gold Coast Banket: Some Aspects of Its Geology in Relation to Mining," *Transactions of the Institute of Mining and Metallurgy* 52 (1942-43): 311-46.

7. The word banket, with an accent on the second syllable, is Afrikaans for "almond rock," a name that refers to the size and shape of the pebbles in the matrix. The term gained wide currency in the mining world after the discovery of the Witwatersrand banket formation in 1885. F. Holmes, "Notes on the Early History of Tarkwa as a Gold Mining District," *Gold Coast Review* 2.1 (January-June 1926): 83.

8. One school argues for a hydrothermal solution and presents evidence that points to igneous beginnings; the second, and majority view, holds to a modified "alluvial" explanation, suggesting that the distribution of gold in most banket systems shows definite sedimentary features. A. W. Rogers, "A Discussion of the Origin of Gold in the Witwatersrand System," *Transactions of the Geological Society of South Africa* 34 (1931): 19.

9. The banket proper was a subdivision within the larger Banket Series. Thus, "[g]old occurr[ed] in varying amounts in the folded and metamorphosed Banket Series conglomerates throughout the Gold Coast." Norman R. Junner, *The Tarkwa Goldfield* (London, 1942), 3, 4-5, 63-64.

10. T. Hirst, "The Geology of the Tarkwa Goldfield and Adjacent Country," *Gold Coast Geological Survey,* Bulletin no. 10 (London, 1938), 6-7.

11. N. R. Junner, "The Geology of the Obuasi Goldfield," *Gold Coast Geological Survey,* Bulletin no. 2 (London, 1932), 5-7. See also Junner, *Gold in the Gold Coast,* 28-31.

12. *Mining Journal,* 31 October 1885.

13. W. R. Feldtmann, "The Mines of the Ashanti Goldfields Corporation." *Mining Magazine* 14 (May 1916): 257-68.

14. See G. O. Kesse, "The Occurrence of Gold in Ghana," in R. P. Foster, ed., *The Geology, Geochemistry and Genesis of Gold Deposits* (Rotterdam, 1984), 652.

15. W. G. G. Cooper, *The Geology of the Prestea Goldfield,* (Colchester, 1934), 5-9.

16. Junner, *Gold in the Gold Coast,* 40-41.

17. For details see T. Hirst, *The Geology of the Konongo Gold Belt and Surrounding Territory, Gold Coast Geological Survey,* Bulletin no. 14 (London, 1942), 7-14.

18. Junner, *Gold in the Gold Coast,* 62-63. See also J. M. Campbell,

"Notes on Some Gold Occurrences in Ashanti," *Transactions of the Institute of Mining and Metallurgy* 24 (1914-15): 252-56.

CHAPTER 3

1. The Twi words used in this study have been checked for accuracy by Dr. Robert Addo-Fening of the University of Ghana and by Dr. Edward Reynolds of the University of California at San Diego. An expert on the languages of Ghana, Dr. Reynolds is presently working on a new Twi-English Dictionary. In cases of disagreement, I have used the Akyem Twi form over the Asante Twi.

2. The present chapter represents a much revised and expanded version of a paper, "Precolonial Gold Mining in Wassa," presented to the Symposium on Asante Kingdom of Gold held at the American Museum of Natural History in 1984, and subsequently printed as *The Golden Stool: Studies of the Asante Center and Periphery* (New York, 1987) under the editorship of Enid Schildkrout. A major difference here is the addition of the recollections of Ghanaian elders from oral field data. I first engaged in research on gold mining in Ghana in a Ph.D. thesis: "British Official Attitudes in Relation to Economic Development in the Gold Coast, 1974-1905" (London University, 1966). Subsequent to this Paul Rosenblum wrote "Gold Mining in Ghana, 1874-1900" (Ph.D. dissertation, Columbia University, 1971). It is important to note that these studies were researched independently of one another. In the course of preparing the present book, I consulted Rosenblum's dissertation. Though in any several studies on a similar topic there is bound to be overlap, the thematic emphasis, methodology, and interpretations in this book differ greatly from those of Dr. Rosenblum. Points of major disagreement are singled out in the endnotes in this and succeeding chapters.

3. K.Y. Daaku and Albert Van Dantzig, "Annotated Dutch Map of the Gold Coast [1629]," *Ghana Notes and Queries* 9 (November 1966): 14.

4. Bosman, *Coast of Guinea*, 164.

5. John Vogt, *Portuguese Rule on the Gold Coast, 1469-1682* (Athens, Ga., 1979), 83-85.

6. Van Dantzig and Priddy, *Forts and Castles of Ghana*, 6, 112-19; A. W. Lawrence, *Fortified Trading Posts: The English in West Africa, 1645-1822* (London, 1969), 147, 160-64.

7. A. Van Dantzig, *Documents Relating to the Gold Coast and the Slave Coast* (Coast of Guinea) 1680-1740, part 1, 1680-1710. (privately printed, Legon, 1971) 1-100.

8. The Dutch from their key bases at Axim and Elmina were in a better position to exploit the southwestern gold trade than their English rivals.

They made several expeditions in the late 1600s and early 1700s to mine directly for gold in the interior, but these ended in failure. For a full discussion of early Dutch efforts, see A. Van Dantzig, "The Ankobra Gold Interest," *Transactions of the Historical Society of Ghana* 14.2 (December 1973): 169-85; and Merrick Posnansky and Albert Van Dantzig, "Fort Ruchaver Rediscovered," *Sankofa* 2 (1976): 7-8.

9. This summary paragraph follows on the detailed work of Larry Yarak. Yarak has worked extensively in unraveling the complexities of early Wassa political history. See his paper "Political Consolidation and Fragmentation in Southern Akan Polity: Wassa and the Origin of Wassa Amenfi and Wassa Fiase, 1700-1840" (typescript, 1976), 1-90.

10. It is also important to point out that guns and powder were two of the European imports most desired by Akan kingdoms and states in this period. See S. Tenkorang, "The Importance of Firearms in the Struggle between Ashanti and the Coastal States, 1708-1807," *Transactions of the Historical Society of Ghana* 9 (1968): 15-16. See also J. Sanders, "The Expansion of the Fante and the Emergence of Asante in the Eighteenth Century," *Journal of African History* 20.3 (1979): 356-59.

11. See Eva L. R. Meyerowitz, *The Early History of the Akan States of Ghana* (London, 1974), 192-93. Meyerowitz states that Wassa Amenfi was established shortly after 1730. Oral tradition gathered by F. G. Crowther also claims that Wassa Amenfi had enjoyed "independence from time immemorial." F. G. Crowther, "Affairs in Wassa," *Gold Coast Review* 2 (July-September 1926): 168-80. Paul Rosenblum in a lengthy summary tends to follow Meyerowitz on the early-eighteenth-century origins for the division into two Wassa kingdoms. (Thesis, 1971, 26-27.)

12. See Yarak, "Political Consolidation," esp. 24-29.

13. Tenkorang, "Importance of Firearms," 15-16; Wilks, *Asante in the Nineteenth Century,* 23-24, 29, 154.

14. This necessarily simplifies much complex history. Although the alignment of states was subject to fluctuations, the Wassas initially sought protection from both the Dutch and the English. The Dutch tried to ameliorate conflict between Asante and Wassa but were drawn increasingly toward siding with Asante as the British became more aligned with the Fante states. H. W. Daendels, *Journal and Correspondence, part 1 (November 1815-January 1817; selected documents from the Furley Collection,* ed. and trans. Edmund Collins (University of Ghana, Legon, 1964), 66-67, 91-92, 102, 113, 127-28. Also see Yarak, "Political Consolidation," 41, 43-45.

15. Thomas E. Bowdich, A Mission from Cape Coast Castle to Ashantee (London, 1819; reprint, 1966), 217.

16. Meredith speaks of two Wassas in 1812 but provides no details. Henry Meredith, *An Account of the Gold Coast of Africa* (London, 1812; reprint, 1967), 74.

17. G. E. Metcalfe, *Maclean of the Gold Coast* (London, 1962), 80, 96–97, 108, 168–69; Yarak, "Political Consolidation," 65–66.

18. G. A. Robertson, *Notes on Africa* (London, 1819), 122–26; Brodie Cruickshank, *Eighteen Years on the Gold Coast of Africa,* 2 vols. (London, 1853; reprint, 1966), 234; Yarak, "Political Consolidation," 65–67, discusses the complicated maneuverings behind these changes.

19. Crowther may have been incorrect in his use of asafohene as a substitute for chief. The asafo were young men's organizations in the Akan states. List of chiefs or omanhene under King Kwamena Enemil of Wassa Fiase, encl. 8 in H. Higgins to Col. Sec., Accra, 30 April 1882, encl. 8 in Moloney to Kimberley, 4 September 1882, *PP* (1883) 8–9 [C.3687]: 58–59. See also appendix in Rept. by M. Rumsey, 9 August 1882, encl. in Moloney to Kimberley, 4 September 1882, ibid., 58–59.

20. Crowther thought that the term asafohene was more appropriate term for chief (than the usual Twi word ohene) in the two Wassas on the grounds that it stressed the military role. F. G. Crowther, a knowledgeable observer, was Secretary for Native Afairs during the administration of Gold Coast Governor Hugh Clifford in the early twentieth century. Nonetheless, some scholars disagree with his terminology, and his conclusions concerning the degree of centralization and subordination of chiefs in the two Wassas are open to question. See Crowther, "Affairs in Wassa," 171.

21. Strictly speaking the ruler of Apinto was a chief under the king of Wassa Fiase. (Crowther, "Affairs in Wassa," 169.) But by the late nineteenth century, with increased wealth and power from gold mining, his own people were calling him king. Field notes, Dumett Collection, Tarkwa, Wassa, 16 May 1987.

22. Indeed, nineteenth-century chiefs of Apinto came to view themselves as more powerful than their superior, the Wassa king. Interview with Nana Faibil III, the Apintohene, and his court, Tarkwa, Wassa, 16 May 1987, Dumett Collection.

23. Olefert Dapper, *Beschreibung von Afrika* (Amsterdam, 1670), 146. Dapper was a medical doctor who lived in Amsterdam. He never visited West Africa. For his information on the Gold Coast, he appears to have drawn largely on de Marees (1602) and on later Dutch documents. In fact few of the classic Dutch and British travelers' accounts are detailed about either the political or the economic history of Wassa. This includes de Marees, Barbot, Bosman, Bowdich, Cruickshank, and Dupuis. For full citations, see the bibliography.

24. Report by Inspector Dudley, "Further Correspondence regarding the Affairs of the Gold Coast," *PP* (1883) 48 [C.3687]: 48.

25. In the early 1800s Robertson observed that the Wassa "country is far more extensive than is commonly supposed by Europeans . . ." ("Notes on Africa," 124).

26. John Phillips, *Agriculture and Ecology in Africa* (London, 1959), 58. Quoted in Ivor Wilks, *Forests of Gold: Essays on the Akan and the Kingdom of Asante* (Athens, Ohio, 1993), 45–46.

27. Frederick Boyle, *Through Fanteeland to Coomassie* (London, 1874), 30. Another issue sometime slighted in the literature is that areas in a number of the "middle" Akan states between the coast and Asante had been depopulated and denuded of agriculture owing to the persistence of internecine warfare.

28. C. H. Armitage and A. F. Montanaro, *The Ashanti Campaign of 1900* (London, 1901), 17; R. A. Freeman, *Travels and Life in Ashanti and Gyaman* (London, 1898; reprint, 1967), 51.

29. J. Muller, Report on Journey around Akyem, 14 June 1881, Kyebi Dist. Correspondence (Paul Jenkins Abstract, no. 152), Basel Mission Archives, Switzerland. This point, confirming the small size of farms and that the European words, plantations, and estates were for the most part misapplied to the Akan forest zone, was confirmed in personal communications with the scholars A. Mawere Opoku and J. H. Kwabena Nketia (October 1984).

30. Wilks, *Forests of Gold*, 45–46.

31. Another neglected point is that many Akan households raised poultry, pigs, goats, and the occasional sheep to help supplement the family income and diet. Meredith, *Gold Coast of Africa*, 74–77; Robertson, *Notes on Africa*, 159. 166.

32. Reginald Hart, "Geological Report on Districts bordering the Bossum Pra," encl. in G.C. Gov. to Kimberley, 5 June 1881; *PP* (1881) 65 [C.3064]: 186–88.

33. Daendels, *Journal and Correspondence*, part 1 (1815–17); 39.

34. V. L. Cameron (a not unbiased commentator who worked for European mining interests) nonetheless traveled to Wassa and reported that some heads of household did not cultivate the land intensively because they disliked the immense work of felling and clearing the huge bombax and other large trees. V. L. Cameron, "The Goldfields of West Africa," *Journal of the Society of Arts*, June 2, 1882, 778.

35. Daendels, *Journal and Correspondence*, 149; quoted in Yarak, "Political Consolidation," 41–42.

36. Boyle, *Through Fanteeland*, 36–37.

37. A number of Dutch and English writers who visited the mining areas in the second half of the nineteenth century were highly critical of the overconcentration by villagers on mining since, they believed, it led to a reduction of crop cultivation and an insufficiency of food. In several areas Vitringa noticed that as one result no food was available to feed the domesticated animals. Coulon J. Vitringa (Dutch Resident at Axim Department), *Report on the Department of Axim*, 26 (1859); original doc. at Library of the Ministry of Colonies, the Hague; edited translation in the Furley Collection, BLG.

38. Robert Addo-Fening, "The Gold Mining Industry in Akyem-Abuakwa, 1850-1910," *Sankofa* 2 (1976): 33-39.

39. Some avoid the use of this terminology because of the overtones of European feudal-style oppression and serfdom. It has, nonetheless, found worldwide application, including by Africanists and Latin Americanists. For an interesting discussion, see Henry Bernstein, "African Peasantries: A Theoretical Framework," *Journal of Peasant Studies* 6:441-43.

40. Louis Binger, *Du Niger au Golfe de Guinée par le pays Kong et le Mossi*, 2 vols. (Paris 1892), 2:282.

41. Interview with Nana Ezonle, Tutohene, Atuabo, eastern Nzema, Ghana, 17 May 1987, Dumett Collection.

42. See also F. W. Sanderson, History of Nzema up to 1874 (Accra, 1925), 100-107. The leading authority on the history of Nzemaland is René Baésjou. See "The Historical Evidence for Old Maps and Charts of Africa," *History in Africa* 15 (1988): 21, 25. Earlier names for this territory were Jomore and Apollonia. Baésjou points out that the term Nzema was not used for the territory until the late nineteenth century. Personal communication, R. Baésjou; October, 1989.

43. One of the few detailed written references on these patterns of settlement comes from E. H. Hobart to Inspector of Gold Coast Constabulary, 8 April 1901, CO Afr. (W) 649, no. 53, p. 113.

44. Fire setting as a central part of traditional mining can be found in the ancient Roman Empire and in medieval Germany; it continued to be used in Europe right up to the invention of dynamite in the 1860s. Some observers contended that the Nzemans first acquired this technique from the Portuguese and that, indeed, the spread of most of the mining techniques described in this chapter was traceable mainly to European influences. Interestingly, this rather extreme Eurocentric diffusionist view on mining technology was put forward by the Eurafrican government commissioner of the Gold Coast Henrik Vroom. See H. Vroom, Q. Dist. Report on Eastern Wassa, 15 October 1891, encl. in Griffith (210) to Knutsford, 25 June 1891, CO 96/217.

45. Norman Junner, the government geologist, a reputable authority, says that this was the local oral tradition. See Junner, *Obuasi Goldfield*, 5.

46. Pieter de Marees, *Description and Historical Account of the Gold Kingdom of Guinée* (1602; new ed., trans. and ed. Albert Van Dantzig and Adam Jones, Oxford, 1987), 189.

47. J. Barbot, *A Description of the Coast of North and South Guinée*, vol. 5 of *Churchill's Collection of Voyages and Travels* (Paris, 1746), 228.

48. Vitringa, Report on the Department of Axim (above), 32.

49. K. Y. Daaku, UNESCO *Project on Oral Data*, no. 2—*Denkyera* (Legon, Ghana, 1970), 215; John Daw, *Lecture on the Development of Gold Mining in Ashanti* (privately printed, London 1902), 76 Cade Papers, LRC.

50. Bosman *Coast of Guinea*, 30, 86.

51. Garrard, "Akan Weights," 359.

52. Interview with Kwame Yeboa, Kyebi, Akyem-Abuakwa, Ghana, 26 May 1987, Dumett Collection.

53. Interview with John Ansah Quinoo, Awiebo, eastern Nzema, 17 May 1987, Dumett Collection.

54. Meredith, "Gold Coast of Africa," 52–66.

55. Skertchly, "Goldfields of Wassa," 278.

56. G. E. Ferguson, Report on Mission to Atebubu (October-December 1890), encl. in Gov. W. B. Griffith, to Knutsford, 9 March 1891, CO 96/215.

57. Interview with Kwame Yeboa.

58. John Beecham, Ashantee and the Gold Coast (London, 1841), 157.

59. Skertchly, "Goldfields of Wassa," 277–79; Ferguson, Report on Mission to Atebubu.

60. Dumett, "Precolonial Gold Mining and the State," 36–68.

61. Oral interviews and field notes from Tarkwa, Wassa, 16 May; plus Obuasi, Asante 21 May, and Konongo, Asante, 26 May and Kyebi, Akyem-Abuakwa 26 May 1987, Dumett Collection.

62. A sizable number of Akan families, perhaps a majority, owned no slaves. According to one knowledgeable Basel missionary who served for a lengthy period in Akyem and Kwahu, most of the people in this region were too poor to purchase or own slaves. Comment by Rossler of 28 May 1893, Basel Mission Slavery Reports, Jenkins Abstracts, no. 168, Basel Mission Archives, Switzerland.

63. Comment by Norman R. Junner on the article by D. A. Sutherland, "The Primitive Uses of Gold," Transactions of the Institute of Mining and Metallurgy 44 (1934–35): 79.

64. See oral interviews, chap. 3, note 61. Comment by Henry Louis on Sutherland, "Primitive Uses of Gold," 82. Also see Henry Louis, "Gold Mining on the Gold Coast, West Africa," Mining Journal (London), 12 December 1885, 1437.

65. Emmanuel Terray, "Long Distance Exchange and the Formation of the State: The Case of the Abron State of Gyaman," Economy and Society 3.3 (1974): 328–31.

66. Extract from Report by C. J. Harvey, 18 May 1878; quoted in Holmes, "Early History of Tarkwa," 84–85.

67. De Marees, Gold Kingdom of Guinée, 190.

68. Skertchly, "Goldfields of Wassa," 278.

69. Clarke, Topography and Diseases, 9–10.

70. Capt. J. S. Hay, "On the District of Ak[y]em, in West Africa," Proceedings of the Royal Geographical Society of London 20 (June, 1876): 476–77; Vitringa, Report on the Department of Axim, 27; Clarke, Topography and Diseases, 10; Junner, Gold in the Gold Coast, 11; Sutherland, Primitive Uses of Gold, 9.

71. Diagram of African pit mines at Tarkwa by E. Wray for Tarkwa and Aboso Mining Co. Ltd., 1879 (Reproduced by Mining Survey, Hq., Accra, 1926). Also see Kwame Arhin, "Political Succession and Gold Mining at Manso-Nkwanta," *Institute of African Studies Research Review* (University of Ghana) 6.3 (1970): 101-9.

72. R. Hart, (Royal Engineers), Report on districts bordering the Bossum Pra, *PP* (1881) 65 [C. 3064]: 184-90.

73. E. A. Cade, "Report on the Obuasi Gold Mine Estate (printed for private circ., 26 August 1895), Cade Papers; (Ashanti Goldfields Corp.) LRC, GHL, and UBL.

74. Report of the Wassa Mining Dists. by Gov. William Brandford Griffith, encl. in Griffith to Knutsford, 25 June 1889, *PP* (1889) 54 [C. 5620-24]: 1.

75. R. Burton and V. L. Cameron, *To the Gold Coast for Gold,* 2 vols. (London, 1882), 2:165.

76. Louis Wyatt, Report on Tarkwa Mining Dist. (1878), encl. in Crown Agents to R. Meade, U.Sec., CO, 14 June 1879, CO 96/129.

77. Interview with Kwesi Frimpong and Joseph Garbrah, Tarkwa, Wassa Fiase, 16 May 1897, Dumett Collection.

78. Ibid.

79. Larry Yarak, "The Dutch Gold-Mining Effort on the Gold Coast, 1841-49" (typescript, 1990), esp. 17-19. I thank him for lending me a copy of this research paper.

80. This diffusion occurred partly as a result of thefts from company storehouses.

81. Junner, *Gold in the Gold Coast,* 11; E. T. McCarthy, "Mining Enterprise in the Gold Coast," suppl. to the *Mining Journal,* 1 July 1882, 797-98; Burton and Cameron, *To the Gold Coast,* 2:246.

82. Comments by the Apintohene Faibil III, and S. K. Cudjoe and others Tarkwa, Dumett Collection.

83. Interview with Opanin Seriboe, Konongo, Dwaben, Asante, 25 May 1987, Dumett Collection.

84. Instances were recorded where kings and chiefs might issue orders forbidding the digging of gold where a certain mother lode was believed to be in the process of expanding and giving birth to many gold offspring. Sutherland, Primitive Uses of Gold, 7.

85. R. F. Rømer, *The Gold Coast of Guinea* (Copenhagen, 1760), part 4, "African History, Customs and Ways of Life," trans. from the Danish by K. Gertelsen (IAS, Legon, 1965), 180. I am grateful to Albert Van Dantzig for access to this typescript.

86. Thomas J. Hutchinson, *Impressions of Western Africa* (London, 1858), 69. Apart from deities and spirits, informants told me that in olden times the people of Wassa also believed in the existence of "little people" or

"dwarfs" who dwelt underground and who could cause trouble. Interviews with the Abontiakoonhene, Nana Blay Adu, and with Kwame Bejisu Blay, Tarkwa, Ghana, 16 May 1987, Dumett Collection.

87. John Beecham, Min. of Evidence (31 May 1842): Report Select Comm. on West Coast of Africa, PP (1842) 11 [551]: 194, (Reprint by Irish Univ. Press: Colonial Africa-2.).

88. J. S. G. Gramberg, Schetsen van Afrikas Westkust (Amsterdam, 1861), 230-31.

89. Bosman, Coast of Guinea, 80; Meredith, Gold Coast of Africa, 179, Sutherland, Primitive Uses of Gold, 7.

90. Barbot, North and South Guinea, 229; Hutchinson, Impressions of Western Africa, 69. Hutchinson, pointed out that that one of the functional purposes of belief in a gold deity or spirits was to put a check on any gold miners avarice.

91. Burton and Cameron, To the Gold Coast, 2:125.

92. While tramping around Tarkwa, friends and I benefited from a wonderful encounter with modern "informal" diggers (outside the control of the companies) who mine in the old ways. Known in Ghana today as galamsey, many come from outside the southwestern region. During the course of our meeting the miners invited our party to descend one of their deep corkscrew shafts: the invitation was respectfully declined. For an interesting short article on the modern resurgence of African traditional mining methods, see Julian Acheampong, "Galamsey Go for Gold," New African, December 1996, 18-19. It is interesting to note the repetition today of many of the economic and social trends noted in the present study. Thanks to Donna Maier for drawing my attention to this article.

93. Ivor Wilks shared with me an interesting diagram of indigenous mines in the Kumasi area that showed nkron at a fairly shallow level (14-15 feet), using ventilation shafts spaced at intervals. Engineers Report, Kumasi, 1960; catalogued at Department of Archaeology, University of Ghana, Legon. This may be a special case and from a more modern time than the period covered in the present study. There are only a few references to such ventilation shafts in the mining literature of the nineteenth century.

94. In West Africa, swish, or sun-dried earth, was commonly used for small structures. Sketch of a cross-section of a concession at Aboso, 23 April 1879, Tarkwa and Aboso Consolidated Mining Co., Ltd. (reproduced by Gold Coast Survey, Accra, 1926).

95. Report and map by Louis Wyatt on Tarkwa and Axim (1878), encl. in Crown Agents for the Colonies to CO, 14 June 1879, CO 96/129.

96. Edwin A. Cade to the directors of the Ashanti Goldfields Corporation, 7 April 1898, Cade Papers, LRC, GHL, UB-CWAS.

97. Skertchly, "Goldfields of Wassa," 37-39; Louis, "Gold Mining in the Gold Coast," 1437.

98. Clarke, *Topography and Diseases,* 9-10. Skertchly, "Goldfields of Wassa," 37-39; Louis, "Gold Mining in the Gold Coast," 1437.

99. Burton and Cameron, *To the Gold Coast,* 2:359.

100. Interview with Nana Efoa Tenkromaa, Konongo, Dwaben, Asante, Ghana, 25 May 1987, Dumett Collection.

101. McCarthy, "Mining Enterprise," 797. The role of indigenous goldsmiths is discussed in many contemporary accounts. See, for example, L. R. Foot and T. F. Jones, *The Gold Coast and the Fantis* (London, 1903), 42-44.

102. The Gold Coast used a mixed currency during the transitional period covered in this study (1870-1900). By Gold Coast Ordinance no. 2 (1880) a wide variety of British, European, and American (including the silver eagle, half-eagle, and quarter) coins were accepted as legal tender. In Asante, the Northern Territories, and other interior states, gold dust was still the most widely used currency in market exchange, even for small purchases. By the 1890s British silver coins were used increasingly in the coastal settlements; and the colonial government was attempting to standardize these. The most widely recognized standard of value on the coast, however, was not the pound sterling but the dollar of the Spanish empire. This would change in the early twentieth century.

103. W. F. Hutchinson, "Report on the Economic Agriculture on the Gold Coast," *PP* (1890) 59 [C.5897-40]: 481.

104. One informant was quite vehement on this subject. He noted that today young people may spend their entire salaries very quickly, "but at that time nobody could do that." We saved and "spent our money wisely." Interview with Kofi Agyepong, Asokore (near Koforidua), Akyem-Abuakwa, Ghana, 1 December 1971, Dumett Collection.

105. Interviews with Opanin Kwaku Adu, Mampong Akrofoso, Asante, 29 December 1971, Dumett Collection, and Kwame Yeboa.

106. The activities of goldsmiths in the history of the Akan people makes for interesting study that lies outside the range of the present volume, and that has been treated at length elsewhere. Known as *sika dwumfo,* the goldsmiths constituted a distinct caste, organized into guilds in which members were related to one another and where sons and nephews followed their fathers and uncles into the profession. These guilds were governed by chiefs, called *ahinfu,* who regulated the members. Their main work was to melt gold dust or remelt old jewelry into new items of adornment for their customers. Some resided permanently in the main towns and cities; others traveled about rural areas from village to village, setting up shop with their forge and bellows, a small anvil, balance scales for weighing gold dust, and tongs and other tools for shaping objects (see photos at the end of chap. 8, this volume). The most honored goldsmiths were responsible for the golden regalia of kings and chiefs; but most goldsmiths worked with other metals as well, including copper, brass, and iron. The famous Akan gold weights, re-

garded as works of art, were graded into some thirty-five different weights and sizes in order to balance various quantities of gold dust ranging from a farthings worth up to the value of £24 or £25 sterling. It was not the custom for Akan miners to take all of their gold winnings to goldsmiths, since this would have exposed their wealth to public view and made them liable for increased taxation by kings and chiefs. (For detailed descriptions of their traditions, see "Petition of Goldsmiths of the Gold Coast Colony to the Secretary of State for Colonies," encl. in Gov. of the Gold Coast (210) to CO, 19 May 1909; CO 96/483. See also H. Coulborn, "Reminiscences of the Gold Coast," *United Service Magazine* 3 (1850): 80.; Timothy Gerrard, *Akan Weights and the Gold Trade*, 99-125.

107. Interviews with Nana Efoa Tenkromaa and Opanin Seriboe. In addition, foreign observers noted that in olden times considerable amounts of gold were buried with the dead, making such grave sites the object of pillage during time of war. H. Colborn, "Reminiscences of the Gold Coast: Extracts from Notes Taken during a Tour of Service in 1847-48," *United Service Magazine* 3 (1850): 74.

108. Dumett, "Precolonial Gold Mining and the State," 48-50

109. Arhin, "Political Succession," 107. Arhin makes the point that the conjugal or nuclear family was the primary production unit in traditional gold mining in Asante, despite what one might suppose from the complexities of the Akan matrilineal descent system. Thus, Arhin contends that a male head of family would take his sons with him on gold-mining expeditions instead of his nephews, as would be expected under matrilineal inheritance. There is some grounds for debate here. My own field interviews in 1987 indicate that although mining crews emphasized spouses, sons, and daughters in mining crews, a man's nephews might also have been included. The use of nephews in mining is also confirmed in the fieldwork of Kwame Daaku. See K. Y. Daaku, *Oral Tradition: Denkyera* (New York, 1970), 4-14, 21-22, 96, 132, 173, 274, and 352. Also see Kwame Y. Daaku, *Oral Traditions of Assin-Twifo* (Legon, Ghana, 1969), 3, 9.

110. Information from interviews in Wassa, Asante, Nzema, and Akyem-Abuakwa in 1971 and 1987, cited above.

111. For an extremely valuable discussion of a wide range of issues surrounding free and unfree labor and the role of ordinary subjects versus royal officials in farming, mining, and various sectors of trade in Asante, see Gareth Austin, "'No Elders Were Present: Commoners and Private Ownership in Asante, 1807-96," *Journal of African History* 37 (1996): 1-30.

112. I am also grateful to Kwame Arhin for written communication and discussions of his views on these questions. See Kwamena Bentsi-Enchill, "Do African Systems of Land Tenure Require a Special Terminology?" *Journal of African Law* 2.9: 114-39; H. C. Belfield, "Report on the Legislation Governing the Alientation of Native Lands in the Gold Coast Colony and

Ashanti," *PP* 59 [Cd.6278], 481–601; Anthony Allott, *Essays in African Law* (London, 1960).

113. Daaku, *Oral Tradition: Denkyera*, 4–14, 21–22, 96, 132, 173, 274, and 352. Also see Daaku, *Oral Traditions of Assin-Twifo*, 3, 9.

114. Dumett "Precolonial Gold Mining and the State," 37–68; Dumett "Precolonial Gold Mining in Wassa," 217–19.

115. K. A. Busia, *The Position of the Chief in the Modern Political System of Ashanti* (London, 1951; reprint, 1968), 44, 49, 54–57; John Mensah Sarbah, *Fanti Customary Laws* (London, 1906; reprint, 1968), 74–75

116. Addo-Fening, "Gold Mining Industry," 33–39.

117. J. A. Dadson, "Land Tenure Reform," in *Background to Agriculture Policy in Ghana* (Legon, Ghana, 1969), 32.

118. See Wilks, "Golden Stool," 1–36; also Wilks, *Forests of Gold,* 127–67; Wilks, *Asante in the Nineteenth Century,* 54–55, 62–71, 414–45.

119. Thomas C. McCaskie, *State and Society in Pre-Colonial Asante* (Cambridge, 1995), 37–49; Wilks, "Golden Stool," 19–21. See also R. S. Rattray, *Ashanti Law and Constitution,* (London, 1929), 108–12; Bowdich, *Cape Coast Castle,* 254, 319–21.

120. Joseph Dupuis, *Journal of a Residence in Ashantee* (London, 1824), lvi–lvii; Terray, "Long Distance Exchange," 328.

121. This was supported in a letter to me from Kwame Arhin, 18 May 1978.

122. Daaku, *Denkyera,* 54.

123. Francis Hart, *The Gold Coast: Its Wealth and Health* (London, 1904), 91.

124. Sarbah, *Fanti Customary Laws,* 74, 92. Also see Burton and Cameron, *To the Gold Coast,* 2:350.

125. Capt. Alfred Moloney to Gov. Strahan, 17 March 1875, encl. in Strahan to Carnarvon, 18 March 1975, *PP* (1875) 22 [C. 1743]: 76–77.

126. This view of more than one mode of production finds support from Emmanuel Terray as well. Raymond E. Dumett, "Traditional Slavery in the Akan Region in the Nineteenth Century: Sources, Issues and Interpretations" in David Henige and T. C. McCaskie, eds., *West African Economic and Social History: Studies in Memory of Marion Johnson* (Madison, Wis., 1990), 18. For Terray's lengthy rejoinder to my basic argument, see E. Terray "Gold Production, Slave Labor, and State Intervention in Precolonial Akan Societies: A Reply to Raymond Dumett," *Research in Economic Anthropology* 5 (1983).

127. Eugenia Herbert, *Iron, Gender, and Power* (Bloomington, Ind., 1994).

128. Burton and Cameron, *To the Gold Coast,* 2:248.

129. E. A. Cade to Directors, Ashanti Goldfields Corp., 22 December 1897, Cade Papers, GHL and UB-CWAS.

130. Campbell, "Gold Occurrences in Ashanti," 253; Whitelaw, "Geological and Mining Features," 16. Paul Rosenblum also discusses these questions in his dissertation, "Gold Mining in Ghana."

131. Extract from Report by Bonnat in Holmes, "Early History of Tarkwa," 81.

132. The generally heavy work load of Akan women, including that in gold mining, is described in many contemporary accounts. See, for example, H. Coulborn, "Reminiscences of the Gold Coast," *United Service Magazine* 3 (1850): 78-80; J. S. Hay, "On the District of Akim in West Africa," *Proceedings of the Royal Geographical Society* 20 (26 June 1876): 477-78.

133. Norman Junner, the government geologist who toured these sites in the 1920s and 1930s, in speaking of peasant mining groups wrote, "It was usual to divide the excavated ore between the workers roughly in proportion to the work done by them." It is probable, however, that Junner was speaking of small groups of adult male miners of approximately equal status. Junner, *Gold in the Gold Coast,* 12.

134. Interview with Efoa Tenkromaa, and other interviews, Dumett Collection.

135. Burton and Cameron, *To the Gold Coast,* 2:298.

136. Kwadwo Enimil Kuma II to Gov. W. B. Griffith, 30 April 1888, encl. in Kuma to A. Woodburn Heron, DC Axim, 30 April 1888, no. 2431/88, ADM 11/11/34, GNA.

137. High Court Records, Cape Coast. Quoted by Rosenblum, "Gold Mining in Ghana," 90.

138. J. Muller, Report on Journey to Akyem, 1881, no. 152, Kyebi Dist. Correspondence (Jenkins Abstract), Basel Mission Correspondence.

139. Wilks, (1978), 529-30.

140. Letter from Capt. Thompson (an eyewitness), 18 November 1873; quoted in Boyle, *Through Fanteeland,* 36.

141. For example, the above comment by Thompson was made during the Sixth Anglo-Asante War, in which much of the land of the intermediate interior was laid waste by warring groups, including the British.

142. Garrard, *Akan Weights,* 145-48. For another pessimistic estimate on returns from traditional gold mining, see Clarke, *Topography and Diseases,* 10; Coulborn, "Reminiscences,", 79.

143. Skertchly, "Goldfields of Wassa," 278, 280.

144. Robertson, *Notes on Africa,* 126.

145. For a more positive picture see, for example, Rømer, *Gold Coast of Guinea,* part 4, 178; Hart, *Gold Coast,* 125; Burton and Cameron, *To the Gold Coast,* 2:112; and Boyle, *Through Fanteeland,* 35. Boyle noted that women could win as many as five or six ounces in gold per day from shallow earth diggings and washings; and he suggested that such results repaid their efforts quite well.

146. Interview with Kwame Yeboa, cited above.

147. George E. Ferguson, Report on Mission to Atebubu (October-December 1890), encl. in W. B. Griffith to Knutsford, 9 March 1891, CO 96/215.

148. Phillip D. Curtin, *Economic Change in Precolonial Africa* (Madison, Wis,, 1975), 205.

149. Polly Hill, *Population, Prosperity and Poverty; Rural Kano, 1900 and 1970* (London, 1977), 164-79.

CHAPTER 4

1. Secondary works that have repeated this story include McPhee, *Economic Revolution,* 50-51; Kimble, *Political History of Ghana,* 15-16. See Henry Brackenbury, *The Ashantee War,* 2 vols. (London, 1974) 2:351; Burton and Cameron, *To The Gold Coast,* 1:ix.

2. One of the leading gold propagandists was Wolseley's own chief of staff. See Brackenbury, *Ashantee War,* 2:216-19, 351-53. Another was Winwood Reade (the *Daily News* special correspondent), *The Ashantee War* (London, 1874), 380-81. Also see G. A. Henty, *The March to Coomassie* (London, 1974).

3. M. F. Ommanney, memorandum of a conversation with Captain Henry Brackenbury, R.A., relative to the Future Policy to be pursued on the "Gold Coast," 27 March 1874, Carnarvon Papers; PRO 30/6/85.

4. For details on this question, see Raymond Dumett and Marion Johnson, "The Suppression of Slavery in the Gold Coast, Asante and the Northern Territories," in S. Miers and R. Roberts, eds., *The End of Slavery in Africa* (Madison, Wis., 1988), 71-116.

5. The Asante problem remained the priority issue on the Gold Coast governments agenda throughout the 1870s, 1880s, and 1890s. For details see the voluminous documentation in the British Parliamentary Papers; for example, "Further Correspondence Relating to Affairs in Ashanti," *PP* (1896) 58 [C.7917]. William Tordoff, *Asante under the Prempehs, 1888-1935* (London, 1965), 8-38.

6. Strahan to Carnarvon, 18 March 1875: "Papers re. to H.M.S Possessions Africa-Part 2. *PP* (1875) 52 [C. 1343]: 75-76. Also see Strahan to Carnarvon, 2 August 1875, *PP* (1876) 52 [C. 1402]: 70.

7. Skertchly, "Gold Fields of Wassa," 274.

8. Interview with the Apintohene Nana Faibel III and his council, Dumett Collection.

9. Extract of letter from W. A. Cuscaden to Col. Sec., Accra. 31 January 1882, encl. 2 in Gov. Sir S. Rowe to Earl of Kimberley, 18 March 1882, *PP* (1885) 48 [C. 3687]: 3.

10. Burton and Cameron, *To the Gold Coast,* 2:123, 140, 160-61, 193, 293; Brackenbury, 2:291-95.

11. Brackenbury, *Ashantee War,* 2:123, 223.

12. Gov. Maxwell (131) to CO, 15 April 1896; CO 96/272.

13. Extracts from Report of M. Bonnat, 12 January 1879, and letter from E. J. Foster, Secretary of the Tarkwa and Aboso Consolidated Mines, Ltd., printed in Holmes, "Early History of Tarkwa," 78, 81.

14. Extract of Report by Bonnat, 12 January 1879, quoted in Holmes "Early History of Tarkwa," 81. See also Skertchly, "Goldfields of Wassa," 275.

15. Extract from a letter by Foster (see note 13, this chap.), quoted by Holmes, "Early History of Tarkwa," 78-79.

16. The fact that most of the European miners, like the Africans, were also using hand tools at this juncture should not go unrecorded.

17. See Godoy, "Peasant Miners in Bolivia," 103-20.

18. See Freund, *Nigerian Tin Mines,* 45-48.

19. Gramberg, *Schetsen van Afrikas Westkust* (Amsterdam, 1861), 233.

20. Asante troops inflicted heavy losses on the Wassas, who were allied with the Fantes and British. Ramseyer and J. Khune, *Four Years in Ashantee* (New York, 1875) 218-19, 221.

21. Skertchly's 1879 description intimates that African mining practices of the late 1870s at Tarkwa were very much a continuation of ancient patterns. Skertchly, "Goldfields of Wassa," 274-83.

22. Burton and Cameron, *To the Gold Coast,* 2:273. For confirmation see Reports by W. A. Cuscaden, 31 August 1882, encl. 1 in Rowe to Kimberley, 13 September 1882, *PP* (1883) 48 [C. 3687]: a-1.

23. Examples are McPhee, *Economic Revolution,* 50; K. B. Dickson, *A Historical Geography of Ghana* (Cambridge, 1969), 184. The story of early European gold mining in Wassa is also covered in Jim Silver, "The Failure of Primitive Accumulation: European Mining Companies in the Nineteenth-Century Gold Coast," *Journal of African History* 22 (1981): 511-21. Silver mistakenly refers to Bonnat as Pierre Bonnat, instead of Marie Joseph Bonnat (513).

24. "Register of Actions of the Commission for Systematic Gold Mining on the W. Coast of Africa as stipulated by his Excellency, the Minister of Colonies, 30 October 1844," Dutch documents, KVG777. Also see "Report on Inspection by Governor, 11 July 1848," from State Archives, the Hague, Netherlands. Possession on the coast of Guinea, ARA/NBKG 777. Copies at Balme Library, University of Ghana. I am grateful to Albert Van Dantzig for providing me with copies and translations of these Dutch documents. See also Yarak, "Dutch Gold-Mining Effort," 4-21.

25. Norman R. Junner reported the gold found in the district of Mpoha on the River Butre as patchy. *Gold in the Gold Coast,* 47-48.

26. An experienced miner and fellow of the Royal Geographic Society,

Skertchly had first traveled to the Gold Coast in 1871 but was diverted from journeying to the gold districts by the political tensions then mounting and so contented himself with a side trip to Dahomey. Returning to the Gold Coast after the Asante War, he commenced digging for gold at Tarkwa in 1877, at a time when Bonnat was still concentrating on placer mining. See J. A. Skertchly, *Dahomey as It Is* (London, 1874), vii-viii.

27. For a full treatment of Bonnat's wider trading and exploration ventures, see Jules Gros, *Voyages, adventures et captivité de J. Bonnat chez les Achantis* (Paris, 1882), 246-58. Also see Marion Johnson, "M. Bonnat on the Volta," *Ghana Notes and Queries* 10 (December 1968): 4-17.

28. Strahan to Carnarvon, 25 October 1875, *PP* (1876) 55 [C. 1142]: 89.

29. For extensive details on Bonnat's mining schemes in Wassa, see H. J. Bevin, "M. J. Bonnat, Trader and Mining Promoter," *Economic Bulletin* (Accra) 4.7 (July 1960): 1-8. Also see E. T. McCarthy, "Early Days on the Gold Coast," *Mining Magazine*, December 1909, 291-95.

30. There has been a resurgence of interest in recent years in the mythology and symbolism of empire, particularly under the aegis of scholars in comparative literature and postcolonial discourse theory. See, especially, Edward Said, *Cultural Imperialism* (New York, 1992); F. Cooper and Ann L. Stoler, eds., *Tensions of Empire: Colonial Cultures in a Bourgeois World* (Berkeley, 1997). One set of ideas, worth further analysis for its psychological as well as economic implications, is the magnetic imagery of Ophir, Golconda, and El Dorado upon mining imperialism and the conquest of wealth.

31. Examples of the very extensive contemporary literature that popularized the apparent ease of placer mining in the post-California gold rush era are Lawson B. Patterson, *Twelve Years in the Mines of California* (Cambridge, 1862) and Raymond Rossiter, *The Mines of the West* (New York, 1869).

32. These riverside sites, Aodua and points south, lay about twenty to twenty-five miles west of the main reef gold sites on Tarkwa ridge. Gros, *Voyages*, 264-67.

33. Unfortunately we have little data on the lives of these men in comparison with Bonnat. See Bevin, "M. J. Bonnat," 1-8.

34. Report by Louis Wyatt on the Tarkwa Mines, encl. in Crown Agent for the Colonies to R. H. Meade, CO, 14 June 1879, CO 96/129, PRO.

35. Bevin, "M. J. Bonnat," 5.

36. Wyatt, Diary of a tour through the Axim Dist. (1879), encl. in Crown Agents to CO, 9 May 1879, CO 96/129, PRO.

37. Wyatt, Report on Tarkwa Mines, encl. in Crown Agent's letter of 14 June 1879, CO 96/129, PRO.

38. There is confusion on this point in Rosenblum, where he says that Moulton had fourteen years prior experience in Australia. But there is no ref-

erence to this supposed fact in W. F. Holmes, which is the source that
Rosenblum gives. In reality, Moulton himself stated that he had no prior
knowledge of geology. Holmes referred to C. J. Harvey as the man who had
the long Australian experience. Rosenblum, "Gold Mining in Ghana," 168;
Holmes, "Early History of Tarkwa," 84-87.

39. Report by M. Moulton to the Directors of the African Gold Coast
Company, Ltd., 3 January 1879, quoted in Holmes, "Early History of Tarkwa," 90.

40. Wyatt, Report on Tarkwa Mines, CO 96/129, PRO.

41. Mine Report by Bonnat, encl. in J. C. Wray to Hicks Beach, 11
March 1879, CO 96/129, PRO.

42. Gros stated that Bonnat died in July 1882 (*Voyages,* 269). But
Bevin, citing other evidence, declares that Bonnat died of malaria in July
1881 ("M. J. Bonnat," 6-7). W. A. Cuscaden to Col. Sec., Accra, 31 January 1882, encl. in Rowe to Kimberley, 18 March 1882, *PP* (1883) 48 [C.
3687]: 81.

43. The best summary of these events is found in J. A. B. Horton, *West
African Countries and Peoples* (London, 1868; reprint Edinburgh, 1969),
238-39; also Bevin, "M. J. Bonnat," 9. We do not know the exact location
of Hughes's mines; but it is possible that Horton later took them over.

44. These developments are also discussed in Rosenblum, "Gold Mining in Ghana," 122-23, which cites the *African Times* (22 February 1862,
53 and 23 November 1866, 51) as sources for these facts. However, a
check of that newspaper shows that there was no page 53 in the 22 February 1862 issue. In the 23 November 1866 issue there is a brief mention
of Hughes's name in reference to politics, but no mention of his mining
activities.

45. I have collected the names of close to 200 indigenous traders and merchants of the Gold Coast who entered exporting and importing between 1865
and 1900. Of these, twenty-five to thirty could be classified as major merchants. In addition a number of African lawyers, teachers, clergymen, and
other professional men can be included in this group. See Dumett, "African
Merchants," 661-93; also Reynolds, *Trade and Economic Change,* 53-63.

46. Kimble, *Political History of Ghana,* 222-67; Francis Agbodeka, *African Politics and British Policy in the Gold Coast, 1868-1900* (London,
1971), 15-35, 123-46, and passim.

47. Several accounts, influenced by neo-Marxist and dependency theory,
tend to view these black businessmen and professional men as a "compra-
dor class," or collaborators in the expansion of the colonialistic economic system, who exploited their own people and were in turn dominated by and
then crushed by European corporate interests. See, especially, Susan Kaplow,
"The Mudfish and the Crocodile: Underdevelopment of a West African Bourgeoisie," *Science and Society,* no. 3 (Fall 1977): 517-33.

48. **Palm Oil and Palm Kernel Exports from the Gold Coast**

	Palm Oil			Palm Kernels	
Year	Quantity (gal.)	Value (£)	Avg. Price (per gal.)	Quantity (ton)	Value (£)
1872	2,246,786	278,642	28.3d	470	5,874
1874	n.r.	n.r.		n.r.	n.r.
1876	3,865,007	305,998	18.7d	7,665	67,645
1878	3,898,917	295,246	18.6d	5,251	48,707
1880	3,420,279	307,113	18.9d	9,511	101,606
1882	1,229,278	178,508	28.8d	8,150	50,317
1884	6,016,189	507,966	18.8d	38,702	403,876
1886	3,163,206	155,979	1/.0d	9,427	47,830
1888	3,410,788	150,361	-1.1d	13,331	68,525
1890	2,932,951	144,788	1/0d	12,650	78,433
1892	3,643,366	178,954	1/0d	15,846	103,295

Source: Gold Coast Colonial Blue Books for the years listed.

49. I discuss the problems of the colony's staple palm product exports and the shift to rubber in R. E. Dumett, "The Rubber Trade of the Gold Coast and Asante in the Nineteenth Century: African Innovation and Market Responsiveness," *Journal of African History* 12.1 (1971): 79-101.

50. Obituary in the *African Times*, 1 March 1884, 30. Also see Kimble, *Political History of Ghana*, 5, 8, 192 (fn. 1).

51. Fitzgerald, Editorial, *African Times*, 23 October 1863.

52. See R. E. Dumett, "Pressure Groups, Bureaucracy and the Decision-Making Process: Slavery Abolition and Colonial Expansion in the Gold Coast, 1874," *Journal of Imperial and Commonwealth History* 9.2 (January 1981): 193-215.

53. *African Times*, 1 April 1880, 42. His middle-of-the-road pragmatic position with respect to colonialism resembled that of his contemporaries Samuel Ajayi Crowther of southern Nigeria and Edward Wilmot Blyden of Liberia. Fitzgerald, though highly critical of British imperial policy, believed that Africans had no choice but to work for improvements within the colonial system. For Blyden's position, see Hollis R. Lynch, *Edward Wilmot Blyden: Pan-Negro Patriot (1832-1912)*. (London, 1967); 140-209.

54. For a very good summary of Horton's career and thought see George Sheppersons introduction to Horton, *West African Countries*, vii-xxiv.

55. Among Horton's medical works are *The Medical Topography of the West Coast of Africa* (London, 1859); *Guinea Worm, or Dracunculus, Its Symptoms and Progress, Causes, Pathological Anatomy, Results and Medical Care* (London, 1868), and *The Diseases of Tropical Climate and Their Treatment* (London, 1874).

56. Far and away the best treatment of Horton's leadership in the Fante

Confederation is still that by David Kimble. See Kimble, *Political History of Ghana,* 71, 94, 230–32, 243–45.

57. Horton had established his London and West African Bank in London in 1882 with a nominal capital of £500,000. Although the project failed owing to Horton's untimely death in 1882, it may be that he had entertained hopes that some of the capital for this enterprise would come from the profits of his mining ventures. J. A. B. Horton, *J. A. B. Horton, Letters on the Political Condition of the Gold Coast,* ed. E. A. Ayandele (new ed., London, 1970), 34–35.

58. Letter from Lt. Gov. Alfred Moloney (Accra) to Gov. Griffith, 20 October 1882, encl. in Griffith (571) to Kimberley, 2 November 1882, CO 96/144. See also Dumett, "Economic Development," 61.

59. For discussions about this group see Dumett, "African Merchants," 678–84. Also see Kimble, *Political History of Ghana,* 225, 229, 244–45.

60. Burton and Cameron, *To the Gold Coast,* 2:237. Also see Claridge, *History of the Gold Coast,* 134; Wilks, *Asante in the Nineteenth Century,* 495.

61. W. A. Cuscaden, report to the acting Col. Secy., 31 December, encl. in S. Rowe to Kimberley, 18 March 1882, *PP* (1883) 48 [C. 3687]: 3.

62. There is an important sub-rosa feature of these relationships that, though muted in direct official Gold Coast correspondence, undoubtedly smoldered beneath the surface in expatriate attitudes of the time. This is the issue of the mixed-race offspring of marriages and unions between people of European and African descent. A growing literature has exposed the fact that the ruling elites of Victorian Britain, Canada, Australia, and the United States were abnormally suspicious of what were variously termed metís, mulattoes, or people of mixed blood. (See Robert J. C. Young, *Colonial Desire: Hybridity in Theory, Culture and Race* [London, 1995], 6–14, 136–40, 141–49.) Militating against such prejudices on the Gold Coast were the pro-British attitudes and obvious abilities of the Eurafricans discussed here.

63. For greater detail on Sarbah's career, see Raymond E. Dumett, "John Sarbah the Elder and African Mercantile Entrepreneurship in the Gold Coast in the Late Nineteenth Century," *Journal of African History* 14.4 (1973): 653–79.

64. Prospectus for G. C. Native Concessions Purchasing Company in the *Gold Coast Times,* 22 April 1882.

65. Interviews with W. S. Kwesi Johnson, Dumett Collection. Personal communication with Dr. S. Sey, former Dean of the Faculty of Agriculture, University of Science and Technology, Kumasi, later deputy governor of the Ghana National Bank, Accra, August 1969.

66. *Gold Coast Times,* 30 September 1882, 3, also regretted the resignation of Brew from the board of directors and asked whether this reflected some deeper problem in the administration of the company.

67. The colonial government deliberately stonewalled the local African

mining company promoters on this issue. See minutes and enclosures in
Moloney (229) to Kimberley, 6 June 1882, CO 96/140. See also Rosenblum,
"Gold Mining in Ghana," 250-59.

68. Horton sold most of his earlier concessions to the Wassa and
Ahanta Gold Mines Syndicate, formed in July 1882. The syndicate issued
£6,500 shares as fully paid up to the main promoters, Horton and Fitzgerald. Registrar of Joint Stock Cos BT 31/3020, no. 1075, PRO.

69. Cooper, *Geology of the Prestea Goldfield,* 10.

70. The directors and major shareholders of the Essaman Mining Company organized in London were: James Labouchere, chairman; Thomas Gillespie; Charles Tuttenham; and Henry Tolputt. Labouchere and Tuttenham
had also backed Horton's Wassa and Ahanta Gold Mines Syndicate, which
was listed as an institutional shareholder in the Essaman Company. B.T.
31/3020, no. 1075, PRO.

71. Records of the Essaman Gold Mining Company, Ltd., 5 December
1885, BT 31/3568, no. 21864, PRO. Also see *Mining Journal,* 9 January
1886, 57.

72. *Mining Journal,* 28 May 1887, 663; also 23 July 1892, 817.

73. Dumett, "African Merchants," 661-93 and "John Sarbah," 653-79.

74. Obituary of William Edward Sam, *Journal of the African Society* 6
(October, 1906): 98-99.

75. The British Companies Act of the 1850s had legalized the limited liability corporation. J. R. Jeffries, "The Denomination and Character of
Shares, 1855-1885," *Economic History Review* 15.1 (1946): 45-55.

76. Ibid., 53.

77. Companies records and shareholders lists, Registrar of Joint Stock
Companies, PRO. See Dumett "Economic Development," 63. Silver, "Primitive Accumulation," 512-21, uses some of the information in my 1966
manuscript for his 1981 article on the weaknesses of capitalization and mismanagement by many of the expatriate companies. His interpretation,
influenced by Marxist theory, is different from the one presented here. He
does not, for example, go into the numerous, complex and very real physical
and technological obstacles faced by the bona fide companies. (See chapters
5, 6, and 7 of the present volume.)

78. For the early history of the Swanzy trading firm, see Henry Swanzy,
"A Trading Family in the Nineteenth Century Gold Coast," *Transactions of
the Gold Coast and Togoland Historical Society* 2, part 2 (Achimota, 1956),
87-120.

79. For details see Brackenbury, *Ashantee War,* 2:306-12.

80. B.T. 31/2925, no. 16316 Company Records, PRO. Also see the
Swanzy Estates and Gold Mines Mining Company, *Mining Journal,* 10 June
1882, 299.

81. See Edward Wilmot Blyden, *Selected Letters of Edward Wilmot Blyden,* ed. Hollis R. Lynch (Millwood, N.Y., 1978), 204-5, 227.

82. No less a champion of rugged individualism than Herbert Spencer did an intensive study unmasking the common fraud and deception in ordinary business dealings of the time. See Herbert Spencer, "The Morals of Trade," *Westminster Review* 71 (1859): 357-90.

83. The term *Gilded Age,* which reflected the materialism and superficial veneer of bourgeois respectability, was coined by Mark Twain in this very period. Mark Twain and C. W. Warner, *The Gilded Age: A Tale of Today* (Hartford, Conn. 1873).

84. See James Irvine, "Our Commercial Relations with West Africa and their Effects on Civilization," Speech before the Royal Society of Arts, 13 March 1877, *Journal of the Society of Arts,* 16 March 1877, 378-88.

85. Walker was a tough old West African hand who had first gone out to West Africa in 1851 and worked at various jobs, including traders agent and merchant seaman before getting to know Irvine. Letter to the editor in *Supplement to the Mining Journal,* 15 April 1882, 468.

86. Hart, *Gold Coast,* 27-28.

87. Burton and Cameron, *To the Gold Coast,* 2:113-32, 154-70, 199-200, and passim.

88. *Mining Journal,* 1 July 1882, 783.

89. Ibid., 18 March 1882, 330.

90. Memorandum of Association, 21 October 1881 and Memo. of Agreement, 22 October 1881, Guinea Coast Gold Mining Company, Ltd., BT 31/2888, no. 1600.

91. Irvine claimed that the mere listing of a company's capital stock (whether paid or unpaid) did not reflect the amount of unlisted investment that a proprietor might put into his companies. And he contended that he had spent a large part of his personal fortune on his companies.

92. For Cameron's earlier career, see W. Robert Foran, *African Odyssey: The Life of Verney Lovett Cameron* (London, 1937), 20-32, 363-73.

93. For the best biography of Burton, see Fawn M. Brodie, *The Devil Drives: The Life of Sir Richard Francis Burton* (New York, 1967), 287-88.

94. *West African Reporter,* 8 April 1882, copy enclosed in Rowe (Conf. 12) to Kimberley, 27 April 1882, CO 96/139. See also Dumett, "Economic Development," 63.

95. *Spectator,* 19 May 1883.

96. *Mining Journal,* 11 December 1886, 1443. This episode is also covered in Rosenblum, "Gold Mining in Ghana," 215.

97. Brodie, *Devil Drives,* 287.

98. Junner, *Gold in the Gold Coast,* 43-45.

99. *Annual Report of the Gold Coast Geological Survey,* 1922-23, 24.

100. *African Times*, 2 October 1883, 1–2 and 1 January 1887, 3–4.

101. Special Resolution of 16 July 1885 that the company be wound up, BT 31/2888, no. 16002, PRO; *Mining Journal*, 30 May 1885, 605; 11 December 1886, 1443–44.

102. The terms *rockers, cradles,* and *long toms* refer simply to various types of sluices (wooden troughs) used for separating gold from sand in alluvial mining (see glossary). Harold Barger and S. H. Schurr, *The Mining Industries, 1899–1939* (New York, 1944; reprint, 1972), 98, 101.

103. Sluices were introduced into California in 1848 and 1849, and it was claimed that two men could scour as much as ten to twenty cubic yards of gravel daily. Walter R. Crane, *Gold and Silver* (New York, 1908), 343.

104. F. Fitzgerald, "Gold Wealth of California and of the West African Gold Coast District," *African Times*, 23 October 1863. Burton and Cameron, *To the Gold Coast*, 2:197, 220–23, 247, 360–64.

105. Paulus Dahse, "Von der Goldküste," *Deutsche geographische Blätter* (Bremen) 1.6 (1882): 286–87.

106. *African Times*, 1 April 1880, 38.

107. Major shareholders were Irvine—1,161; Solomon Hecht—1,150; P. Dahse—729; Charles Hecht—666; and Fitzgerald—714. Memorandum of Association, 1 October 1879; also Summary of Capital and Shares, 17 October 1882; Registrar of Joint Stock Companies, BT 31/2576, no. 13495, PRO.

108. The initial nominal capital was £50,000, divided into 10,000 £5 shares. The company was formed in October 1879; by March 1880, 3,980 partially paid up shares had been sold, making a paid up capital of £11,940. By October 1882, 11,540 fully paid shares had been sold for £57,700. Effuenta Company, Summary and Capital and Shares, RJSC, BT 31/2576, no. 13495.

109. Agreement of October 1879 between Fitzgerald and Paulus Dahse. Records of the Effuenta Company, RJSC, BT 31/2576, no. 13495.

110. McCarthy knew Bonnat, having traveled to Wassa about the same time as the representatives of the Anglo-French Company in 1879.

111. Commander Rumsey to Act. Col. Sec., Accra, 9 August 1882, encl. 1 in Moloney to Kimberley, 4 September 1882, CO 96/140, 53.

112. Cameron, "Goldfields of West Africa," 780.

113. Dahse and McCarthy were apparently oblivious to the fact that the copper surface on their Appleby plates, over which the crushed sludge passed, had to be coated with mercury in order to draw off the gold particles.

114. *Mining Journal*, 23 May 1883, 577; *African Times*, 1 August 1883; Griffith (Conf.-26) to Kimberley, 22 November 1882, CO 96/144, PRO.

115. Memorandum of Association (9 March 1880) and Concession, Agreement (8 March 1880) between J. A. B. Horton, Fitzgerald, A. B. Walton (engineer), and Chief Ango of Apinto, BT 31/2620, no. 13859, PRO.

116. Report by Rumsey, 9 August 1882, 54.

117. Fourth Monthly Report on Tarkwa by H. Higgins, 31 July 1882; encl. in Moloney to Kimberley, 61-62.

118. For example the board chairman of this company predicted a crushing rate of 100 tons daily, but the actual rate in late 1882 was 100 tons over the course of two months. *Mining Journal,* 27 January 1883, 95; also 17 February 1883, 207, and on January 1882, 21.

119. *Mining Journal,* 26 January 1884, 100; also Rosenblum, "Gold Mining in Ghana," 202.

120. For example, the first hint of gold on the Upper Yukon River reached the South in 1867, and the first stream of prospectors reached the territory between 1873 and 1878. Profitable mining, including deep shafts for lode gold, did not get underway until 1898 to 1902.

CHAPTER 5

1. Michael Tanzer, *The Race for Resources.* (New York, 1980), 22-29; J. H. Chileshe, *Third World Countries and Development Options: Zambia* (New Delhi, 1986), 2-13; T. M. Shaw and M. J. Grieve, "The Political Economy of Resources: Africa's Future in the Global Environment," *Journal of Modern African Studies* 16.1 (1978): 1-32.

2. General histories of mining in Africa, which have tended to overlook or give insufficient attention to problems of operating costs and other basic constraints to effective mining such as technology, accessibility, and grade of ore, include Greg Lanning with Marti Mueller, *Africa Undermined: Mining Companies and the Underdevelopment of Africa* (Harmondsworth, 1979); Silver, "Primitive Accumulation," 517-21; O. Ogunbadejo, *The International Politics of Africa's Strategic Minerals* (London, 1985).

3. E. H. Davies, "Some Hints on Mine Management," *Mining Journal, Railway and Commercial Gazette,* 2 December 1893, 1334.

4. James H. Batty later became Chairman of the Board of the Ashanti Goldfields Corporation. James Batty to Gov. Mathew Nathan, appendix A., 9 June 1902, Nathan Papers, Correspondence, 305-6, RHO.

5. This remains a daunting task for future research that could cast light on a vital segment of British overseas investment. We lack information on exact purchase prices of machines from major manufacturers, even for the important Ashanti Goldfields Corporation and at later periods, for which some papers exist. Prices were not listed in machinery advertisements—but it is possible that contemporary price lists in catalogues and company order books will one day be unearthed.

6. At the end of the 1880s, the Gold Coast governor, W. B. Griffith, put forward a figure of £975,000 total nominal capital listed by all companies in

the gold rush, out of which £510,000 nominal capital was his figure for mines still active. He did not trouble to calculate either the total paid up capital or the actual capital invested in West African mines for properties, plants, equipment, and buildings. See Report on the Mining Companies of Wassa, encl. in Griffith to Knutsford, 25 June 1889 PP (1889) 54 [C. 5620-24]: 14-15.

7. Leases passed through many hands, with each party receiving a share of the take, before they reached their ultimate destination in London. Often (1) a chief would lease a property to a West African concessions dealer; (2) the dealer would sell the lease to a European agent on the coast; (3) the agent would sell the lease to company directors in London; (4) the company directors would then charge their own companys capital for the transfer of the lease in question.

8. Even a weak company like the Akankoo had as many as 700 stockholders. "The Akankoo (Gold Coast) Mining Company," Mining Journal, 16 December 1882, 1515.

9. Warnings about investments in Gold Coast companies can be found in Mining Journal, 4 February 1882, 145; 7 April, 1883, 403.

10. See for example, C. E. Harvey, The Rio Tinto Company (Penzance, 1981) and Colin Newbury, "The Origins and Function of the London Diamond Syndicate 1889-1914," Business History Review, xxix, No. 1 (1987), 5-20. It is questionable whether these models are applicable at all to expatriate mining organizations prior to the 1930s.

11. Thomas Cornish, "Gold Mining Prospects and Management on the West Coast of Africa," Mining Journal, 31 December 1881, 1615.

12. As Rosa Luxemburg put it, "In the extractive industries, mines, etc. the raw materials form no part of the capital advanced. The subject of labor is in this case not a product of previous labor, but is furnished by Nature gratis, as in the case of metals, minerals, coal, stone, etc." Rosa Luxemburg, The Accumulation of Capital (London, 1951), 356.

13. Diamond-tipped exploration drills were used in Canada as early as the 1870s. See Dianne Newell, Technology on the Frontier: Mining in Old Ontario (Vancouver, 1980) 15-17, and passim. There is no evidence that such drills were ever discussed for use in the Gold Coast in the 1880s. They appear to have come into limited use only after about 1905.

14. The whole science of assaying was imprecise and subject to error. For these reasons, assays by the best London houses were often inaccurate. Note by Louis Gowan, Mining Journal, 7 January 1882, 21.

15. Mining Journal, 31 October 1889; Report on the Tarkwa Mining Dist. (1875), encl. in Crown Agents to CO, 14 June 1879, CO 96/129, PRO.

16. Black powder was a mixture of sulfur, nitrate, and charcoal. While the invention of nitroglycerin by Sobrero in Italy in 1847 put awesome detonating power within the reach of miners, little practical progress was

achieved until Alfred Nobel's perfection of dynamite in 1867. Progress in the systemization of underground blasting came even more rapidly after the first blasting gelatin came into production by Nobel in the early 1880s. J. K. Mercer, "The History of Industrial Explosives in Australia," paper delivered to the International Mining History Conference, University of Melbourne, 27–30 August 1985, 6.

17. Tarkwa, Q. Dist. Report, encl. 13 in Hodgson (41) to CO, 21 January 1898, CO 96/310.

18. Wassa Dist. Mining Report, 1 April 1897, encl. in Maxwell (330) to CO, 23 July 1897, CO 96/297. The first patented "Cornish" steam-powered drills appeared between 1880 and 1882. They became common between 1900 and 1910. See "The Rise of a Great Cornish Industry: Holman Brothers," *Mining Journal*, 30 July 1910, i–iv.

19. Interview with Jacob Eduam-Baiden, former tailings clerk for the AGC at Obuasi. (Interview at Saltpond, Ghana, 5 August 1969, when he was eighty-eight years of age.) According to this informant, the Ashanti Goldfields corporation continued to use hand-powered drills until 1905 to 1910 and perhaps later.

20. Report on the Gie Appanto, Gold Mining Company, Ltd., *Mining Journal, Railway and Commercial Gazette*, 22 July 1893, 805.

21. Interview with T. Rowe and B. Lockyear of the Ashanti Goldfields Corporation, London, 15 June 1982.

22. Q. Dist. Report for Wassa, encl. 13 in Maxwell (18) to CO, 14 June 1897, CO 96/288.

23. Wassa DC's Report, encl. 13 in Maxwell (33) to CO, 23 July 1897, CO 96/297.

24. *Mining Journal*, 23 July 1892, 819.

25. Ibid., 26 December 1885.

26. McCarthy, "Early Days on the Gold Coast," 293–94.

27. U.S. Bureau of Census, "Mines and Quarries," *1902 Special Reports* (Washington, D.C., 1902), 394–95.

28. Hopkins, *Economic History*, 14, 34.

29. I have found no analysis and scarcely any mention of the serious problem of corroded machinery in tropical regions in such standard works on the diffusion of technology in the Third World as T. R. DeGregori, *Technology and the Development of the Tropical African Frontier* (Cleveland, 1969) or Daniel Headrick, *The Tools of Empire* (New York, 1981). Not even Headricks acclaimed second book, *The Tentacles of Progress* (Oxford, 1988), which does stress mining machinery, goes into the basic problem of corrosion.

30. C. P. Larrabee, "Atmospheric Corrosion of Iron" plus K. C. Compton, "High-Humidity and Condensation Tests," in Herbert H. Uhlig, ed., *The Corrosion Handbook* (New York, 1948), 120–21 and 1006–8.

31. R. K. Swandby, "Corrosives," plus C. P. Larrabee and W. L. Mathay, "Iron and Steel," in F. L. LaQue and H. R. Copson, eds., *Corrosion Resistance of Metals and Alloys,* 2d ed. (New York, 1963) 45-50, 323-39.

32. Report on Tarkwa Gold Mining Dist., 31 July 1882, *PP* (1883) 48 [C. 3687]: 61.

33. In Wassa Mining Company to CO, 6 September 1897, CO 96/305.

34. T. R. Rickard, "The Utah Copper Enterprise," *Mining and Scientific Press* 117 (28 December 1918): 848; quoted in Barger and Schurr, *Mining Industries,* 115.

35. Thomas Cornish (consulting engineer for the Akankoo Mining Company), "Gold Mining Prospects and Management on the West Coast of Africa," letter to the editors of the *Mining Journal,* 31 December 1881, 1615.

36. Silver, in his "radical" interpretation of these events, does not go into the problem of death and disease at all. He focuses almost entirely on company stupidity as the cause of failure. He touches briefly on "the severity of the climate" as a subject for complaint, but states that its role in the failure of the mines "has been seriously over-estimated." By focusing on the mistaken words used at the time, it is easy to poke fun at the attitudes of a century ago. However, the genuine issue was not the Victorian concern with "climate," but rather disease. Silver, "Primitive Accumulation," 517-18. Similarly, Rosenblum, in his 396-page dissertation, devotes little attention to the disease factor. Rosenblum, "Gold Mining in Ghana," 293.

37. This is confirmed in *G.C. Mining Dept. Reports* and *G.C. Medical and Sanitary Dept. Reports,* when the issue of African miner's illness and mortality was first taken up systematically. Also see "Vital Statistics for Europeans in the Gold Coast and Lagos, 1881-97," CO Afr. (W) Conf. Print 727, p. 102.

38. For details on the basic problem of data retrieval even in the twentieth century, see Raymond E. Dumett, "Disease and Mortality among Gold Miners of Ghana: Colonial Government And Mining Company Attitudes and Policies, 1900-1938," *Social Science Medicine* 37.2 (1993): 213-32.

39. "Vital Statistics Respecting Europeans Employed by the Governments of the Gold Coast and Lagos, 1881-1897," Co. Afr. (W) Conf. Print. 727, p. 102.

40. *Mining Journal,* 31 October 1885.

41. In 1887, Patrick Manson first isolated the plasmodium parasite that causes malaria. In 1897, Dr. Ronald Ross identified mosquitoes of the genus *Anopheles* as the principal malaria vector. See Raymond E. Dumett, "The Campaign against Malaria and the Expansion of Scientific and Sanitary Services in British West Africa, 1898-1910," *African Historical Studies* 1.2 (1968): 153-97.

42. H. Higgins, 1st Monthly Report on Tarkwa, 30 April 1882, *PP* (1883) 48 [C. 3638]: 10.

43. Second Monthly Report on Tarkwa Dist., encl. in Moloney to Kimberley, 24 June 1882, 18.

44. H. Louis, "Gold Mining on the Gold Coast," 1437; Q. Dist. Report on Axim, encl. 7 in Rowe (213) to Derby, 29 March 1884, CO 96/156.

45. The issue of depression was recognized in the diary of Lewis Wyatt (1879), above. Dr. Charles Easmon, one of Ghana's leading physicians, told me that many of the psychological and physical ailments that were combined in colonial times under the label of tropical neurasthenia were undoubtedly a genuine force behind European depression, despondency, and poor work performance. Interview with Dr. C. O. Easmon, Chief Medical Officer of Ghana and president of the Medical School of Korle Bu Hospital, Accra, Ghana, July 1969. Also see L. E. Napier, *The Principles and Practice of Tropical Medicine* (New York, 1947), 47. One or two recent publications by writers in the colonial-discourse or "deconstruction" mold have dismissed "nuerasthenia" as a kind of malingering or sham that was a product of the nineteenth-century colonial culture in the tropics. Obviously the label was archaic, and some outlandish pseudoscientific explanations were put forward for misunderstood symptoms, just as they were at this time for "malaria." This does not, however, rule out the strong possibility that many such patients suffered from genuine psychological disorders of the sort that today would be scientifically understood and treated as "depression."

46. Part of the problem with European alcoholism, as with psychological depression, is that it is difficult to measure and no records were kept. Even when company managers were sure that this lay behind a European workers dereliction of his duties, they covered up the fact.

47. Comment in *Mining Journal,* 22 July 1893, 805. Also see McCarthy, "Early Days on the Gold Coast," 219.

48. Among the vast number of comments that fit the closed-minded Eurocentric and racially biased category were the following. "As I have stated in former reports, the natives of these parts are bad workers, and are employed as little as possible in the mines." Henry Higgins, 5th Report on Tarkwa Dist., 31 August 1882, encl. in Moloney to Kimberley, 21 September 1882, PP (1883) [C.3687]: 73. Later Governor William Maxwell, after only a brief period on the coast, wrote that the laborers employed by the mines were "not only idle but also absolutely unskilled in the use of tools given to them and also in acquiring the necessary dexterity." W. E. Maxwell, "Affairs of the Gold Coast and Ashanti," address to the African Trade Section of the Liverpool Chamber of Commerce (1 July 1906), 15, 19.

49. One of the most blatantly racist views on the so-called worthlessness of African mines labor ever put forward was by the eminent mining engineer and later U.S. president, Herbert Hoover, in his textbook *Principles of Mining* (London, 1909), 162–63. And because his book had such a wide influence throughout the world, one must assume that this attack on African

miners ("one white man equals to two or three of the colored race and in skilled positions the ratio is one to seven or even one to eleven") also had wide support among the general European and North American mining fraternity. For another similar random observation, see "The Labor Question in the Gold Coast," *Economist,* 27 July 1903, 1127.

50. Letter to editor in *Supplement to the Mining Journal,* 14 April 1882, 458. Richard Burton, with characteristic arrogance, purported to write extensively and with great assurance on "the Labor question in Western Africa." The two main problems, he proclaimed, were laziness and a predilection to thievery. He concluded that it was "useless to preach industry" to Africans. His solution was to import foreign labor, including Chinese "coolies." Burton and Cameron, *To the Gold Coast,* appdx. 1, 2:326-30.

51. See comments in *African Times,* 1 October 1889. Also see W. B. Griffith (329) to CO, 13 November 1894, CO 96/249. Several commentators expanded on this by saying that colonial proclamations and laws against African domestic slavery had made it doubly difficult to procure manual labor on a wage basis. John Duncan, *Travels in Western Africa in 1845 and 1846,* new ed. (London, 1968), 40-42.

52. W. F. Hutchinson in "Report on the Economic Agriculture in the Gold Coast," *PP* (1890) 48 [C. 5897-40]: 9, 12.

53. Easmon suggested that some coastal peoples, including the Kru, were more vigorous because they ate a more balanced and nutritious diet, including a great amount of green vegetables. Report by J. F. Easmon, Act. Med. Off., encl. in Griffith (111), 5 April 1887, CO 96/180. Dr. James Easmon was a respected African medical doctor in the Gold Coast at this juncture, and he had the support of the colonial government. (Part of the reason, of course, was that so few European physicians were willing to take up extended service in West Africa.) With the advent of the "new imperialism" in the 1890s, these tolerant and respectful attitudes toward African M.D.s would change. The story of how a growing colonial racism would impede the advancement of African physicians in the colonial medical service has been well told by Adell Patton in *Physicians, Colonial Racism, and Diaspora in West Africa* (Gainesville, Fla., 1992).

54. Easmon stated that this conclusion is based on modern research. Dr. Charles Easmon is the grandson of the eminent nineteenth-century physician James Farrel Easmon. Interview, Korle Bu, Accra, 7 August 1969.

55. For details, see Wilks, *Asante in the Nineteenth Century,* 52, 70, 83-85, 176-77, 308, and passim; and Joseph La Torre, "Wealth Surpasses Everything: An Economic History of Asante" (Ph.D. dissertation, University of California, Berkeley, 1974), 98-99, 136-41, and passim.

56. Rattray, *Ashanti Law and Constitution,* 114.

57. "A plentiful supply of labor is the great difficulty this colony has to contend with . . . in a climate like this, existence becomes practicable on a

very small amount of labor. . . . Most of the work that is done is performed by the female portion of the community. . . ." *African Times*, 1 April 1885, 59-60. Also see Hutchinson, "Economic Agriculture" (note 52, this chap.).

58. Hopkins, *Economic History*, 15, 24-25. See also David Northrupp, *Beyond the Bend of the River* (Athens, Ohio, 1988), 213-16.

59. Cameron, "Goldfields of West Africa," 781.

60. Remi Clignet, *The Africanization of the Labor Market.* (Berkeley, 1976), 10-14, 18-26.

61. Interview with J. W. S. Hammond (retired Ghanaian mines supervisor), Tarkwa, Wassa, Ghana, 4 August 1969, Dumett Collection.

62. For the use of slaves as porters, see Marion Johnson, "The Slaves of Salaga," *Journal of African History* (1986): 27, 341-62. Gold Coast labor recruitment by the government for military expeditions has been discussed by a number of writers. This could involve the use of former slaves and outright forced labor. David Killingray, "Guarding the Extending Frontier: Policing the Gold Coast, 1865-1913," paper presented at the 33rd Annual Meeting of the African Studies Association of the United States, Baltimore, 1-4 November 1990, 9.

63. Skertchly, "Goldfields of Wassa," 275.

64. Ordinance no. 2 of 1883: the Public Labor Ordinance. W. B. Griffith Jr., *Laws of the Gold Coast Colony in Force, April 1887* (London, 1887), 541-44.

65. The Kru men were universally regarded as superb canoemen and praised for their work in a variety of other vocations. See Jane Martin, "Down the Coast: Liberian Migrants on the West African Coast in the Nineteenth and Twentieth Centuries," *International Journal of African Historical Studies* 18.3 (1985): 401-23. Also see George Brooks, *The Kru Mariner* (Newark, Del., 1970); and B. Harrell-Bond, Allen Howard, and D. Skinner, *Community Leadership and the Transformation of Freetown, 1801-1976* (The Hague, 1978), 72-75, 98-99.

66. Kru laborers normally hired on for six- to twelve-month contracts. Initially these contracts were negotiated between mine managers and Kru headmen.

67. See, for example, George Orwell, *The Road to Wigan Pier* (London, 1937), 26-58, and passim. Also see Shaftesburys speech on conditions in English coal mines, in A. A. Cooper, *Speeches of the Earl of Shaftesbury*, 2d ed. (Shannon, Ireland, 1977), 34-47.

68. Interview with Issah Busonga, Obuasi, Asante, Ghana, 21 May 1987, Dumett Collection.

69. Among those who held to this reactionary view was H. M. Stanley, *Coomassie and Magdala: The Story of Two British Campaigns in Africa* (New York, 1974); 140-41. Burton and Cameron did not specifically stress flogging in their Gold Coast book, but they doubted whether "the African"

could be made to mine for gold for Europeans except by force. Burton and
Cameron, *To the Gold Coast*, 2:165, 205-6. Throughout this volume other
examples demonstrate that physical punishment was used right up to the
1920s and 1930s (see chap. 17).

70. Comment quoted in the *Gold Coast Chronicle*, 11 March 1893, 3.

71. Agreement. between Chief Enemil Kuma and M. J. Bonnat, 18 April
1879, appendix to Holmes, "Early History of Tarkwa," 114-15.

72. As the two explorers reported it, the Anglo-French company fell
back on the *abusa* share system purely as a stopgap measure, not as a methodical approach to the establishment of regularized wage labor. Burton
and Cameron, *To the Gold Coast*, 2:333.

73. Report by Cuscaden, 3 January 1882, encl. in Sir S. Rowe to
Kimberby, 8 May 1882, *PP* (1883) 48 [C. 3687].

74. Africans could still use three other land routes from the Tarkwa mining districts to the coast. The first followed a narrow and indefinable trail
from the port of Axim directly overland to Tarkwa, a distance of about sixty
miles. Even under the best of conditions this route was limited to Africans
carrying light loads. A second and better-defined road ran from Tarkwa in a
southeasterly direction through Manso to Shama, west of Cape Three
Points. This was the ancient gold route to the coast used since Portuguese
times—a distance of about seventy miles. The third and far longer route ran
overland in a southeastern direction from Tarkwa to the port of Cape Coast,
a distance of 107 miles. All these distances were as the crow flies. Owing to
unpreventable detours the real mileage was far greater.

75. Comment by W. H. Swift in *Journal of the Society of Arts* 47.2 (24
February 1899): 312.

76. Griffith (Conf.) to Knutsford, 2 June 1891, CO 96/217. Also see
Hodgson to Knutsford, 3 October 1889, CO Afr. (W) 451, no. 32, p. 72.

77. M. Jones, Asst. Surveyor to Col. Sec., Accra, 8 August 1882, encl. 6
in Moloney to Kimberley, 4 September 1882, 48 (1883) [C.3687], pp. 56-57.

78. T. J. Price, "Missionary Travelling on the West Coast of Africa,"
Work and Workers in the Missionary Field 1 (1892): 87. Fifty to sixty miles
was the official mileage, Axim to Tarkwa, as the crow flies. Because of the
numerous detours for portage, the journey was always longer. This helps to
explain Price's figures.

79. Report by Louis Wyatt, DC at Axim, ends in letter from Cramer
Agents to CO, 14 June 1879, CO 96/129.

80. Tarkwa Dist. Roads Report, (March 1890), encl. 1 in Griffith to
Knutsford, 2 June 1891, CO Afr. 451, no. 41, pp. 90-99.

81. Richard Burton reported that the Anglo-French (African Gold
Coast) Mining Company paid only £2.0.0 to £2.10.0 per ton for transporting machinery from England, but as high as £24.0.0 per ton for shipping

and same weight seventy miles by combined canoe and headload to Tarkwa. Burton and Cameron, *To the Gold Coast,* 2:282.

82. Report by R. G. Rogerson, appendix A, encl. 1 in Crown Agents to CO, 23 August 1897, CO 86/301. Also see *The Gold Coast Annual Report for 1897,* 12. Another contemporary report presented figures that showed that transport costs within the Gold Coast alone added up to 31 percent of the original invoice price of that same machinery in the United Kingdom. Report by Stanley Clay on Wassa (G.C.) Mining Co. to CO, 7 March 1900, CO 96/369.

83. Sixty pounds was the average weight load that an individual porter could carry; but they were frequently asked to carry heavier loads. In some instances two men could carry still heavier loads of crated machinery by hanging them on poles. But these loads also consisted of sectionalized parts. Rosenblum tends to minimize the problem of sectionalized machinery and hypothesizes that larger canoes or surfboats could have been used more effectively to transport large units of heavy machinery a longer part of the distance from the coast to the mines by using the Ankobra. Rosenblum, "Gold Mining in Ghana," 135, 185, 188, 190, 247, 281-85.

84. J. T. F. Halligey, "A Visit to the West African Gold Mines," *Work and Workers in the Missionary Field* 2 (1893): 23-24.

85. Rosenblum, "Gold Mining in Ghana," 135, 185, 188, 190, 247, 281-85; also Silver, "Primitive Accumulation," 518-19.

86. M. Jones, Report on Tarkwa and Neighborhood, 8 August 1882, chap. 6 in Moloney to Kimberley, 4 September 1882, *PP* (1883) 48 [C 3687]: 57.

87. For example, "After four days on the river during which 3 of his boats capsized, he was forced to complete the journey on foot." Rosenblum, "Gold Mining in Ghana," 134-36. See also Hart, *Gold Coast,* 30.

88. A number of contemporary mining company critics of the existing transport system maintained that the average cost of transport from Axim to Tarkwa was £24 to £26 per ton. This is true only if companies used head porterage at a rate of 4s. to 5s. per ton-mile on a totally overland route to Tarkwa, which was normally not the case.

89. For a Prestea mining company, such as the Gie Appanto, that could rely almost exclusively on boat transport to the mining site, transport of machinery cost £10 per ton for the entire journey. For the more typical Wassa companies, which used boat transport as far as Tomento and human porterage to Tarkwa or Aboso, total transport costs were quite similar, about £11 to £15 per ton for boat transport combined with a group of 23 men (carrying 100 lbs. each) to carry the 2,300 lbs. over the final fifteen miles. (My calculations. These figures are corroborated in Report by F. Shelford, 23 August 1897, encl. in Crown Agent to CO, 23 August 1897, CO 96/301.)

90. W. R. Feldtmann, "The Ashanti Goldfields Corporation Ltd.," *Mining Magazine* 14.5 (May 1916): 258. Feldtman early in his career worked for the Wassa (G.C.) Mining Company.

CHAPTER 6

1. Among specialists, the appropriate term for the greater part of the nineteenth century is *interest group*. These scholars argue that the terms *pressure group* and especially *lobby* appear in common British usage only in the twentieth century. Nonetheless, the three terms are used interchangeably here.

2. Burton and Cameron, *To the Gold Coast,* 2:259; Dumett, "Pressure Groups," 193-215.

3. The notion that so-called unoccupied lands or wastelands ever existed was blatant Eurocentrism and usually a smoke screen for imperialist takeovers—first by the Crown and then by corporate interests. In this period the Colonial Office refused to consider such proposals on grounds that the British colonial government possessed no sovereign control over lands in a "protectorate." Two decades later (in 1895), however, the Accra government put forward an abortive Crown Lands Bill. This brought on a storm of protest from both traditional chiefs and the educated African communities of the coastal towns. For details, see Kimble, *Political History of Ghana,* 330-57; and Olumefi Omosini, "The Gold Coast Land Question, 1894-1900," *International Journal of African Historical Studies* 5.3 (1972): 453-69.

4. Ferdinand Fitzgerald to CO, 9 April 1877, CO 96/122. For similar views held by the contemporary Pan-African nationalist Edward Wilmot Blyden, see Lynch, *Edward Wilmot Blyden.*

5. Report by E. Wray, encl. in J. C. Wray to Hicks Beach, 11 March 1879, CO 96/129.

6. Louis Wyatt, Report on Axim Dist. and the Tarkwa Mines, encl. in Crown Agents to R. H. Meade, CO, 14 June 1879, CO 96/129.

7. Verney L. Cameron to Alfred Moloney, 30 April 1882, CO Afr. (W) 249, no. 3, p. 9.

8. Min. by Carnarvon, 13 October 1876, on Actg. Gov. Lees (167) to Carnarvon, 10 August 1876, CO 96/118; min. by Carnarvon, 30 October 1877 on Freeling (226) to Carnarvon, 13 September 1877, CO 96/122.

9. When an exuberant Gold Coast governor made an overoptimistic revenue forecast for the year 1877 (based on a meager 4 percent customs duty), he unwittingly gave the imperial government an excuse to cancel a £35,000 grant-in-aid for public works that had been approved as a move to rebuild the colony in the aftermath of the Asante War. Freeling (65) to Carnarvon, 2 March 1877; draft reply CO to Freeling, 22 June 1877, CO 96/121; min. by Meade, 4 June on Freeling (112) to Carnarvon, 28 April 1877, CO 96/121.

10. For details see D. C. M. Platt, *Finance, Trade and British Foreign Policy, 1815-1914* (Oxford, 1968), xix, 272-73, 306-7.

11. For detailed analysis of the impact of the lobby on slavery abolition on the Gold Coast, see Dumett, "Pressure Groups," 204-5.

12. Cain and Hopkins, *British Imperialism,* 1:122-27, 143-48, 158-57, 351-70. Most of the generalizations in this seminal work have too broad and global a focus for easy application to the work here. Indeed Hopkins and Cain argue that West Africa invariably ranked low on the priorities of the rulers of the Empire. This would certainly ring true for the Gold Coast up to 1895. For other general discussions of colonial policy in the mid-Victorian period, see B. S. Blakely, *The Colonial Office, 1868-1892* (Durham, N.C., 1972); W. D. McIntyre, *The Imperial Frontier in the Tropics, 1865-1895* (New York, 1967); John Cell, *British Colonial Administration in the Mid-Nineteenth Century: The Policy-Making Process* (New Haven, 1970); John D. Hargreaves, *Prelude to the Partition of West Africa* (London, 1963).

13. There exist reams of printed memoranda and correspondence on Gold Coast roads and proposed railway schemes, which were considered by the Colonial Office but not acted upon in the late 1870s and early 1880s. See, for example, Correspondence Regarding the proposed Constructions of Railways, Colonial Official Confidential Print (West Africa) 451, CO 879/39, PRO.

14. For details, see Dumett, "Pressure Groups," 196-99; Dumett, "Economic Development," 50-94.

15. See, for example, B. Berman, and J. Lonsdale, "Coping with Contradictions in the Development of the Colonial State in Kenya," *Journal of African History,* 20 (1979): 487-506. Also see G. B. Kay, *The Political Economy of Colonialism in Ghana* (Cambridge, 1972), 8-11. I do not suggest that we get rid of the term *colonial state,* only that we refine our criteria and time periods for application of the concept so that it has a more definite meaning.

16. In line with the dominant emphasis on revenue collection plus law and order, the three largest departments were the Customs and Treasury Department, the Judicial Establishment, and Constabulary.

17. From 1876 to 1885 the governors (including those acting) were:

Sanford Freeling	May 1878-June 1879
H. T. Ussher	June 1879-Dec. 1880*
W. B. Griffith	Dec. 1880-Mar. 1881
Sir S. Rowe	Mar. 1881-May 1882
C. A. Moloney	May 1882-Oct. 1882
W. B. Griffith	Oct. 1882-Dec. 1882
Sir S. Rowe	Dec. 1882-Apr. 1884
W. A. G. Young	Apr. 1884-Apr. 1885*

*died in office

18. Min. by Hemming, 9 March 1880, on Ussher (22) to Hicks Beach, 22 January 1880, CO 96/130.

19. Ussher (182) to Hicks Beach, 5 August 1879; and (205) 25 August 1879, CO 96/127.

20. *Gold Coast Times*, 25 January 1885, 2–3

21. Min. by Robert Meade, 17 April 1877, on F. Fitzgerald to CO, of April 1877, CO 96/122; min. by Hemming, 22 November 1882 on Commander Cameron to R. Meade, 8 November 1882, CO 96/146.

22. The law governing "Protectorates" set down by Britain according to her own criteria were contained in the various Foreign Jurisdiction Acts. Edward Fairfield, "Origins and Extent of the British Obligations towards the Native Tribes on the Gold Coast" (24 March 1874); CO Conf. Print, no. 49, Carnarvon Papers; PRO 3/6/85; min. by Bailey Hamilton, 10 January 1885 on Crown Agents to U. Sec., CO, 7 January 1885; CO 96/169. See also Kimble, *Political History of Ghana*, 302–5.

23. These issues were addressed in numerous interoffice communications; see, for example, Strahan (Secret) to Carnarvon, 27 March 1875, CO 96/115; min. by Bramston, 18 July on Griffith (Conf.) to Knutsford, 14 June 1888, CO 96/192.

24. Moloney (511) to Griffith, 20 October 1882, encl. in Griffith to Kimberley, 2 November 1882, CO 96/144; Moloney (415) to Kimberley, 4 September 1882, CO 96/143.

25. Min. by Hemming, 15 March 1879, on Lt. Col. J. C. Wray to Hicks Beach, 11 March 1879; CO 96/129.

26. Min. by Meade, 17 March on Lt. Col. J. C. Wray.

27. W. B. Griffith to Kimberley, 1 November 1882, *PP* (1883) 48 [c. 3687]: 76; reported in Ussher (146) to Hicks Beach, 10 May 1880, CO 96/131.

28. See Ord. no. 1 of 1874, "An Ordinance to Provide for the Abolition of Slave-Dealing," W. B. Griffith, *Ordinances of the Settlements on the Gold Coast and of the Gold Coast Colony in Force April 1887* (London, 1887), 23–30.

29. For details, see Dumett and Johnson, "Suppression of Slavery," in Miers and Roberts, *End of Slavery in Africa*, 71–95.

30. In practice, "pawning," the placing of a family member in the hands of another family as security for a debt for a period of time, was barely distinguishable from other forms of household slavery. For a more detailed discussion of these and other matters related to household slavery, see Dumett and Johnson, "Suppression of Slavery," 283–328; and Gareth Austin, "Human Pawning in Asante c. 1820–1950: Markets and Coercion, Gender and Cocoa," in T. Falola and P. Lovejoy, eds., *Pawnship in Africa* (Boulder, 1994).

31. In fact nineteen chiefs or captains of Wassa signed a petition protesting the selection of King Impira; encl. 110 in C. C. Lees to Carnarvon, 1 May 1876, CO 96/118.

32. Over the next decade the London humanitarian lobby would continue to badger the Gold Coast government and the Colonial Office for dragging their feet in the arrest of inland slave dealers. Aborigines Protection Society to CO, 20 August 1890, CO 96/214.

33. For details, see Agbodeka, *African Politics and British Policy,* 104–8.

34. Henry Higgins, Report on Tarkwa, 30 April 1882, encl. in Moloney to Kimberley, 7 June 1882, *PP* (1885) 48 [C. 3687]: 8.

35. The latter figure was the dry season estimate. Report by Travelling Comdr. Murray Rumsey, August 1882, encl. in Moloney to Kimberley, 4 September 1882, 54. I discuss the history of the Gold Coast mining towns in R. E. Dumett, "The Gold Mining Centers of Tarkwa and Obuasi: Colonial Administration and Social Change at Company Towns in an African Setting," in Klaus Tenfelde, ed., *Towards a Social History of Mining* (Munich, 1993).

36. "Foreigners" in this context did not mean Europeans only, but also African peoples from other regions. *Gold Coast Times,* 9 September 1882, 2.

37. Nearly every trader in the mining district turned a nice profit, since mark-ups ranged from 500 to 1,000 percent. R. G. Rogerson, appdx. A to the Shelford Report 1897, encl. in Crown Agent to CO, 23 August 1897, CO 96/301.

38. Burton and Cameron, *To the Gold Coast,* 2:292–93; extract from letter by Cuscaden to CO, 31 December 1881; *PP* (1883) 48 [C. 3687]: 3.

39. Despatch from Chas. D. Thompson to Asst. Col. Sec. for Native Affairs (Accra), 14 April 1883, Tarkwa Native Affairs, no. 112, ADM 11/845, GNA.

40. W. B. Griffith to Kimberley, 1 November 1882, *PP* (1883) 48 [C. 3687]: 76.

41. *Gold Coast Times,* 11 February 1882, 2. For a more critical comment, see Henry Higgins, 2nd Monthly Report on Tarkwa, 31 May 1882., 19.

42. For example, Petition of the newly organized Mercantile Association of Saltpond to Gov., 29 July 1890, sub-encl. 25 in 1, Charles Fraser to Gold Coast Col. Sec., 30 July 1890, encl. in Griffith to Knutsford. The formation of the Cape Coast Chamber of Commerce and the Accra Chamber of Commerce consisting of leading African merchants also occurred in the 1890s. But informed associations of African merchants and professional men had been meeting at the towns since a much earlier period. See Kimble, *Political History of Ghana,* 28n., 285, 337.

43. I have examined the Synod Minutes and the General Correspondence of the Gold Coast Methodist Missionary Society 1880–1897, housed at the Wesleyan Missionary Society, London. These documents deal almost entirely with religious matters and schools. There is little in the way of commentary on the cultural, economic, and social life of the local African people

in any district, even though there were religious circuits and schools in every important coastal district and also, for a time, at Tarkwa. See also Halligey, "West African Gold Mines," 23-26.

44. We have, for example, rare government reports on the State of Krobo and the Volta River Dist. suggesting that violence was far more frequent than either the Accra government or the Colonial Office cared to admit. It was stated that both the European and African agents for major European trading houses at the river port of Akuse "beat up" African female palm oil sellers for failing to bring the best quality oil to them. See testimony of E. Turnbull in Ussher (146) to Hicks Beach, 10 May 1880, CO 96/131.

45. Oral interviews with European staff at the Ashanti Goldfields Corporation, main plant, Obuasi, 20-21 May 1987.

46. See, for example, Donald F. Foster, "Labor and Superintendance on the Gold Coast," *Mining and Scientific Press,* 3 February 1912, 202-3. Use of an eyewitness account from a somewhat later period seems justifiable here, on the grounds that if treatment by European foremen was harsh in 1910 through 1912 (when government regulation and protection was better), then methods of treatment were at least equally, and probably more, abusive in the 1880s.

47. Min. by Meade and Ashley, 12 and 13 April, on letter from Aborigines Protection Society to CO, 2 April 1883, CO Afr. (W) 249, no. 53, p. 119.

48. *Gold Coast Times,* 30 September 1882, 3. Some allowance should be made for the fact that this was an African-owned newspaper that espoused ardent nationalist views. On the other hand, from what we know of the techniques of European concessionaires in Wassa and elsewhere in West Africa, these accusations have the ring of truth.

49. Kimble, *Political History of Ghana,* 72, 227-29. Ussher had totally misinterpreted the meaning of the Fante Confederation, which was opposed to the extension of Dutch influence in the central coastal states, and was not initially anti-British. He had botched an opportunity to associate the colonial government with a legitimate movement for African nationalism and self-government.

50. It was pointed out that most of Ussher's predecessors had never bothered to visit even distant coastal towns, let alone interior districts far from the seat of government.

51. Ussher (Private) to Hicks Beach, January [n.d.] 1880, Hicks Beach Papers, PCC/60.

52. Ussher (22) to Hicks Beach, 21 January 1880, CO Afr. (W) 3, no. 4, pp. 86-90.

53. Ussher (86) to CO, 25 March 1880, CO 96/130.

54. Min. by W. B. Hamilton, 29 February 1884, on Gov. Rowe (45) to Derby, 21 January 1884, CO 96/155.

55. Ussher (40) to Hicks Beach, 4 February 1880, CO 96/130.

56. Ussher (22) to Hicks Beach, 21 February 1880, CO Afr. (W) 379, no. 4, pp. 86–90.

57. Orders in Council of 2 September 1880, establishing the Volta River Dist. embracing Eastern and Western Krobo and the territory of Akuapem up to the frontiers of Akyem. G.C. Annual Report for 1880, 62.

58. Copy of letter from Sir Michael Hicks Beach to Ussher (private), 11 November 1879, Hicks Beach Papers; box PCC/60, no. 182; Ussher (305) to Hicks Beach, 3 December 1870, CO 96/128.

59. Min. by Hemming on Ussher (146) to Hicks Beach, 10 May 1880, CO 96/131.

60. Crowther (336) to Derby, 18 September 1883, CO 96/151. Two of the traveling commissioners whose reports are used here were Louis Wyatt and W. A. Cuscaden.

61. Ussher (162) to CO, 25 May 1880; CO 96/131.

62. Rowe (81) to Kimberley, 18 March 1882; printed in CO Africa (W) 249, no. 1, P.A.

63. W. B. Griffith Jr., *Ordinances of the Gold Coast Colony in Force in 1903*, 2 vols. (London, 1903), 1:406–7

64. James Brew of Dunquah to CO, 23 October 1897, CO 96/307.

65. Ord. no. 2 of 1883; cited in Griffith, *Laws of the Gold Coast Colony*, 541–44.

66. Revised Ord. no. 3 of 1894, in W. B. Griffith Jr., ed., *Ordinances of the Gold Coast in Force in 1898* (London, 1898), 977–84.

67. Maxwell (205) to CO, 18 May 1895, CO 96/257; mins. on Griffith (44) to Ripon, 5 February 1895, CO 96/255.

68. Griffith (329) to CO, 13 November 1894, CO 96/240.

69. For the use of forced labor by the colonial state in connection with military expeditions, see Killingray, "Guarding the Extending Frontier."

70. See, for example, the Fiji Islands in the 1860s and 1870s in J. D. Legge, *Britain in Fiji, 1858–80* (London, 1958), 64–65. The misapplication of East Indian and later Northern Nigerian principles of Indirect Rule to other African states and small-scale societies, where they had little meaning, has been discussed in numerous books and articles. For more detailed criticisms of the Native Jurisdiction idea in the Gold Coast, see Anthony Allot, *Essays in African Law* (London, 1960), 105–6; Lord Malcolm Hailey, *An African Survey* (Oxford, 1938), 468.

71. Min. by Meade, 12 April on Aborigines Protection Society to CO, 2 April 1883, CO Afr. (W) 249, no. 53, p. 119.

72. For a full discussion, see Thomas J. Lewin, *Asante before the British* (Lawrence, Kans., 1978), 85–222.

73. In another statement, typical throughout this period, Meade wrote in 1883, "[I]f the Ashanti Kingdom breaks up, all the better for its neighbors.

We don't want a strong United Ashanti." Min. by Robert Meade, 6 September 1883, on Rowe (Conf.), 1 September 1883, CO 96/151.

74. For the best treatments of Asante history in the period, see Wilks, *Asante in the Nineteenth Century,* 52; Rattray, *Ashanti Law and Constitution,* 175-76.

75. W. B. Griffith (teleg.) to Kimberley, 24 January 1881, no. 3, and Kimberley to Rowe, 21 July 1881, no. 36; *PP* (1881) 65 [C. 3064].

76. A. B. Ellis, *The Land of Fetish* (London, 1883), 211-49; Claridge, *History of the Gold Coast,* 219-45.

77. Draft letter from CO to Gold Coast Mining Company, 19 March 1880, on Gov. Ussher (40) to Hicks Beach, 4 February 1880, CO 96/130.

78. Editorial, *Gold Coast Times,* 11 February 1881, 2.

79. Hansard, *H. of C. Debates,* 24 February 1881, col. 1653.

80. Ussher (86) to Hicks Beach, 25 March 1880, CO 96/130. Ussher had argued that the "bush magistrates," in particular, required government regulation because they operated independently of any authority, levying illegal fines and otherwise victimizing the local African people and mine workers.

81. Four Africans—Peter Alexander, Abokay, and Rolla, all miners; and William Andrews, a clerk of the Aboso Mining Company—were accused and later convicted of murdering John Barrow while in the act of robbing the company safe. *Gold Coast Times,* 20 January 1883; see also R. J. Roulston, M.D., Actg. Civil Commr. Tarkwa to Col. Sec., Accra, 13 January 1883, encl. in Rowe to Derby, 5 February 1883. There were one or two other cases of robbery or attempted robbery at the offices of local mining companies. Rept. on Tarkwa, 30 September 1882, encl. in Lt. Gov. Griffith to Kimberley, 1 November 1882, *PP* (1883) 48 [C. 3687], 77.

82. Aborigines Protection Society to CO, 2 April 1883, *PP* (1883) 48 [C. 3687]: 98-99, CO Afr. 249, no. 53, p. 119.

83. Some of the events described here are placed in a more Whiggish evolutionary mold by Jeff Crisp, who includes them on a list with later events and interprets them as the seeds for organized worker protest movements and for the ultimate development of class consciousness. This is quite easy to do if one selects certain events out of their wider contexts, telescopes time, and lists them in outline form. Crisp, *African Working Class,* 17-19, 30-31.

84. A petition headed by the Aboso Company's foreman, E. T. McCarthy, his assistant, David Gowans, and the two Africans William E. Sam and Joseph Dawson, blamed the incident, not on the cruelty or oppressiveness of the mining companies, as alleged in humanitarian circles and the local African press, but simply on the audacity of some members of the working population on account of the absence of a regular district magistrate's court. Petition, 1-12 January 1883, encl. in R. J. Roulston to Col. Sec., Accra, 22 January 1883, encl. in Rowe to Derby, 3 February 1883, CO 96/155.

85. Min. by Meade, 12 April, Draft despatch, CO to Rowe, 13 July 1883, CO 96/152.

86. Rowe (275) to Lord Derby, 11 August 1883, CO 96/151.

87. Burton and Cameron, *To the Gold Coast,* 2:292-93.

88. Reports by L. Wyatt (1879) and W. A. Cuscaden (1882), quoted in chap. 2.

89. *Gold Coast Times,* 20 September 1884, 4.

90. Report on Eastern Wassa by H. Vroom, encl. in Griffith (191) to Knutsford, 6 June 1891, CO 96/217.

91. K. David Patterson, *Health in Colonial Ghana: Disease, Medicine and Socio-Economic Change, 1900-1955* (Waltham, Mass., 1981), 5-7, 33-83.

92. See J. F. Easmon, Report on Mortality in the Gold Coast, encl. in Griffith (111) to CO, 5 April 1887, CO 96/180.

93. Report by Stanley Clay to Directors, Wassa (G.C) Mining Co., 5 January 1900, encl. in WGCMC to CO, March 1900, CO 96/89.

94. Raymond E. Dumett, "Disease and Mortality," 213-17.

95. Ibid., tables 1 and 2, pp. 219-23.

96. For a full discussion of the power of these later Anglo-West African pressure groups, see Raymond E. Dumett, Joseph Chamberlain, Imperial Finance and Railway Policy in British West Africa in the Late Nineteenth Century," *English Historical Review* 90 (April 1975): 287-321.

97. For general background see Hargreaves, *Partition of West Africa,* 34-37, 184-88, 274; also *West Africa Partitioned,* vol. 1, *The Loaded Pause, 1885-1889* (Madison, Wis., 1974), 26-28, 30-31, 86-87, 215-19, 239. Hargreaves's excellent work focused on international diplomacy. However gold mining would play a part in military expeditions and boundary demarcation for the hinterland of the Gold Coast during the aggressive "new imperialism" of the post-1895 period. I shall deal with this in a subsequent volume.

98. The first informal meetings of the West African Trade Section of the London Chamber of Commerce were held in March and May 1884. London Chamber of Commerce, *Annual Report for 1884* (London, 1885), 121.

99. A. LeBrun to Col. Sec., Accra, 18 January 1881, each in Griffith (44) to Kimberley, 11 February 1881, CO Afr. (W) 451, no. 5, pp. 37-38.

100. Despatch from Lt. Gov. Griffith (44) to Kimberley, 11 February 1881 (see previous note).

101. F. Barry to CO, 28 July 1881; and response by Rowe to CO, 11 September 1882, CO Afr. (W) 451, no. 7, p. 29 and no. 13, pp. 46-47.

102. Hicks Beach to F. Fitzgerald and W. Mercer, 6 September 1879, CO Afr. (W) 451, no. 4, p. 36. The circumspect attitude of British authorities at this time is interesting in view of the imperial government's willingness to ride roughshod over African land rights during railway construction twenty years later.

103. Kimberley to Rowe, 4 April 1880, CO Afr. (W) 451, no. 6, p. 39.

104. Min. by Meade, 13 August 1881, on F. Barry to U. Sec., CO, 28 July 1881, CO 96/136; min. by Meade, 20 July 1883, on Rowe (186) to Derby, 19 May 1883, CO 96/150.

105. Reference in Moloney (Conf. 17) to Kimberley, 6 June 1882, CO 96/140.

106. Manchester Chamber of Commerce to Derby, 7 December 1883; and Petition from London merchants, encl. in F. and A. Swanzy to CO, 7 December 1883, PP (1884) 41 [C. 4052]: 94-96.

107. Derby to Gov. Rowe, 25 December 1883, CO Afr. (W) 451, no. 23, p. 63; CO to Charles McIver trading firm, 4 April 1885, 24 November, p. 65.

108. Recent research on the history of mining technology shows that diamond-tipped ore-prospecting drills suitable for deep-level sampling were in use on the U.S. and Canadian mining frontiers as early as the 1870s. See Newell, *Technology on the Frontier,* 15-17.

109. Min. by Derby, 12 June 1883, on Griffith (557) to Kimberley, 29 November 1882, CO 96/144.

110. *Mining Journal,* 2 December 1889, 185.

CHAPTER 7

1. Some readers may wish to know why I have written about African Labor in conjunction with company management, technology, and production in a single chapter instead of providing a separate chapter on labor, which is a common practice in other books of this type. The reason for this is that the recruitment, treatment by management, and working conditions for labor for each of the three groups of mining companies discussed here were all very different and, therefore, these conditions cannot be discussed in a simplified, uniform manner, as if they were a single mines labor force. Labor cannot be understood apart from the policies of individual companies.

2. J. E. Tilton, *The Future of the Non-Fuel Minerals* (Washington, D.C., 1977), 27.

3. Report to the shareholders of the African Gold Coast Company, Ltd., Paris, 1 March 1874, encl. in Lt. Col. J. Copely Wray (Private) to Sir Michael Hicks Beach, 11 March 1879, CO 96/129.

4. Report by Comdr. M. Rumsey, 9 August 1882, encl. 1 in Moloney to Kimberley, 4 September 1882, "Further Corres. rel. to the Gold Coast," PP (1883) 48 [C. 3687]: 53.

5. Report by Foster, quoted in Holmes, "Early History of Tarkwa," 90, 205.

6. Gov. Rowe to Kimberley, 18 March 1882, CO 96/138; *African Times,* 1 March 1881, 29; 1 April 1881, 37.

7. Report by Rumsey to Col. Sec., 9 August 1882, PP (1883) 48 [C. 3687]: 54.

8. *African Times,* 2 May 1881 and 1 June 1881. Also see Burton and Cameron, *To the Gold Coast,* 2:199, 299.

9. This is summarized in detail in Rosenblum, 171-71

10. Burton and Cameron, *To the Gold Coast,* 2:289-99.

11. Report by Rumsey, 9 August 1882, 54.

12. H. Higgins, Fifth Monthly Report on the Tarkwa Dist., 31 August 1882, encl. in Moloney to Kimberley, *PP* (1883) 48 [C. 3687]: 72.

13. Like most of its competitors, this company lacked fitters and greasers who knew how to repair the machines and spare parts. Seventh Monthly Report for Tarkwa (mechanics), encl. in Griffith to Kimberley, 1 September 1882, *PP* (1883) 48 [C. 3687].

14. W. C. Cuscaden to Col. Sec., Accra, 31 January 1882, encl. in Rowe to Kimberley, 4 September 1882, CO 96/138, 1-4.

15. Tarkwa and Aboso Gold Mining Co., Ltd., Articles of Incorporation, 1888, BT 41/4160, no. 26872, PRO. Also see G. Macdonald, "Gold in West Africa," *Journal of the African Society* 1.2 (January 1902): 422.

16. *Stock Exchange Yearbook,* 1890 (London, 1890), 488. See also Henry Wallach, *The West African Market Manual* (London, 1890), 29.

17. The firm of Radcliffe and Durant later played an important role as political intermediaries in Great Britain, representing the government of the Asante Kingdom. Ivor Wilks has investigated this connection. For details see Wilks, *Asante in the Nineteenth Century,* 612-13, 643.

18. Reported in "Tour of the Wassa District," in Gov. Maxwell (389) to CO, 28 September 1895, CO 96/260.

19. Report on Eastern Wassa for 1891, encl. 6 in Griffith (278) to Ripon, 12 October 1892, CO 96/226.

20. Report on the Gold Mines (1889), encl. in Gov. W. B. Griffith to Lord Knutsford, 25 June 1889, *PP* (1889) 54 [C. 5620-24]: 10-11.

21. Interview with Tommy Rowe and Bruce Lockyear, London, 8 May 1987. Rowe and Lockyear were longtime staff members of the Ashanti Goldfields Corporation.

22. In December 1891 there were on the job at the Tarkwa and Aboso 83 underground miners and a total African workforce of 258. Report on Eastern Wassa, encl. in Griffith (278) to Ripon, 12 October 1892, CO 96/226.

23. From the mid-1890s it became possible to buy a cyanide plant, but this method would not become widely operational in the Gold Coast until construction of a railway after the turn of the century. Wm. Bourke to Gov.

W. E. Maxwell, 17 December 1895, encl. in Maxwell to CO, 12 March 1896, CO 96/271.

24. Report by R. G. Rogerson, 6 August 1897, appdx. A, encl. in Cr. Agents to CO, 23 August 1897, CO Afr. (W) 531, no. 190, p. 214.

25. Q. Dist. Report for Wassa, encl. in Maxwell (454) to Chamberlain, 4 November 1896, CO 96/278.

26. Rosenblum suggests total gold returns of £125,000 during the period of the Anglo-French company's management (approximately for 1880 to 1887). Rosenblum, "Gold Mining in Ghana," 184, n. 3. He bases this on a statement in Hart, *Gold Coast* (84-85), partly a promotional tract, which is not the best source for data of this type. He also suggests an estimated overall production of £161,174 for the period of early British company management (presumably 1888-1900), but he provides no exact annual figures. Rosenblum's estimate runs too high, and his scattered annual figures do not square with the series presented here. See table 7.1 in the present text.

27. Griffiths 1889 Report on the Gold Mines, *PP* (1889) 54 [C. 5620-24]; Dumett, "Economic Development," 69.

28. Figures in encl. 1, appdx. A to Rogerson Report in CO Afr. (W) Conf. Print, no. 190, p. 214.

29. DC's Report, Wassa, encl. 13 in Gov. Maxwell to CO, 14 January 1897, CO 96/288.

30. This claim was certainly one of the first to be registered in Tarkwa, as early in time as the negotiations by Harvey, Lightfoot, and Bonnat with Chief Ango for the Tarkwa and Aboso Mine. Initially the company tried to extend old African shafts in the vicinity of Crockerville; but when these flooded out, the company concentrated its attention more on Aja Bippo.

31. There was less of a problem about recruiting Fante men from the central coast for hard labor, provided it was above ground. The main problem was always underground wage labor.

32. Excerpts from Report of the Wassa (Gold Coast) Mining Company, Ltd., *African Times,* 1 April 1886, 51.

33. "The Wassa (G.C.) Mining Company, Ltd.," *African Times,* 1 July 1886, 99. For earlier extravagant hopes, see also Burton and Cameron, *To the Gold Coast,* 2:235.

34. The Swanzy Estates and Gold Mining Company, Ltd., Memorandum and Articles of Association, 21 January 1882, RJSC, BT 31/2925; no. 16316, PRO.

35. Special Resolution of the Swanzy Estates and Gold Mining Co., 17 October 1883; Summary of Capital and Shares as of 14 January 1887, RJSC, BT 31/2925, nos. 16316/6 and 16316/11, PRO.

36. Wassa (G.C.) Mining Company, Ltd., BT 31/2926, no. 16317, PRO.

37. *Stock Exchange Yearbook,* 1890, 494.

38. Cameron, "Goldfields of West Africa," 541, 750.

39. Report by F. J. Crocker in *Mining Journal,* 13 February 1886, 185. Also see extract from Louis Gowans Diary, encl. in Wassa Mining Co. to CO, 3 September 1897, CO 96/306; Burton and Cameron, *To the Gold Fields,* 2:277-78.

40. Gov. Rowe (Conf. 22) to Derby, 14 May 1883, CO 96/150.

41. Sam's appointment was welcomed by the African-owned journal *Western Echo,* 16-30 September 1887, 2. Also see *Mining Journal,* 9 April 1887, 439, and 21 April 1888, 441-42.

42. Report on tour of the Wassa gold mines of the Gold Coast in Griffith to Knutsford, 25 June 1889, PP (1889) 54 [C. 5620-24]. "Tarkwa" Sams second son, W. E. Sam Jr., also worked for the WGCMC as assistant deputy manager.

43. See T. B. F. Sam, "On the Origin of the Auriferous Conglomerates of the Gold Coast Colony (West Africa)," *Quarterly Journal of the Geological Society of London* 54 (August 1898): 20. G. E. Ferguson also had a knowledge of mining, having taken courses at the Royal School of Mines. See R. G. Thomas, "George Ekem Ferguson," *Transactions of the Historical Society of Ghana* 13 (1972): 181-215.

44. Unfortunately the second son, W. E. Sam Jr., died from a mining accident in 1899. Interview with W. S. Kwesi Johnson, Cape Coast, 3 August 1969, Dumett Collection.

45. While most historians have assumed a growing and more virulent racism in the Gold Coast during the late nineteenth and early twentieth centuries, there appear to have been several opposing cross-currents between this and a more tolerant treatment toward the African educated community by some Europeans on the Gold Coast. See *Gold Coast Chronicle,* 7 January 1892. See also a laudatory send-off signed by some twenty-five leading African gentlemen (chiefs, lawyers, merchants) on the departure of W. Waters, Chief Agent for the Swanzy Company, to England. *Gold Coast Independent,* 31 October 1896. One elderly Ghanaian informant told me that, as far as the early twentieth century was concerned, the issue of white racism in the Gold Coast had been exaggerated. He thought that it was an individual rather than a group malady. He stated that he personally had never experienced it from British officials. Interview with P. K. Arthur Badoo, July 1972, Mampong, Akuapem, Ghana, Dumett Collection. Mr. Arthur Badoo worked in the colonial government agricultural service in the 1930s, 1940s, and 1950s; however, such members of the African coastal elite knew nothing of the experiences of unskilled and illiterate miners.

46. Hendrik Vroom, Q. Dist. Report for Wassa, 19 January 1991, encl. in Griffith (210) to Knutsford, 25 June 1991, CO 96/217.

47. Holmes, "Early History of Tarkwa," 107.

48. Report by Rumsey, 9 August 1882, encl. in Moloney to Kimberley, 4 September 1882, PP (1883) 48 [C. 3687]: 53-54.

49. Griffith, "Report on the Gold Mines," *PP* (1889) 54 [C. 5620-24]: 11. The exact details on the financial relationship between the company and Chief Enemil Kuma, between Kuma and subordinate village chiefs and headmen, and between these leaders and their workers will probably never be known.

50. Rumsey Report, in Moloney to Kimberley, 4 September 1882, *PP* (1883) 48 [C. 3687]: 53-54.

51. Ord. no. 16 of 1877, an ordinance for regulating the relations between employers and employed under contract. Griffith, *Ordinances of the Gold Coast in Force in 1887*, 406-16. One of the avowed central motives behind this law was to train young men as apprentices.

52. Hillard Pouncy, "Colonial Racial Attitudes and Colonial Labor Laws in British West Africa" (Ph.D. dissertation, Massachusetts Institute of Technology, 1981), 72-75.

53. Some mine managers allowed workers to come back after three to six months absence in their home villages at the same wage levels, as if nothing had happened. Detailed quarterly district reports show the size of the labor force on duty fell to extremely low levels during the rainy seasons at the very time they were needed to bail out flooded mines. Tarkwa Dist. Report for March-December 1891, encl. in Griffith (278) to Ripon, 12 October 1892, CO 96/226.

54. Report on attitudes at Tarkwa by Higgins, encl. in Griffith to Kimberley, 27 October 1882, no. 29 of "Further Corres. on G.C." *PP* (1883) 48 [C. 3687]: 74.

55. Jeff Crisp argues that the Wassa companies of the nineteenth century should have paid their workers a higher wage. If they had done this, he argues, then they would have attracted more indigenous Akan men as unskilled laborers. Crisp, "African Working Class," 16. Evidence supplied elsewhere in this chapter shows that the assumed "lowness" of the average wage is a subjective and frequently Eurocentric twentieth-century construct. African miners of the time did not necessarily view it that way. This subjective argument is also divorced from the realities of mines management and available working capital. Even in modern times, with the most sophisticated forms of extractive machinery, reef gold mining companies have found it difficult to maintain steady profits owing to the low yield of most ores coupled with high labor costs. In the late 1970s and early 1980s a number of mines that were milling marginal gold ores were able to make it only because of skyrocketing world gold prices that reached unprecedented levels (e.g., 8.50 per ounce in January 1980). After this the price subsided and these mines returned to dormancy.

56. John Sarbah to Thomas Jeffrey, 25 May 1877, John Sarbah Letterbook, Sc. 6/4, Sarbah Papers, GNA.

57. Interview with Nana Akodaa Kwadwo Ofor, 28 December 1971, Ayisan, Akyem-Abuakwa, Ghana, Dumett Collection.

58. Oral interview with Issah Busonga, Obuasi, Asante, Ghana 1987, Dumett Collection. It is extremely difficult to get accurate information on African food prices because prices varied greatly with the season, the particular town where the prices were quoted, and the sources of supply. For this reason I have not quoted Gold Coast Blue Book annual statistics, which, though available for the 1880s and 1890s, look as if they were copied by rote from year to year and do not conform to other accounts. One somewhat more sophisticated source for a later period is nonetheless revealing about the very low prices that must have prevailed also around 1900: "There is very little produce grown at or near Accra. Yams from Kpandu are sold at 1s.6d. to 2s. each; cocoa yams from Suhum are 4 or 5 for 6d.; sweet potatoes from Ada are 4 or 5 for 3d.; plantains from Suhum are 6 for 3d.; bananas from Aburi are 12 for 3d. . . . millet from Lagos at 6d. a pound . . ." (G.C. *Municipal Annual Reports* for 1927-28, 10). These figures for the 1920s support statements gathered in oral interview from retired miners that they could live adequately on the average daily wage and have some money left over.

59. Report by W. H. F. Migeod, Transport Labor Officer, 1 January 1904, encl. in Nathan (13T) to Lyttelton, 9 January 1904, CO 6/416.

60. For a good definition of exploitation under colonialism, see David Landes's statement: "imperialist exploitation consists in the employment of labor at wages lower that would obtain in a free bargaining position; or in the appropriation of goods at prices lower than would obtain in a free market." Landes, "The Nature of Economic Imperialism," *Journal of Economic History* 21 (1961): 499.

61. Hart, *Gold Coast,* 151.

62. Report on Kru labor by E. Wray, encl. in J. C. Wray to Sir Michael Hicks Beach, 11 March 1879, CO 96/129.

63. In 1893 the colonial legislature passed a Master and Servant and Foreign Employment Ordinance. The law stated that no written contract of service could be enforced against any party who was unable to read or understand English writing and unless it bore the seal of a district commissioner who was present at the reading. But this law was designed to protect not the Kru or other immigrants seeking employment in the Gold Coast, but rather Gold Coastans then being recruited to work in other European colonies, such as the Congo Free State. Ord. no. 8 of 1893: Master and Servant and Foreign Employment Ordinance; Sir W. B. Griffith Jr., *Ordinances of the Gold Coast in Force in 1903,* 782-93.

64. Encl. 1 in Maxwell to Chamberlain, 26 May 1897, CO 96/290.

65. Burton and Cameron said that the work routine at the Tarkwa and

Aboso mine was "decidedly loafy." Burton and Cameron, *To the Gold Coast*, 2:290.

66. Interview with E. W. Morgan, Layham, Ipswich, Suffolk, 30 June 1982, Dumett Collection; also Actg. Gov. Bryan (103) to CO, 8 March 1908, CO 96/467.

67. Letter from the West African Youth League, 14 January 1937, encl. in Sec. for Mines to Col. Sec., Accra, 27 January 1937, ADM 716/33 SF1, file 19/2, GNA.

68. Memorandum of Agreement, Cinnamon Bippo Gold Mine, Ltd., BT 31/3882, no. 24, 506, PRO.

69. Encl. 3 in Griffith (187) to Ripon, 23 June 1894, CO 96/246; encl. 3 in Maxwell (175) to Ripon, 4 May 1895, CO 96/257.

70. "The Wassa (G.C.) Mining Company," *Mining Journal Railway and Commercial Gazette*, 16 June 1894, 650; R. G. Rogerson, Tarkwa Mines Survey for 1896, appdx. to F. Shelford, Report on the Tarkwa Railway Survey, 6 August 1897, encl. in Crown Agents to CO, 23 August 1897, CO 96/301.

71. Report on the Aja Bippo Mine, 12 November 1885, printed in *Mining Journal*, 13 February 1886, 185.

72. Report on a tour of the Wassa Gold Mines of the Gold Coast in Griffith to Knutsford, 25 June 1889, *PP* (1889) 54 [C. 5620-24]: 12; Dumett, "Economic Development," 69.

73. Rogerson, Survey of Mines (1897), encl. in Crown Agents to CO, 23 August 1897, CO 96/301.

74. Ordinary General Meeting of Shareholders, WGCMC, 15 March 1886, reported in *Mining Journal*, 20 March 1886, 320.

75. The cable link was completed on 24 August 1886. Griffith (328) to Granville, 25 August 1886, CO 96/175.

76. Report of General Meeting of Shareholders, *Mining Journal*, 16 June 1894, 650.

77. Report by independent consulting engineer, 5 January 1900, encl. in Wassa (G.C.) Mining Co. to CO, 9 March 1900, CO 96/369.

78. Wassa (G.C.) Mining Co. to CO, 3 May, 1897, CO Afr. (W) 531, no. 97, p. 68.

79. Report of Ordinary General Meeting, WGCMC, *Mining Journal Railway and Commercial Gazette*, 16 June 1894, 650.

80. First reported in *Mining Journal Railway and Commercial Gazette*, 15 May 1897, 59; also Rosenblum, "Gold Mining in Ghana," 289.

81. *Mining Journal Railway and Commercial Gazette*, 16 March 1901, 325.

82. Report by Stanley Clay, encl. in Wassa (G.C.) Mining Co. to CO 9 March 1900, CO 96/89.

83. Cooper, *Geology of the Prestea Goldfield*, 10.

84. The Essaman Mining Co., Ltd., Memorandum of Association 188 and Summary of Capital and Shares. May 1885, RJSC, BT 31/3568, no. 21864, PRO. Also see *Mining Journal,* January 1886, 4; 28 May 1887, 663; Dumett, "Economic Development," 10.

85. Report on Annual General Meeting of Essaman Company shareholders, *Mining Journal,* 29 March 1890, 361.

86. A major contract came with the leasing of the fabulously rich Obuasi concession by the Ashanti Goldfields Corporation in the mid-1890s, which I shall discuss subsequently. In that instance the rent that the British company paid to the African rulers was miserly indeed. In the case at hand it may be doubted whether the Gie Appanto mine of Prestea continued to pay the rent originally stipulated. A later government report stated that Chief Kofi Kyei received about £800 per year from the successor company. Even this was a more equitable amount than most expatriates paid local chiefs for gold producing properties. Wassa Dist. Report, encl. in Maxwell (389) to CO, CO 96/260.

87. Certificate and Articles of Incorporation, Gie Appanto Gold Mining Co., Ltd., 30 October 1886; and Summaries of Capital and Shares, 22 May 1889, 9 January 1891, and 12 January 1893, RJSC, BT 31/374, no. 23365, PRO.

88. E. T. McCarthy was son of the early-nineteenth-century Gold Coast governor Sir Charles McCarthy. A mining engineer, he had worked on the Gold Coast in the early 1880s. Form E, Gie Appanto Company, capital and shares up to January 1893, RJSC, BT 31/374, PRO.

89. This did not mean that the journey up the Ankobra River and the emplacement of machinery to Prestea was ever easy. It was regarded as a record when the engineering staff transported a second ten-head battery of stamps (total weight: 7,500 lbs.) upriver, implanted in its foundations and in good working order in three months. Furthermore, during the dry season, when rocks and snags were exposed, the Ankobra was impassable much of the way to Prestea.

90. Griffith, Report on the Gold Mines (1889), in Griffith to Knutsford, 25 June 1889, *PP* (1889) 54 [C. 5620-24]: 8.

91. Report by Hendrik Vroom on Wassa, encl. in Griffith (210) to Knutsford, 25 January 1891, CO 96/217.

92. Report by F. Cogill, 7 September 1904, encl. in Rodger (481) to Lyttelton, 7 October 1904, CO 96/240.

93. Q. Dist. Report for Tarkwa, encl. 13 in Gov. Hodgson (312) to Ripon, 10 September 1893, CO 96/23.

94. Meeting of Shareholders, reported in *Mining Journal,* 23 July 1892, 817.

95. Report on the reconstruction of the Gie Appanto Mining Company, *Mining Journal,* 23 July 1892, 817.

96. Wassa Dist. Report, encl. 13 in Maxwell (18) to CO, 14 January 1897, CO 96/288. Also see encl. 13 in Hodgson (41) to CO, 21 January 1898, CO 96/310.

97. *Mining Journal,* 23 July 1892, 817; 30 July 1892, 85. See also Rosenblum, "Gold Mining in Ghana," 243.

98. As noted in chapter 6, far more miners than could have been diagnosed at this time suffered from chronic lung disease. V. L. Cameron, among others, deplored labor coercion by the companies because it "makes the miner work even when he is unfit for exertion." Burton and Cameron, *To the Gold Coast,* 289.

99. The Abontiakoon Company had an abysmal record on wage payments. No wages were paid during July to October 1882. Wages were paid from January to October 1883, when £1,965 in gold was sent home. Wages were again discontinued after October 1883. *Mining Journal,* 29 March 1884, 385; 16 May 1885, 550.

100. Jacob Eduam-Baiden, who worked for the Ashanti Goldfields Corporation, insisted in oral interview that the first serious miners' strike occurred at that company's facility when Baiden was a young man in 1904. Interview with Jacob Eduam-Baiden, 5 August 1969, Saltpond, Ghana, Dumett Collection.

101. Draft dispatch from Lyttelton to Board of Trade, 20 December 1904, on Gov. Rodger (Conf.) to CO, 16 October 1904, CO 96/420; also H. Bryan (134) to Elgin, 27 March 1908, ADM 1/2/69, GNA.

102. Min. by R. H. Meade, 13 August 1881, on F. Berry to U. Sec., CO, 28 July 1881, CO 96/136; min. by Meade, 20 July on Gov. Rowe to Derby, 19 May 1883, CO 96/150; Chas McIver to CO, 26 March 1885; CO to Bircham and Company, 25 March 1887, CO Afr. (W) 41, no. 24, p. 65 and no. 27, p. 69; James Irvine to Gov., encl. in Hodgson to CO, 23 September 1891, CO Afr. (W) 4578, no. 43, pp. 10–14 and no. 48, p. 118; African Concession Trust to CO, 24 January 1891, CO Afr. (W) 451, no. 36, p. 79.

103. Dumett, "Economic Development," 135–55.

104. Griffith to Ripon (123), June 1893; *PP* (1893) 60 [C. 7225]: 37.

105. Clearly the cocoa-growing revolution had endogenous roots and was self-generating under the leadership of African smallholders. But the Swiss Basel Mission, and to a lesser degree the colonial government, played a part in it. In traveling through the eastern districts as early as the late 1880s and early 1890s, Griffith observed that farmers were already cultivating substantial numbers of cocoa trees in Akuapem and Krobo. Griffith to CO, 22 August 1888, extract in the *Kew Bulletin,* no. 44 (July 1891): 171. Also see Hodgson to Knutsford, 9 November 1891, CO 96/219. Coffee cultivation proved a failure.

106. W. B. Griffith, "Report on the Gold Mines, 1889," encl. in F. M. Hodgson to Knutsford, 5 July 1889, *PP* (1889) 54 [C. 5620–24]: 173–95.

107. Formation of new Wassa Dist., Gold Coast Order in Council, no. 15 of 31 October 1892, posted in *Gold Coast Government Gazette,* 27 October 1892.

108. Griffith (Conf.) to Ripon, 24 October 1892, CO 96/226.

109. Actg. Gov. F. M. Hodgson to Lord Knutsford, 30 October 1889, CO Afr. (W) 451, no. 32, p. 73. The results of this pledge continued in recommendations by the Gold Coast government to the Colonial Office. "Further Reports Relative to Economic Development on the Gold Coast," Colonial Reports Miscellaneous, *PP* (1891) [C. 6270]: 6.

110. *Gold Coast Chronicle,* 18 February 1893, 2.

111. For details on policy shifts toward the new imperialism during the period of Lord Rosebery's foreign secretaryship and prime ministry, see Robert Rhodes James, *Rosebery* (London, 1963), 258–77, 283–93.

112. See, for example, Liverpool Chamber of Commerce to Knutsford, 17 October 1890, CO 96/214; Liverpool Cham. of Comm. to CO, 29 December 1992, CO Afr. (W) 451, no. 15, p. 9; West African Trade Section, London Cham. of Comm. to Ripon, 11 January 1893, CO 96/240; Manchester Cham. of Comm. to Ripon, 22 February 1893, CO 96/240; Resolution from the Congress of Chambers of Commerce of the British Empire, encl. in London Cham. of Comm. to CO, 25 October 1892, CO 96/338.

113. London Cham. of Comm. to CO, 21 May 1894, CO Afr. (W) 464, no. 11, p. 63; Meeting between Liverpool Cham. of Comm. and member of Parliament reported in *Liverpool Journal of Commerce,* 19 October 1895, 5; Glasgow Merchants to Lord Ripon, 7 May 1893, CO 96/240.

114. Knutsford to Griffith, 19 February 1890, CO Afr. (W) 451, no. 33, p. 75.

115. Min. by Hemming, 18 December 1892, on John Holt (African Association) to Lord Ripon. 13 December 1892, CO 96/229.

116. Draft letter from CO to John Holt, 31 December 1892; John Holt to Lord Ripon, 16 December 1892, CO 96/229. For a discussion of the role of the Colonial Office, Treasury, Parliament, and the Crown Agents for the Colonies in West African railway construction, see Dumett, "Joseph Chamberlain."

117. Draft Letter from CO to John Holt, 31 December 1892.

CHAPTER 8

1. The often retold story of the journey of Jason and the Argonauts (ca. 1,200 B.C.) points to the supposition that the land of Colchis on the eastern shores of the Black Sea was probably an early and important source of gold for the ancient Mediterranean world. Sheepskins were used to entrap grains of gold in ancient placer mining.

2. This information derives from numerous sources, including two extended interviews with the venerable W. S. Kwesi Johnson, businessman of Cape Coast, who, with other family members, was an eyewitness to many of the events and developments described here. Field Interviews in 1969 and 1971, Cape Coast, Ghana, Dumett Collection. See also Gold Coast, *Annual Blue Book Reports* for the years; Robert Szereszewski, *Structural Changes in the Economy of Ghana, 1891-1911* (London, 1965), 25-26.

3. The cargo manifests of nearly every steamer bound for Europe from Accra, Cape Coast, and other ports in these years showed considerable quantities of gold. The greater portion of gold produced by the Wassa companies was still shipped from the old port of Axim. African peasant-produced trade gold was shipped from nearly every small port along the coast where the steamers stopped in those days.

4. Hesketh J. Bell, "The History, Trade, Resources and Present Condition at the Gold Coast Settlement," address delivered to the West African Trade Section of the Liverpool Cham. of Comm., 1 May 1893; printed in *Topographical Tracts* (1877-95), 14. See also *Gold Coast Annual Report* for 1894, 15. These official assumptions that the "emancipation of slaves [administered] a death blow to the export of gold through the native economy" have been repeated in other publications. See K. B. Dickson. "Cocoa in Ghana" (Ph.D. thesis, University of London, 1960), 36. Production of gold by independent African farmer-miners continued until the First World War and even after. It is possible that in the 1920s and 1930s the gradual fall-off in the number of slaves and the fading out of traditional slavery may have had a limited effect on indigenous gold mining, especially in Asante. By that time, however, a number of other constraints were also at work. The early sources, criticized here, spoke of an immediate impact of the antislavery ordinances on gold mining between 1875 and 1900.

5. Q. Dist. Report for Cape Coast, March 1895, encl. in Maxwell to Ripon, 20 June 1895, CO 96/258.

6. Q. Dist. Report on Eastern Wassa for December 1891, encl. in Griffith (278) to Ripon, 12 October 1892, CO 96/226.

7. See Griffith, Report on the Gold Mines (1889), in Griffith to Knutsford, 25 June 1889, *PP* (1889) 54 [C. 5620-24]: 10.

8. Oral interviews with Daniel Adu and Kwame Yeboa, Kyebi, Akyem-Abuakwa, Ghana, 26 May 1987, Dumett Collection.

9. Lewin makes clear that this resurgence of trade also owed a great deal to the rising profitability of rubber tapping. Lewin, *Asante before the British*. See also Q. Dist. Report, Cape Coast (1895), encl. in Maxwell to Ripon, 20 June 1895, CO 96/258.

10. See Charles Perrings, *Black Mineworkers in Central Africa* (London, 1979), 238-42.

11. W. H. F. Migeod to Gov. Mathew Nathan, 12 March 1903, Nathan Papers, 307-9, RHO.

12. Reference to the activities of Kofi Accra, originally from Gwira, seen as representative of other Akan miners at Tarkwa in Letter no. 19, from A. Bowden Page, Gen. Mgr. of the African and Aboso Gold Mining Company, to Chas. B. Turton, Asst. Col. Sec. (Accra), 10 February 1883, ADM 11/845, GNA. I am grateful to Mr. Augustine Mensah of the Ghana National Archives for recovery of this document.

13. Reference in Cape Coast Cham. of Comm. to Gov. Nathan, encl. 17 in Nathan to Chamberlain, 25 March 1902, CO 96/395.

14. H. Vroom, Tarkwa Dist. Report for December 1897, encl. in Hodgson (41) to CO, 21 January 1898, CO 96/310.

15. In contrast to a number of recent works in mine labor history (e.g., Freund, *Nigerian Tin Mines*, 49) the present study does not stress the stealing of tools, dynamite, and especially of gold dust by mine workers as early examples of "proletarian resistance" against mine management. Rather it views such acts at face value, as random acts of minor theft or smuggling in response to human temptations that are common among employees at factories, warehouses, as well as mines in most countries of the world. For support on this position see Lentz and Erlmann, "A Working Class in Formation." Lentz concedes that Marxist writers cover themselves by stating that the "resistance" element in these acts of thievery is usually "unconscious." But she adds that this strains the evidence with too much "ideological freight."

16. The classic statement for West Africa is still that by Elliot J. Berg, "Backward-Sloping Labor Supply Functions in Dual Economies: The Africa Case," *Quarterly Journal of Economics* 75 (1961): 468-92. The limitations that Berg placed on the concept of target incomes need to be restated. His study of the historical evidence led him to the conclusion that this concept *did* apply in the short term for smallholders in subsistence or peasant economies that were just beginning to be absorbed into a capitalistic labor market. But his use of the concept was in no way designed to lend support to the policy prejudice of some expatriate corporate managers that to offer wage increases or other incentives to workers would lead to a reduction in the supply of labor. Nor did he believe that the theory had much applicability to modern African labor markets. He concluded that neither the target incomes nor the backward-sloping supply curve concepts had validity in long-term analysis, since experience with the receipt of higher wages, coupled with extended exposure to the capitalist economy and the inculcation of new consumer wants, inevitably would raise target income thresholds. Ibid., 477-79.

17. Oral Interviews with Kwaku Wangara and Charles Bathurst, Obuasi, Asante, Ghana, 30 December 1971, Dumett Collection; interview with

Mallam Muhamma, August 1984, Tamale, Northern Region, Ghana, Dumett Collection.

18. This includes the luck of finding nuggets, which eyewitness observers tell me was not all that rare. Field interviews at Tarkwa, Wassa, and Kyebi, Akyem; above.

19. Lentz, "Working Class in Formation?" 21. For similar conclusions concerning the slow or nongrowth of a genuine working class in cocoa farming, see Gareth Austin, "The Growth of Cocoa Farming in South Ashanti, 1896–1914" (Ph.D. thesis, University of Birmingham, 1984), 480–90.

20. Introduction to H. C. Belfield, "Report on the Legislation Governing the Alienation of Native Lands in the Gold Coast . . . ," *PP* (1912–13) 59 [Cd. 6278]: 44–45.

21. Reference to this rent agreement emerged in a subsequent dispute over payments. Kwadwo Enemil Kuma II, successor chief of Aboso, to Gov. W. B. Griffith, 30 April 1888, encl. in DC, Axim, to Gov., 8 May 1888, ADM 11/11/34, file 2432/88, GNA

22. C. K. Meek pointed out that in the Akan region "[t]he ownership of land, therefore, by a family is not analogous to that of tenancy in common under English law. . . . Every grown-up male has a right to an individual share of land and as long as he behaves himself he enjoys perpetuity of tenure. But he cannot sell the land. Nor is he permitted to alienate land permanently to strangers." C. K. Meek, *Land Law and Custom in the Colonies* (London, 1946, 1968), 178. See also W. F. Hutchinson, Report on the Economic Agriculture on the Gold Coast, *PP* (1890) 48 [C.5897]: 10. Hutchinson was a respected Eurafrican merchant of Cape Coast with close ties to the rural African community.

23. There would of course be a parallel movement involving the commercialization of land in eastern Ghana as a consequence of the burgeoning cocoa industry of Akyem, Akuapem, and Krobo in eastern Ghana. There is an extensive discussion of this in Polly Hill, *Migrant Cocoa Farmers of Southern Ghana* (Cambridge, 1963), 138–60. She says "Wholesale alienation by Akim Abuakwa chiefs seldom occurred until the eighteen-nineties, by which time the practice of out-and-out sale had been well fortified by established usage, being part of (not alien to) customary law" (139). My own interpretation emphasizes the radical and disconcerting aspects of the commercialization of land transfers in southwestern Ghana, which appear to have resulted in greater upheaval because of the expatriate mining capitalist and concessionaire element. Hill tends to stress how quickly and easily the changes toward individual ownership in Akyem were absorbed and became a part of customary procedures and land law.

24. The Gold Coast timber export industry, utilizing indigenous woods (especially *Khaya ivoriensis,* broadly labeled West African mahogany), owed

a great deal to the entrepreneurship of both the African and European traders at the port of Axim and especially to up-country timber cutters, large numbers of whom were from Nzema, who floated logs downriver to the coast for overseas export. Gold Coast timber exports rose markedly from 476 cubic feet in 1888 to 3,567,337 cubic feet in 1895. Information on how this affected land sales in Summary of Q. Dist. Reports, enclosure in Griffith (278) to Ripon, 12 October 1892, CO 96/226; also Crown Agents for the Colonies to CO, 23 August 1897, CO 96/301. Information on early Nzeman upcountry timber cutters from interviews at Awiebo and Atuabo, Ghana, May 1987, Dumett Collection.

25. Even after the first decade of the twentieth century, an expert on the lands question could write: "The chiefs and their advisers have no idea, even at the present time, what extent of a country is given in a given number of square miles. They always imagine that what they are granting is a mere fraction of what they actually dispose of." Belfield, "Report on the Legislation Governing the Alienation of Native Lands . . . ," *PP* (1912-13) 59 [C. 6278]: 9.

26. Gov. W. B. Griffith, Report on the Gold Mines (1889), encl. in Griffith to Knutsford, 25 June 1889, *PP* (1889) 54 [C. 5620]: 1-15.

27. King Enemil Kuma of Aboso lodged a complaint in the colonial law courts against Joseph Dawson on the grounds that Dawson had sold his original lease of the Aboso gold-bearing land to Bonnat's African Gold Coast Company without consulting the king or paying him any of the proceeds from the assigned lease. Furthermore, Kuma complained that the company had refrained from paying him any annual rent. The case was decided against the king and in favor of Dawson. Summary in *Gold Coast Assize* 2.5 (February 1884): 16.

28. The accepted Akan tradition here was that whereas a chief did not have to share the proceeds from land leases to strangers with individual people of his stool, he was nonetheless under obligation to consult with subchiefs prior for approval of a lease and also to reserve the use of such moneys for state or public purposes and not for his own private uses or aggrandizement.

29. Letter from A. Woodburn-Heron, DC at Axim, to King Enemil Kwadwo Kuma II of Aboso, 28 March 1888, ADM 11/11/34, file 2432/88, GNA. Kwamena Faibil was destooled as Chief of Apinto in 1904. Rodger (600) to CO, 16 December 1904, CO 96/421.

30. In statements made to the Belfield Committee on these problems in 1912, Chiefs Kwamena Enemil IV of Bensu and Essel Kwadwo of Apinto bitterly condemned the coastal lawyers, and they made it clear that problems connected with excessive litigation had commenced at least a decade earlier under their predecessors. Belfield Report, *PP* (1912-13) 59 [C. 6278]: 75-76.

31. Kwamena Faibil was destooled as Chief of Apinto in 1904. (Rodger) [600] to CO, 16 December 1904, CO 96/421. For continuing reports on the status of kings and chiefs Wassa Fiase and Apinto, see also G. C. *Reports on the Native Affairs Dept.* for 1902, 5; for 1904, 5; for 1912, 4.

32. I shall treat Gold Coast attempted lands legislation and regulations more fully in a future publication. This is a vast topic. For details on the legislative history of the crown lands and concessions bills see Kimble, *Political History of Ghana,* 334–39.

33. See for example Min. by Hemming and Meade on Ussher (75) to CO 17 March 1880; CO 96//130.

34. Nearly all the senior civil servants at the Colonial Office at this time were Oxford educated. Robert Meade was particularly close to Sir Edward Hamilton at the Treasury (the two had been both to public school [Winchester] and college together), and they and their immediate circle of friends in Whitehall were dubbed by one wag as the Treasury Ring. Sir Edward Hamilton, *Diaries* 74 (9 January 1898): 93, BL Mss. (48672). For Meades views on colonial expenditures see Letter to Lord Ripon, 13 December 1894, Ripon Papers, BL Addl. Mss. (43558).

35. In their milestone work *British Imperialism,* Peter Cain and A. G. Hopkins stress the commonalities and bridges—which they call gentlemanly capitalism—between civil service mandarins in Whitehall and business and financial interests in the City of London. I raise the question of whether greater distinctions should be made between the backgrounds and interests of diverse City subgroups—merchants, commodity brokers, and particularly mining company share pushers, as well as merchant bankers. I also raise questions about the modus vivendi of the linkage to Whitehall.

36. Min. by Knutsford, Meade, and Hemming, 11–12 November 1889, on Griffith to Knutsford, 3 August 1889, CO 96/204.

37. These ordinances sanctioned penalties against both employers and employees who reneged on labor contracts. Ord. no. 16 of 1877, Griffith, *Ordinances of the Gold Coast* (1887), 412; Ord. no. 12 of 1902, encl. 2 in Gov. Nathan (344) to CO, 11 August 1902, CO 96/398.

38. Examples of heavy criticism in the British House of Commons of anything that smacked of coercive labor in the Gold Coast are seen in Parliamentary Questions by Sir Charles Dilke, 22 July 1897, to Sec. of State for Colonies, CO 96/301; and by Henry Labouchere, 28 March 1901, CO 96/387.

39. Pouncy concludes that there was again, as noted in early chapters, no meaningful correlation between convictions under these ordinances and possible efforts by the colonial state to regulate mining labor on behalf of the companies. Pouncy, "Colonial Racial Attitudes," 72–75.

40. Ord. no. 8 of 1893, the Master-Servant and Foreign Employment Ordinance, was designed to protect Gold Coast workers employed in the Congo State or other African colonies. An official later claimed it was used

to protect Kru workers in the Gold Coast. *G.C. Annual Report* for 1908, 49. But I have seen no proof of this.

41. Two later examples that show some changes are found in J. F. Furley, DC, to Messrs. Proctor and Hayles, Tarkwa, 28 September 1909; and Furley to Tarkwa Mining Company, 4 October 1909, Tarkwa Dist. Records, ADM 27/1/14, GNA. In most other instances, where complaints were entered, the Colonial Office responded that there was little or nothing that they could do to compel delinquent British managers to remit back pay to workers because so many of their companies had gone into bankruptcy.

42. Magnus J. Sampson, *Gold Coast Men of Affairs* (London, 1937), 96–100.

43. Interview with Jacob Eduam-Baiden, Saltpond, Ghana, 5 August 1969, Dumett Collection.

44. Deed to Obuasi lands, 3 March 1890, no. 23 vol. 2, *Register of Deeds and Conveyances and Leases,* Cape Coast, Gold Coast.

45. Cade and Fry to Col. Sec., Accra, 19 June 1895, encl. in Maxwell (267) to Ripon, 21 June 1895, CO 96/258.

46. In his diary, Cade noted that his actions "appear[ed] to them to be very highhanded." Edwin A. Cade, typescript of a visit to Bekwae and Adanse, entries for 31 July 1895, 102 and for 14 August 1895, 117–18, encl. with a Report on the Obuasi Gold Mining Estate from Cade to Directors of the Côte d'Or Co., Ltd., Kumasi, 22 August 1895, Cade Papers, UB-CWAS.

47. The exact amount of the transaction between the three owners and Edwin A. Cade, as representative of the Côte d'Or Company for purchase of the Obuasi leases has never been disclosed before. In pertinent documents on the agreement at both the Public Record Office (Kew) and in the archives of the Ashanti Goldfields Corporation, the consideration money for the purchase was excised from the record. But Mr. Eduam-Baiden told me, "I have seen the document." Cade made an additional offer of £40,000 total. Ellis, Brown and Biney responded that they hoped to receive an offer of £250,000. In fact, Mr. Eduam-Baiden told me that the ultimate figure that Cade paid for the purchase was £60,000–£30,000 in cash on the spot and £30,000 by check. In addition, each of the three partners were awarded several hundred shares each in the Ashanti Goldfields Corporation. By 1900 Biney owned 1,000 shares. Interview with Jacob Eduam-Baiden, 5 August 1969, Saltpond, Ghana Dumett Collection.

48. Agreement for purchase of lease, 27 August 1895, encl. in Cade to Chamberlain, 17 February 1896, CO 96/297. Agreement for occupation of certain lands in the territories of Bekwai, encl. in Maxwell (357) to CO, 16 August 1897, CO 96/297.

49. This was the George Reckless Concession. See letter from Kesham, Saxon, Sampson and Company to CO, 23 October 1895, *PP* (1896) [C. 7918], 107; quoted in Wilks, Asante in the Nineteenth Century, 107.

50. In some ways it appears strange that the three African entrepreneurs did not proceed through F. and A. Swanzy (with offices in Accra and Cape Coast as well as London) to advise them on how to raise capital. After all, both J. P. Brown and their fellow African entrepreneur and mining engineer, W. E. Sam, worked for Swanzy. It may be that Brown, Ellis, and Biney simply felt too close to the Swanzy firm and that they sought to demonstrate their total independence.

51. Chamberlain, in turn, demanded his "pound of flesh" in the form of payment to the imperial government of a substantial annual royalty of 5 percent on the corporations gross profits before giving his consent to the agreements. Revised Agreement Allowing for the Occupation of Certain Lands in the Ashanti States between W. Maxwell, Gov. of the Gold Coast, J. Biney, J. E. Ellis, and J. P. Brown and the Côte d'Or Company. Final executed agreement, encl. in Maxwell (357) to CO, 16 August 1897, CO 96/297.

52. Dumett, "Rubber Trade," 79-101.

53. Interview with Nana Ezonle, Atuabo, Ghana, Dumett Collection.

54. Junner, *Gold in the Gold Coast,* 12.

55. Alfred Strauss, Pres. Bibliani Co., to Gov. Nathan, 22 September 1902, Nathan Papers, RHO.

56. Report by Traveling Commissioner Lang to U.S., CO, 17 November 1892, CO 96/137.

57. Richard Austin Freeman, who traveled widely in Asante and Brong-Ahafo, contended that southwestern Gyaman was perhaps "the most highly auriferous portion of the region." Freeman, *Ashanti and Jaman,* 529.

58. Binger, *Du Niger au Golfe de Guinée,* 2:175-80.

59. Report on a journey through Ashanti and surrounding areas; encl. in Gov. Clifford to Harcourt, 9 January 1914, CO 96/542.

60. Interview with Peter Lamptey, May 1971, Ajumako, Ghana, Dumett Collection.

61. This phenomenon was described by the well-known Eurafrican merchant W. F. Hutchison, who had conducted an export-import business from Cape Coast since the mid-1800s. He dated the beginning of the modern cash and currency revolution to the early 1870s. See W. F. Hutchison, "The Gold Trade of the Gold Coast, 1826 to 1890," *Elder Dempster Magazine,* March 1925, 10.

62. In fact there was a drop in the export of nearly all Gold Coast products as a result of the 1900 Yaa Asantewa War. See Précis of District Commissioners Reports, encl. in Nathan (26) to CO, 17 January 1901, CO 96/377.

63. "[T]he largest increase in the exports at Cape Coast is owing to the price of rubber having more than doubled in value. . . . This has caused natives to leave [other branches] of trade." Report from DC at Cape Coast, 1 December 1890, encl. 4 in Griffith to Knutsford, 6 June 1891, CO 967/217.

64. Extract from diary of Louis Gowans, encl. in Wassa (G.C.) Mining Company to CO, 6 September 1897, CO 96/306.

65. James Irvine to the *African Review,* 5 August 1896, encl. in F. and A. Swanzy to CO, 14 August 1896, CO 96/287.

66. Report on the Wassa (G.C.) Mining Co. for 1899, encl. in the WGCMC to CO, 9 March 1900, CO 96/369.

SELECTED BIBLIOGRAPHY

Primary Sources

Manuscript Sources

ADM 11/series and ADM 27/series. Tarkwa District Records. Ghana National Archives.

AGC/series. Ashanti Goldfields Corporation (now controlled by the Lonrho Corporation, Ltd). Papers housed at the Guildhall Library, London, and at the Centre for West African Studies, University of Birmingham, England.

Basel Mission Documents. Slavery Reports. Abstracts translated by Paul Jenkins, Basel, Switzerland.

BT/series. Records of limited liability companies, formerly the property of the Registrar of Joint Stock Companies, London. Public Record Office, London.

Cade Papers. Papers of Edwin A. Cade, Guildhall Library, London and Centre for West African Studies, University of Birmingham, England.

CO 96/series. 351 volumes. Original correspondence on the Gold Coast Colony, the Colonial Office (London), other departments of state, and miscellaneous individuals, plus minutes by the CO staff, 1874 to 1905. Public Record Office, Kew, Richmond, Surrey.

CO 100/series. Sessional Papers of the Gold Coast Legislative and Executive Councils. Public Record Office, London.

Furley Collection. Balme Library, University of Ghana.

Ocansey Trading Papers, GNA Sc. 8/64. Private papers of Gold Coast business and political leaders. Ghana National Archives, Accra.

Papers of Sir Matthew Nathan. Nos. 277-321. General Correspondence as Governor of the Gold Coast. Rhodes House Library, Oxford University.

Papers of the Wesleyan Missionary Society, London. Library of the School of Oriental and African Studies, London.

Ripon Papers. Papers of the First Marquess of Ripon. British Library, Addl. Mss., London.

Sarbah Papers, GNA Sc. 6/4. Private papers of Gold Coast business and political leaders. Ghana National Archives, Accra.

Printed Primary Sources

Gold Coast Blue Books. Annual Statistical records. British Library, London.

Gold Coast Departmental Reports

The following reports were viewed in bound volumes at the Balme Library, University of Ghana, Legon.

Mining Department Reports.

Native Affairs Department Reports.

Colonial Office Confidential Prints

These are available in larger bound volumes listed in the CO 806/, the CO 879/, and the CO 885/series. (Viewed at the Public Record Office, Kew, and the former Colonial Office Library, Great Smith Street, London.) In the list below the words *Confidential Print* can be assumed in the titles of individual papers.

CO African 321. Gold Coast Affairs; Further Correspondence, 9 June 1885 to September 1886.

CO African 326. Correspondence re. proposals by C. S. Salmon, Esq., for the development of trade with the interior of the country in the vicinity of the British Settlements on the West Coast of Africa, October 1886.

CO African 333. Gold Coast Affairs; Further Correspondence, 25 August 1886 to 15 February 1888.

CO African (West) 379. Financial Conditions (Gold Coast); Correspondence 28 May 1887 to 1 January 1890.

CO African (West) 451. Proposed Construction of Railways; Further Correspondence, 23 June 1879 to 8 November 1893.

CO African (West) 464. Proposed Construction of Railways; Further Correspondence, 20 July 1894 to 6 January 1896.

CO African (West) 513. Land Grants and Concessions; Correspondence 24 July 1889 to 31 December 1896.

CO African (West) 532. Land Grants and Concessions; Further Correspondence, 1 January 1897 to 30 December 1898.

CO Conf. Print 47. Memo by E. Fairfield, "Domestic slavery: The Jurisdiction of the Judicial Assessor and the Legal Character of the Limitations on British Power upon the Gold Coast," 19 March 1874.

British Parliamentary Papers

Papers in this series were examined at the British Library, London, and also at the Library of the University of Illinois, Urbana. (In the endnotes to this book all the references to the Parliamentary Papers, no matter what their origins or subdivisions, are abbreviated simply as *PP.*)

Belfield, H. C., Report on the Legislation Governing the Alienation of Native Lands in the Gold Coast Colony and Ashanti. *PP* (1912-13) 59 [Cd. 6278]: 481-601.

Colonial Reports Annual. Gold Coast, 1874 through 1906.

Correspondence Relating to the Queens Jurisdiction on the Gold Coast and the Abolition of Slavery within the Protectorate. *PP* (1875) 52 [C. 1139]: 277.

Further Correspondence Respecting Affairs of the Gold Coast. *PP* (1883) 48 [C. 3687]: 453.

Further Correspondence Respecting Affairs of the Gold Coast. *PP* (1884) 56 [C. 4052]: 283.

Report from the Select Committee on the Western Coast of Africa: *Reports of Committees* (1865) 5 [412]: 1.

Report on the Economic Agriculture on the Gold Coast. *PP* (1890) 48 [C. 5897-40]: 355.

Report on the Gold Mines of the Gold Coast (June, 1889). *PP* (1889) 54[C. 5620-24]: 173.

Statistical Abstracts and Tables for the Colonial and Other Possessions of the United Kingdom, 1964-1878. *Accounts and Papers* (1878) 77 [C. 2029]; *Accounts and Papers* (1880) 76 [C.2520]; *Accounts and Papers* (1906) 132 [Cd. 3253].

Hansard, Parliamentary Debates
Third Series (1874-91).
Fourth Series (1892-1905).

Contemporary Newspapers and Periodicals
African Review
The African Times
The African Times, Railway and Commercial Gazette
The Anti-Slavery Reporter
The Economist
The Examiner
Gold Coast Chronicle
Gold Coast Independent
Gold Coast Review
Gold Coast Times
Journal of the African Society
Journal of the Society of Arts
Liverpool Journal of Commerce
Mining and Scientific Press
The Mining Journal

The Mining Magazine
Proceedings of the Royal Geographical Society
Quarterly Journal of the Geological Society of London
The Spectator
Transactions of the Institute of Mining and Metallurgy
United Service Magazine
The West African Reporter
Western Echo
Westminster Review
Work and Workers in the Missionary Field

Other Printed Primary Sources:

Gold Coast Annual Geological Surveys. (Published in the twentieth century.)
Griffith, William Brandford Jr., ed. *Ordinances of the Settlements on the Gold Coast and of the Gold Coast Colony in Force in 1887.* London, 1887.
———. *Ordinances of the Gold Coast Colony in Force in 1903.* 2 vols. London, 1903.
London Chamber of Commerce Annual Reports. Guildhall Library, London.
Manchester Monthly Record. Monthly reports of the Manchester Chamber of Commerce.
Stock Exchange Official Intelligence. (Published in London for the years.) Guildhall Library, London.
Stock Exchange Yearbooks. (Published in London for the years.) Guildhall Library, London.

Oral Evidence and Field Notes

Daaku Collections

Daaku, Kwame Y. *Oral Traditions of Assin-Twifo.* Legon, Ghana, Institute of African Studies, 1969.
———. *Oral Traditions of Denkyera*, UNESCO Project on Oral Data, no. 2. Legon, Ghana, 1970.

Dumett Collection

Adu, Daniel Edmund. Asikan (near Kyebi), Akyem-Abuakwa, Ghana, 26 May 1987.
Adu, Nana Blay (Abontiakoonhene). Tarkwa, Wassa, Ghana, 16 May 1987.
Adu, Opanin Kwaku. Mampong Akrofoso, Asante, Ghana, 29 December 1971.
Agyepong, Kofi. Asokore, Akyem-Abuakwa, Ghana, 1 December 1971.
Akwase, Osei. Essumeja, Asante, Ghana, 25 July 1969.
Arthur Badoo, P. K. Mampong, Akuapem, Ghana, 1 December 1971.
Blay, Kwame Bejisu. Tarkwa, Ghana, 16 May 1987.
Busonga, Issah. Obuasi, Asante, Ghana, 21 May 1987.

Cudjoe, S. K. Tarkwa, Wassa, Ghana, 21 May 1987.

Eduam-Baiden, Jacob. Saltpond, Ghana, 5 August, 1969.

Ezonle, Nana (Tutohene). Atuabo, eastern Nzema, Ghana, 17 May 1987.

Faibil, Nana, III (Apintohene; king of Apinto substate). Tarkwa, Wassa, Ghana, 16 May 1987.

Frimpong, Kwesi. Tarkwa, Wassa, Ghana, 17 May 1987.

Garbrah, Joseph. Tarkwa, Wassa, Ghana, 17 May 1987.

Hammond, J. W. S. Tarkwa, Wassa, Ghana, 4 August 1969.

Johnson, W. S. Kwesi (merchant). Cape Coast, Ghana, 3 August 1969 and 27 December 1971.

Lamptey, Peter. Ajumako, Fante region, Ghana, 4 January 1972.

Morgan, E. W. (retired mining manager). Ipswich, Suffolk, England, 30 June 1982.

Muhamma, Mallam. Tamale, northern region, Ghana, 10 August 1984.

Ofor, Nana Akodaa Kwadwo. Ayisan, Akyem-Abuakwa, Ghana, 28 December 1971.

Otu, Kwamena. Ajumako, Fante region, Ghana, 28 December 1971.

Pong, Kwesi. Onwi village, Ejisu, Asante, Ghana, 27 July 1969.

Quinoo, John Ansah. Awiebo, eastern Nzema, Ghana, 17 May 1987.

Rowe, Tommy, and Bruce Lockyear (staff of the Ashanti Goldfields Corp.). London, 15 June 1982.

Seriboe, Opanin. Konongo, Dwaben, Asante, Ghana, 25 May 1987.

Tenkromaa, Nana Efoa. Konongo, Dwaben, Asante, Ghana, 25 May 1987.

Wangara, Kwaku, and Charles Bathurst. Obuasi, Asante, Ghana, 30 December 1971.

Yeboa, Kwame. Kyebi, Akyem-Abuakwa, Ghana, 26 May 1987.

Secondary Sources

Addo-Fening, Robert. "Asante Refugees in Akyem Abuakwa 1875-1912," *Transactions of the Historical Society of Ghana* 14.1 (1973): 39-64.

——. "The Gold Mining Industry in Akyem-Abuakwa, 1850-1910," *Sankofa* 2 (1976): 33-9.

Agbodeka, Francis. *African Politics and British Policy and British Policy in the Gold Coast, 1868-1900.* London, 1971.

Agricola, Georg. *Georgius Agricola de re metallica.* 1556. New ed., trans. Herbert Hoover. New York, 1950.

Allen, G. Keith. "Gold Mining in Ghana." *African Affairs* 57.228 (July 1956): 221-24.

Allen, V. L. "The Meaning of the Working Class in Africa." *Journal of Modern African Studies* 10.2 (1972): 169-189.

Allot, Anthony. *Essays in African Law.* London, 1960.

Anquandah, James. *Rediscovering Ghanas Past*. Harlow, Essex, 1982.

Arhin, Kwame. "Political Succession and Gold Mining at Manso-Nkwanta, 1850–1910." *Institute of African Studies Research Review* (University of Ghana) 6.3 (1970): 101–9.

Asante, S. K. B. "Law and Society in Ghana." In T. Hutchinson et. al., eds., *Africa and Law: Developing Legal Systems in African and Commonwealth Nations*. Madison, Wis., 1968.

Austin, Gareth. "The Growth of Cocoa Farming in South Ashanti, 1896–1914." Ph.D. thesis, University of Birmingham, England, 1984.

———. "Human Pawning in Asante c. 1820–1950: Markets and Coercion, Gender and Cocoa." In T. Falola and P. Lovejoy, eds., *Pawnship in Africa*. Boulder, 1994.

———. "'No Elders Were Present: Commoners and Private Ownership in Asante, 1807–96." *Journal of African History* 37 (1996): 1–30.

Austen, Ralph. *An Economic History of Africa*. London, 1987.

Barbot, John. *A Description of the Coast of North and South Guinée*. Vol. 5 of Churchills *Collection of Voyages and Travels*. Paris, 1746.

Barger, Harold, and Sam H. Schurr. *The Mining Industries, 1899–1939*. New York, 1944. Reprint, 1972.

Barros, J. de. *Da Asie de Joao de Barros e de Diogo do Couto*. 13 vols. Lisbon, 1552–88. Reprint, trans. and ed. G. R. Crone, Hakluyt Society, 2d ser. 80. London, 1937.

Bauer, P. T. *West African Trade*. Cambridge, 1954.

Bean, Richard. "A Note on the Relative Importance of Slaves and Gold in West African Exports." *JAH* 14 (1977): 351–56.

Beecham, John. *Ashantee and the Gold Coast*. London, 1841.

Bernstein, Henry. "African Peasantries: A theoretical framework." *Journal of Peasant Studies* 6:421–43.

Baésjou, René. "The Historical Evidence for Old Maps and Charts of Africa." *History in Africa* 15 (1988).

Bevin, H. J. "M. J. Bonnat, Trader and Mining Promoter." *Economic Bulletin* (Accra) 4.7 (July 1960): 1–8

Blainey, Geoffrey. *The Rush That Never Ended: A History of Australian Mining*. 3d ed. Melbourne, 1978.

Blakely, B. S. *The Colonial Office, 1868–1892*. Durham, N.C., 1972.

Binger, Louis. *Du Niger au Golfe de Guinée par le pays Kong et le Mossi*. 2 vols. Paris, 1892.

Boahen, Adu. "The Origins of the Akan." *Ghana Notes and Queries* 9:3–10.

Bosman, William. *A New and Accurate Description of the Coast of Guinea*. 1st English ed., London 1705. Reprint, London, 1967.

Bowdich, T. E. *A Mission from Cape Coast Castle to Ashantee*. London, 1819. Reprint, 1966.

Boyle, Frederick. *Through Fanteland to Coomassie*. London, 1874.

Brackenbury, Henry. *The Ashantee War.* 2 vols. London, 1974.

Brodie, Fawn. *The Devil Drives: The Life of Sir Richard Francis Burton.* New York, 1967.

Brooks, George. *The Kru Mariner.* Newark, Del., 1970.

Burton, Pierre. *Klondike Fever.* New York, 1958, 1985.

Burton, Richard, and V. L. Cameron. *To the Gold Coast for Gold.* 2 vols. London, 1883.

Busia, K. A. *The Position of the Chief in the Modern Political System of Ashanti.* London, 1951. Reprint, 1968.

Cain, Peter. "Financial Capitalism and Imperialism in Late Victorian and Edwardian England." In A. N. Porter and R. F. Holland, eds., *Money, Finance and Empire, 1790-1860.* London, 1985.

Cain, Peter J., and A. G. Hopkins. *British Imperialism,* 2 vols. London, 1993.

Cameron, V. L. "The Goldfields of West Africa." *Journal of the Royal Society of Arts* 30.1 (2 June 1882): 541.

Campbell, J. M. "Notes on Some Gold Occurrences in Ashanti." *Transactions of the Institute of Mining and Metallurgy* 24 (1914-15): 252-56.

Casely Hayford, J. E. *Gold Coast Native Institutions.* London, 1903.

Cell, John. *British Colonial Administration in the Mid-Nineteenth Century: The Policy-Making Process.* New Haven, 1970.

Claridge, W. W. *A History of the Gold Coast and Ashanti.* 2 vols. London 1915. Reprint, 1964.

Clarke, R. *Remarks on the Topography and Diseases of the Gold Coast.* London, 1860.

Clignet, Remi. *The Africanization of the Labor Market.* Berkeley, 1976.

Cooper, W. G. G. *Geology of the Prestea Goldfield.* Colchester, 1934.

Crane, Walter R. *Gold and Silver.* New York, 1908.

Crisp, Jeff. *The Story of an African Working Class.* London, 1984.

Crowther, E. G. "Affairs in Wassa." *The Gold Coast Review* 2 (July-September 1926): 168-180.

Cruickshank, Brodie. *Eighteen Years on the Gold Coast of Africa.* 2 vols. London, 1853. Reprint, 1966.

Curtin, Philip D. *Economic Change in Precolonial Africa.* Madison, Wis., 1975.

———. "Africa in the Wider Monetary World, 1250-1850." In John F. Richards, ed., *Silver and Gold Flows in the Medieval and Early Modern Worlds.* Durham, N.C., 1981.

Daaku, Kwame Y. *Trade and Politics on the Gold Coast, 1600-1720.* London, 1970.

Daaku, Kwame Y., and A. Van Dantzig. "Annotated Dutch Map of the Gold Coast [1629]." *Ghana Notes and Queries* 9 (November 1966): 14.

Dadson, J. A. "Land Tenure Reform" In *Background to AgriculturalPolicy in Ghana*. Legon, Ghana, 1969.

Dahse, Paulus. "Von der Goldküste." *Deutsche geographische Blätter* (Bremen) 1.6 (1882): 286-87.

Dapper, Olefert. *Beschreibung von Afrika*. Amsterdam, 1670.

Davidson, Basil. *Africa in History: Themes and Outlines*. New York, 1974.

Davies, E. H. "Some Hints on Mine Management." *Mining Journal, Railway and Commercial Gazette* 2 (December 1893): 1334.

Davis, Lance, and R. Huttenbach. *Mammon and the Pursuit of Empire: The Political Economy of British Imperialism, 1860-1912*. Cambridge, 1987.

Daw, John. *Lecture on the Development of Gold Mining in Ashanti*. London, 1902 (privately printed).

DeGregori, Thomas. *Technology and the Development of the Tropical African Frontier*. Cleveland, 1969.

Dickson, Kwamina B. *A Historical Geography of Ghana*. Cambridge, 1969.

Dumett, Raymond E. "British Official Attitudes in Relation to Economic Development in the Gold Coast, 1874-1905." Ph.D. thesis, University of London, 1966.

———. "The Campaign against Malaria and the Expansion of Scientific Medical and Sanitary Services in British West Africa, 1898-1910." *African Historical Studies* 1.2 (1968): 153-197.

———. "The Rubber Trade of the Gold Coast and Asante in the Nineteenth Century: African Innovation and Market Responsiveness." *Journal of African History* 12.1 (1971): 79-101.

———. "John Sarbah the Elder and African Mercantile Entrepreneurship in the Gold Coast in the Late Nineteenth Century." *Journal of African History* 14.4 (1973): 653-679.

———. "Joseph Chamberlain, Imperial Finance and Railway Policy in British West Africa in the Late Nineteenth Century." *English Historical Review* 90 (April 1975): 287-321.

———. "Precolonial Gold Mining and the State in the Akan Region with a Critique of the Terray Hypothesis." In George Dalton, ed., *Research in Economic Anthropology* no. 2 (1979): 37-68.

———. "Pressure Groups, Bureaucracy and the Decision-making Process: Slavery Abolition and Colonial Expansion in the Gold Coast, 1874." *Journal of Imperial and Commonwealth History* 9.2 (Winter 1981): 193-215.

———. "African Merchants of the Gold Coast, 1860-1905: Dynamics of Indigenous Entrepreneurship." *Comparative Studies in Society and History* 25 (October 1983): 661-93.

———. "Precolonial Gold Mining in Wassa: Innovation, Specialization, Linkages to the Economy and to the State." In Enid Schildkrout, ed., *The Golden Stool: Studies of the of Asante Center and Periphery.*

Anthropological Papers of the American Museum of Natural History (New York) 65, pt. 1 (1987): 209-24.

———. "Sources for Mining Company History in Africa: The History of the Ashanti Goldfields Company." *Business History Review* 62 (Autumn 1988): 502-15.

———. "Disease and Mortality among Gold Miners of Ghana: Colonial Government and Mining Company Attitudes and Policies, 1900-1938." *Social Science Medicine* 37.2 (1993): 213-32.

———. "The Gold Mining Centers of Tarkwa and Obuasi: Colonial Administration and Social Change at Company Towns in an African Setting." In Klaus Tenfelde, ed., *Towards a Social History of Mining.* Munich, 1993.

Dumett, Raymond, and Marion Johnson. "The Suppression of Slavery in the Gold Coast, Asante and the Northern Territories." In S. Miers and R. Roberts, eds., *The End of Slavery in Africa.* Madison, Wis., 1988.

Dupuis, Joseph. *Journal of a Residence in Ashantee.* London, 1966.

Edelstein, Michael. "Rigidity and Bias in the British Capital Market, 1870-1913." In D. M. McCloskey. ed., *Essays on a Mature Economy after 1840.* London, 1971.

Ellis, A. B. *The Land of Fetish.* London, 1883.

———. *The Tshi-Speaking Peoples of the Gold Coast of West Africa.* London, 1887.

Fetherling, Douglas. *The Gold Crusades.* Toronto, 1988.

Foran, W. Robert. *African Odyssey: The Life of Verney Lovett Cameron.* London, 1937.

Freeman, Richard Austin. *Travels and Life in Ashanti and Jaman.* London, 1898. Reprint, 1967.

Freund, Bill. *Capital and Labour in the Nigerian Tin Mines.* Atlantic Highlands, N.J., 1981.

Fynn, J. K. *Asante and Its Neighbors, 1700-1807.* Evanston, Ill., 1971.

Garrard, Timothy F. "Studies in Akan Goldweights." Parts 2-4. *Transactions of the Historical Society of Ghana* 13.2 (1972); 14.1 (1973); 14.2 (1973).

———. *Akan Weights and the Gold Trade.* London, 1980.

Godinho, V. Magalhaes. *L économie de lempire portugais aux xv, xvi siècles.* Paris, 1969.

Godoy, Ricardo. "Technical and Economic Efficiency of Peasant Miners in Bolivia." *Economic Development and Cultural Change* 34.1 (October 1985): 103-20.

Gramberg, J. S. G. *Schetsen van Afrikas Westkust.* Amsterdam, 1861.

Gros, Jules. *Voyages, aventures et captivité de J. Bonnat chez les Achantis.* Paris, 1882.

Halligey, J. F. T. "A Visit to the West African Gold Mines." *Work and Workers in the Missionary Field* 2 (January 1893): 23-26.

Hargreaves, John D. *Prelude to the Partition of West Africa.* London, 1963.

———. *West Africa Partitioned.* Vol. 1, *The Loaded Pause, 1885-1889.* Madison, Wis., 1974.

Hart, Francis. *The Gold Coast: Its Wealth and Health.* London, 1904.

Harvey, Charles E. *The Rio Tinto Company.* Penzance, 1981.

Harvey, Charles E., and Jon Press. "Overseas Investment and the Professional Advance of British Metal Mining Engineers," 1851-1914." *Economic History Review,* 2d ser., 42.1 (1989).

Headrick, Daniel. *The Tools of Empire.* New York, 1981.

———. *The Tentacles of Progress.* Oxford, 1988.

Herbert, Eugenia. *Red Gold of West Africa.* Madison, Wis., 1984.

———. *Iron, Gender and Power.* Bloomington, Ind., 1994.

Hill, Polly. *Migrant Cocoa Farmers of Southern Ghana.* Cambridge, 1963.

———. *Population, Prosperity and Poverty; Rural Kano, 1900 and 1970.* London, 1977.

Hirst, T. *The Geology of the Tarkwa Goldfield and Adjacent Country.* Gold Coast Geological Survey, Bulletin no. 10. London, 1938.

———. *The Geology of the Konongo Gold Belt and Surrounding Territory.* Gold Coast Geological Survey, Bulletin no.14. London, 1942.

Hobson, G. V., and A. M. Robinson. "The Gold Coast Banket: Some Aspects of Its Geology in Relation to Mining." *Transactions of the Institute of Mining and Metallurgy* 52 (1942-43): 311-46.

Hobson, J. A. *Imperialism: A Study.* London, 1902.

Holmes, F. "Notes on the Early History of Tarkwa as a Gold Mining District," *Gold Coast Review* 2.1 (January-June 1926): 78-117.

Hopkins, A. G. *An Economic History of West Africa.* London, 1973.

Horton, James Africanus B. *West African Countries and Peoples.* London 1868. Reprint, Edinburgh, 1969.

———. *J. A. B. Horton, Letters on the Political Condition of the Gold Coast.* Ed. E. A. Ayandele. New ed. London, 1970.

———. *The Medical Topography of the West Coast of Africa.* London, 1859.

Hudson, John C. "Theory and Methodology in Comparative Frontier Studies." In David O. Miller and J. O. Steffen, eds., *The Frontier: Comparative Studies.* Norman, Okla., 1977.

Hutchinson, Thomas J. *Impressions of Western Africa.* London, 1858.

Irvine, James. "Our Commercial Relations with West Africa and Their Effects upon Civilization." Speech before the Royal Society of Arts, 13 March 1877. *Journal of the Royal Society of Arts,* 16 March 1877, 378-88.

Johnson, M. "M. Bonnat on the Volta," *Ghana Notes and Queries* 10 (December 1968): 4-17

Junner, Norman, R. *The Geology of the Obuasi Goldfield.* Gold Coast Geological Survey, Bulletin no.2. London, 1932.

———. *Gold in the Gold Coast.* London, 1935.

———. *The Tarkwa Goldfield.* London, 1942.

Kaplow, Susan. "The Mudfish and the Crocodile: Underdevelopment of a West African Bourgeoisie." *Science and Society,* no. 3 (Fall 1977): 517-33.

Kay, G. B. *The Political Economy of Colonialism in Ghana.* Cambridge, 1972.

Kea, Ray. *Settlements, Trade and Politics in the Seventeenth-Century Gold Coast.* Baltimore, 1982.

Keegan, Timothy. "The Dynamics of Rural Accumulation in South Africa: Comparative and Historical Perspectives." *Comparative Studies in History and Society* 28:4 (1986): 628-50

Kesse, G. O. "The Occurrence of Gold in Ghana." In R. P. Foster, ed., *The Geology, Geochemistry and Genesis of Gold Deposits.* Rotterdam, 1984.

Killingray, David. "Guarding the Extending Frontier: Policing the Gold Coast, 1865-1913." Paper presented at the 33rd Annual Meeting of the African Studies Association of the United States, Baltimore, 1-4 November 1990.

Kimble, David. *A Political History of Ghana.* Oxford, 1963.

Kyerematen, A. A. Y. *Panoply of Ghana.* London, 1964.

Lanning, Greg, with Marti Mueller. *African Undermined: Mining Companies and the Underdevelopment of Africa.* Harmondsworth, 1979.

LaQue, F. L., and H. R. Copson, eds. *Corrosion Resistance of Metals and Alloys.* 2d ed. New York, 1963.

La Torre, Joseph. "Wealth Surpasses Everything: An Economic History of Asante." Ph.D. dissertation, University of California, Berkeley, 1974.

Lentz, Carola, and Veit Erlmann. "A Working Class in Formation: Economic Crisis and Strategies for Survival among Dagara Mine Workers in Ghana." *Cahiers détudes africaines* 113 (1989): 69-111.

Lewin, Thomas J. *Asante before the British.* Lawrence, Kans., 1978.

Lewis, G. R. *The Stanneries: A Study of the Medieval Tin Miners of Cornwall and Devon.* Truro, Cornwall, 1968.

Louis, Henry. "Gold Mining on the Gold Coast, West Africa." *Mining Journal* (London) 12 December 1885, 1437.

Luxemburg, Rosa. *The Accumulation of Capital.* London, 1951.

Lynch, Hollis R. *Edward Wilmot Blyden: Pan-Negro Patriot (1832-1912).* London, 1967.

Maier, Donna, *Priests and Power: The case of the Dente Shrine in Nineteenth-Century Ghana.* Bloomington, Ind., 1983.

Marees, Pieter de. *Description and Historical Account of the Gold Kingdom of Guinée*. Dutch ed., the Hague, 1602. Annotated ed., the Hague, 1912.

Martin, Jane. "Down the Coast: Liberian Migrants on the West African Coast in the Nineteenth and Twentieth Centuries." *International Journal of African Historical Studies* 18.3 (1985): 401-23.

McCarthy, E. T. "Mining Enterprise in the Gold Coast." Supplement to the *Mining Journal*, 1 July 1882, 797-98.

———. "Early Days on the Gold Coast." *Mining Magazine*, December 1909, 291-95

McCaskie, Thomas C. *State and Society in Pre-Colonial Asante*. Cambridge, 1995.

McIntyre, W. David. *The Imperial Frontier in the Tropics, 1965-1895*. New York, 1967.

McLeod, M. D. *The Asante*. London, 1981.

McPhee, A. *The Economic Revolution in British West Africa*. London, 1926.

Meredith, Henry. *An Account of the Gold Coast of Africa*. London, 1812. Reprint, 1967.

Metcalfe, G. E., ed. *Great Britain and Ghana: Documents of Ghana History, 1807-1957*. London, 1964.

Meyerowitz, Eva L. R. *The Early History of the Akan States of Ghana*. London, 1975.

Mickssell, Marvin. "Comparative Studies in Frontier History." *Annals of the Association of American Geographers* 51 (1961): 62-74.

Miers, Suzanne, and Richard Roberts. *The End of Slavery in Africa*. Madison, Wis., 1988.

Morrell, W. P. *The Gold Rushes*. London, 1940.

Mota, A. Teixeira da, and P. E. H. Hair *East of Mina: Afro-European Relations on the Gold Coast in the 1550s and 1560s*. University of Wisconsin Studies in African Sources, no. 3. Madison, 1988.

Napier, L. E. *The Principles and Practice of Tropical Medicine*. New York, 1947.

Newell, Diane. *Technology on the Frontier: Mining in Old Ontario*. Vancouver, 1986.

Orwell, George. *The Road to Wigan Pier*. London, 1937.

Owusu, Maxwell. *Uses and Abuses of Political Power: A Case Study of Continuity and Change in the Politics of Ghana*. Chicago, 1970.

Patton, Adell. *Physicians, Colonial Racism and Diaspora in West Africa*. Gainesville, Fla., 1992.

Patterson, K. D. *Health in Colonial Ghana: Disease, Medicine and Socio-Economic Change, 1900-1955*. Waltham, Mass., 1981.

Patterson, Lawson. *Twelve Years in the Mines of California*. Cambridge, 1862.

Pereira, Duarte Pacheco. *Esmeraldo de situ orbis*. Lisbon, 1505-8. Reprint, trans. G. H. T. Kimble. Hakluyt Society (London), 2d ser., 29 (1937): 114-21.

Phimister, Ian. *An Economic and Social History of Zimbabwe, 1890-1948*. London, 1948.

———. "Alluvial Gold Mining and Trade in Nineteenth Century South Central Africa." *Journal of African History* 15.3 (1974): 445-56.

Platt, D. C. M. *Finance, Trade and British Foreign Policy, 1815-1914*. Oxford, 1968.

Posnansky, Merrick, and Albert Van Dantzig. "Fort Ruchaver Rediscovered." *Sankofa* 2 (1976): 7-8.

Pouncy, Hillard. "Colonial Racial Attitudes and Colonial Labor Laws in British West Africa." Ph.D. dissertation, Massachusetts Institute of Technology, 1981.

Ramseyer, F. A., and J. Kuhne. *Four Years in Ashantee*. New York, 1875.

Rattray, R. S. *Ashanti*. London, 1923.

———. *Ashanti Law and Constitution*. London, 1929.

Reinhart, Herman Francis. *The Golden Frontier: Recollections of H. F. Reinhart, 1851-69*. Ed. N. B. Cunningham and D. B. Nunis. Austin, Tex., 1962.

Reynolds, Edward. *Trade and Economic Change on the Gold Coast, 1807-1874*. London, 1974.

Richards, John F., ed. *Precious Metals in the Later Medieval and Early Modern World*. Durham, N.C., 1982.

Rickard, T. A. *Men and Metals: A History of Mining in Relation to the Development of Civilization*. New York, 1932.

———. *The Romance of Mining*. Toronto, 1944.

Robertson, G. A., *Notes on Africa*. London, 1819.

Rodney, Walter. "Gold and Slaves on the Gold Coast," *Transactions of the Historical Society of Ghana* 10 (1969): 14-28.

Rømer, R. F. *The Gold Coast of Guinea*. Copenhagen, 1760. Part 4, "African History, Customs and Ways of Life." Trans. from the Danish by K. Gertelsen. University of Ghana, Institute of African Studies, Legon, 1965.

Rosenblum, Paul. "Gold Mining in Ghana, 1874-1900." Ph.D. dissertation, Columbia University, 1971.

Rossiter, Raymond. *The Mines of the West*. New York, 1869.

Rowe, Tommy. "E. A. Cade: 1856-1903." Typescript, ca. 1985.

———. "John Daw: 1851-1934." Typescript, ca. 1985.

———. "John Daw Report, 1898." Typescript, ca. 1985.

Said, Edward. *Cultural Imperialism*. New York, 1992.

Sam, Thomas Birch Freeman. "On the Origin of the Auriferous Conglomerates of the Gold Coast Colony (West Africa)." *Quarterly Journal of the Geological Society of London* 54 (August 1898).

Sanderson, F. W. *History of Nzema up to 1874.* Accra, 1925.

Sarbah, John M. *Fanti Customary Laws.* London, 1906. Reprint, 1968.

Schildkrout, Enid. *The Golden Stool: Studies of the Asante Center and Periphery.* Anthropological Papers of the American Museum of Natural History, vol. 65, part 1. New York, 1987.

Silver, Jim. "The Failure of Primitive Accumulation: European Mining Companies in the Nineteenth-Century Gold Coast," *Journal of African History* 22 (1981): 511-21.

Skertchly, J. A. "A Visit to the Goldfields of Wassa, West Africa." *Journal of the Royal Geographical Society* 48 (September 1979): 274-83.

Spence, Clark S. *British Investments and the American Mining Frontier.* Ithaca, N.Y., 1958.

Spencer, Herbert. "The Morals of Trade." *Westminster Review* 71 (1859): 357-90.

Spude, Robert. "Native Americans and the Gold Rushes." In K. Tenfelde, ed., *Sozialgeschichte des Bergbaus im neunzehnte und zwanzigste Jahrhundert.* Munich, 1992.

Summers, Roger. *Ancient Mining in Rhodesia.* Salisbury, 1969.

Sutherland, D. A. "The Primitive Uses of Gold." *Transactions of the Institute of Mining and Metallurgy* 44 (1934-35).

———. *The Primitive Uses of Gold and Methods of Gold Mining.* Accra, 1952.

Swanzy, Henry. "A Trading Family in the Nineteenth Century Gold Coast." *Transactions of the Gold Coast and Togoland Historical Society* 2, part 2 (1956): 87-120.

Tanzer, Michael. *The Race for Resources.* New York, 1980.

Tenfelde, Klaus, ed. *Sozialgeschichte des Bergbaus im neunzehnte und zwanzigste Jahrhundert.* Munich, 1992.

Tenkorang, S. "The Importance of Firearms in the Struggle between Ashanti and the Coastal States, 1708-1807." *Transactions of the Historical Society of Ghana* 9 (1968): 1-16.

Terray, Emmanuel. "Long Distance Exchange and the Formation of the State: The Case of the Abron State of Gyaman." *Economy and Society* 3.3 (1974): 315-45.

———. "Gold Production, Slave Labor, and State Intervention in Precolonial Akan Societies: A Reply to Raymond Dumett." *Research in Economic Anthropology* 5 (1983): 95-192.

Tilton, J. E. *The Future of the Non-Fuel Minerals.* Washington, D.C., 1977.

Tordoff, William. *Ashanti under the Prempehs, 1888-1935.* London, 1965.

Twain, Mark, and C. D. Warner. *The Gilded Age: A Tale of Today.* Hartford, Conn., 1873.

Van Dantzig, Albert. "The Ankobra Gold Interest." *Transactions of the Historical Society of Ghana* 14.2 (December 1973): 169-85.

———. *The Dutch and the Guinea Coast, 1674-1742: A Collection of Dutch Documents from the General State Archive at the Hague.* Accra, 1978.

Van Dantzig, Albert, and B. Priddy. *A Short History of the Forts and Castles of Ghana.* Legon, Ghana, 1971.

Vogt, John. *Portuguese Rule on the Gold Coast, 1469-1682.* Athens, Ga., 1979.

Wallach, Henry. *The West African Market Manual.* London, 1890.

Ward, W. E. F. *A History of Ghana.* London, 1958.

Weeks, John, "Epochs of Capitalism and the Progressiveness of Capital Expansion." *Science and Society* 49.4 (Winter 1985-86): 414-36.

Whitelaw, O. A. L. *The Geological and Mining Features of the Tarkwa-Aboso Goldfield.* Gold Coast Geological Survey, Bulletin no. 1. Colchester, 1929.

Wilks, Ivor. *Asante in the Nineteenth Century.* Cambridge, 1975.

———. "The Golden Stool and the Elephant Tail: An Essay on Wealth in Asante." In G. Dalton, ed., *Research in Economic Anthropology* 2 (1979): 1-36.

———. "Wangara, Akan and the Portuguese in the Fifteenth and Sixteenth Centuries." Part 1, "The Matter of Bitu." *Journal of African History* 23.3 (1982): 333-49.

———. "Wangara, Akan and the Portuguese in the Fifteenth and Sixteenth Centuries." Part 2, *Journal of African History* 23.4: 463-72.

———. *Forests of Gold: Essays on the Akan and the Kingdom of Asante.* Athens, Ohio, 1993.

Wolfson, Freda. "British Relations with the Gold Coast." Ph.D. thesis, London University, 1951.

Yarak, Larry. "Political Consolidation and Fragmentation in Southern Akan Polity: Wassa and the Origin of Wassa Amenfi and Wassa Fiase, 1700-1840." Typescript, 1976.

———. *Asante and the Dutch.* New York and Oxford, 1990.

———. "The Dutch Gold-Mining Effort on the Gold Coast, 1841-49: European Failure, Akan Success." Typescript, 1990.

Young, Robert J. C. *Colonial Desire: Hybridity in Theory, Culture and Race.* London, 1995.

INDEX

abirempom, 44

Abontiakoon: concession, 113; mines, 113, 119-20, 121-22, 250

Aborigines Protection Society (London), 167, 180, 188

Aborigines Rights Protection Society (Gold Coast), 99, 281

Aboso (town and mines), 12, 19, 32-34, 71, 87, 90,153, 154, 165, 176, 205, 209, 261

abosum, 61

Abrade, 45

abuna (share), 70, 221

Abura state, 96

abusa (share system), 69, 71, 75, 76, 122, 153, 208, 221, 222

Accra, 21, 24, 91, 172

Adanse, 187, 281, 282

Addo-Fening, Robert, 49, 318 n. 38

Adom, 43

Afrenen Asante, 87

Africa (continent of), 1, 10

African (and Africans): bourgeois (middle) class, 22, 99, 105, 184, 280-81; capitalist class (development of), 23, 100, 104, 281, 283; democracy, 98; entrepreneurs, 98-109, 240, 281-82; farmers, 17, 47-49, 79, 147; labor (recruitment of), 144-50; miners' frontier (indigenous), 19, 90, 262, 264, 284-87; precolonial mining, 6, 17 (see also traditional mining); traditional mining, 6-

7, 37, 49-74, 88-90, 264-66, 284-87; working class, 18-19, 147-48, 269-72

African Aid Society, 100

African Gold Coast Mining Company, 93-95, 205

African Gold Coast Syndicate, 113, 123

African (Gold Coast) nationalism, 96, 100-102, 181, 281

African innovations: adzes (aso), 19, 53; deep shafts, 57-58; explosives, 59, 134, 268, 271; fire setting, 50, 58-59; lagging, 58; lamps, 57; loaming, 73; mullerstones and bedstones, 64; soso toa, 53; soso tupre, 53; timbering, 58-59; tunneling, 58

African religion, 59-61

African Trade Sections (of chambers of commerce), 194

African Times, 100, 194

African Times Railway and Commercial Gazette, 194

Agbodeka, Francis, 99

Anyi (people and region) 49, 285

agriculture, 44-49, 79; bush fallow, 47-49; cocoa, 3, 24, 99, 360 n. 105; large-scale commercial, 21, 146, 252

Agyepong, Kofi, 322 n. 104

Ahafo region, 36, 285

Ahanta, 42, 43, 49, 75, 88, 91, 115

Aja Bippo (mine), 215-16, 219, 237

Akan: family and household, 74; gold (or brass) weights, 4, 27, 293; land law 67-